KHURASAN AND SISTAN

KHURASAN AND SISTAN

BY

LIEUT. COLONEL C. E. YATE
C.S.I., C.M.G.

Indian Staff Corps

GYAN

Published by

Gyan Publishing House
5, Ansari Road
Daryaganj, New Delhi-110002
Phone: 011-47034999, 9811692060
E-mail: books@gyanbooks.com

Distribution Network
gyanbooks.com
India, USA, Canada, UK, Australia, France

ISBN : 978-81-212-1244-1 (PB)
First Published, 1900

2nd Impression 2021

Printed at: Gyan Press, Delhi.

Khurasan and Sistan
Author: Lieut. Colonel C. E. Yate

KHURASAN AND SISTAN

BY

LIEUT.-COLONEL C. E. YATE

C.S.I., C.M.G.

INDIAN STAFF CORPS;
AGENT TO THE GOVERNOR-GENERAL AND CHIEF COMMISSIONER OF BALUCHISTAN;
FORMERLY AGENT TO THE GOVERNOR-GENERAL OF INDIA AND HER
BRITANNIC MAJESTY'S CONSUL-GENERAL FOR KHURASAN
AND SISTAN IN PERSIA; F.R.G.S., ETC.

WITH MAP AND ILLUSTRATIONS

WILLIAM BLACKWOOD AND SONS
EDINBURGH AND LONDON
MDCCCC

INTERIOR OF THE SHRINE OF IMAM RAZA AT MASHHAD.

PREFACE.

In "Northern Afghanistan" I gave a description of Afghan Turkistan from Kabul on the east to Herat on the west. I now carry on the description farther west into Persia, and describe each district of Khurasan and Sistan in detail, from the Kurd and Turkoman country along the Russian frontier on the north, to the confines of Baluchistan on the Indian frontier to the south.

A full account is given of the time I spent amongst the Goklan and Yamut Turkomans, hitherto comparatively unknown; their life and character is described, and an account is given of my trip to the source of the river Gurgan, never before visited by any European traveller.

An account is also given of the Afghan troops and soldiers as I saw them at Kandahar, Farah, and Herat; of the Persian troops and officials; and of the various tribes on the Afghan and Persian frontiers. The state of trade with Persia through Sistan and Bandar Abbas is described, and the question of the disappearance of hereditary chiefs and of the power of the priesthood in Persia is entered into; as well as that of the difference in the number of native followers in India and in Russia; the different modes of life in India and in Central Asia; the contrast between the employment of natives in the army and in the civil administration of the country under the British Government in India and the Russian Government in Central Asia, and various other subjects connected with India.

The proposed junction of the Indian and Russian railways is also discussed.

The shrine of Imam Raza and the history and antiquities of Mashhad, Nishapur, and other places, the tomb of Umar Khaiyam, and the turquoise mines at Mádan are described; and a general account is given of the people I saw and the life I led during the three years I held charge of the office of agent to the Governor-General of India and H.B.M.'s Consul-General at Mashhad, in the hope that it may prove of use to my brother officers in the Indian army who may think of visiting Khurasan and Sistan, or who may take an interest in Central Asia.

CHAS. E. YATE.

25th September 1900.

CONTENTS.

LIST OF ILLUSTRATIONS.

KHURASAN AND SISTAN.

CHAPTER I.

KANDAHAR, FARAH, AND HERAT.

On the 5th April 1893 I left Chaman, the British frontier station in Baluchistan, as her Majesty's Commissioner for the settlement of certain disputes with Russia regarding the Kushk river canals on the Afghan frontier to the north of Herat, and with orders, after settling those disputes, to proceed on to Mashhad in Persia and take up the post of agent to the Governor-General of India and H.B.M.'s Consul-General for Khurasan and Sistan.

Riding out accompanied by the officers of the 40th Pathan Regiment, then quartered at Chaman, and escorted by a troop of the 6th Bombay Cavalry, we were met at the frontier by Abdul Hamid Khan, a Tajik from Logar, the Amir's agent deputed to escort me to Kandahar, with thirty Afghan cavalry and twenty Khawinin or irregular sowars. Saying good-bye to our British comrades, the Afghans formed up and took charge, and for the fourth time in my life I found myself launched on a journey through Afghanistan. We were soon on the best of terms with our Afghan guardians, and all who have ever travelled under an Afghan cavalry escort will join me in testifying what excellent fellows Afghan soldiers are when taken the right way. A cheerier, heartier, and more willing man than the Afghan sowar in his own country is hard to find.

The road to Kandahar is well known. On arrival at Kandahar I was met by Mirza Taki Khan, the British agent, and the Afghan colonel of artillery, a son of Wali Ahmad Khan, the Amir's former representative and envoy with the Government of India. Escorted by them we entered the city by the Bar Durani gate, and wended our way to the main entrance of the citadel. Crossing the open space inside that, we rode up to the residence of the Naib-ul-Hukumat, as the governor is styled, in a court-yard on the western side. A guard of honour of the 3rd Herat Regiment was drawn up opposite the reception-room under the command of a subadar who wore a pith sun-helmet, of which apparently he was very proud, while his men were possessed of every sort of head-covering, including foxskin hats, sheepskin hats, and hats of various other kinds of skins.

The governor, Abdulla Khan Timuri, appeared resplendent in a bright red coat, one mass of gold embroidery; and shortly afterwards "Brigade," as the Afghan general commanding was locally called, Muhammad Sádik Khan, appeared, accompanied by the "kurnél" oı commandant of the 1st Herat Regiment; both similarly gorgeously got up in gold. About a dozen "kapitáns" were also brought in and introduced and shook hands, but were then marched out again.

On returning I rode back down the bazar to the "Chaharsú," the large central dome on which the main roads of the city converge, and then out by the Kabul gate. The city seemed more crowded than even when we were in occupation of it during the war of 1879–80, and trade seemed brisk; the Juma Musjid had been newly repaired, and the whole city looked in a more flourishing condition than I had ever seen it before.

The Bagh-i-Manzil, which had been assigned to me as my residence during my stay, was a new garden-house constructed by order of the Amir just behind the village of Deh Khojah, the scene of our sortie during the siege of 1880. The house itself was a large square building. The lower storey consisted of vaulted kitchens and servants' rooms. Mounting the stairs, we found ourselves in a huge hall, in the shape of a Maltese cross, with a small room at each corner, and another room above each of those again. The garden was full of apricot, peach, pomegranate, and quince trees, giving a green and pleasant prospect, while a cuckoo was calling loudly, and there were lots of small birds about, giving life to the place. In the hall I found breakfast ready spread. There was enough to feed a regiment, and all my men had a grand feast.

Two "kapitáns" were put on duty with me, one of artillery and one of an Herat regiment, both good fellows, and I spent the evening walking round the garden and chatting with them.

One thing that particularly struck me during my stay was the curious ignorance of all the Afghan officials I came across of our ways and customs across the frontier. None of them had ever been permitted to cross the border or to mix with our people in any way, and their ideas of British rule were crude in the extreme. The official is apparently the only class that is tied down in this respect. The lower classes, fruit-sellers and traders generally, visit India in large numbers every year, and some even extend their travels beyond it.

I remember one man in Baluchistan accosting me in

English in the airy manner of a colonial workman, and I found he had been with camels to Australia, while another came back from there with an Australian wife, a widow with two little girls, who insisted upon accompanying him across the border into Afghanistan, and is now, I presume, living in the usual nomad's low black tent on some arid plain.

At dusk the Afghan artillery colonel arrived to dinner, and brought with him an invitation for me to a parade of the Afghan troops in garrison the next morning. We rode out together at the time appointed, and found the governor already there, gorgeously attired in his red and gold coat. The brigadier and colonels took up their position as I approached, and the parade commenced at once by a march past in slow time. I ranged myself alongside the governor, and there we sat for an hour or an hour and a half watching the manœuvres. The force on parade consisted of one field battery, one mountain battery, and two regiments of infantry. The horses of the field battery looked light for the work they had to do, but they wheeled and moved about with the infantry without difficulty. The mountain guns were mounted on good, strong *yábus* or ponies; but, strange to say, the ponies were not used on parade at all, and the screw guns, some of those given by the Viceroy to the Amir at Rawal Pindi, so they said, were dragged about by the gunners in line with the infantry the whole time. The gunners were all Kabulis, and fine stalwart men too, and they showed their metal in this work. They had a cross-bar fixed to the trail of the gun, and they lifted this up and walked away with the gun as if it was nothing. I always think a Kabuli is worth two Kandaharis and about four Heratis for real work. After much marching and countermarching the parade came to an end with a general salute. For this the brigadier dismounted, carefully handed his pith helmet with a cock's feather in it to his bugler, and stood bareheaded with his hand to his forehead at the salute the whole time that the band played what I suppose was "God save the Amir!" When this was over the governor and I rode forward and went down the line, shaking hands with the colonels and plentifully distributing our "Mánda na báshid" (May you not be tired) and other salutations amongst the men, who grinned and replied in due form, and seemed to be highly delighted. When we had gone down the whole line the governor drew up again in front with me by his side. He then removed his grey Astrakhan hat, and the generals and I took off our helmets and the men took off their turbans, and the governor giving the lead, we all went through an invocation for the welfare of his Highness the Amir with much devotion. The troops then marched home, the band still playing. I must say one word for that band. It was a bugle band, and the men were dressed in short red coats with white trousers, and I think it played steadily throughout the whole proceedings without ceasing. I was on the ground for nearly two hours. How many hours it played before I got there I don't know.

The next day I rode round the city and cantonments to visit the old familiar scenes of our occupation during the war. I first inspected the cemetery and found the graves all in perfect order. The only thing was that the tombstones and inscriptions had all been removed, and it was impossible to tell who the graves belonged to. The cemetery was surrounded by a high mud wall and the gate was bricked up, but a part of the wall fell down at one time, and before the British agent in the city had time to report the fact and to get sanction for money to rebuild it, the villagers around had stolen whatever bricks and stones they were able to remove. The governor, I believe, as soon as the matter was reported to him, put a guard on the place; but I presume it was too late to save the tombstones.

Our old cantonments were occupied to a certain extent by the Afghan troops, but the domes in the hospital and in some of the other squares that we left in perfect order in 1881, had fallen in, and there was a general look of decay; but still with a little cleaning up it seemed to me that the majority of the old barracks could be brought into use again without much difficulty. The various gardens and houses occupied during the war by the general officer commanding, the staff, the engineers and others, all looked much the same as of yore. One great improvement I noticed, and that was that the road made by us round the west and south faces of the city had been widened and planted with trees, and the main Kokeran road, too, from the Herat gate had also a fine avenue of trees.

These improvements spoke well for the Amir's Government, and formed a marked contrast between the Afghan and Persian rule. At Mashhad or any town in Persia no governor thinks of making a road or of planting a tree. His whole thoughts are apparently concentrated on making money, and public works of any sort are unknown. The Afghan governors struck me as much better in this respect.

At Kokeran I inspected Sartip Nur Muhammad Khan's house where Sir Hugh Gough's cavalry brigade was quartered after the battle of Kandahar in September 1880, and I found it a complete ruin, all the domes of the building having fallen in. From there we made our way down to the Argandab river, which turned out to be only up to the men's waists, and not so deep as we expected. We got the baggage across on camels without mishap, and camped for the night on the open ground beyond. The next day at Sinjari we passed a large camp just getting under way, which I was told was that of the Wali of Maimana, Muhammad Sharif Khan, son of the late Wali Husain Khan, who with his wives and family was on his way to Kabul under a guard of Kandahar cavalry. What has become of him since I have never heard.

On the 18th April 1893 we arrived at the banks of the Helmund and crossed over to Girishk in the ferry-boat. This boat is manned by a colony of Farsiwans—Raisani Baluchis they called themselves—who were brought here, they said, by Nadir Shah seven generations ago. The way they swam all the horses and mules across the river was deserving of every praise. They rode the animals into the water till they got out of their depth, and then, holding on to the mane by the right hand, they swam alongside with their left, splashing water into the horse's face to keep its head up-stream if it showed any intention of turning. Then, mounting again on the other side, they galloped the animal about to warm him up after his bath. On the far bank I found the Hákim's brother waiting to receive me with tea and sweets, and we sat and chatted with him till the baggage had all been brought over and reloaded, and then we all rode on to the fort together. This fort is a most important-looking structure from the far side of the river, standing on the edge of a conglomerate rise with low ground, green and grassy, below it, stretching right away down to the river. By no means a healthy place, I should imagine. The Hákim or governor of Pusht-i-Rud, as the district is called, met me in the fort and gave me tea in a room he had prepared for me to live in, but I preferred to camp in my own tent outside. There was no garrison in the fort; a battery of field artillery and the other troops were all camped outside, and the only occupants of the fort itself were the Hákim and his family. In the evening I had some snipe-shooting in the rice-swamps down by the river, near a *ziarat* or shrine. This *ziarat* was the tomb of some famous Saiyid, and was surrounded by a fine clump of big trees. Noticing that these trees were all dead at the tops, I asked why the dead wood had not been removed, but I was told that no one could touch it. One man, it was said, had once committed the sacrilege of stealing the sacred wood, but he was punished on the spot in some awful way, I forget how, and no one had ever dared to touch a tree since.

At Girishk the governor appointed an Alizai Khan named Ata Muhammad from Zemindawar, with some half-dozen local sowars, to pilot me on to Farah. Our first halting-place was at Sádat, and there I found a curious water-mill. The water channel, which was on the surface, dropped some 15 feet down a brick well and turned the mill in a hole in the ground at the bottom, the water running on underground in a fresh channel till it came to the surface again lower down. In the mill I found an Arab, as he called himself, who, seeing me shoot some pigeons, came up with great glee and fraternised at once. "I am a shikari; I shoot too," said he; and he went on to tell me that the country was full of gazelle, locally known as *áhú*, and that he used to sit up over his crops and shoot them at night as they came to feed. That deer were plentiful I had learned from the governor at Girishk, who told me that the Amir had sent a circular round to the different provinces ordering all deerskins to be sent to Kabul to be tanned, and that he had replied by sending off 500 skins there and then. How the deer were not extinct I cannot think.

It was at Sádat that I first began to get some hold on

the plundering propensities of my Afghan entertainers. I was the Amir's guest, and at every stage supplies were laid in for me and my party with the utmost profusion. I soon found, however, that these supplies were not paid for, but owing to the strict guard kept over the camp no villager could get in to make any complaint. At Sádat, though, the Arab women were not to be daunted, as, despite the guards, they forced their way into camp, clamouring loudly for payment for the fowls and milk that had been taken from them. This was my chance. On making inquiries I found that while my modest demands had been satisfied with two seers of milk and six eggs, the servants and followers had required nothing less than a fowl or two apiece; while as to the Afghans, their requirements were wholesale. No wonder the poor villagers had a bad time of it. However, I was able to help them a little by insisting upon paying for what my own camp required.

Our marches beyond Sádat were mostly uninteresting and very hot. The country was almost entirely deserted, the inhabitants being Nurzai nomads who spent the whole of the summer with their flocks up in the hills to the north. At this season hardly a soul was to be seen except the one or two men left to irrigate the crops. Many of the low hills we crossed were covered with a small bush bearing a fruit something resembling a sloe, but it was still green, and it was difficult to say what it was. The Afghans called it *zirga*, and they said the poorer people often lived on it for a considerable time while their grain was ripening. At Bar, on the right bank of the Khash Rud, I was met by Muhammad Sharif Khan, who had been sent out to meet me by the governor of Farah. The river here runs in a good stream some thirty-five yards across and two feet deep. It looked so inviting that I got out my rod and tried for a fish, but I could not get a rise, and finally a man volunteered the information that there were no fish in it, as it dried up completely in the hot weather, and even in flood did not get down to the Helmund. The river-bed was some half-mile in width and full of grass and tamarisk jungle, and I had better luck with my gun, as I found some black partridges, hill partridges, little partridges, hares, and wood-pigeons. There were also traces of pig.

After rounding the solitary peak known as the Koh-i-Duzdan, or the thieves' hill, our route led for forty miles straight on end across the Dasht-i-Bakwa, a dead-level plain without a tree, stone, or bush to vary the monotony, and almost utterly deserted during the summer months. The western end of this plain is just about half-way between Kandahar and Herat, and here it is on the Dasht-i-Bakwa that the Afghans say is to be fought the great battle of the future between the English and the Russians. I first heard this tradition in 1886 in Afghan Turkistan,[1] and I have been told the same story in various other places, the different tellers invariably finishing up by adding that so severe was to be the fight that after the battle 12,000 riderless horses would be found wandering over the plain. No one could ever tell me who was to be the victor, but as part of General Skobeloff's scheme of 1877 for the attack of India was "to organise hordes of Asiatic horsemen, who to a cry of blood and plunder were to be launched against India," it would seem to be clear, from the numbers of horses mentioned, that it is to be these Asiatic horsemen who are to get the worst of it. As to the Afghans, they firmly believe in this prophecy and look upon a battle on the Dasht-i-Bakwa in the future as a certainty; but of all the men in Afghanistan who quoted the prophecy to me I could never find one

[1] *Vide* Northern Afghanistan, p. 320.

who could tell me who was the author of it. I subsequently found out the author by accident at Mashhad. My assistant, Khan Bahadur Moula Bakhsh, was talking to a Herati priest there one day when the latter quoted this identical prophecy and named the author, Shah Ni'-Amat Ulla, Wali of Kirman. This man was a native of Kuchan, who travelled a good deal in Iran, Turan, and Arabia, lived in Yezd for a time, then went to Shiraz where he was the friend of Háfiz, and afterwards to Herat at the invitation of Shah Rukb Mirza. His later years he passed at the village of Mahan, near Kirman, and there he died in the year 1430 A.D., at the age of ninety-seven. He was an author, philosopher, and saint, who preached a form of religion of his own, and he is mentioned in various Persian books; but I have never been able to obtain a copy of his works, which are apparently very rare, and of course only exist in manuscript.

According to the Herati priest, the Dasht-i-Bakwa was at one time the headquarters of one of the ancient rulers of Afghanistan, and the inhabitants were Persian-speaking people. At another time it was occupied by Timuris, who were removed to the neighbourhood of Kabul by one of the Amirs, and since then it had formed the camping-ground of Nurzais. It is clear, though, that it has not always been the home of nomads. I found the plain covered with the marks of old *karezes* or underground water-channels, and it had evidently been thickly populated by a cultivating class at some time, while water was said to be obtainable all over it. When I passed it was all a waste. There was no cultivation, but the grass that grew there was said to be so good that the ghee from it fetched a higher price than any other.

The Nurzais who now hold Bakwa are all nomads and *maldars*—that is, cattle-owners and graziers in contradistinction to cultivators. Consequently they are never so inclined to join in a fray as the cultivating classes are, as they cannot leave their flocks and herds with no one to look after them. In this lies the difference between the Nurzais of Bakwa and the Alizais of Zemindawar. The latter are cultivators pure and simple, and at off-times are free to go away and join in any expedition that may be on hand. In this possibly is the secret of the help given by the Zemindawaris to Ayub Khan on his advance to Maiwand in 1880, and the contrary by the Bakwa Nurzais.

On the 30th April 1893 we arrived at Farah, and never shall I forget the picture of desolation that met my eyes as we rode in at the Kandahar gate. Farah is a square walled place standing out in the middle of the plain something like Kandahar, but with the ramparts of Herat. It is no longer a town. It has long been deserted by all inhabitants, and is now simply occupied by the men of the regiment quartered in it. The governor does not even live there. He holds his court there in the daytime, but his family and the families of all the sepoys and people live in the villages outside. The houses that formerly existed have all tumbled down, and the whole ground within the walls is nothing but a succession of mounds and heaps varied by pits and holes. Dotted about here and there were a few mud huts occupied by the sepoys, and what is called the bazar was a row of some half-dozen miserable-looking shops near the Herat gate. The only building in the place was the governor's court-house.

The colonel and the "Kumedan"—as the second in command was called—came out to welcome us, and all the men thronged out to see us pass. The regiment had only just returned from the Hazarahjat, and what with cholera and service against the Hazarahs, its ranks had been greatly thinned.

We rode through the fort, and then camped in a garden built by the former governor, Sirdar Muhammad Yusuf Khan, to the north of it, and there in the afternoon the governor, Moula Dad Khan Charki of Logar, came to call. I returned his visit the same evening, and after that, at the request of the colonel, I inspected his regiment on parade, and finally made a tour round the walls.

Our next camp was at a place called Kilah-i-Sam, or the fort of Sam, the grandfather of Rustam the hero of Sistan—a high square mound with a swamp all round it, the remains apparently of the ancient moat.

Our marches were all made in the very early morning, starting well before dawn on account of the heat of the sun; but the nights were always cool and pleasant, and very amusing it was at times to hear the conversations that went on round the camp fires in the evening after dinner. The head-men of the tribes in the neighbourhood would come in to join their Afghan brethren on duty with me, and all would chat away for hours. I remember one night we were talking of Sistan and the grain it produced, and an Afghan soldier who had been across the frontier and seen what the Persian administration was like, at once burst out with, "Ah, if it was not for you and the Russians we would take Sistan to-morrow," and I could not help thinking what truth there was in his words. The Persians if left to themselves in Sistan could not stand against the Afghans for a day; but believing that they will be protected, they treat the Afghans, when they meet them, with all the scorn they can, and this is bitterly resented by the latter.

Another night we had representatives of the Ishakzais, Nurzais, and Barakzais all together round the fire and talking of the results of the Afghan Boundary Commission of 1885–87 I was glad to hear them unanimous in the expression of their sense of what good that Commission had done for them. It has been supposed by some that we lost territory for the Amir by the giving up of Panjdeh, but the tribesmen took a very different view. According to them, miles and miles of land along the Herat frontier, which none of them had either seen or heard of before, had been recovered for them by the Commission, and the Nurzais were flocking there at the time in numbers. Far from Panjdeh being considered as a loss, the acquisition of Badghis, that rolling pasture-land on the northern slopes of the Parapomisus, was looked upon by them as pure gain. Before the time of the joint Commission, they said, not a man had dared to go there for fear of his life. Now all was perfect security.

The Nurzais had many tales to tell of the Amir, and from what I could gather the latter had greatly strengthened his position amongst them. They had been much pleased by receiving a message from him not long before to say that he was a Durani and a nomad as well as themselves, and asking them to send him one of their *khizdis*, or black nomad tents, to live in, which they did. The Amir had also betrothed his eldest son, Habibulla Khan, to a Nurzai girl, and his second son to an Ishakzai girl, thus bringing both of these important tribes to his side.

Some twenty-five miles from Sabzawar I was met by Muhammad Akbar Khan, Kakari, and a Duffadar and sixteen sowars of the Chahar Yari Cavalry Regiment, who had been sent out by the governor of Herat to meet and escort me through his district. They also brought twenty *yábus* or baggage ponies for me in case I was in want of carriage. I recognised Muhammad Akbar Khan's face, and found he had been with us at Bala Murghab when the Boundary Commission was encamped there in the winter of 1884. Some time after his arrival a fresh body of sowars came into sight, and this turned out to be the governor of Sabzawar, Yasin Khan, Barakzai, and we all rode into the town together. The Sabzawar Valley seemed to be rich in water, and the whole place smiled with cultivation. The town, which is a high-walled structure, was so hid by its surrounding gardens that one could hardly see anything of it, except those portions of the walls that towered up above the trees. To call Sabzawar a town, though, is a misnomer, as all the people live outside. I camped in a garden close to the Hauz-i-Ambar at the gate, and in the evening I paid my visit to the governor. Passing through the so-called bazar inside the gate, which consisted apparently of only some half-dozen shops of Shikarpuri Hindus, we found ourselves in the midst of desolation. The main fort is uninhabited, and contains nothing but a few ruined houses, empty spaces, and holes full of water. In the centre of all this stood a square, lofty building, which was the governor's residence—a more wretched place to live in I never saw, but the view from the top was grand. The whole ground below the town, as I saw it that May evening, was one sheet of green, and everything looked peaceful in the light of the setting sun. The air was cool and pleasant after the heat of Farah, and the place was said to be healthy. The most notable feature was the ruin of a grand old fort, called the Kilah-i-Dukhtar, that crowned the last hills of a ridge some three miles to the south of the town. The walls of this ancient fortress apparently enclosed a large area, as they ran right down to the water's edge at the elbow of the river. They were said to be built partly of stone and partly of brick, and were accredited by local tradition to Zál, the father of Rustam. Opposite the fortress, and out in the plain on the other side of the river, were the ruined mud walls of some ancient city, and in the hills beyond there was said to have been another fortress. The present Sabzawar is said to be only the citadel of the former city, the walls of which are still to be traced to the west, and are accredited by local tradition to fire-worshippers.

At Hauz-i-Mir Daoud, fourteen miles from Herat, we found a large square *robat* or caravanserai of burnt brick, and, strange to say, not in ruins like the majority of these ancient buildings. It was filled with the litter of ages, and too dirty for occupation; but still it was roofed and apparently water-tight, and would afford welcome shelter in a storm. Here I was met by Khan Bahadur Mirza Yakub Ali Khan, the British agent at Herat, and shortly afterwards a note arrived from the governor himself to say that he had detailed the colonel of artillery and a troop of cavalry to meet and escort me in next morning, and that he had also sent out the *mirab* to see that everything was arranged for my crossing of the river. On arrival at the river bank next morning we accordingly found a number of *aobazis* as they are here called, *i.e.* expert swimmers, to help the baggage across. We had three channels of the river to cross, but in each the water was only up to about the horses' girths, and the baggage was all got over without accident or wetting. On the right bank, near the remaining arches of the old bridge, the Pal-i-Malun, I found the colonel of artillery in a gorgeous blue uniform and the governor of Herat's son waiting to receive me; behind them again was drawn up a squadron of Turki sowars of the Chahar Yari Regiment under a Risaldar and other irregulars. We had an imposing entry into the city. We were marched right through the bazar, and thence by the citadel to the governor's house. Two companies of infantry were drawn up as a guard of honour at the gate, and at the door I was met by the governor himself, our old friend Kazi Sasadudin Khan, Barakzai, of the Boundary Commission days, and also by the Sipah Salar, or commander-in-chief, Faramorz Khan. I was taken in and introduced to General Allahdad Khan Firozkohi, whom I recognised as an old acquaintance, and to the various colonels and commandants of the different regiments, and then we all sat down to tea and sweets.

The artillery colonel and the cavalry escorted me back to the quarters that had been prepared for me in the Bagh-i-Karta, and about midday I was joined by the party sent to meet me from Mashhad, under Lieutenant the Hon. H. Napier.

In the evening the Naib-ul-Hukumat, as the governor is locally called, came down to pay me a formal visit. He was carried down in a sedan chair, having been far from well; so much so, in fact, that I had begged him not to come, but he would insist upon it.

The next morning Napier and I rode out, escorted by the artillery colonel and some twenty sowars, to call on the Sipar Salar in the citadel. There all the colonels and commandants were assembled, and we paid quite a long visit, chatting away about the troops, &c. After this we just had time to have a look at the Musalla before going in to breakfast with the governor at his house.

The next two days were mostly employed in inspecting the fortifications, and on the evening of the 15th May 1893 we went up to the citadel to witness a parade of the Afghan troops in garrison. This was a fine sight, and one that I was very pleased with. We—that is to say, the governor, the commander-in-chief, Napier, the British agent, and myself—all sat in an open room overlooking the new citadel parade-ground, and the troops were paraded below us. The men drilled steadily, and General Allahdad Khan manœuvred his division quietly and well. Finally the battalions were formed up and gave a general salute, after which they all marched past on their way to their various lines. The general and colonels all then came up and joined us at tea, after which we bid each other farewell. That same afternoon I started for the frontier.

Riding out on the road to Parwana, I could not help contrasting the Herat, as I had known it, of 1885 with the Herat of 1893. In the former year the greater part of the houses in the city were uninhabited and mostly in ruins; while as to citizens, scarcely a soul was to be seen, and had it not been for the garrison, the place would have been like a city of the dead.[1] That was the Herat represented in the accompanying picture. In 1893 I found it much more flourishing, and vastly improved in every way. The houses formerly in ruins had been rebuilt, and there was said to be a civil population of some 3000 families, in addition to the troops resident in the town, while the cultivation and population in the valley outside appeared to have also considerably increased.

Outside the city walls I found the principal men of the Kandahar Cavalry Guard, who had escorted me from Kandahar, waiting for me by the roadside to say good-bye. The Herat officials were very jealous of these Kandahar men, and directly they were relieved by Herat troops they were no longer allowed to come near me. The men felt this, and sent me a message to say that they did not wish to let me go without making their salaam, and the only way they could manage to see me was by meeting me on the road, which they did. This showed good feeling on their part, and I mention it as wherever I have been associated with Afghan troops I

[1] Northern Afghanistan, p. 29.

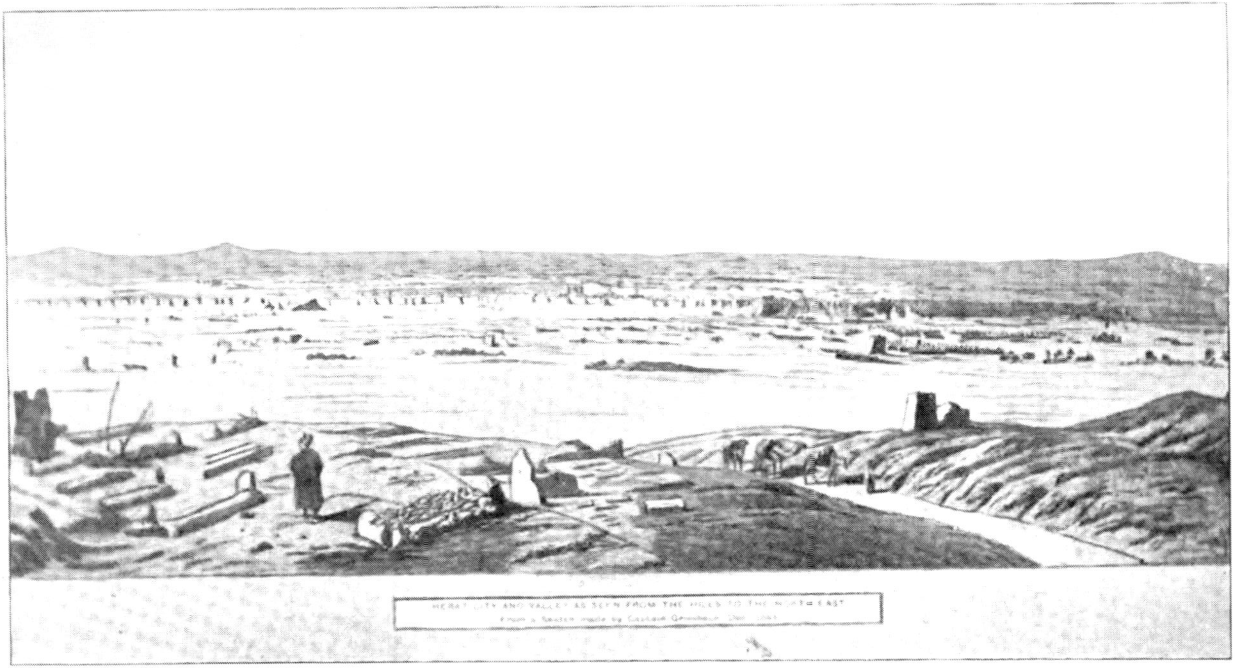

HERAT CITY AND VALLEY AS SEEN FROM THE HILLS TO THE NORTH-EAST.

have always found them one and all respectful, willing, and obliging, and I have never had occasion to notice a single case amongst them of that sullenness that we were so used to at the time of the war.

So far as I have had an opportunity of judging, I should say that the Afghan army is imbued with a feeling friendly to the British, and that this feeling is gaining ground more and more every year, not only in the army, but amongst the people of the country generally, and that the animosity against us caused by the losses inflicted by us upon them during the war is year by year dying out. In the south this is less marked than in the north. In Kandahar, for instance, the people know nothing of and think little of the Russians. They have heard of them but nothing more, and have no immediate knowledge of or dread of them. The farther north one goes the more this is altered, and the more one hears of complaints against the Russians. I have several times had it said to me by Afghans, "Well, if we are to come under a European Power we hope it may be under you." "Why?" said I. "Because," was the reply, "with you our women are safe; see what it is with the Russians." There is no doubt, I think, that the excellent discipline in this respect, preserved throughout the British army during the Afghan War of 1879–81, was productive of the best results in the minds of the Afghan people. During our two years' occupation of Afghanistan, so far as is known, not a woman of the country was touched or molested in any way; whereas, so the Afghans say, the Turkomans bitterly complain that the Russian soldiers are perpetually pursuing their women, and that when they do bring this to notice they can get no redress.

As to the troops themselves, I found that at Herat an attempt had lately been made to get the men into some sort of uniform. Almost all had got old British red tunics, and each regiment had a distinctive trouser of some light material. The Amir gives no uniforms to his troops as a general rule, but such is the spirit of the men that they buy these tunics and trousers for themselves. The trade between India and Afghanistan in cast-off tunics must be very large, but it is not with India alone that this trade exists, as I remember once seeing a whole squadron of Afghan cavalry clad in the cast-off coats of guards and ticket-collectors of the South-Eastern and Metropolitan Railways, which shows that there must be a regular trade in old uniforms with England as well. One thing is certain, and that is, the Afghan soldier is never happy without a uniform; get it he will, and his pride in this respect is an excellent trait in his character. At Herat all the men wore a round brown felt cap as their head-dress, while the officers, under the Amir's orders, were to provide themselves with Indian helmets. We saw no formations or manœuvres in extended order during our stay, but the ordinary company and battalion drill was well done, and I could not help being struck by the general steadiness on parade. The words of command were all in Pushtoo, and the drill, though antiquated, was good. The spirit of the Afghan soldiery, to judge by the way they talk, is excellent. In various places on my journey through Afghanistan I heard the sentiment expressed by the men that they were looking forward to have an opportunity to wipe out their defeat at Panjdeh. "Then," they said, "we were few in numbers and had nothing but old muzzle-loading muskets, and those were so drenched in the rain they would not go off. Now the Sirkar has given us breechloaders, and we can hold our own on even terms, and when the time comes for the fight the result will be very different." All expressed their reliance on British aid in what they considered to be the coming struggle, and said they were confident of victory. Afghan officers and officials of all ranks, though are very jealous of any intercourse or communication between their men and British officers. This is due, I think, to the fear that the men might draw conclusions between British rule and Afghan rule unfavourable to the latter. Nothing keeps a British Indian subject more loyal than to see somebody worse off than himself in a neighbouring native state; and so, conversely, is the fear of the effect on the Afghan subject of seeing somebody better off than himself in the British officers' camp always present in the mind of the Afghan governor.

CHAPTER II.

THE RUSSIAN-AFGHAN FRONTIER.

Marching north from Herat into Badghis, which may be described as the country stretching north from the Parapomisus to the Russian frontier and bounded by the Band-i-Turkistan Mountains on the east and the river Hari Rud on the west, I was again struck by the difference between the Badghis of 1885 and the Badghis of 1893. In the former year it was the home of the wild pig and the pheasant, and hardly a man dared to show his face in it. The few inhabitants it possessed had only just arrived, and the country was mostly a waste, the hunting-ground of Turkoman raiders. In the latter year the old *karezes* and canals had been opened out and hamlets were springing up in every direction. After crossing the Ardewan Pass we emerged on to rolling grassy downs covered with vegetation of all kinds, and beyond that we wound our way through almost continual cultivation and a succession of hamlets. At many of these the villagers were waiting for us with pots of *dogh*, a kind of sour milk very cool and refreshing. Our road ran down a valley almost due north most of the way, and we could see by the long straight depression existing in places that we were travelling on what must have been once a great highway, probably the high-road from Herat to Merv, when the latter was at the height of its glory. The size of the buildings still extant, such as the huge caravanserai known as Khush Robat, testified to the traffic of former days, and we wondered where all that traffic had gone which once made it worth while to erect such works along this route. Jamshidi hamlets were mostly confined to the neighbourhood of Herat, but beyond them again in the valley of the Kushk I found a large number of Durani tribesmen from Pusht-i-Rud and Zamindawar, whilst Nurzais were established to the west of them again. The Amir appeared to have pursued a settled policy in thus peopling his northern frontier with pure Afghan tribes. It is only the non-Afghan tribes, such as the Maimanah Uzbegs and the Herat Hazarahs and Jamshidis that have intercourse or communication with the Russian Turkomans, and apparently it had been determined to encircle these with a cordon of Pushtu-speaking races. These Afghan cultivators are never likely to break away from Afghanistan or to willingly fall under Russian influence, and this colonisation of the northern provinces during the last few years has consequently worked a considerable change in Afghan border politics.

On tho 18th May, the date originally named by me before leaving India, we duly arrived at Chihal Dukhtaran, on the banks of the river Kushk, which here marks the Russian frontier. We pitched our camp under the clump of trees known as the Chihal Dukhtar Ziarat. A spring here bubbles up out of the side of a mound beneath a tangled mass of reeds, and below that again were a row of mulberry trees which afforded grateful shade for our tents. On the opposite or eastern bank of the river stood the southernmost pillar of the boundary marked out by Colonel Peacocke and myself in 1887.

Not finding any news of the Russian Commissioner, I

wrote to the Russian officer commanding the Kushk post, twelve miles farther north, asking him to forward on a letter from me to the Russian Commissioner, telling of my arrival, and also asking him to let me know what news there was of the Russian Commissioner's movements, and when he was likely to arrive. The messenger returned the same evening with a reply from Lieutenant-Colonel Khomichevski, commanding the post, acknowledging receipt of my letter, and saying that the Russian Commissioner ought to arrive shortly, and on his arrival would himself inform me of the fact; adding that many telegrams had been sent concerning my arrival.

Next day Napier and I put on our uniforms, and, accompanied by my orderlies and the usual escort of Afghan cavalry, we rode over to the Kushk post to call upon Colonel Khomichevski. Remembering the pleasant time of it Colonel Peacocke and I had in Transcaspia on our return from the demarcation of the Afghan frontier in the spring of 1888, and the kindness and hospitality with which we were then received at Karki, Chaharjui, Merv, and Ashkabad, I was looking forward with pleasure to the chance of renewing my acquaintance with Russian officers; but, alas, my anticipations were doomed to sad disappointment. We had a ten-mile ride down the valley of the Kushk to the Afghan frontier post at Kara Tappa, where we found a *bairak*, or company, of Khasadars, or Afghan irregulars, posted on the banks of the river near the boundary pillar. Leaving them we crossed the river and rode up to the Russian outpost on the opposite bank. Here we found a sergeant and three Russian soldiers, who fixed bayonets and refused to permit us to pass. A Cossack who was with them had saddled up his pony and mounted as we approached, and Napier having explained to him in Russian who we were, and that we had come to call on the colonel, he galloped off as hard as he could to announce our advent, saying that he would soon be back. However, we sat on and sat on by the roadside there, and it was not till an hour had elapsed that our Cossack was at last descried; but he returned at a walk, and with quite a different manner. Instead of the respect with which he had saluted us before, he now sauntered up and told us that he had reported our arrival to the colonel, but that the latter had said that he supposed we were merely a couple of English private soldiers, and that he had given him no orders to let us pass. All we could do, therefore, was to leave our cards for the colonel at the outpost and ride back again.

On my return I wrote to Colonel Khomichevski, informing him of what had occurred; but my letter was never replied to and my visit was never returned, and though day after day during our stay in the Kushk Valley we spent hours in the Russian Commissioner's camp at that same outpost, within a couple of miles of the Kushk post station, never once did we set eyes on either the commandant or on a single officer of the garrison.

Our Afghan escort were very angry at the rudeness with which we were turned back, and the way they showed their resentment was amusing. They waited till the Russian Commissioner arrived and came to call on me, and then, instead of turning out as a guard of honour to salute him, they let him pass unnoticed, and after he was gone I found them quite cheery, and full of the idea that they were even with those Russians at last.

A week passed before we received any news of the Russian Commissioner, and then a note came in from M. Ignatiev to say that he and his assistant had arrived and would call the next day, which they did. On returning M. Ignatiev's visit he was kind enough to ask us to stay to dinner, and we passed a pleasant evening at his camp, starting to ride back at 9 P.M. The following days were spent in examining the various canals and cultivated fields which formed the subject of our inquiry. We finished off work at the Chihal Dukhtar Canal, close to our camp, and then the Russian Commissioners came in to dine with us. We sat down a party of nine, consisting of M. Ignatiev, Russian Commissioner; Lieutenant-Colonel Artamanov, Assistant-Commissioner; Lieutenant Graf Armfeld, English Interpreter, and Topographer Nassibiantz; Painda Khan, the Afghan agent with me and my assistants, Lieutenant Napier, Mir Shams Shah, and Ghulam Murtaza Khan. Outside, my Baluchistan police orderlies entertained the Cossacks, and our Turkoman postal couriers from Mashhad entertained their Turkoman brethren on the Russian side.

The month of June was a very sickly one for almost all of us. Both Napier and myself and most of the people in camp suffered badly from fever, and the heat was great, ranging from 98 to 103 each day in our tents, despite the shade of the trees.

In July we were gladdened by the arrival of Captain Duke, the Residency Surgeon at Mashhad. His hospital was soon thronged with patients from all the surrounding Afghan hamlets, and what with our own and the Afghan agent's camp, and the Afghan troops and villagers, his hands were pretty full. The Russian Commission were just as sickly as ourselves. M. Ignatiev was very ill, and, like myself, he did not shake off that horrible Kushk fever for the next six months. At the Kushk post 400 men were in hospital out of the Russian battalion quartered there, and the Kushk Valley proved itself a most unhealthy place for all.

Our work brought us into constant intercourse with the Afghan settlers in the hamlets around, and it was curious so see how these men, even in this remote corner of their country, still dwelt on their connection with India. One of the Maliks boasted that he had formerly lived at Hoti Mardan in the Punjab, and others had connections in India. All the intercourse of Afghans and all their interests seem to lie with India. With India is almost all their trade. In India they enlist in the army and work on the roads and railways, and thus numbers of men who have been in India are scattered throughout Afghanistan. Hundreds of Ghilzais and Hazarahs used to come in to Quetta every year when I was there, to work on the railway, and this constant intercourse all tends to turn the minds of the Afghan people to India. On the Russian side there is nothing of the sort. There is comparatively little trade, no enlistment, and little work, though the Murghab Railway, I believe, attracted a certain number of Afghans for a time.

I remember contrasting the difference in the employment of native labour, as shown in the Russian frontier station of Karki, on the Oxus,[1] with our own frontier stations in Baluchistan. Karki was occupied in May 1887, and Colonel Peacocke and I visited it in March 1888. We found the soldiers all housed in capital barracks and the officers' houses all built, and yet there was not a single native of the country in the whole cantonment. The Russian troops had built their own barracks and their officers' houses as well. They cooked their own food, drove their own water-carts, and washed their own clothes.

In the Indian frontier station of Loralai, in Baluchistan, which had a garrison of a similar strength to that of Karki in 1888—viz. a regiment of cavalry, a regiment of infantry, and a battery of artillery—and was built nearly about the same time, all this was altered. Loralai

[1] Northern Afghanistan, p. 400.

took a much longer time to build, it cost a large sum of money, and not a hand was put to it by the troops themselves. The whole station was built by civil labour, and when built the garrison, although all Indians and not Europeans, employed on an average a native follower for every fighting man to keep itself going. In India doubtless a certain number of followers are required, but when I saw a European regiment straight from Quetta in camp at the Pyramids, and the men driving their own water-carts, cooking their own dinners, and doing everything for themselves—though in quite as hot a climate as that of Quetta—I came to the conclusion that followers, even for European troops, were not everywhere in India an absolute necessity. Native troops, and Indian cavalry especially, employ a large number of followers, but the Afghan cavalry have none, and what the Afghan cavalry can do the Indian cavalry can do. A certain number of followers will always be necessary on service, but I should like to see as many of these as possible trained and enlisted men, capable to a certain extent of defending themselves. A light carbine slung on their backs and a small knife-bayonet in their waistbands would enable them to assist in repelling attacks on their convoys by day or their camps by night, and yet would not incommode them in their work.

However, to return to our frontier tribesmen. Once a week we used to collect them about us for sports, and it was astonishing with what eagerness they entered into the fun. Before long, under Napier's supervision, a steeplechase course was marked out, jumps erected, and regular races inaugurated. One day the Russian Commissioners came over to join us, and we all spent the afternoon together at the sports. We commenced with goat-cutting with swords for the Afghan cavalry. We ourselves joined in this, and so did the Cossacks, but nothing would induce the Russian officers to try a run. When the goat was disposed of we took up our position on a little mound that formed the grand stand for the occasion, and started the races. The Afghan cavalrymen were as keen as possible over it. We had two races—one for the regulars on escort duty with myself, and one for the Khawanin or tribal levy sowars on duty with the Afghan agent. Each was run in two heats, with a final race for the first three in each heat. There were eight jumps of sorts, not big ones of course, as not a man of the lot had ever jumped his horse in his life till we began to teach him, but sufficiently high to give some fun.

The Cossacks, too, joined in and had their race, and went round the course in good style, not a pony refusing. They also gave us an exhibition of their horsemanship, but this consisted almost entirely in bending over in their saddles and picking up handkerchiefs off the ground at a gallop, and in jumping off and vaulting on to their saddles again. They seemed to show little proficiency with their swords. There were about fifteen of them on the ground altogether, and after the races Colonel Artamanov put them through some movements to show us how they worked. Their ponies were well in hand and wonderfully under control. One manœuvre, supposed to show what they did if caught in the open, was when cantering along in line they suddenly swung round inwards, and each man jumped off and in a few seconds was firing away, resting his rifle on his pony's saddle. They formed a ring, ponies outside and men inside, wonderfully quickly, and not a pony moved. Again advancing at a canter, they suddenly halted and made all their ponies lie down with a rapidity that showed uncommon good training. The Cossacks of the Caucasus are without doubt capital, hardy, handy men. They are in their element as scouts and foragers, and as a screen to an army. I have heard Cossack officers say that in war their rôle is to go ahead and to be the scouts and outposts of the army, both infantry and cavalry having complete rest while they are in front, and thus coming up fresh to do the fighting. Their rôle, they say, is not to fight, and certainly they are armed and equipped neither as infantry nor cavalry, and would be at a disadvantage when opposed to either.

About the middle of August the weather began to change, and the nights got cool. The young sand-grouse then began to appear, and formed a welcome addition to our larder. We had various expeditions into the *chul*, as the rolling, undulating ground on either side of the river was called, after deer; but though lots were seen, none were bagged. We turned out all the Afghan sowars, too, to try and beat the wild pig out of the reed swamp up the river above our camp, but without success. The reeds were so thick that neither men nor horses could get through, and they were not dry enough to burn. Towards the end of the month teal, snipe, and quail began to make their appearance. All this time work was steadily progressing, and on the 3rd September 1893 the final protocol was signed. We dined for the last time with the Russian Commission, and they dined with us, and that was the end of our festive evenings together.

M. Ignatiev started for Petersburg, and I to join my appointment at Mashhad. Instead of returning to Herat and going round by the high-road I struck off due west across Badghis. Leaving the Kushk Valley on the 6th September 1893 we crossed the hills into the valley of the Moghor stream, which was under cultivation by Jamshidis, and thence to Gulran, where I was visited by the Hákim of Ghorian, who had been posted to watch the frontier with fifty Afghan sowars on the look-out for a refugee named Abdul Majid, a grandson of Sultan Ahmad, the last independent ruler of Herat. This man had lately escaped from Mashhad, where he had been living on a pension from the Persian Government, and was said to be in Russian territory organising a raid on Herat. However nothing came of the attempt, and the last heard of Abdul Majid was that he was living at Samarkand, where he had been granted an allowance by the Russian Government.

Gulran we found in the occupation of Afghan nomads, and the road on from there to Robat-i-Surkh was very hilly. We found the hoof-marks of wild asses which had evidently come in from the *chul* to drink, but we had not the luck to come across any, and apparently they were getting very scarce.

We struck the Hari Rud at Kaman-i-Bihisht on the 10th September 1893. The bed of the river was mostly dry, with pools of salt-water here and there, and we had to send some distance to get water fit to drink. A gale of wind blew all day and we were covered with dust.

The Russian frontier post on the banks of the Hari Rud is at Pul-i-Khatun. The old bridge there has been rebuilt by the Russians, and free communication across the river into Persian territory has thus been obtained at all times of the year. It was from Pul-i-Khatun that the Cossacks were despatched into Persia in 1897, and the place will be an important one in any future advance.

CHAPTER III.

THE PERSIAN NORTH-EAST FRONTIER.

THE nearest inhabitants on the Persian side to the Russians at Pul-i-Khatun are the Jamshidis at Shuriya. These Jamshidis originally came from Herat with the Hissam-us-Sultanah after the siege of 1857, and they afford a good instance of the wandering nature of the tribesmen of these parts. They numbered about 2000 families at that time, and were first settled in the Sar-i-Jam district under their chief Allahyar Khan. They were driven from there to Khanagusha and Karrabukha near Mashhad by Turkoman raids, and from there a large number returned to Herat. Allahyar Khan himself at last went back as well, and then the remaining families were moved by the Persian Government away back to Kushkhana, in Kuchan, and placed under the Routi chief, Ismail Khan.

Eventually Allahyar Khan fled back from Herat, returned to Mashhad and was reinstated as chief of the Jamshidis in Khurasan, but the numbers of the tribe were reduced to 150 families by the famine of 1871. Allahyar Khan died at Karrabukha, and was succeeded by his son, Zulfikar Khan. In 1885 the tribes were moved to Paskamar, where their numbers still further dwindled down to 80 families. Zulfikar Khan subsequently opened negotiations with the Russians, and he and his tribesmen were sent back in 1889 by the Persian Government from Paskamar to Karrabukha. Zulfikar Khan shortly afterwards fled from there to Russian territory, whereupon his younger brother, Muhammad Azim Khan, was appointed chief of the tribe in his place, and they were settled at Jellalabad and Jizaabad, some ten farsakhs to the south-east of Mashhad. Zulfikar Khan, however, afterwards returned from Russian territory and settled with his tribe at Shuriya and Paskamar on the Kashaf Rud, and both he and his younger brothers now receive allowances from the Persian Government, and the tribe has a service of 50 sowars.

The Jamshidis in Herat still apparently have a hankering after Persia. Though they were removed by the Amir from their more distant quarters at Kushk in 1885, and settled near Herat itself under close supervision, they still get away at times. In 1893 about 50 families managed to make good their flight from Herat to Khurasan, and were settled by the Persians in the Zurabad district under their chief Saiyad Ahmad Beg, and others possibly may follow if they get the chance.

The Routis are another tribe that have had wanderings very similar to the Jamshidis, and are now located with them at Paskamar on the Kashaf Rud. They came originally from Derawat in Kandahar, and after many wanderings in Khurasan and Badghis they finally were settled in 1857 to the number of 700 families in Sar-i-Jam. They were driven from there with the Jamshidis to Khanagusha and Karrabukha by Turkoman raids, and were also moved with them to Kushkhana in Kuchan. They then numbered some 550 families, but were reduced to 200 in the famine of 1871. They returned from Kushkhana to Khanagusha, and were moved to Paskamar in 1885.

These constant changes of residence show what little ties frontier tribesmen as a rule have to the land they occupy, and how devoid they are of all sense of patriotism or devotion to any particular country.

Immediately to the north of the Jamshidis, the only residents on the Persian side are in the extreme north-east corner at Sarakhs.

Persian Sarakhs consists of nothing but a walled enclosure or fort. Inside is the residence of the Hákim or Persian governor, and also of the Karguzar and the Persian telegraph clerk. The remainder is mostly, I believe, a ruin. Some two or three hundred *sarbazes* or Persian infantry and a few *topchis* or artillerymen are quartered in the place. In addition to the Persian garrison there are some 150 families of Arab descent located in the place. These Arabs were settled at Sarakhs in 1874, and have a service of 50 horsemen. About 100 families of Sistanis were also settled there in 1888 with a service of 60 footmen, but their numbers have now dwindled down to about 60 families. All these people are nominally cultivators, but they eke out a miserable existence by all accounts. At the time of the Russo-Persian boundary settlement, one-sixth of the water of the river was assigned to Persian Sarakhs and the remaining five-sixths to Russia, consequently there is little or no water for cultivation on the Persian side. On the Russian side this is all changed, and there is plenty of cultivation. The bazar and the Salor Turkomans to the number of some 2000, who live about a couple of miles beyond the cantonment, and the small colony of Russian families of German descent located beyond them again, are all under the charge of the Pristav, who apparently is a sort of revenue collector and police magistrate rolled into one. The pay of these appointments as Pristav is only some 180 roubles or about £19 a month,

BARRACKS AT RUSSIAN SARAKHS.

I believe; but this is large in comparison to the pay of the Russian military officers, who at the outside only get fifty per cent. on the pay of their rank in Russia proper. The Russian garrison in 1894 consisted of one infantry regiment, the 5th Transcaspian battalion, and one company of a reserve battalion, and the photograph gives a picture of their barracks. Russian regiments in Transcaspia in ordinary course never change stations, consequently the officers at Sarakhs are there for their lives, so to speak. The men hate the place, I have been told, and attempts at desertion are frequent; but though the heat is great it is not unhealthy, and they do not get the fever there that rages so terribly at Merv and at the Kushk post. The Russian telegraph line to Sarakhs has been brought down to the river and joined on to the Persian line from Mashhad, which has been considerably improved and is now in fair working order. A considerable amount of Russian traffic now passes along it. The Russian Government, however, do not subsidise the Persian Government on that account as we do—on the contrary, the Persian Government have to go to considerable expense in repairing the line to meet Russian requirements.

On leaving Afghan territory at Kaman-i-Bihisht we crossed the Hari Rud to the banks of the Jam in Persian territory, and followed the course of that river up to Amirabad. We found the Jam very narrow, hardly ten yards in breadth in fact, full of dense reeds and utterly impassable, so deep was the mud. The water too was brackish, and though we beat both banks we only saw two pheasants in the whole twelve miles. We found lots of *chakor* though, or red-legged hill partridge, called *kabk* in Persia, and bagged eight or ten brace of them and a hare and a teal.

Our ride the next day to Turbat-i-Shaikh Jam was

across a waste plain the whole way. Here we struck the high-road from Herat to Mashhad, and came into direct communication with both places by means of the line of postal couriers kept up by the Indian Government for the conveyance of the Indian mails from Herat to the agent to the governor-general at Mashhad. The post-bag is despatched by the Amir's post from Chaman through the British agents at Kandahar and Herat, and thence these couriers take it on to Mashhad. On the Afghan side Afghan sowars are employed, but on the Persian side of the border the couriers are mostly Turkomans, mainly Sariks from Panjdeh, who were employed as guides and couriers by the Afghan Boundary Commission before Panjdeh was taken possession of by Russia, and who have remained on in British service ever since, many of them having become naturalised British subjects. These men are posted in relays along the road, three men at each stage, about 6 farsakhs or 24 miles apart, and Turbat-i-Shaikh Jam being about half-way between Herat and Mashhad, the British agent in charge of the line was stationed there, and was present to meet us on arrival. We had a great parting at Amirabad with our Afghan hosts, the Mehmandar and the Jamadar and men of the cavalry. They had accompanied us thus far to see us safe to the first inhabited village in Persian territory, and then took leave and returned to Herat. They were good fellows all round, and we were sorry to part with them. On their departure the Turkoman postal sowars took up their duty and kept watch over our camp at night.

The village of Turbat-i-Shaikh Jam, or Jam as it is locally called, consisted only of some 250 houses of people known as Jámis. The tribe was said to number some 4000 families, all cultivators, and formerly had a chief of its own. Alizar Khan, the head-man of Faraiman, was the representative of the chief's family, but he had no power. His father had been deprived of the chiefship, and the tribe were under the control of the governor of the district for the time being. Those of them at Turbat-i-Shaikh Jam lived inside a square mud fort. Around this were a number of gardens, where quantities of fruit were grown. The shrine or tomb of the holy man who gave his name to the place lies to the east of the town, and the lofty *aiwan* or arch surmounted by the usual square superstructure, with a couple of domed minarets, stood up clear above the surrounding trees, and was visible from afar. The face of this arch was originally covered with tiles, but these had been greatly destroyed, and the Kufic inscription was quite illegible. Some of the flower patterns remaining, though, were good. The enclosure in front was full of graves, but the whole place looked dirty and deserted, and the musjid, corridors, and buildings around were mostly in a state of ruin. Khanikoff gives a short biography of the saint, and according to him Shaikh Jam was the thirty-eighth in descent from Abraham, and was born near Turshiz, of Arab origin, in A.D. 1048, and died in 1141. An inscription inside the dome of the mausoleum bears date A.D. 1456, and some lines of poetry engraved on a stone are said to have been placed on the grave by the Emperor Humaiyun in 1544. Around the tomb were the graves of various holy men, dating from 1612 to 1642, but there was no record of anything specially ancient.

From Turbat-i-Shaikh Jam to Mashhad is a distance of 96 miles. At Langar (15) we found the ruins of a fine old shrine in a garden and a big reservoir full of water. I was too ill with Kushk fever to go out, but Napier and Duke shot over the snipe jheel there, and made a good bag. Our next camp was at Karez-i-Nou, 18 miles beyond. The principal feature of the country was the number of ruins about and of old *karezes* that ran for miles across the plain, showing that at some time or other the land was much more flourishing than it is now. Faraiman (23) consisted of a good-sized open village, surrounded by fields of lucerne. To the north-west of the village, close to the high-road, a fine new *robat* or rest-house was being built by the Nusrat-ul-Mulk, the chief of the Timuris in Persia.

These Timuris are said to be of Tartar origin, but to have come to Khurasan from Syria, whence some 20,000 families of them were moved by Amir Timur (1369–1405), after whose name they were called. Timur first settled them in Balkh and gave them in dowry to his daughter, who was married to one Mir Saiyid Kalál, a holy man of Arab descent who lived on the banks of the Oxus, and was Timur's spiritual guide. On Mir Saiyid's death the tribe was distributed amongst his sons. Among these was one Saiyid Mir Shahid, or Mir Shah Khan, who got about 4000 families, and moved them from Balkh to Herat. There apparently they increased in numbers, as after his siege of Herat in 1883 Muhammad Shah Kajar moved some 8000 families of them to Khurasan under their chief, Kilich Khan, a great-grandson of Mir Shah Khan, who subsequently obtained great power, and became the ruling chief of the Jam, Bakhurz, Khaf, and Zorabad districts under the title of Amir. About 2000 families are said to be still in Afghanistan in the Herat, Sabzawar, and Farah districts, and in 1897 some 120 families of these suddenly crossed the border into Persian territory, before the Afghan authorities got news of their flight. The latter followed them up and did their best to persuade them to return, but they refused to do so. The Timuris in Persia are now supposed to number about 6000 families all told.

About a mile out of Bakirabad we passed a ruined

brick *robat* and then the village of Sangbast, and away to the right of that again was a tall minaret and a dome, locally said to be the mausoleum of Agaz the slave and minister of Mahmud of Ghazni, whose native place it was. The Tarikh-i-Yamini, however, states that the founder of the *robat* at Sangbast was Arsalan Jázib, Wali of Tus under Sultan Mahmud of Ghazni (997–1028), whose mausoleum was also there. The probability, therefore, is that these are the remains of those buildings. Beyond this we came to a low rise at the end of some hills topped by a tower, from which we looked down on the Mashhad plain. Here it is that the pious pilgrim from the Herat side gets his first glimpse of the distant shrine.

At Turuk (17) we camped close to a building to the south of the village, consisting of a lofty *aiwan* or portico between fifty and sixty feet in height, with a domed enclosure behind it, presumably the mausoleum of some famous man, but now utterly in ruins and unrecognisable. The inscription had gone, and nothing was known as to who built the place or what it was built for. In front of it were three large and beautifully carved tombstones in black marble, but broken and defaced. One of these, according to the Sani-ud-Dowlah, has an inscription in Arabic to one Darwesh Yahiya dated A.H. 716 (1317 A.D.), but none of us could make out the name or date at all.

CHAPTER IV.

MASHHAD.

AT Turuk I received the Persian programme of the reception that was to be accorded to me on my arrival at Mashhad the next morning, and I cannot do better than give a translation of the document as a specimen of Persian official etiquette. It ran as follows:—

The reception party will consist of the following officials:—

On the part of the Governor-General.

A sartip (colonel) in full uniform, head of the reception party.
A yuzbashi (non-commissioned officer), with ten Persians dressed as Cossacks.
A led horse with gold trappings.
A riding-horse with gold trappings and English saddle (for the Consul-General).
One mustaufi (financial secretary).
Two munshis (secretaries).
A naib mir akhor (assistant-master of the horse).
One jilaudar (head-groom).
Two yawars or majors of the army.
Four ardals (orderlies) mounted.
Four ardals (orderlies) on foot.

On the part of the Beglarbegi (Police Magistrate of the Town).

The kalabegi (collector) of the town.
Two kadkhudas (heads of quarters).
The darogha (city magistrate).
A led horse.

THE BRITISH CONSULATE AT MASHHAD.

On the part of the Karguzar (Persian Foreign Office Agent).

A naib (assistant) of the Karguzar in full uniform.
One munshi (secretary).
Farashbashi with ten Farashes (messengers).
A led horse.
One jilaudar (head-groom).

The Governor-General of Khurasan and Sistan will provide the following things at the Bagh-i-Musalla:—

Reception tent (large)	1
Tent for putting on uniform	1
Tent for preparing tea in	1
Chairs	40
Table (large)	1
Sweetmeats (trays)	2
Tea	—
Coffee	—
Kalyans (pipes)	—

On the morning of Thursday the 21st September 1893 the reception party will be present in the reception tent when the Consul-General arrives at the small tent made ready for changing clothes.

After putting on his uniform the Consul-General will proceed to the reception tent accompanied by the officers of the British Consulate-General. On his arrival at the reception tent the head of the reception party and his companions will come out to meet him and conduct him inside the tent, where the Consul-General will occupy the central chair, the reception party sitting to his right, the officers of the British Consulate-General to his left, and respectable British subjects, present to receive the Consul-General, towards the door on the right and left.

After partaking of tea, coffee, &c., the procession will start towards the town in the following order:—

Farashes.
Persian Cossacks.
Led horses.
Consul-General's own orderlies.
Consul-General (riding on horse with gold trappings).
Head of reception party.
Officers of the British Consulate-General.
Naib Karguzar.
Others.

At the entrance to the town a Naib Farash Bashi and some Farashes of the Karguzar and of the Governor-General will meet the Consul-General.

After conducting the Consul-General to his house and partaking of tea, &c., the reception party will depart.

After the Consul-General's arrival at his house, two trays of sweetmeats will be sent by the Governor-General with a Sartip (colonel) to inquire after his health; sweetmeats will also be sent by the Karguzar.

The next morning the Karguzar, having given notice, will call upon the Consul-General in full uniform.

The Governor-General's wazir will also call upon the Consul-General the same day, in full uniform, after giving notice.

On the third day the Consul-General will call on the Governor-General in full uniform in the following manner:—

A naib of the Ishik Aghasi (master of ceremonies) will call for the Consul-General on horseback with

A riding-horse with gold trappings for the Consul-General.

A Yuzbashi with ten Persian Cossacks and four Ardals (orderlies) at an hour appointed by the Karguzar, and will conduct the Consul-General to the Ark (citadel).

Some Sarhangs (lieutenant-colonels) Ghulam Peshkhidmats (mounted orderlies), Tufangdárs (musketeers), &c., will be drawn up in a row in front of the reception room.

After partaking of refreshments the Consul-General will depart, and return the visits of the Governor-General's wazir and the Karguzar the same day.

The Governor-General will pay a return visit to the Consul-General on the third day.

This programme was duly carried through in all details. We rode in the five miles next morning to the Bagh-i-Musalla, outside the Páin Khiaban gate of the city. First of all appeared Duffadar Shahzadah Taimus and the five orderlies of the Guides Cavalry on duty with the consul-general at Mashhad, who came out to escort me in. After them we were met by the Persian Cavalry, dressed in red Cossack uniform, and the Farashes in black, who conducted us into the garden. A Farash in Persia answers to the Chuprassi or Peon in India to a

THE ENTRANCE TO THE BRITISH CONSULATE AT MASHHAD.

certain extent, but he is more than that. He is a lictor, a messenger, a tent-pitcher, a carpet-spreader, an everything in fact all in one.

At the entrance to the Musalla garden I found Mr. Thomson, the vice-consul, Khan Bahadur Moula Bakhsh, the attaché, and the remainder of the British consular staff awaiting my arrival. The Persian Sartip received me at the tent inside, where the British-Indian subjects and pensioners residing in Mashhad had also assembled, and we all sat down together to tea and sweets and cigarettes. This over, we mounted our horses again and rode into the town. After proceeding up the Páin Khiaban street we wended our way through the lanes and by-ways at the back of the shrine to the British Consulate near the citadel at the south-west corner of the city, where the same tea-drinking was again gone through, the only difference being that we were the hosts this time instead of the guests.

I now had time to look around at my new domain. I found myself in an enclosure some six acres in extent, surrounded by a high wall. Towards the centre of this stood the consulate, a large white square building in two storeys, with a verandah round the lower storey. The house had only been built the year before, and had never been occupied. The furniture belonging to the old consulate down in the town had been brought over and put into it, but that was all. The main gate of the garden opened out towards the citadel. On the opposite side of the garden were the dispensary, the consulate office, and the attaché's house, with the clerks' and orderlies' quarters on the third side. Behind the office again were the stables and the vice-consul's house, so that all was very compact, and when the doctor's house was subsequently built in the remaining corner of the enclosure, the consul-general and his staff were all brought together; a much better arrangement than being scattered about in hired houses in various parts of the town, as had been the case before.

Life at Mashhad at first starting was almost entirely taken up with receiving and returning visits. First of all to come and call was the Karguzar or Persian Foreign Office agent. This official takes precedence of all others, and is independent of the Local Government. All consular business is transacted through him, and all cases in which foreign subjects are concerned are settled by him. He is also one of the highest paid of all Persian officials. The Karguzar at Mashhad received two hundred tumans a month. This included everything, that is to say, all sumptuary and other allowances, as well as the pay of the office establishment. Out of this sum the Karguzar had to keep up his staff, which at the time consisted of his son, as assistant, and a clerk, the latter a permanent man, who was taken on by one Karguzar after another. Two hundred tumans represent about £40, or 600 rupees, not a large sum to provide everything on, but a large sum for Persia, where actual pay by no means represents the total emoluments received.

On this his official visit the Karguzar appeared in full uniform with three stars on his breast and a ribbon over his shoulder. These were the badges of his rank, and showed his promotion from Sarhang, or lieutenant-colonel of the second class, to Sarhang of the first class, and thence to Sartip or colonel of the third class. This was my first introduction to Persian badges of rank, and I had to learn the difference between them and decorations proper. At first sight they looked all the same.

After the Karguzar came the Wazir, who held the rank of Mustaufi, or revenue accountant of the first class. Mustaufis in Persia hold a rank of their own, and are of considerable importance, as they are the only men in the

H.H. THE MUAIYID-UD-DOULAH, GOVERNOR-GENERAL OF KHURASAN AND SISTAN.

country who understand the revenue accounts. These are kept in the Siák character, which is a speciality of its own, and no one but a Mustaufi can interpret accounts thus written. The system has its advantages at times, as I heard of one governor who on removal from office had his accounts made up, and was found to be a debtor to Government to the extent of 80,000 tumans (£16,000). He got another Mustaufi to examine his accounts, and the latter brought him out a creditor to the amount of 40,000 tumans, thus showing to what an extent both the Government and the governors are at the mercy of their Mustaufis.

The Muaiyid-ud-Doulah, the governor-general, received me in the uniform of an Amir-i-Tuman, or general of ten thousand, with its star and sash. His Highness wore the jewelled portrait of the Shah round his neck, the highest decoration in Persia.

My noxt visitor was the Hakím Bashi, the governor-general's doctor, who spoke French. In Persia no man of any position is known by his name, but by his title, and to get a title from the Shah is the one thing that gives a man admission into society. The doctor at the time of my arrival rejoiced in the title of Muawin-ul-Atibba, or the Supporter of Physicians, but after his return to Teheran I heard that he had dropped the physician and joined the Persian Foreign Office, and had blossomed into the Muntazam-ul-Mulk, or the Manager of the Country.

After the doctor came the Nusrat-ul-Mulk, the chief of the Timuris in Persia and the governor of the frontier districts of Jam, Bakhurz, and Khaf on the Herat border, in which his tribesmen were mostly located. He was an old and faithful servant of the Persian Government, and had been given his title and the rank of Amir-i-Tuman by Nasir-ud-din Shah on his first visit to Mashhad in 1867, for services rendered during the Turkoman raids on the

Persian frontier. He was subsequently nominated the deputy to the governor-general and also commander-in-chief of the forces in Khurasan, but in 1895 the poor old man had a terrible fall. The then governor-general, the Asaf-ud-Dowlah, sent for him one day to the citadel, and there suddenly seized and deported him from Mashhad. Things might have gone hardly with him had not the Shah sent for him to Teheran, where he found a safe retreat.

Another chief of the Timuris whom I subsequently made the acquaintance of was Mir Asadulla Khan, the Shaukat-ud-Dowlah. He was the head of some 300 families who emigrated from Herat to Khurasan at the time of the siege of Herat by the Hissam-us-Sultanah in 1858. He received his title and the rank of Amir-i-Tuman from Nasir-ud-din Shah in 1893, and after the Nusrat-ul-Mulk's deposition he was appointed governor of Jam and Zorabad in his place, Bakhurz and Khaf being given to others.

One of my next visitors was the Malik-ut-Tujar, the head of the merchants, a fine-looking long-bearded old man belonging to Ispahan, and a brother of the mint-master at Teheran. He told me that he had lived for two years at Constantinople, and another brother of his had lived and died a silk merchant in France. He himself was the farmer of the turquoise mines, out of which he was supposed to have made a fortune. He had a partner at Marseilles and another at Moscow, and when I returned his call I met the latter, who had only just arrived back, in Russian clothes, and had barely had time to change into Persian ones before I came in.

The head of the Persian telegraphs in Khurasan, a Kajar prince, also came to call, and so did the chief of the post-office. This man's grandfather was a Kizil-bash of Kabul in the service of Amir Dost Muhammad

MIR ALI MARDAN SHAH, NUSRAT-UL-MULK, CHIEF OF THE TIMURIS IN PERSIA.

at the time of the first Afghan war, but subsequently migrated to Mashhad, where his two sons, and afterwards his grandson, were in turn British agents under the orders of various British ministers at Teheran. The grandson entered the Persian service and opened the first post-office at Mashhad in 1875. For his services he received from the Shah in 1894 the rank of Sartip of the first class and the title of Mushir-ul-Wazarah, or the Adviser of Ministers. I also made the acquaintance of the Hafiz-us-Siha or the Protector of Health, a Persian doctor educated in the Teheran College, who held the post corresponding to our sanitary commissioner. This gentleman for his services shortly afterwards, during an outbreak of cholera, got the high-sounding title of Malik-ul-Hukama, or King of Physicians

I must not forget to mention either our next-door neighbour at the British Consulate, the Muhandis or Persian engineer. He held no diploma, but apparently that is not necessary to become an engineer in Persia. He had been first of all the surveyor and afterwards the Persian commissioner on duty with General MacLean during the settlement of the Hashtadan boundary dispute on the Afghan-Persian border. In 1895 he was sent down to Sistan, and that killed him. He died soon after his return, and his son succeeded him as the local engineer. The son is now a Sarhang or lieutenant-colonel, and will doubtless rise as his father did, and leave just as big a case full of stars. He showed me his father's badges, commencing with the little star of a Yawar and going right through the six grades to Sartip of the first class. A Yawar is commonly translated "Major," but it does not correspond to that, and answers more nearly to our Indian rank of Subadar major. A Yawar has no rank or position, and in the army he often rises from the ranks. In civil departments, a man when first appointed may be given the rank of Yawar, but officials in these departments never rise higher than Sartip or colonel. Any further promotion as a rule is given in titles.

The visits that I have mentioned give a fair idea of Persian official society in a provincial town. From my colleague, M. Vlassow, the Russian consul-general, and his wife and family we all received the kindest of welcomes. Our party at the British Consulate was reduced before long by the departure of Napier to India. He was able to obtain permission through M. Vlassow to travel by the Transcaspian Railway from Ashkabad to Uzunada, the then terminus on the Caspian, and the driver of a small phaeton, with four ponies harnessed abreast, contracted to drive him the 160 miles from Mashhad to Ashkabad in four days for 22 tumans, or £4, 10s. Some hours after his departure a telegram arrived for him. One of our Turkoman postal sowars started off in the evening, caught him up 60 miles out the next morning, delivered the telegram, and was back again the day after, all on the same horse, and as fresh as if he had only been out for an ordinary stage. I must say our Turkoman couriers were excellent men at long-distance rides. I never knew better. Shortly before Napier left us, a Russian traveller, Prince Galitzin, arrived at Mashhad, and we were all invited by M. and Madame Vlassow to the Russian Consulate to meet him. He had been travelling through Siberia and showed me his route on the map—along the Chinese frontier from Tomsk and down through the Cossack settlements there to Samarkand and Bokhara, and thence to Merv and Bala Murghab. Having seen this, he was going to spend his leave the next year, he said, in a trip to Canada, to compare that country with Siberia.

With Prince Galitzin came Captain Lomakin, the

M. VLASSOW, RUSSIAN CONSUL-GENERAL AT MASHHAD.

Pristav or police officer of Russian Sarakhs, who was kind enough to invite Thomson to pay him a visit at Sarakhs, and subsequently entertained him most hospitably during his three days' stay there.

On the 17th November 1893 we had a severe shock of earthquake in Mashhad, the same that destroyed the town of Kuchan, 92 miles away. I was sitting at dinner at the time, and despite the 3½-feet thickness of the walls of the house everything shook so that I was by no means sorry to find myself out in the verandah. The shock was a long one, and when it ceased a roar of "Allah-u-Akbar" came up from the town, and many a man, I fancy, was calling louder on his God than he had ever done before.

Shortly after this Major Massy of the 19th Bengal Lancers, who had been travelling in Persia, arrived at Mashhad. He had hoped to travel through Transcaspia and see something of Russian territory before returning to India, but permission was refused, so he then arranged to travel down with me to Sistan, and to return to India by the Quetta route. Why the Russian authorities in Central Asia should prohibit British officers travelling there it is difficult to say. Russians have told me the reason was that Russian officers were not permitted to visit India, but that, I assured them, was all a mistake on their part, as not only were Russian officers free to visit India whenever they liked, but they did not even require a passport, much less a special permit, to do so, and they would be warmly welcomed by the British officers in India whenever they did come. The only difficulty that I know of is that Russian officers are not permitted to travel to India through Afghanistan, but the Amir has been perfectly impartial in that respect. He does not permit the Englishman to travel through to Russian territory any more than he permits the Russian to travel through to India. Russian officers can travel freely through Persia or else round by sea, and the pity is that they do not take advantage of their opportunities to come and see us oftener. As it is the Russian affects to believe that India is closed to him, and this justifies in his mind the closing of Transcaspia and Turkistan to the Britisher. The consequence of this want of intercourse between Russians and English in Asia is that each has the most erroneous ideas about the other. Both sides would learn to appreciate the other more did they know each other better, and there can be no doubt that a little more friendly intercourse would greatly tend to eliminate the suspicion and distrust with which the Russian frontier officer is now apt to regard everything done by the English. For Englishmen in Mashhad the general prohibition to travel by the Transcaspian Railway is specially hard. The difficulties and delay in getting leave simply to pass through to Europe are often so great that I have known a man take the twenty days' march to Astarabad, to embark on the Caspian from there, rather than wait on the chance of a permit to go to the Caspian by rail from Ashkabad. I must say, though, that when permission has once been granted, Englishmen as a rule are treated with every kindness and civility throughout Russian territory.

CHAPTER V.

TURBAT-I-HAIDARI AND TABAS.

MASSY'S leave was limited, so I determined to start for Sistan without delay. Our arrangements for the march were soon complete. In Persia one soon learns to discard the palatial tents used in India. Large Indian tents are excellent things for standing camps, but they take many men and much time to pitch, and after many years of constant travelling I have come to the conclusion that they are too big for every-day marching. I have often wondered, indeed, why the Indian Government, in their desire for economy, have not long ago substituted the more handy and less expensive Swiss cottage and Kashmir tents for the big double-pole and single-pole tents that are now kept up for the use of district officers when on tour. Except one Swiss cottage-tent for the mess, we took nothing with us but small Kashmir and Kabul tents, and these we found ample for all our wants. However, after cutting down all impedimenta to the lowest, we still found that we had by no means a small camp. First of all we had to get extra Farashes as tent-pitchers, and these were a mixed lot. We had amongst them a Herati farrier, a Kandahari tailor, a Turk carpenter, and a Persian tent-mender; two Hazarahs, men who had worked on the Bolan Railway in India, and a Kabuli. Then we had to take with us ten or a dozen Turkoman couriers to keep up our postal communication on the road, and also to help as camp watchmen at night. A Persian guard of a vakil and four surbazes, corresponding to a naik and four Sepoys of our Indian army, formed the official escort, but as they had only rusty old muskets and neither cartridges nor clothes, they were not of much use for either protection or show. The only really armed men were my three Indian cavalry orderlies. The party consisted of Major Massy, Dr. Duke, and my Indian assistant, Khan Bahadur Moula Bakhsh, with a couple of Indian clerks and a hospital compounder, and a total all told of some 50 men, including servants, couriers, orderlies, guards, Farashes, grooms, &c., with 24 horses, 30 mules, and 38 camels, and some 18 or 20 muleteers and camelmen. We all moved out into camp at Turuk on the 11th December 1893.

The last to arrive just as we were starting were the guard of Persian soldiers, and the poor men when they did turn up had nothing but their ragged thin blue cotton suits. There was not such a thing as even a greatcoat for them in Mashhad, and all the Wazir could say was that warm clothing should be made up for them, and sent after us. To take men on a journey in midwinter in such attire was an impossibility; so when the promised warm clothing did not turn up we did what best we could on the road to clothe the men ourselves. I must say that in the end the Wazir was as good as his word, for some two months afterwards, one day towards the end of February, in Sistan, just as the hot weather there was commencing, a sowar turned up with the promised suits tied up on his horse behind him, having travelled after us some 500 miles, a fair example of Persian military efficiency.

From Turuk we went first to Sharifabad, fifteen miles

along the Teheran high-road, and then struck south into the country of the Karai, a local tribe who at one time held a position of considerable importance.

According to the Sani-ud-Dowlah, Amir Khan, chief of the Karais, was appointed to the charge of Mashhad under Shah Rukh by Ahmed Khan Durani in 1749. At the beginning of the present century the tribe came to great prominence under their chief Ishak Khan, who in 1813 incited the various tribes to rise in rebellion and to advance on Mashhad. They were apparently worsted, however, and Ishak Khan had to beg for forgiveness in 1816. Both he and his son, Hasan Ali Khan, were subsequently killed in Mashhad. Muhammad Khan, another son of Ishak Khan, then took up the rebellion, and the Karai and Hazarah tribes combined to take Mashhad. Peace was not restored till the governor Muhammad Wali Mirza was recalled. In 1827 Halaku Mirza was appointed governor, and advanced on Turbat-i-Haidari, but owing to the opposition of the other Khurasani nobles he was unable to do anything against the Karai, and had to return to Mashhad. Muhammad Khan became more powerful than ever, and took possession of the town of Mashhad in 1829, but was at last subdued by Ahmad Ali Mirza, son of Fateh Ali Shah. He, however, retained a sort of semi-independent existence, and never thoroughly acknowledged the authority of the Kajars. After his death the tribe lost their independence, and gradually the hereditary chiefship was abolished and the tribe placed under the Persian governors for the time being of Turbat-i-Haidari. The Karai now number about three thousand families. They are said to be of Turk origin, to have originally been brought from Turkistan by one of the Mongol kings, and to have been taken to Syria. Amir Timur (1369–1405) located them in Fars, whence they were brought to Khurasan by Shah

Ismail Safavi (1499–1523), and after residing for some time at Merv and Herat they finally settled at Turbat-i-Haidari. The tribe now provides one regiment of infantry. Of these half are on duty, and the other half on furlough, the detachments being relieved every six months.

We crossed the pass known as Gudár-i-Muhammad Mirza at a height of 6540 feet, and camped at Asadabad, in wet and cold weather. The next day the rain turned to snow, with a bitter east wind, and we had to push on to Kaskak to get over the Bedar Pass before the snow melted. This pass, 6700 feet in height, has a steep descent on the southern side through soft earth, and the camels just got over it in time. Next morning, some three miles from Turbat-i-Haidari, we were met by the governor, accompanied by Sarhang Ali Muhammad Khan Karai, his son Sultan Abdur Raza Khan and some thirty Karai horsemen, and we all rode in together.

The Karai horsemen consist of 150 sowars, armed mostly with old muzzle-loading guns carried on their backs, and they serve locally in the Turbat-i-Haidari district. Their establishment comprises one Sarhang, one Yawar, three Sultans or Resaldars each in command of fifty men, one pay clerk, and one writer. Each sowar receives pay at the rate of 17 tumans (£3, 8s.) in cash and 2½ kharwars or 1625 lbs. of grain a year, which would not go far towards keeping a man and his horse, with a wife and family as well, if he had not land to cultivate in addition.

Turbat-i-Haidari presents a very tumble-down appearance when first seen. The walls are high, and were formerly strong, but are now broken in all directions. In former days the people had all to live within the walls to save themselves from Turkoman raids. Now most of them have moved out into the surrounding villages, and the present town only occupies a fraction of what was formerly inhabited, and probably does not contain more than 500 houses. The ruined citadel marked the residence of the last chief of the Karais. Half the town, and certainly all the boys, were assembled on the top of the ancient rampart to see us come in as we passed along to the caravansarai at the south-west corner of the town, where most of our party secured quarters. I myself was put up in a couple of rooms close by, and the governor, having escorted us thus far, took leave for the time, and came back to pay his formal visit in the afternoon. Haji Muhammad Mirza Kashif, now the Káshif-us-Sultanah, to give him his last title, had spent ten years of his life in Paris attached to the Persian Legation there, and spoke French well. When I returned his call we rode through the bazar, which was some 150 yards in length, and of the usual shape of four streets radiating from a large dome in the centre, each street being covered with a domed roof throughout. I was astonished to see so much business going on. I found the bazar thronged with people, and showing every sign of commercial activity. Several Russian Armenians were settled in the town engaged in the wool trade, which was said to be almost entirely in their hands, and there was also a large trade in dried plums and fruits of sorts. On return from my visit I received the old Karai Sarhang and his son, and in the evening the governor came to dine with us. It was here at Turbat-i-Haidari that I first came in for the ceremony of having a sheep's throat cut in front of me on my arrival at the town, a custom which I afterwards found was almost universal throughout the country. The sacrifice is supposed to bring good luck, and the ceremony is apparently gone through on the arrival of any special visitor. The sheep is thrown down on its back on the road, and its throat is cut right in front of the visitor in whose honour it is sacrificed, and the blood is allowed to flow in front of him, so that he crosses it on his way in.

The town of Turbat-i-Haidari derives its name from the *turbat* or tomb of a saint named Kutb-ud-din Haidar, who is buried in a large, domed, red-brick mausoleum. When visiting this tomb I found several darweshes or religious mendicants established there, and thinking that one man looked like an Indian, I addressed him in Hindustani, and he replied at once. He turned out to be an old sowar of the 1st Bengal Cavalry, and he said that he had left Peshawur thirty years ago. The way these mendicants wander about the world is very curious, and most of them seem to have no home or home ties of any description. One can understand Muhammadans flourishing in Persia, but it has always struck me as particularly curious how the Hindus made their way from India to Baku on the Caspian Sea and back again in former years. The Hindu temple where they kept up the perpetual fire was still intact when I first visited Baku in 1881, but the Hindu Fakir was no longer the custodian there. Petroleum factories had driven him out, but only just before my arrival. The revenue of the Turbat-i-Haidari district was said to be 70,000 tumans (£14,000), but this did not include the Khalisa or crown lands, which were supposed to yield another 10,000 kharwars of grain. The district was at one time famed for its silk, but disease destroyed the silkworms, and the industry has been almost put an end to. Tea, indigo, tin and copper sheets, and some piece goods were imported from India, but we found that most of the piece goods in the bazar were Russian, and that all other things came from Russia.

On leaving we sent all the baggage on ahead, and then

remained behind ourselves for breakfast, the servants afterwards packing up the breakfast things on their mules and riding on with us. The Persian *abdári*, as it is called, is an excellent institution in this respect. It consists of two large leather bags joined together and made to fit the two sides of a mule or pony, and the man rides on the top. These bags are fitted up for all culinary appliances, there being one place for the spit, another for the *samovar* or hot-water urn, and a box containing tea cups and saucers strapped on behind. The cook and the two *peshkhidmats* or table servants who had these *abdári* mules could always stop and give us a meal at any time anywhere on the roadside. It was marvellous the amount of things these bags of theirs seemed to contain.

We reached the southern limit of the Turbat-i-Haidari district at Miandeh, and there the official deputed by the governor to accompany us took his leave. Tabas territory, we were told, commenced just beyond.

At the village of Ghujd we apparently formed quite a show, as all the people were out to see us pass, the women, all clad in white, sitting on the tops of the walls, and the men in the streets below. A little way beyond we were met by the chief of Tabas's Názir and Mirakhor, with a carriage and pair for our use, but it was as much as the horses could do to pull the carriage through the sand as it was, and we allowed it to precede us in state. Two miles out from Jumand I was met by the chief's two grandsons and the deputy-governor with led horses and some twenty sowars, who escorted us into our camp on the south of the town, where the old chief sent presents of sheep and fruit to meet us on our arrival. The weather was cloudy and cold, and the thermometer went down to 23° F., which is as low as one cares for in tents. The next day was Christmas Day, and it opened brighter, and we had the sun out again. In the morning the chief's eldest son, with the Wazir and the chief's two grandsons, paid their formal visit, and in the afternoon I paid my visit to the old chief, accompanied by Massy, Duke, and Moula Bakhsh. We rode through the village to the ark, or so-called citadel, a walled enclosure in the centre of the village, now mostly in ruins, where the chief was living. The son and grandsons met us outside the door, and inside we found the old man seated. He was just able to rise from his chair to receive us, that was all; but though so weak physically, he showed himself a clever and well-informed old man in conversation, and it was a pleasure to talk to him. Duke had already been to see him in the morning at his special request, but he was seventy-seven years of age, and his life was evidently running out fast, and there was little that a doctor could do.

The old chief asked lots of questions about England and India, and told us that he had a turquoise mine in his territory, which he had formerly worked at a profit, but the turquoise veins spread about through the rock, and when they had got down some thirty yards they could get no farther, and the works were abandoned. He was pressing in his invitations to us to return viâ Tabas, promising us excellent oorial and ibex shooting in the hills around, but unfortunately I was unable to go that way.

The village of Jumand, the headquarters of the Gunabad district, turned out to be a straggling, thinly-inhabited place, consisting mostly of enclosures of pollard mulberry trees, though there was comparatively little silk culture remaining. The total revenue of Tabas was said to be only 30,000 tumans (£6000) per annum, of which the districts of Gunabad contributed 10,000, Tun 10,000, and Tabas and Bijistan 5000 each.

HAJI MUHAMMAD BAKIR KHAN, IMAD-UL-MULK, CHIEF OF TABAS.

In the evening the eldest son came to dine with us, accompanied by the two grandsons and the Wazir. The second and third sons of the chief we did not see, one being the deputy-governor of Tabas and the other of Tun, where they then were.

The Government of Tabas for a long time past had been in the hands of the chief's family. Originally of Arab origin, and said to have been brought to Persia from Arabia by one of the kings of the Safavian dynasty (14991–736), they made themselves practically independent as the governorship became hereditary under the title of the Vakil-i-Tabas. Mir Muhammad Khan, the last Vakil-i-Tabas, is said to have taken Nadir Mirza, son of Shah Rukh, prisoner in 1776, and also to have defended Mashhad against the Afghans under Madad Khan.

He was succeeded by Haji Muhammad Bakir Khan, the chief who received me and who was granted the title of Imad-ul-Mulk by Nasir-ud-din Shah during his first visit to Khurasan in 1867; by which title the chiefship has ever since been known. I may here add that I never saw Muhammad Bakir Khan again, as he died in 1894. He was generally believed to have been one of the wealthiest chiefs of Khurasan, and to have possessed large hordes of treasure and jewels, but whether this was the case or not it is impossible to say. He did not trust any of his sons, and died without confiding his secrets to any one or even making a will. On his death the hidden treasure was either never found or else it was made away with. What jewels were found by his sons were at once disposed of to raise cash. The amount realised being only 29,000 tumans (£5800), landed property was disposed of to make up the amount to 40,000 tumans (£8000), which sum was expended by them in presents to the Shah, the prime minister the governor-general, and the Wazir of Khurasan for permission to retain their father's government. The eldest son, Ali Akbar Khan, was accordingly given his father's title of Imad-ul-Mulk and the government of Tabas. The second son, Muhammad Raza Khan, and the third son, Abul Kasim Khan, were given the titles of Imad-i-Diwan and Mu'in-i-Diwan respectively, and were appointed deputy-governors of districts under their brother. This arrangement, however, only lasted for a short time. It was not long before the eldest brother lost the government owing to his own incompetence, combined with the intrigues of his brothers and the enmity of the priests, who denounced him as a Babi. He was summoned to Teheran, and his next brother, who managed to give a good present by selling his landed property, was appointed to succeed him. In 1896 the latter was also dismissed, and the district of Tabas was then given to the Hashmat-ul-Mulk, the chief of Sistan, who had married a grand-daughter of the old Imad-ul-Mulk, and who gave large cash presents for the appointment. The Hashmat-ul-Mulk, however, only remained in possession for about a year. By that time the Imad-ul-Mulk, the eldest brother, who was at Teheran, had contrived to raise enough money to get himself reinstated. The Hashmat-ul-Mulk, however, was not to be beaten. He outbid the Imad-ul-Mulk and was reappointed. When the Rokn-ud-Dowlah arrived at Mashhad in 1897 as governor-general of Khurasan, the Hashmat-ul-Mulk was again dismissed and the second brother, the Imad-i-Diwan, was re-appointed governor of Tabas in his place. This appointment, however, was not confirmed by the Persian Government, who ordered the eldest brother, the Imad-ul-Mulk, who by this time had raised sufficient money to give a third present, to be again reinstated, the second brother's title being raised from Imad-i-Diwan to Imad-ul-Mumalik in compensation. Thus the case stood when I left—what will happen the future alone can tell, but it looks as if the various brothers will soon be impoverished, and that a generation hence their descendants will probably be found occupying a position little removed from that of peasant.

The road to ruin is a rapid one in Persia, and the case of Tabas is a typical one of the fall of many of the hereditary families of Khurasan who were so powerful at the beginning of the present century.

CHAPTER VI.

KAIN AND BIRJAND.

From Jumand we had a bare stony plain to cross to Kakhk, a good-sized village lying at the foot of the Siah Koh hills, that here bound the Gunabad district on the south. The land was neatly terraced up the slope to the village, and full of pollard mulberries. We passed a fine building domed and covered with tiles, the mausoleum of Sultan Muhammad, said to have been a brother of Iman Rasa at Mashhad, and we noticed a number of *mullas* and *saiyids* about. Our camp was besieged all day by crowds of villagers, who seemed to be quite content so long as they could sit and look at the unusual sight of *faringhis* in their midst. Their only work seemed to be the manufacture of curious little inlaid pocket-saws.

At the villages of Khizri and Dasht-i-Piaz the whole population turned out to see us pass, and we noticed a decided difference in the people. The men mostly wore sheepskin hats, and only a few of them turbans. The women were darker and redder in the face, and wore a checked scarf instead of the white one we had hitherto seen. Supplies were plentiful and cheap—so cheap, in fact, that I was told fowls could be bought at the rate of three for a kran, or about a penny-halfpenny apiece.

At Nughab we were met by the deputy-governor of

Kain and a party of eight sowars who had been sent out by the chief to meet us and escort us into Birjand.

The old town of Kain we found consisted of only a few poor houses inside the walls, while the bazar, the musjid, the madrasa, and the greater part of the town was outside. We rode through the so-called bazar, but it consisted of nothing but a few dyers' and bootmakers' shops. The musjid was the only building that rose above the rest, and that, according to an inscription on a stone over the arch, was built in A.D. 1368.

The silk trade had greatly decreased during the past ten years, and the growing of saffron had taken its place. Owing to the high prices prevailing, the cultivation of this was increasing year by year. Formerly, I was told, the price was six or seven miskals for a kran—say fourpence an ounce, but it had gone up to two and a half miskals or one Indian tola per kran. The inhabitants largely consisted of *saiyids* and *mullas*, neither of whom in Persia can be reckoned among the working-classes. Since the cultivation of opium had been introduced, they had taken greatly to the smoking of it, and the sad results were only too visible.

No tax other than the usual land revenue is levied on opium cultivation in Persia, and the extraordinary cheapness of the drug tends greatly to the excessive use of it. The custom of smoking opium is becoming universal amongst men, women, and children, and must have a baneful effect on the country generally before long. It is the smoking, not the eating of opium that seems to have such very bad effects.

The trade of Kain I found to be larger with Bandar Abbas on the Persian Gulf than with Mashhad and Sabzawar on the north. Saffron, opium, silk, and skins were exported to Bandar Abbas; and drugs, iron sheetings, spices, indigo, and tea imported in return. Roughly speaking, two-thirds of the trade was said to go to Bandar Abbas and one-third to Mashhad and Sabzawar. The sugar was all Russian, and came direct from Sabzawar.

I ascended the hills to the south of the town to examine the old ruined fort. The walls were all built of stone and mortar, and enclosed a space of considerable extent. We had a climb over the hills to see a second and similar, but smaller, fort to the east, known as the Kila-i-Dukhtar. We saw fresh traces of ibex and oorial on the way, but did not come across any. One curious thing on the top of the hills was a hole in the ground from which emanated hot air or steam. The rocks round the hole were all wet and covered with green moss, which could not have existed in such a place except in a hot-house atmosphere. There had been twelve degrees of frost the night before, and the ice had not thawed in the shade all day.

Next morning, New Year's Day, 1894, we divided up into two parties. Massy and Duke went off on a trip to Durukhsh to see the carpet-weaving there, while I went on with Moula Bakhsh by the direct road to Birjand. My first march was to Rúm, crossing a pass in the hills on the way, and then on through more hills to Sehdeh, which turned out to be the home of the Naib of Kain, who was escorting us, and who showed me with much pride the caravansarai he had built, for which good work, as I told him, I trusted he would get due reward in heaven. The village contained some 150 houses, and we had to take supplies with us for the next day at Ghip, a small place of only 15 houses where nothing was procurable. The road gradually ascended through hills the whole way, and the cold was so great that the ice did not even melt in the sun the whole day. I was clad in about half-a-dozen layers of the thickest things I had, and an

MIR ISMAIL KHAN, SHAUKAT-UL-MULK, CHIEF OF KAIN AND BIRJAND.

Afghan Barak greatcoat on the top of all, and it was not a bit too warm.

On the 4th January 1894 I arrived at Birjand. About two miles from the town I was met by the Shaukat-ul-Mulk, the chief of Kain, as he is called, though he lives at Birjand, his father having been the Amir of Kain. That title, though, has not been continued to the son by the Persian Government, a fact which of itself marks one step in the gradual reduction of the independence of this formerly hereditary chiefship.

With the Shaukat-ul-Mulk were his cousin Haji Abdul Ali Khan, the Sarhang commanding the Persian artillery stationed at Birjand, and some thirty mounted and twenty footmen and led horses, &c. The chief himself drove out in a carriage and invited me to drive back with him, but I persuaded him to ride instead, and we rode in together through the bazar to my camp on the other side of the town, where he came in and had tea. The chief had prepared his garden house for us, but this I declined, as, with so many men and animals, damage, I thought, might possibly be done to the garden.

Directly the Shaukat-ul-Mulk had left, his brother, the Hashmat-ul-Mulk, the chief of Sistan, sent to express his regret at having been prevented by illness from coming out to meet me, and here I must give some of the family history. The two brothers, Mir Ismail Khan, Shaukat-ul-Mulk, chief of Kain and Birjand, and Mir Ali Akbar Khan, Hashmat-ul-Mulk, chief of Sistan, are now both about fifty years of age. The founder of the Kain family, Mir Ali Khan, of the Arab tribe of Khuzaima, is said to have been forced to emigrate from Arabia to Khurasan in the time of the Khalifa Harun-ul-Rashid (786–809), and to have settled in the Kainát district. The tribe were wealthy flockowners, and gradually increased in power till Mir Alam Khan, their chief, became

Amir of Kain about the end of the seventeenth century. His son, Mir Masum Khan, is said to have been in the service of Nadir Shah (1736–1747), and his grandson, Mir Alam Khan II., is said to have been the man who deprived Shah Rukh, the grandson of Nadir Shah, of his eyesight at Mashhad in 1748. In the disturbances that subsequently ensued Mir Alam Khan II. gained great power, and even proclaimed himself Amir of Khurasan, but was forced by Ahmad Shah Abdali to take refuge in flight. He is said to have been succeeded as Amir of Kain by Mir Ismail Khan, and the latter by Mir Alam Khan III., the grandfather of Mir Alam Khan IV., Hashmat-ul-Mulk, the father of the present brothers, who was the Amir of Kain so well known in the days of General Sir Frederick Goldsmid's mission to Sistan in 1872. He died at Mashhad in 1891, and on his death the title of Hashmat-ul-Mulk was given to his elder son, Mir Ali Akbar Khan, with the governorship of Sistan, and a new title, that of Shaukat-ul-Mulk, was conferred on the second son, Mir Ismail Khan, with the governorship of Kain. The Persian Government, by thus splitting the family up, were enabled to reduce its power and also to drop the title of Amir, and the sons are now simply designated the Hukmráns or governors of Kain and Sistan respectively. Once the power of the family has thus been broken, the probability is that the hereditary government in time will go too, and in the end the governors of Kain will come to be ordinary Persian officials with no local connection, who will come and go with each new governor-general, just as the governor of Turbat-i-Haidari does at present.

The day after my arrival Massy and Duke rejoined me from their trip to Durukhsh. They told me that they found carpet-weaving in full swing there, and the carpets manufactured were said to command high prices at Teheran and Constantinople. The colours were too glaring, though, for English taste, and the use of aniline dyes was universal; but the texture was good, some of the finer carpets being very beautiful, with a velvety nap rare in other Persian carpets. The prices asked, though, were prohibitive. Shortly after their arrival I received formal visits from both the Hashmat-ul-Mulk and the Shaukat-ul-Mulk. The former drove over in his carriage from the village of Hajiabad, six miles out, where he lived. He came alone, his eldest son, then some fourteen years of age, being away in Sistan, acting as deputy-governor for his father. The Shaukat-ul-Mulk came accompanied by his younger brother, Muhammad Ibrahim Khan, his cousin, and the Sarhang of artillery. The old Amir of Kain was said to have left 60,000 tumans (£12,000) in cash, as well as a large amount of jewellery and arms and considerable landed property, and when I was at Birjand the division of this amongst the sons had not yet been arranged, and was giving rise to much friction between the brothers.

I returned the Shaukat-ul-Mulk's visit at his residence in the village of Abidin, about 1½ miles out of the town. The chief had here built for himself a reception-room some 25 feet in length, with verandahs on either side and a fortified enclosure at the back of it for his *andarun*, or family quarters. The village formerly occupied by his father, named Akbarabad, a mile to the east, was left uninhabited. The chief told us his territory extended as far as Bandan on the Sistan side, and to the village of Sar Chah-i-Amari at the edge of the desert, 12 farsakhs from Birjand, on the Kirman side. Beyond that there intervened a waterless tract 60 farsakhs across, and the Kirman territory commenced on the other side. Camel *kafilas*, he said, crossed this desert tract in three days and three nights, the men taking water for themselves, but the camels getting none the whole way. By this route caravans could reach Bandar Abbas in twenty-eight days, viz., thirteen days from Birjand to Kirman, and fifteen days from Kirman to Bandar Abbas. The longer route more to the east, round by Neh and Bám, took fifty days. Caravans, though, only went to Bandar Abbas once a year, going and returning during the winter. No one could go in summer, he said, on account of the heat. Finally the chief showed us his collection of guns and rifles, in which he took great interest. The majority of these, I believe, he inherited from his father, and he had some good ones as well of his own. He also showed us some Snider cartridges that he had had made by hand in Birjand. These had a solid brass base, and his workmen had turned out about a thousand of them. The Sistan chief, the Hashmat-ul-Mulk, received us in tents. With our tea he gave us some excellent macaroons and sweetmeats, which he said had been specially prepared for us by his family.

While at Birjand I received a visit from the Mustaufi of Kain, a young man, who had taken part in the assessment of the revenue of both Kain and Sistan, and had thus acquired a thorough knowledge of both districts. I also went, at the request of the Sarhang of artillery, to inspect his guns. He received us in full uniform—a dark tunic and trousers tucked into huge boots with spurs, and his white sash and star of Sarhang on his breast, while a guard of honour of about a dozen of his men presented arms. They had the usual blue calico artillery uniform, with blue shoulder-straps and a blue band on the hat and trousers. All the men were Azarbaijanis, and apparently the whole of the artillery in Persia is recruited from the Turks of that province. The guns consisted of six brass pieces, five of which were smooth-bores, with inscriptions showing they had been manufactured at Teheran some fifty years before. The sixth was rifled, having been manufactured so late as 1865, but two of the gun-carriages were broken, and most of the limbers. The guns had no horses, were much honeycombed, and seemed of little use. I subsequently heard that better guns were sent in their place the following year.

Birjand itself was a good-sized town, and was said to contain 25,000 people. The town had a flourishing look, in so far that all the houses appeared to be inhabited, and few ruins were to be seen about, as is generally the case in most Persian towns. There were few gardens around it, owing to the general want of water. The Kanat water in the town was brackish, and sweet water had to be brought from springs near the chief's village at the foot of the Kuh-i-Bakiran. These hills, which bound the Birjand plain on the south, are said to be twelve farsakhs in length and four in breadth, and to have numbers of small springs in the upland villages, to which many people move up in the summer. This may account for the want of game in them, as both ibex and oorial were said to be scarce.

As to trade in Birjand, the preponderance was said to be with Bandar Abbas, but this did not appear to be a certainty. The wool trade was mostly in the hands of the Armenian merchants at Sabzawar, who had agents in Birjand, and 5000 camel-loads of wool and other goods were said to have been exported during the year to Sabzawar for shipment on the Caspian. Sugar appeared to be pretty evenly divided between Russian from Sabzawar and French from Bandar Abbas, the former selling for 6½ krans, and the latter for 7 krans per man of 6½ lbs.

English piece goods were said to preponderate over Russian in the proportion of 5 to 3, but how far that was actually the case I had no means of testing. However, during the year 3800 camel-loads of dried fruit, skins, saffron, and opium had been despatched, it was said, by Birjand merchants to Bandar Abbas. These camels mostly went the long round via Neh and Bam, by which they took two months going and the same returning, and they brought back with them piece goods, as well as tea, spices, iron, indigo, sugar, and copper.

Regarding the revenue of Birjand, I found that for the whole Kain district the amount of 32,300 tumans (£6660) was levied in cash from the Shaukat-ul-Mulk by the Persian Government.

On leaving Birjand I called on the Shaukat-ul-Mulk to say good-bye, and to thank him for the arrangements that had been made for our comfort during our stay. Both he and his brother had done their best to show their hospitality and make us welcome in every way. Though I declined with thanks their offer to supply the whole camp with free rations throughout my stay, still they made such a point of my accepting their hospitality that it would have been discourteous to have refused a dinner, and a fine feast all the men had in consequence. When I mention that the two brothers between them sent something like 100 lbs. of sweetmeats, 50 lbs. of sugar, 100 lbs. of ghee, 20 sheep, 300 lbs. of rice, 300 lbs. of bread, 10 lbs. of tea, with bottles of sherbet and lime-juice, and a large supply of saffron and other luxuries, it will not be doubted that our men had their work cut out for them to do justice to it all. As for myself, the difficulty was to find sufficient presents to give in return.

I camped at Bujd, seven miles out, on purpose to say good-bye to the Hashmat-ul-Mulk at his village of Hajiabad, and then went on with the Shaukat-ul-Mulk's Farashbashi, who was sent to accompany us to the limits of the Kain district. The part of the road from Birjand to Bandan was very bleak and cold. Our first march, to a place called Múd, was across a bare stony plain with a gradual ascent till we got to snow level. The village we found contained some 300 houses, and the chief work of the place was the weaving of a fine sort of Barak or woollen cloth. The next stage to Sarbisha was a long one across a bleak upland plain. We rode through snow the whole distance, and the only sign of mankind was a small water reservoir about half-way. Sarbisha contained some 700 houses, and stretched in a long strip of mud domes all along the end of a spur in the hills, and standing at a height of something like 5700 feet, the cold was great. Snow fell the whole time we were there, and we were glad to get down to a lower altitude beyond it. The principal occupation of the people seemed to be the manufacture of *namad* or felts. Some miles beyond the village we met a Herati camelman who came up and made friends at once, having been formerly employed with us on the Afghan Boundary Commission. He was on his way to Narmashir. This, he said, was the principal henna-growing district in Persia, and thousands of camel-loads of it were sent annually from there to Yezd, where the leaves were ground into powder before being distributed over the country.

From Sarbisha we had a drop of some 1500 feet down to Sahlabad, a small village of some sixty families. Here the snow changed to rain, and then it froze so hard that our tents were as stiff as boards, and could not be struck till they had thawed.

The plain beyond was quite different from the bleak uplands near Sarbisha, in so far that it was covered with bushes; and two of them, the *ták*, said to be eaten by camels when green, and the *kich*, a darker-coloured wood, both ran up to four and five feet in height. There was also a small shrub called *tirikh*, about a foot in height, which I was told was readily eaten by all animals.

At the village of Tark we rose again to a height of something like 6000 feet, and found ourselves once more above snow level. The cold continued great, and my Caucasian *bashlik* was the greatest comfort on the march. No one travelling in winter through Central Asia should be without one. They keep the head, neck, and ears warm, despite wind, cold, rain, or snow. Tark contained about sixty houses, mostly of shoemakers, and the water was good, but there was not enough of it for much cultivation.

Two stages farther brought us into Neh, which lay in a hollow in the middle of a plain at a level of some 2300 feet below that of Tark. The principal building in the place was a mud fort on a mound, with a citadel held by a few men. The village lay around a mass of mud domes, and was said to contain about 500 houses. To the north was a long row of some fifty windmills, which were worked in summer when a north wind blows. The fort was utterly in ruins, but the citadel had been kept in repair and stood high, well overlooking the village, and there was a good view from it. Neh was the residence of a Naib, or deputy of the Shaukat-ul-Mulk, and he came out to meet us accompanied by one of the local Khans. In the bazar I found that Russian sugar was selling for 6 krans a man, whereas Marseilles sugar from Bandar Abbas was 7 krans. This was even cheaper than the Russian sugar was selling at Birjand, and showed how the Russian bounty system enabled dealers to undersell the French sugar and drive it from the market, even so far south as this. Russian cotton goods were also for sale in the bazar, though in less quantity than English. Wool and skins seemed to be the only export, and of these some 200 camel-loads were said to be sent down annually to Bandar Abbas. The principal work of the place seemed to be the manufacture of woollen socks and gloves.

From Neh we made a short march of five miles to Khunik-i-Pain, or Lower Khunik. Here we found another row of about a dozen windmills similar to those at Neh. Curious-looking things they were too. Each windmill consisted of an upright pole standing between two side-walls open at the back to the south, but with two-thirds of the space closed to the north. The pole in the centre was fixed in a cross-beam at the top, and ran down through the millstones in a room below to a pivot fixed in the ground. The upper millstone was fixed to the pole by wedges and was worked by it, but the pole went through the lower stone without moving it. This pole was some twenty feet in height, and the sails, made of straw, were affixed to it by rods sticking out horizontally. The mill was then spun round horizontally by the wind blowing in through the opening to the north.

From here we had a longish march across a bare plain to Aliabad, a walled village of some twenty houses. According to our aneroids we got down here to an elevation of only some 2000 feet, but the cold still continued great, and the Kushk fever still continuously pursued me. We camped the next day at a place called Shutargardan, where there was no village or habitation of any sort, simply some brackish water in a river-bed; and the day after we reached Bandan, a walled village at the mouth of a gorge in the hills, containing some thirty houses. To the east lay a curved line of high cliffs. The elevation was about 1500 feet, and there was a considerable grove of date trees in the valley just above the village; but for all that it did its best to snow all day. A stream of brackish water ran down from the village of Zainulabad to Bandan, and thence away southwards. It was along the banks of this that the date groves lay up a narrow valley in the hills, and good dates we found were procurable at the rate of about 4½ lbs. per kran, or say a penny a pound. Massy purchased a large bagful for his trip across the Baluchistan desert. We had now arrived at the limit of the Kain territory, and the Shaukat-ul-Mulk's Farashbashi and Ghulam, who had accompanied us from Birjand, accordingly here took leave and returned.

CHAPTER VII.

SISTAN.

EIGHT miles out from Bandan, at a spot called Bal-i-kamab, we were met by Sultan Abu Turab on the part of the Hashmat-ul-Mulk, the chief of Sistan. He left Birjand the same day that we did, and rode through to Sistan in seven days. There he arranged about our reception and collected the necessary supplies for us, and then came back to meet us and escort us in. Three inches of snow had fallen during the night, an almost unknown occurrence in these parts, but the farther we got out the thinner it became, till by the time we arrived at Bahrang there were only a few thin patches to be seen. The road led across a dry plain, and before we had gone far out the famous Koh-i-Khwajah of Sistan, a low, flat-topped, isolated hill, came in sight, and just before we got in to Bahrang we struck the edge of the Naizar. The reeds could be seen from our tents, and the water of the Hamun was visible some two miles off. Our camp was pitched near some pools of brackish water, but there was no habitation or anything but a few bushes anywhere near, and the supplies had all been sent out from Sistan. This being a dry year, we were able to cross into Sistan on dry land; but Mr. Merk in 1885 described the water as reaching right up to Bahrang and several feet in depth, and the passage across in *tutins* or reed-rafts took a couple of hours.

It was on the 27th January 1894 that we arrived at Násirabad or Shahr-i-Sistan, the City of Sistan, as it is called. For the first ten miles the road led over soft ground, which was generally inundated, but had then been dry for some eighteen months. Then we entered a narrow, sunken lane through the Naizar or reed-beds, called locally the *kúcha* or street, which is the route for the reed-rafts when the reeds are under water. When we emerged on the more open ground beyond we crossed a level expanse with short grass here and there, and some two miles out from Násirabad we were met by the *istikbal* or reception party, which surprised me greatly by its size. All the Sirdars, Kadkhudas, and leading men of villages had been called in, and the result was that we were greeted by a body of horsemen numbering nearly 150 all told. I did not think that there were so many horses in the whole of Sistan, knowing of its ancient reputation for poisonous flies and horse disease, but here they were. At the head of the party was the young chief Sartip Mir Masum Khan, and with him were Sirdars Sa'id Khan, Khan Jan Khan, and Purdil Khan, and they all escorted us into camp, and then came in and sat down with us to tea. Our camp was pitched near the garden, or rather enclosure, called the Chahar Bagh, a little distance from the town, and as we rode in, our numerous escort galloped around, firing off their guns in every direction.

Sirdar Sa'id Khan, the maternal uncle of the young chief, was the son of the late Sirdar Sharif Khan, Nahrui, who held a prominent position in Sistan politics at the time of the Goldsmid Boundary Settlement in 1872. He subsequently submitted to the Afghans, and died at Kabul about 1889. The Hashmat-ul-Mulk had married his daughter, and she was the mother of Mir Masum Khan. Sharif Khan's two sons were both summoned to Kabul by the Amir after their father's death, and were sent off by him to Turkistan, but they escaped on the road. Sa'id Khan made his way to Peshawar, and thence to Sistan via Quetta. The other brother, Muhammad Ali Khan, came down the Helmund to Sistan, and since then had lived mostly with the Baluchis in Sarhad.

Sirdar Ibrahim Khan of Chakansur, also a well-known man in former days, the father of Sirdar Khan Jan Khan, had died in Sistan just two months before my arrival, after having lived in huts a wanderer in the jungle for many years, and, like him, all the other old Sirdars of Sistan were dead and gone, and there was no one left with any power or following.

Later on the young chief came to pay me his formal visit, accompanied by the Peshkar, and I duly returned it. We rode along outside the walls to the gateway of the fort, and then through it to the ark or citadel in which he lived. The Sartip met us at the door, and took us into his reception room—a cold place for winter, as I remember I was seated on a raised dais at the end just under the *bádgir* or windshaft, which, though excellent in summer, was a trifle too draughty for the cold weather then prevailing. Almost all the better-class houses in Persia have these windshafts to catch the air in hot weather. The Sartip told us that the fort or citadel had been built by his grandfather, the late Amir of Kain, some twenty-five years before, and that the garrison consisted of a regiment of Kain infantry 800 strong and 500 *iliyáts* or irregulars. These iliyáts or nomads, he said, all came from Kain. They paid no revenue, but performed service instead, and were sent to serve in Sistan. Both these and the *sarbazes* or soldiers were all quartered in the fort or Násirabad, as it is called.

This fort is purely a Kain settlement. No Sistanis are allowed to live in it, and those that come in by day to the bazar are not allowed to take in arms, and are turned out again at night when the gates are shut. There were said to be about 1400 people altogether in the place, including sarbazes, irregulars, and followers of sorts. The pay of the sarbazes, or soldiers of the Kain regiment was seven tumans, or £1, 8s. in cash, and three Kain kharwars, or 1095 lbs. of grain, per annum. With these sarbazes were also twenty Persian artillerymen, mostly Azarbaijanis like those at Birjand, and the Sartip took me round to show me the guns. They consisted of two old brass smooth-bores cast at Tabriz seventy-five and fifty years before respectively, and one mortar. Two other guns were mounted on bastions, and one was in store, but most of the wheels had fallen to pieces, and it was doubtful if any one of them could be fired or moved. When I looked at these guns and at the so-called Kain Regiment, a lot of miserable, sickly-looking men armed with rusty old muskets, without the faintest idea of drill or discipline, and utterly devoid of all soldierly instincts, I could not but acknowledge the truth of the Afghan soldier's remark that were it not for us and the Russians they would turn the Persians out of Sistan to-morrow.

In a small tank in the courtyard of his house the Sartip had some wild swans—six were fine large white birds caught young the year before; two others were cygnets in brown plumage caught that year. There were also three grey geese caught young before they could fly, and I was surprised to find that wild swans and geese bred in such a hot country as Sistan. The Sartip also had some red-headed pochards and mallards, but these he said had been caught in nets, and did not breed in Sistan. We then bade good-bye to the young chief, and rode back through the fort bazar. This was a poor place, but all the people we saw were wonderfully civil. Passing out of the fort at the far side, we rode through Husainabad, the adjoining village, now simply a collection of domed mud hovels. The village was originally walled, and was the main town, but the walls were destroyed during the rebellion in 1873, and had never been rebuilt. On the way back I was taken to see what is called the new citadel, a square, high-walled enclosure with a garden inside, which the late Amir of Kain had built on to the citadel of the fort some fifteen or sixteen years before, but which had never been properly finished, and was quite untenanted, except by the guard at the gate.

The shooting in the inundated country two or three miles to the south-west of Násirabad was sadly disappointing work. We found water in every direction and swarms of duck and geese away far out of shot, but no cover or means of getting near them. We tried sending men on horseback round to drive the birds, but that was a long and rather tiresome business, as the men found it so difficult to get across the various water-channels, and at last, when the drive did come off, and we got the birds well on the wing, the result was again disappointing, as almost all the birds we shot fell into deep water, and we had no means of getting them out. At last I got hold of two men, the *arbabs* or head-men of all the netters and fishermen of the country, and they promised us good sport in the Naizar to the north, and so off we went. The 1st of February 1894 saw us encamped seventeen miles out at a place called Tishakáni; our road led due north for the first seven or eight miles through villages and numerous ruins, and then we got out on to the open plain and finally into the Naizar. We rode for some miles through dry reeds, and finally came to our tents pitched by the waters of the Hamun. We all got on to *tutins*, the reed-rafts of the country, each of us being propelled about by a man with a pole. We found lots of ducks of sorts, and bagged some thirty in an hour or two before it got dark, but few were of really good kinds, and the loss of wounded birds amongst the reeds was very exasperating. We found that we were camped on the southern shore of the western Hamun or lake, known as the Hamun-i-Sáwari, after some traditional king of Sistan named Sawar Shah, who built a palace in it which is now under water, but can still be seen, so the fishermen told me, when the waters are low. They described it as a large building of burnt brick on the western side of the lake.

Next day we were out early, directly after breakfast, and first of all were shown how the Saiyáds, as the Shikaris of Sistan are called, netted wild-fowl. In the open pools of water dry reeds are stuck in the mud, in rows at short intervals, and bent down one on to the next so as to form long lines along the surface of the water, by which an obstacle is created. The ducks, when swimming, follow along these lines, and are thus diverted over the net. The net is fastened in the centre and at the corners to sticks driven firmly into the ground. These sticks are then bent down outwards, two on one side and two on the other, under the water, and hitched into nicks in four stakes fixed in the ground opposite to each corner of the net when thus spread out, the sticks thus forming a powerful spring. The Saiyád sits concealed in the neighbouring reeds, and when a flock of ducks swim over the submerged net, he pulls a rope which releases the four sticks. These at once spring upright, thus bringing the two sides of the net together and enclosing the birds between them. The ducks caught are then pinioned in an ingenious manner by crossing their wings at the back of their heads and putting their feet up on their backs, and so sent to the town for sale, where ten or a dozen of the commonest sorts can be bought for a kran, or at say a halfpenny apiece.

The two headmen of these Saiyáds, Arbab Ali and Arbab Muhammad, told me that the tribe under them numbered from a hundred to a hundred and fifty families, and they subsisted almost entirely by netting. They were divided into *mahallas* or groups of families, generally seven or eight in a group, to each of whom a separate beat or piece of water was assigned. In the winter they lived by catching wild-fowl and in the summer by catching fish, and I must say they were the wildest and poorest set of men I had seen in Persia. They paid a tax of a few krans a year for the right of netting. This they easily made in ordinary years, when the roads across the Naizar were inundated, as they had the monopoly of plying the *tutins*, and no passengers or *kafilas* could pass to or fro without employing them. They inhabited the southern shores of the Hamuns and the Naizar as far as the inundations extended, but they never worked on the river. A glance at the map will show that the Helmund, flowing from south to north along the eastern side of Persian Sistan, empties itself into the Hamuns or lakes on its north. When the snow in the mountains melts and the river is in flood these lakes overflow, and the surplus water flows back again from north to south along the western side of Sistan, eventually emptying itself into the Gaud-i-Zarih, the lake on the south. Just to the south of the two Hamuns is the large tract of country covered with high reeds known as the Naizar. The water in these reeds advances and recedes with the level of the lakes. We for instance had to pass through several miles of dry reeds before we got to the edge of the water on our way out from Násirabad, and we also got in to Násirabad from Bandar dryshod, but then 1893 was an exceptionally dry year. Under ordinary circumstances we should have had to employ these Saiyáds to transport the whole of our camp—men, tents, baggage, and everything—in their little reed-rafts across the inundated portion of the road, the camels, horses, and mules being tied on to the rafts behind, to wade or swim as the case might be. Owing to the dryness of the year we found the Saiyáds in exceptionally unfortunate circumstances, and not having been able to make any money as ferrymen they were reduced to great straits. In high flood the charge is as much as two krans per trip for each *tutin*, whereas fish and duck were selling so cheap that little could be made by netting. The Turkomans, for instance, purchased fifteen good large fish one day from them for a kran, which works out about three for a penny. The *tutins* made by these Saiyáds are works of art of themselves. They are handy, excellent little rafts made up of bundles of reeds skilfully bound together, and they are poled along in the water with ease. The difficulty with them out shooting is that the ducks get into the shallow water near the edges, and there these *tutins* cannot follow them. At one place called Puza-i-Daraz, a long stretch of open water some six miles to the west of Tishakani, the water was so shallow that we could not get into the reeds at all, and consequently had very poor sport. There were lots of ducks, but all up at the end in shallow water where nobody could get near them, or else in the reeds at the side. The number of common black coots in these pools in the Naizar was something marvellous. Blue coots also were very plentiful, as well as shovellers, and a curious small stiff-tailed duck that I had never seen before; really good ducks were comparatively scarce.

On our return to Násirabad continuous rain set in. The country was soon flooded, and our camels starting out with the tents could not cross the water-channels and had to return. There was nothing for it, therefore, but to sit quiet. On inquiring about the country I found that the revenue was mostly levied in kind, and was fixed at 24,000 kharwars of 649 lbs. of grain per annum. Of this I was told 6850 kharwars were paid out locally in allowances to officials and troops, and the balance had to be accounted for by the Hashmat-ul-Mulk to the Government at the rate of 7 krans per kharwar, resulting in a fixed payment of 12,000 tumans (£2400), for which he was responsible whether the crops were good or bad. The fact that the Government rate for grain should be so low as 7 krans, or little more than half-a-crown per kharwar, showed of itself how extraordinarily cheap grain was in Sistan at the time when the rate was fixed. The Government rate, of course, is always much below the market value, as for instance in Khurasan, where the average value of wheat was 50 krans a kharwar, while the rate at which the revenue grain was accounted for to the Government was only 25 krans; the difference being one of the perquisites of the governor-general, who made what he could by the sale. In addition to the 24,000 kharwars of grain, a sum of 2600 tumans was also levied in cash. This represented taxes on sheep and cattle at the rate of one kran per 20 sheep and 2½ krans per 100 cows. Bullocks I found were not taxed at all, and curiously enough none of the cultivators or villagers kept bullocks of their own, but hired them when required for ploughing from the Maldars or nomads, who kept large herds of them in the Naizar. What with their debts to the cattle-owners for hire of bullocks, and their debt to the Kadkhudas who advanced their grain, the cultivators and people of Sistan generally were in a wretched state of poverty. I do not think I ever saw a more miserable-looking lot. There were no landowners in Sistan. All the land and water belonged to the Government, who took a third share of the produce. Consequently the revenue fixed at 24,000 kharwars would represent an annual out-turn of 72,000 kharwars of grain, but the total out-turn was said to be about 85,000 kharwars, as there were 500 Sistani sowars who got no pay, but paid no revenue and were given each one plough of land free; the produce of one plough being estimated at 18 kharwars of grain. Of the total produce, about half was supposed to be consumed in the country, the other half being exported, some 80,000 camel-loads of grain having been sent out of Sistan at the time of my visit. The prices ruling in the Násirabad bazar were as follows:—

Wheat, 25 krans,	or about 10 shillings,	per kharwar of 649 lbs.	
Barley, 20 "	" 8 "	" "	
Bhoosa 4 "	" —	" "	
Firewood (tamarisk), 4 krans		" "	
Bread, 1 kran	—	per 2 mans or 13 lbs.	
Ghee, 4 "	—	" 1 " " 6½ "	
Milk, 1 "	—	" 2 " " 13 "	
Sugar, 6½ "	—	" 1 " " 6½ "	
Fowls, 2 or 3 for a kran.			
Eggs, 40 " "			

As to trade, I found that there were no regular traders in Sistan at all, nor any foreigners, except a few Kainis who dealt in skins and wool. As a rule the different villages clubbed together and sent a *kafila* to Bandar Abbas or to Quetta once a year in the autumn, returning in spring. About 3000 camel-loads were said to leave Sistan in this way annually, 500 of which went to Quetta with ghee and a little wool, and all the remainder to Bandar Abbas with wool and goatskins, bringing back in return tea, indigo, spices, sugar, and a small quantity of piece goods. The things thus brought did not as a rule come into the town bazar, but were taken by the camel *kafilas* to the villages direct. The supply was said to be generally not sufficient to last out the year, and the people had to eke out the last few months with goods from Birjand which were mostly Russian. The Sistan bazar at Násirabad I found absolutely empty. There was nothing in it at all but a small quantity of Russian sugar, with, curiously enough, the British arms on the label, and two packets of Belgian candles. Some 7000 camel-loads of hides, wool, and goatskins were said to be sent to Sabzawar every year for exportation to Russia, and the imports from Russia in return were iron cooking-pots, piece goods, and sugar. Russian sugar I found was sold in Sistan at a little less price than it was sold in Birjand. It was curious to see how the farther it went the cheaper it got.

As soon as the rains ceased we made a fresh start. At the village of Afzalabad we came across an enormous flock of some thousands of pelican in the shallow water. Beyond that we passed for some miles across a plain where there were a good many sand-grouse, and finally we entered the tract marked on the map as liable to inundation. This was dry, but reeds were within a short distance on either side. On arrival at Koh-i-Khwaja, some eighteen miles out, we found there was no water to be got there, and that all supplies had to be brought from the village of Ali Akbar, two miles off. Koh-i-Khwaja is a name derived from the saint Khwaja Sara Sarir, who is said to have been a direct descendant of Abraham, and whose *mazár* or mausoleum stands at the northern end of the hill where all Sistan assembles on the festival of the Nauroz, or New Year's Day (21st March). Of the origin of the fortifications on the hill, or of the ancient history of Sistan, I make no mention here. I can only refer the reader to Sir Henry Rawlinson's "Notes on Sistan," at page 272 of vol. xliii. of the Royal Geographical Society's *Journal* for 1873.

The Sistanis with me considered the fortress to be the Kila-i-Mirbád mentioned in the Sháhnáma as the residence of the Kak-i-Kuhzad who was attacked and conquered by Rustam. The hill, which looks quite flat on the top as seen from below, is some 200 or 250 feet high, and is surrounded on all sides by a steep scarp, and is only accessible at three places on the south-west, the south-east, and the north-west. The main entrance and ancient fort is on the south-east. The outer walls of this fort apparently extended right down to the water's edge, and when the floods were out the Koh-i-Khwaja must have been an island, and a difficult island to get at, as not only did the inundations from the Hamun wash it on the east, but at the back of it, to the west, lay an expanse of white-coloured dry mud, stretching apparently right away to the foot of the Koh-i-Palang hills in the distance, called the Hamun-i-Sanjal, which, though dry at that time, retained water in it, so my guides told me, for a whole year after all the rest of the inundated ground had dried up. It had been dry for two years at the time of my visit. Ascending from the outer line of walls we came first of all to the ancient gateway, and behind it to a huge square structure all of unburnt brick. This was mostly in ruins, and consisted of domes, rooms, and archways in endless confusion, and mostly fallen in; but there was sufficient to show what a strong place it once had been. Working our way through this we ascended the remains of what had been a ramped causeway leading up the side of the cliffs to the summit of the hill, and guarded at the top by another and smaller fort. Horses could not get up this. They had to go round to the south-west side of the hill and come up a ravine, which was also guarded by a third fort on the point overlooking the passage. The summit of the hill, when reached, turned out not to be level, but all up and down in little hollows. There were no walls, nor any signs of fortification or of habitations on the top; but there were a large number of curious graves above-ground, built of stones some three feet in height and roofed with slabs of stone covered with earth. In many cases rows of these graves extended in one long line all in one building, so to speak, with separate compartments for each body side by side. Many of these had been opened at the end, and one could see a shallow vault inside with the bones of the deceased lying barely covered with a thin layer of dust at the bottom, and an open space of a foot or so between the bones and the roof. I never heard of the custom of burying the dead above-ground in these countries before, but the loose stones of which these receptacles were composed were mostly in perfect order, and the bits of cloth visible in some that had been opened gave the idea that the graves were not of any very great age. One of our guides told me that the old men of his village had a tradition that some really ancient graves once existed below the hill on the south-west, which, when opened, had been found to contain arms, necklets, and coins, and had all been rifled in consequence. I could find no trace of any inscription or engraved stone or tile or anything to give a clue to the date of these graves, and General Lovett, in his narrative of a visit to Koh-i-Khwaja, published at page 145, vol. xliv. of the Royal Geographical Society's *Journal* for 1874, the only other account of the place that I have seen, mentioned the same thing.

The view from the top of Koh-i-Khwaja was unique. Away to the north-east lay the open horizon of the Hamuns, while all the land to the east and south looked as flat as a board, just as if it had all been the bed of some ancient lake.

On our ride from Koh-i-Khwaja to Chilling we

passed through what appeared to be about the most thickly-populated portion of Sistan, but Chilling itself and all the other villages around were built on the level plain, and there was not a sign of the *tappahs* or artificial mounds so common in other parts of the country. The only hillocks about were the three mounds on which the village and fort of Sehkoha was built. About a mile from there we passed through the ruins of a thick walled fort called Kala-i-Sám. Here I was met by the Kadkhuda of Sehkoha, Pasand Khan, a Gurgej Baluch and his two sons, and, escorted by them, I was taken through the village and up to the top of the fort, where I was shown the room in which Ali Khan Sarbandi was murdered by his nephew, Taj Muhammad, the uncle of Sirdar Purdil Khan—a well-known scene in Sistan local history, which has been already related by Bellew in his "Record of the March of the Mission to Seistan," published by the Government of India in 1873, No. civ. p. 145. Bellew has so fully entered into the history of Sistan, and has so graphically described its ruins and antiquities, that it is needless for me to refer to either here further than to say that this Ali Khan was the man who first gave in his submission to the Persians, and who first hoisted the Persian flag on the fort at Sehkoha in 1852. This Sehkoha fort occupies two out of the three mounds, but though the outer walls are in good repair all the rooms inside have been allowed to go to ruin, and the place was nothing better than a stable, and filthily dirty. It was garrisoned by a sultan or Subahdar and a few Persian Sarbazes of the Kain Regiment. The Kadkhuda lived in the top of the third mound, and there was originally a wall round the village below, but that was mostly in ruins too. The Kadkhuda declared that the village contained 300 houses, but it did not look to me as if there were so many. The majority of the villagers were Sistanis, the Baluchis being confined to a few relatives of the Kadkhuda, though there were some Baluch settlements scattered about outside. There were a good many walled enclosures around the village, but there were no shops inside it nor any shopkeepers, and the place altogether had a deserted look. Four traders were said to live in Sehkoha, but they were all away with their annual caravans, and no information was obtainable regarding trade. A few packets of Belgian candles and a little Russian sugar were the only commodities we could find in the place. The Kadkhuda Pasand Khan did his best to put difficulties in our way, and had it not been for Sultan Abu Turab Beg, the Hashmat-ul-Mulk's representative, we should have had much trouble in getting the supplies we required.

I here determined to split up our party. Duke was to remain with the main camp to devote himself to the Sistan sick, who were flocking in for treatment, while I and Moula Bakhsh went on to the Baluchistan border to see Massy as far as we could on his way to India. We had to collect provisions and to make up Massy's caravan. His mules and muleteers who had accompanied him throughout his travels in Persia were to return, and camels had to be hired in their place for the journey across the desert to Quetta, at that time a comparatively unknown road. The Afghans, it was known, had encroached far to the south into Baluchistan territory, and were levying taxes on caravans and otherwise making themselves objectionable, and consequently a longer round than necessary had to be taken to avoid them. Since then the boundary between Afghanistan and British Baluchistan has been defined. The Afghans have been relegated to their side of the border now fixed, and the Indian Government have opened up a new route from Quetta across Baluchistan, running through British territory the whole of the 508 miles to the Persian frontier, viz. Quetta to Nushki, 80; Dalbandin, 110; Amir Chah, 184; and Koh-i-Malik Siah, the British frontier post, 134 miles, or some 24 marches, altogether averaging a little over 21 miles each. All along this route wells have been dug, and levy posts established to secure the safety of caravans and to facilitate traffic, and the journey is now accomplished with a comfort and safety that was formerly unknown. This desert bit has hitherto been the most difficult portion of the whole route. The total distance from Quetta to Mashhad is 1092 miles, or 54 marches, averaging 20¼ miles each, as against the 966 miles or 46 marches, averaging 21 miles each, from Bandar Abbas to Mashhad; but then traders have the advantage by the Quetta route of avoiding the delay and extra expense entailed by the shipment of their goods from Karachi to Bandar Abbas, and again at Quetta camels can be engaged for the whole journey to Mashhad, and the goods are thus delivered much quicker than by the Bandar Abbas route, where carriage is scarce at the best of times, and camels can never be engaged for more than a portion of the way. Goods have thus to be consigned to agents, who send them on from place to place, as opportunity offers, and months and months very often elapse before they arrive at Mashhad. Now that the hitherto unknown Baluch desert has been opened out, there is every prospect of this overland route coming into general use. In 1894 things were very different. Massy on starting had little knowledge of the different stages, and had to trust to such guides as he could get locally. Nothing was then to be procured on the way, while now provisions are stored at the different posts. The question of supplies was one of our greatest difficulties. With the exception of Warmal, a village of about one hundred houses, seven miles off, where we camped on the 11th February, Sehkoha marks the southern limit of habitation in Sistan, and both Massy and myself had to take everything with us from there. No bags were procurable in which to carry grain and fodder for the horses, so we sewed up all the *salitas* or covers of the tents and made them into bags. We set the whole village to work to bake bread, and finally, thanks to the Hashmat-ul-Mulk's man, Massy got the required number of camels. Pasand Khan, the Kadkhuda who had written beforehand offering to supply as many camels as were required, no sooner got us at Sehkoha than he commenced with a demand for hire at the rate of five rupees per day for each camel. He next came down to five krans, the proper local rate being one kran a day, and finally sent off and concealed his camels, thinking he had us in his power. Captain Massy offered two krans a day, and Sultan Abu Turab Beg eventually got camels from other men and put an end to the obstruction on the part of Pasand Khan, who proved himself a thoroughly unreliable man. All that the Sistanis could say for him was that he was not a Sistani, but a Baluch. The Baluchis on the other hand looked on him as a renegade, as they were mostly Sunnis, and he had turned Shiah some three years before to ingratiate himself with the Persians. Which tribe, whether Sistani or Baluch, holds the palm for honesty I cannot say, but the Baluch certainly does not as a rule bear a good character in that respect. Pasand Khan, however, was a man of some standing, as he was the head of the Gurgej tribe, a nomad race said to number about a thousand families, scattered between Gudar-i-Shah and Band-i-Sistan, some in Afghan territory and some in Persian.

From Sehkoha we were to launch ourselves into an almost unknown tract of country extending down to the

Gaud-i-Zarih, as the lake is called which forms the last receptacle for the overflow waters from the Hamuns on the north. The water does not get down to this lake every year, far from it, only at long intervals at the time of exceptional floods; and the country about it was a sort of no-man's-land, inhabited by a few wandering nomads who paid taxes to no one and cared for no one. Neither Persia nor Afghanistan nor Baluchistan at the time of my visit had made the least attempt to establish control in this portion of their territories, and not a Persian or an Afghan or a Baluchistan official, so far as I could ascertain, ever visited it. It was an unknown waste except to a few wandering Baluchis, and few travellers had passed through it. The boundary between Persia and Afghanistan had indeed been fixed by the Goldsmid Mission of 1872, but this was only by an imaginary line drawn at haphazard on paper from the Band-i-Sistan on the Helmund to the Koh-i-Malik Siah, a hill to the west of the Gaud-i-Zarih, and this line had never been marked out on the ground, and neither Persia nor Afghanistan had the least idea where it lay, nor indeed did they seem to care. As a matter of fact, neither side had any interests there. The Persians had never occupied any land to the south of that portion of Sistan watered by the Band-i-Sistan canal from the Helmund, and the Afghans occupied no land beyond the valley of the Helmund itself, and thus Baluchis and anybody else could wander over the country at will. The direct route to Quetta lay down the banks of the Shela to the Gaud-i-Zarih, but the Afghans being in the occupation of Chagai to the east of that again, the direct route beyond that lake had to be abandoned for one farther to the south, and what between the wild inhabitants of the district known as Sarhad to the south-west—which though nominally under Persia was quite independent of all authority—and the Afghans with their forcible exactions on the east, caravans, we were told, had a difficult and dangerous task in getting through at all, and generally travelled at night and hid away in the desert as much as possible during the day.

Once beyond Varmal we had to trust ourselves entirely to the Baluch guides we got in Sistan. They alone knew where water was to be found, and I must say right well they guided us. One of them, Muhammad, a Baluch Shikari of Sehkoha, proved himself an invaluable man.

Our first march was to Hauzdar, a distance of some fifteen miles. The sun was very hot—a great change after the cold days we had had—and it seemed to us as if the cold weather of Sistan was now over. Not a man was to be seen all the way, but a few black tents of some nomads were visible in the distance from the fort when we got in. The fort itself we found to be about 200 yards in length and 130 in breadth, and the buildings inside it to be still in a fair state of repair. The mud domes to the houses were still standing, and the walls were thick and in good order, but when it was deserted no one with us could say. We pitched our tents close beside it, as our only water supply was a pool of rain-water just in front of the gateway, and another in the ditch on the far side. The water was shallow, but clear and good, and all that was necessary was care in scooping it up.

Hauzdar must have been a thickly-populated district in its day. A mile or so to the south-east of it lay a long stretch of ruins known as Machi and Kalacha-i-Rais. These marked the site of an open town, and the buildings were all standing, mostly roofed with domes, and quite deserted except by numerous flocks of pigeons, which seemed to have taken up their abode in the place. For a mile or more in length were to be seen large halls with galleries and many fine buildings, and the place was by no means the shapeless mass of ruined mud walls that one generally sees. The town had apparently been surrounded by gardens and large groves of date-trees, as the roots of the latter were still visible. It is these which give the name of Machi to the place, *mach* being a date-tree in Baluchi. Nowadays there is not a single date-palm left in Sistan, and one wonders where they have gone to and why they have gone. If date cultivation was possible there in olden days, why should it not be possible now, and what was the reason of its stoppage? To all of this we could get no clue; Sistan seemed to be a country without any local history. As to Hauzdar itself, the only thing I could hear about it was a vague idea some of the people had that it was deserted about a century ago when a flood in the Helmund washed away the head-works of the Taraku canal, from which these places received their water, and when that ran dry the people had to move north into Sistan proper, as Goldsmid called it.

At Machi there was a graveyard containing four domed mausoleums still standing, and the graves in them and around them were all above-ground, and had apparently at some time been opened and rifled. There was also a similar cemetery to the west of the Hauzdar fort. Here, too, the people were apparently all buried above-ground. The graves were all of sun-dried brick, and consisted simply of an arched vault some three feet high, in which the body had been enclosed. Every one of those graves had apparently been opened by a hole at the end. I did not see a single grave intact, and though I looked into several I could see no bones. There was not a stone or anything to give a clue as to who or what the people buried here were.

The next day we marched thirteen miles to Ramrud, or rather to a pool of water in a nullah some two miles to the north-east of the ruined fort of that name. The road led across the inundation plain and some rough ground full of small clay mounds for the first ten miles, and then entered a sandy tract covered with tamarisk. Striking straight through this, our guide brought us to a pool of brackish water, and by digging some small wells about three feet deep just below the pool, we found sweet water and camped by it.

In the afternoon I walked over to Ramrud and found the fort to be a rectangular structure somewhat similar to, but about half the size of, the Hauzdar fort, and much more decayed. The highest wall standing was apparently that of a Masjid. There were the ruins of a smaller fort a little way to the east, and every here and there could be seen the remains of smaller buildings scattered about for several miles. All were of mud or sun-dried brick. Although the country generally was strewn with fragments of broken pottery, I could hear of no ruins of stone or burnt brick. Standing on the top of the fort there was nothing to be seen but a waste of tamarisk jungle, some six feet in height, as far as the eye could reach over the plain on every side. A few nomad Baluchis were scattered around getting their water from rain-pools, which were still fairly plentiful, but they were all to leave for the hills very shortly, after which the country, they said, would be absolutely deserted. All these villages now in ruins, such as Hauzdar, Machi, Kundar, Ramrud, and others, drew their water in former days from the Taraku canal, which took off from the Helmund somewhere above

Bandar-i-Kamal Khan.[1] The land on which they stood was said to be on a higher level than the at present inhabited portion of Sistan farther to the north, now watered by the Band-i-Sistan canal, and it thus was impossible to irrigate it from Persian Sistan. Consequently, under present circumstances, so long as this land remains with Persia it can never be re-cultivated, and must always lie waste, as the head of any canal to irrigate it would have to be in Afghan territory.

Another thirteen miles next day took us on to Gumbad-i-Sar-i-Shela, or the domes at the head of the Shela, as the river-bed is called that carries the water from the inundated tracts on the north down to the Gaud-i-Zarih, the lake on the south-east. The road led for the first ten miles through tamarisk jungle which gradually got thinner and thinner till we arrived at Náwar, so called from a pool of fresh water on the roadside. The guide at first thought of camping there, not being sure of finding sweet water farther on, but he agreed to push on, and we found a plentiful supply of rain-water in a pool close to the ruined domes where we camped. On the road we passed a Baluch graveyard on a low mound to the left of the road. The graves, which were apparently fresh, were decorated and covered with curious stones. One grave was entirely covered with small pieces of clear white felspar carefully arranged, so different to the ordinary unkept graves one sees in Persia. Other graves had on them broken bits of stone vases which had been well cut from some red-streaked, jade-coloured stone. These presumably had been collected from some ancient ruins, but where those ruins were I could not find out. We passed various nomads on the road, one party of whom were Kharut Ghilzais, who said that their grandfathers had emigrated from their own country near Ghazni, and that they had

[1] Bellew, p. 51.

lived about here ever since. They said they spent the winter in the plains here, and in another ten or fifteen days they would move up into the hills, going via the Koh-i-Malik Siah to Sarhad. So far as I could gather, there were something like 600 families of Baluchis and Brahuis who frequented this tract along the Shela in the winter, and moved up into the hills in Persian territory to the west in the summer, where they apparently had to pay grazing tax. Gumbad-i-Sar-i-Shela, or Gumbad as it is locally called, consisted of four domed mausoleums of sun-dried brick on a low rise surrounded by an ancient graveyard. The graves were all vaults built above-ground, and like those at Hauzdar they had all been opened and the bones could be seen lying inside. To the east was another domed mausoleum by itself, the graves in which had also been opened. Between the two were some Baluch graves on a mound, and here too were collections of the curious stones I had noticed before. In addition to the felspar and bits of vases, I found here in one heap a collection of large and curious cylindrical stones carefully cut and polished, and varying in size from a foot or more to six inches in length, and from five to two inches in diameter, shaped something like a dice-box. These were all cut from different and peculiarly coloured stones, and were perfectly smooth and round, but where they came from, and what they had been made from, nobody could tell me. One man said that stone vases had been found at Gumbad-i-Shah, and that the felspar or whatever it was came from Rubat, on the road to Chagai. We were also told by one of the men that he had heard there were some ruins to the east of these domes where gold coins used to be found, but that the sand had come and buried the whole, and not a trace of them was now to be seen. We also were told that there were mines in the hills at a place called Mádanak, presumably of copper, and that on the top of Laṙ hill, just to the south of the Koh-i-Malik Siah, there were some buildings of cut stone or houses cut in the rock which Shikaris had seen but could not get at; unfortunately we had no time to put the truth of these tales to the test.

In the afternoon I walked down to the Shela, a little more than a mile to the west of the domes, and I found it full of bitterly salt water, which is said always to remain in a pool just there. The bed of the river was some 150 to 200 yards in width, with precipitous banks 30 and 40 feet high, and it is only when the Hamuns overflow and a flood flushes out the salt water that sweet water is to be obtained. The soil is evidently salt hereabouts, as we passed through a good deal of soft ground covered with a white saline efflorescence.

Another march of thirteen miles brought us to Dasht-i-Shela, though there was nothing to mark our camping-place but a small pool of muddy water in the bed of a nullah. Our road led through the same waste as the day before, covered thinly with tamarisk, and the glare from the white saline ground and hard-baked clay was trying to the eyes. Not far from camp we passed some low mounds covered with pieces of black-coloured slag, which the guide declared were the remains of an ancient furnace for smelting ore, and he pointed out to us various little thin bits of a green-coloured metal lying about which was said to be copper and would seem to show that formerly a copper mine did exist in the hills about. About seven miles out the road crossed the Shela at a place called Gardanrig, and continued down the right bank. On the left bank ran a succession of sandhills which appeared to be only stopped by the river from encroaching beyond it.

Fifteen miles farther on the next day brought us to Gudar-i-Shah, somewhere near the place so vividly described by MacGregor in his "Wanderings in Baluchistan."[1] The road led down the right bank of the Shela across a sandy plain. At the fourteenth mile we crossed the Shela again just at the head of a stretch of salt water on which we found a good many wild-fowl of sorts. The banks on both sides were thickly covered with tamarisk, and the bed was about 150 yards in width, with sloping banks some 20 feet high and full of sand, there having been no flood waters down for the last five years. Continuing about a mile down we camped below the first long pool of salt water, and between that and another, at a place where there were some shallow wells in the river-bed, which on being dug out, strange to say, afforded a good supply of sweet water at a depth of only 3 or 4 feet. The land about here was said by the guides to have been irrigated formerly by a branch of the Taraku canal, and in very high floods in the Helmund water was said still to find its way along the old canal-beds, which would seem to show that the place might be repopulated at no very great expense could the canals in Afghan territory only be opened again. Just opposite our camp and some 500 yards to the north lay the ruins called by the guides Shah Mardan, comprising a *ziarat* or place of pilgrimage at the tomb of a saint of that name, and also the ruins of some building. The guide said that similar ruins formerly extended a considerable way both north and south, but that they had been enveloped in sand of late years.

The tomb of the Pir or saint was surmounted with the usual sticks covered with rags, the mementoes of the pilgrims who had visited it, and the grave itself was covered with a most curious collection of stones of all shapes and sizes, with bits of white and blue tiles and odds

[1] P. 179.

and ends of sorts. The principal things were the large dice-box-shaped cylinders of smooth polished stone of many and various colours, a foot or more in length, but generally thicker at one end than the other, and with a groove cut across one or both ends. These the guides maintained were brought from Rubat, near Koh-i-Malik Dukand. Wherever they were brought from they must have been brought at considerable trouble and expense, and unfortunately a good many of them had been chipped and broken by Baluchis and pilgrims, who ground the pieces chipped off into powder as a medicine for their sick. Many of the bits of stone on the tomb looked like broken bits of stone pestles and mortars, and one of the tiles had a portion of an inscription burnt into it, just sufficient to show that it had been part of the headstone of some grave, but not sufficient to give the name or date.

Next day we moved camp six miles farther down the Shela, to a place some two miles to the north-east of the domes, described by MacGregor[1] as the Gumbaz-i-Shah, but our men gave that name to the ruined buildings at the shrine of Shah Mardan, and these they called the Gumbad-i-Sar-i-Zarih, or the domes at the head of the Zarih, which certainly seemed an appropriate name, whether correct or not. The banks of the Shela were some 15 to 20 feet high, but the water in flood-time evidently overflowed them here, as the reed-beds, marked by the roots then standing, were all on the top of the banks, forming a fringe in places half a mile wide. The bed of the Shela still continued from 150 to 200 yards in width, but these reed-beds evidently marked the commencement of the lake when full. We obtained our drinking-water, as before, from some shallow wells dug in the sand in the bed of the river just below

[1] P. 185.

another long pool of salt water, but the water in this I found was not nearly so salt as in the pools higher up. A few families of Baluch nomads were camped in the neighbourhood who called themselves Afghan subjects from Kila-i-Fath, across the Helmund, but, as our guides explained to us, all nomads in these parts called themselves alternately Persian and Afghan subjects, so as to escape the payment of revenue to either. One man a little bolder than the rest, apparently concluding that we were not Persian tax-gatherers, called himself a Raiyat-i-Khuda, or a subject of God. He would not own to dependence upon any man. I walked over to the domes, which stand on a low ridge now much covered with sand, with a sprinkling of minute black pebbles about the size of flower seeds on the top, which makes the ridge appear black in the distance. The buildings we found to be five in number, and none of our guides had ever heard of the name of Gumbad-i-Shah Maksud that MacGregor's men gave them. Only part of the walls of sun-dried brick were standing; the domed roofs, which apparently had been built of burnt brick, had all fallen in. The buildings appeared to me to have been mausoleums, and the whole ridge, I imagine, was once an extensive graveyard, but the graves on it were almost entirely covered up by the sand. From what I could see, it looked as if they had been of the same above-ground type before described. I saw no signs of a fort, as there were no ruins or signs of habitations about, and none were said to exist farther east than this. I noticed a few black partridges in the vicinity, and hares were comparatively plentiful in the tamarisk jungle wherever sweet water was obtainable.

From here we made an expedition down to the Gaud-i-Zarih. The guides could give us no idea as to how far we should have to go to get to the lake itself, as all they knew was that the waters were rapidly drying up. As it turned out we found the distance was about nine miles. Following down the course of the Shela, the banks gradually got lower and lower till they disappeared altogether. About six miles out the tamarisk jungle ceased, and we came to an open plain forming the bed of the lake, covered with white saline efflorescence. For about a mile over this the roots of reed-beds extended, and beyond that again the plain was covered every here and there with dead tamarisk bushes which had apparently been killed by the water. In these were numerous old nests of some sort of diver, but of what species I could not tell. They were built of twigs and reeds, about eighteen inches in depth and the same in width, and firmly fixed in a fork of the branches at a uniform height of from four to five feet from the ground. Our guide told us that he came here with other Baluchis in the breeding season a couple of years or so before, when this ground was all under water, and caught and ate numbers of the young birds, of which there must have been thousands, to judge by the numbers of nests. It was hopeless, though, to gather from his description what the bird was. We had to approach the edge of the water on foot, as the horses' hoofs sank deep in the soft damp soil. This soil, however, was not so salt as it looked, and the covering of saline matter on the top was of the thinnest, just sufficient to give it a glare. The water of the lake itself we found to be beautifully clear, and only slightly salt. Having heard that water drawn in the centre of the lake was quite drinkable, I sent a man to wade out as far as he could, and to fetch a bowlful, and what he brought back was certainly not so very salt. To the east the water extended as far as the eye could see. To the south we could trace a long line of sandhills, and to the north the low edge of the *dasht* or plateau extending to Taraku. When we arrived we found a large flock of pelicans on the bank, and numbers of white sheldrakes were swimming about in the water, but there was no sign of any other fowl. There were no *tutins* or reed-rafts on the lake, and the Baluchis apparently do not know how to make them. A party of Saiyáds from the Hamuns to the north would have to be brought down on purpose to make these if required. We had breakfast on the banks of the lake, and then rode back to camp.

This lake marked the most southerly point of my tour, and now our party was to break up—Massy to make his way to India, and the rest of us to return to Mashhad. Massy was in luck in getting twelve good camels just at the last moment to take him to Kharan, from one Rustam, a Zarizai Baluch from Sarhad, who turned up and offered his services as he was going himself to Kharan. The Sistani camels accordingly returned, and Rustam went on with his in their place—an arrangement that seemed to please all. Sunrise on the 19th February 1894 saw us saying good-bye and starting our several ways. I myself had intended to march across the *dasht* or gravelly plateau, to a place called Fakirband Náwar, and thence to Taraku, by a route that the guides said they knew; but just before starting a Baluch shepherd turned up on his way to the hills and reported that the pool of rain-water at Fakirband was dry, and that there was no water at Taraku either. We found ourselves thus just about a fortnight too late, and the conclusion I came to was that January was the month to spend in Sistan, not February. Goldsmid's Mission noted that the weather changed and they began to complain of the heat on the 10th February.[1] I noticed the same on the 12th, and a week later all the pools of rain-water were rapidly

[1] Goldsmid's "Eastern Persia," vol. i.

drying up. We went straight back to our former halting-place at Dasht-i-Shela, and just in time, as we found the pool of rain-water there, that had supplied our wants so well only four days before, almost exhausted.

Next day we made a march of eighteen miles to a place called Kachuli. We followed up our former road as far as the crossing of the Shela at Gardanrig, and then taking a line a mile or two to the east of the domes at Gumbad-i-Sar-i-Shela, we came to a well called Chah-i-Kachuli, some eight feet deep, with a good supply of sweet water about four miles farther on. Eight miles beyond that again we came to some pools of rain-water, and there we camped. The name of the place, Kachuli, is derived from the Baluchi word for pottery; broken pottery being found in quantities on the mounds near by.

Here we turned east, and took a march of twenty miles to Burri Kila. For the first seven miles the road ran through tamarisk jungle, and then emerged on to a bare gravel-covered plain. At the tenth mile we crossed a broad shallow depression, containing an ancient canal which the guide told us came from Taraku. Eight miles beyond we arrived at the Burri wells, which we found were six in number and about twelve feet deep, and contained sweet water. A shepherd, however, gave us the news that there was good rain-water close to the Kila or fort, so we pushed on there, two miles to the north, where we struck the depression again. The so-called Kila consisted of nothing but four ruined walls with a tower at each corner, and we camped close to it. We found various nomad Baluchis camped about. Like the rest they spent the winter hereabouts and the summer in Sarhad, and paid taxes to nobody if they could help it.

Leaving our camp standing, Moula Bakhsh and I made our way from here to the famous old fort of Taraku, said by local tradition to have been the birthplace of Rustam.

The road lay east following the course of the depression, down which we could trace the marks of two canals that must have formerly run parallel to each other. At the seventh mile we came to an old ruined fort, some seventy yards by fifty in size, called Gina. Here the depression or trough widened out, and there was a large expanse of arable land, but no water. Three miles farther on we reached the Taraku fort, which stands high on the top of a scarped and precipitous mound in the middle of this depression, and is some 200 yards in length and ranging from 60 to 120 yards in breadth; the walls ranging in height from some 50 or 60 feet above the ground at the north to double that height at the south. Under the shade of these walls we sat down and had our breakfast.

The ancient canals, which were taken off from the Helmund at Bandar, or Band-i-Kamal Khan, as it is marked on the maps, having all gone to ruin, there is no water nor any habitation or cultivation now at Taraku. The guides told us that rain-water pools never lasted long at either Gina or Taraku, and consequently the whole country was uninhabited, even by nomads, and lay a perfect waste. That it could be repopulated is proved by the fact that water from the Helmund, during the floods of the spring of 1885, found its way down the trough or depression that I have described, which shows that in all probability water might be brought down it again without much difficulty, if there was only some one to bring it. At present there is no one, and it does not look as if there ever will be so long as present conditions continue. The Afghans will do nothing, and the Persians cannot even if they would. The Persian Government will do nothing even for Persian Sistan. The great necessity there is a proper masonry dam across the Helmund at Kohak to control the water, instead of the present makeshift of tamarisk twigs that now exists. The

Persian Government will not give a penny towards such a work, and all they do is to tell the local governor that if he wishes for a *band* he had better build it himself. That he cannot do, as directly he had built it others would rush in and outbid him for the government, and he would then lose both that and his money as well. No public works or improvements of any sort can thus be carried out in Persia so long as the present insecurity of tenure continues.

However, to return to the Taraku fort. Inside everything was in ruin. The rooms or chambers could all be traced, and though most of the domed roofs had fallen in, some were still intact. The most curious piece of work in the fort was the well, which was square, and lined with burnt brick throughout. It was sunk, near the highest point of the mound, at least 100 feet above ground level, and went right down through the hard stone of the mound. To the east of this was a sloping vaulted passage, which must have been excavated at great labour, leading down apparently into the well at water level. The fort looked as if it had been deserted by its inhabitants, but why and wherefore no one could tell me. From the fort I rode on a couple of miles to a small heap of earth, surmounted with sticks and rags, known as the Ziarat-i-Sultan Sakhi. On this mound I found two white stone pedestals of pillars some 18 inches in height, and also a square piece of beautifully-carved white marble, the only relics of cut stone that I came across in Sistan. What they belonged to no one could say.

On my way back to Burri Kala I had a look at the mausoleums, tombs, and ruined buildings of sorts that seemed to be scattered about all along the banks of the depression. To the east of Taraku was a domed mausoleum and various above-ground graves all opened.

Another mausoleum that I entered had six of these vaulted tombs in it all in a row. They were in perfect condition, having been protected from the weather by the building, but they had all been opened at the end, and the skulls and bones and bits of cloth could be seen lying on the floor within. Bits of old cloth were also lying outside, which looked as if the graves had been rifled, and that not so long ago. It was curious to see a place that must have been thickly populated now so utterly deserted, and yet, although the banks of the Helmund at Bandar were only some twenty miles from Tarakun, I was told there was not a man within a dozen miles of the place.

Next day we marched twenty-one miles almost due north to a place called Khanduk, where water was obtainable from four or five wells some 10 feet deep dug in the open plain. The first half of the way we travelled over a hard plain covered with small gravel. After that we came on a lumpy, hard, clay soil. All this ground was apparently formerly inhabited, as there was not a mound that did not bear traces of broken pottery. As we neared Khanduk the country became more level and open till we came to the raised ground known by the name of Shahr-i-Sukta or the burnt city, not that there were any visible signs of a city, but the whole extent of ground hereabouts, stretching far on every side, was one thick mass of broken pottery, and one could only wonder where it all came from. Most of it was of a pale red colour, while some was ornamented with patterns in black, but the enormous quantity of it was astounding. Hunting about, we found bits of copper and an old axe-head, and also fragments of marble vases; and the guide, Muhammad, who was with us turned up the ground in various directions to show me that it was black and burnt, to prove that we were really on the site of a burnt city.

The wells at which we encamped lay about a mile to the north of Shahr-i-Sukta, and some twenty-five families of Baluchis were also camped around them with their flocks. The water was brackish, but drinkable. During the day a caravan of thirty camel-loads of tea and sugar passed through on return from Bandar Abbas to the village of Jazinak. This was the first arrival of the season.

On our return to Sehkoha we were gladdened by the sight of a Mashhad post-bag awaiting us. This had been exactly a month on the way, the road, as the post-master at Birjand reported, having been almost completely blocked by a heavy fall of snow nearly three feet deep. We found Duke still busy in his dispensary, which had been thronged with patients from far and near, over 500 having come in for treatment during the fortnight we had been away.

Talking to the people, I was told that the climate of Sistan had changed considerably of late years. The heat was not so great, and the plague of flies had considerably decreased, the flies being now confined to the neighbourhood of the Naizar or reed-beds. The horse disease, known as *sargin surkh*, formerly so prevalent, was also said to have much abated, only a few cases occurring now and then in the spring and autumn. The number of horses in the country had accordingly considerably increased, and the Kadkhudas and others were taking to horse-breeding.

Our next move was to Burj-i-Kuhna, a village of good size, consisting of something like 1000 houses, with gardens and vineyards round it, and belonging to one Saiyid Ali, an influential Mulla or priest, to whom it was given by the late Amir of Kain after Sardar Sharif Khan, to whom it had belonged, went over to the Afghans and his lands and villages on the west of the Helmund were confiscated. Six miles out from Sehkoha we came to a branch of the Band-i-Sistan canal, here some thirty yards in width, and unfordable except at one place on the road to Lúf. The road then led along the top of a long, high bank built to keep the canal from overflowing to the south, where there was already a good-sized lake in a hollow. There was a lot of flood water about, and plenty of ducks, but as usual it was impossible to get near them.

CHAPTER VIII.

THE BANKS OF THE HELMUND.

We were now on our way to inspect the Band-i-Sistan, or the dam across the Helmund at the head of the canal, and thence to explore the eastern side of Persian Sistan. Rain again the next morning kept us back for a time, but starting in the afternoon we crossed a plain covered with *kirta*, a kind of grass, for the first three miles to Kila-i-Nau, a good-sized village formerly belonging to Sardar Sharif Khan Nahrui, whose fort here formed a stronghold for the people during the rebellion, and had been destroyed by the late Amir of Kain in consequence. From Kila-i-Nau the road ran for another seven miles across the gravelly plateau till we arrived at the left bank of the main canal, here some 50 yards broad and 9 feet deep, where we camped. We had passed a large extent of inundated ground on the way, and the waters were by no means confined to the canal, which ran here with a swift stream. We found two old *tutins* collected for us, and Sardar Sa'id Khan had had a new one made for us as well, and on these we started the men to ferry the baggage across. While they were employed on this, Duke and I beat the tamarisk bushes for black partridge and bagged a few. Next morning commenced the business of swimming the camels, horses, and mules across. Our Turkomans were invaluable at this, far better than any of the local men. Their method of swimming camels across a river I had not seen before. Their theory is that a camel is so heavy in front in comparison to what he is behind, that when swimming he cannot keep his head above water unless a man is mounted on his hind-quarters to balance him. They do not take the camels across singly like horses, but a whole string at a time, each with a man on behind. One man plunges in and swims ahead holding the nose-string of the leading camel, and the rest all follow in due course, and very comical they look. The body of the camel is entirely submerged when swimming, and one can see nothing of the animal but its head and the body of the man seated behind, up to his waist in water and holding on for dear life.

Having seen everything across, and leaving the camp to be pitched at Khwaja Ahmad, we ourselves rode on to see the Band-i-Sistan, on the Helmund, upon which the life of the province depends. The new village of Khwaja Ahmad consisted of some 300 wattle-and-daub huts scattered along the right bank of the canal, and belonged to Sardar Sa'id Khan, to whom it had been given by the Hashmat-ul-Mulk. About half-way to the Band lay the old village of Khwaja Ahmad, now nothing but a ruin with the remains of a circular wall round the top of a mound. A mile or so beyond that we came to the small fort of Kuhak, on the top of another mound, but quite deserted. Beyond that again lay the Band or dam, some 15 to 20 yards wide at the top, and formed entirely of tamarisk boughs laid horizontally and lengthwise along it. The river was in considerable flood owing to recent rains, and about a quarter of the Band had been washed away and the river was flowing freely through it. These floods continue through the spring and summer while the snows are melting in the Hazarajat, but about August or

September, we were told, when the floods subside, every village in Persian Sistan would send its quota of men to repair the Band. The whole country round, though, had been so entirely denuded of tamarisk that the bringing in of the wood alone must be no small task. I noticed how much barer the country looked than it did when I first visited the place from the Afghan side in 1884, and every year the people will have to go farther and farther afield.

On the 1st March 1894 we moved ten miles to the north, down the left bank of the Helmund, and camped near an old mud pillar on a slight rise called the Mil-i-Milak. We passed the ruins of Shahristan, on an island between two branches of a canal. A little to the north was the village of Sharifabad, and away on the opposite bank of the river were the ruins of Nad-i-Ali, consisting of three mounds which could be seen from afar. Most of the way lay through tamarisk jungle, and a *gúra* or embankment of earth had been constructed all the way along to prevent the inundation of the country from the river, and the villagers were busy repairing it. The embankment did not look strong enough to stand any very severe strain, and the people told us that when the river overflowed its banks four years before, the embankment gave way, and the flood destroyed the whole of the villages and harvest of Milak. The crops had been cut and thrashed, and the grain was to be divided into its various shares the very next day, when in burst the river and swept grain and village and everything clean away. Milak is the name of a district rather than of a village. All the villages, or rather hamlets, along the river-bank here are inhabited by Baluchis of various tribes, and each hamlet or cluster of tamarisk matting, wattle-and-daub huts has no distinctive name, but is simply called by the name of the Kadkhuda or head-man for the time being, and a man from Milak means that he comes from that district. Milak belonged to Sirdar Khan Jan Khan, the son of the late Sirdar Ibrahim Khan, Saujurani, the man who murdered Dr. Forbes the traveller. Khan Jan Khan at one time, I believe, went over to Afghanistan, but fled from there, and afterwards appealed to the British authorities at Quetta for help. Finally he returned to Sistan, and was given the charge of this district by the Hashmat-ul-Mulk. He visited me with his two sons and a nephew on my arrival in camp, and so did Sardar Sa'id Khan, both of whom were busy superintending the repairs to the embankment through their respective villages.

I rode off in the afternoon to have a look at Zahidan and the pillar known as the Mil-i-Kasimabad. I had not time to reach the latter, but it has already been described, both by Euan Smith in Goldsmid's "Eastern Persia"[1] and by Bellew.[2] I could see the pillar in the distance, and also the ruined fort, supposed by the people to have been the citadel of the great city that once stretched for miles along here. The curious thing is that no coins or relics ever seem to be found in these ruins. All the people say that Sar-o-Tar on the Afghan side of the river is the only place for such things, and we were shown a few small coins and some engraved seals, said to have come from there, by a trader whom we found at our camp who had recently returned from Karáchi with goods.

Our next move was ten miles farther down the river to Deh Ghulam, the last village of the Chilingak district, of which also Khan Jan Khan had charge. We had a hard march, crossing one branch of the river and camping on a second. The first branch was some three miles out, and Sirdar Khan Jan Khan kindly sent out *tutins* for our use, and his son, Muhammad Hussain Khan, and

[1] P. 301. [2] P. 61.

nephew, Shamsuddin Khan, accompanied us. Our Turkoman sowars and camelmen worked splendidly, and we got everything across in a couple of hours. The stream was some 60 yards broad and 5 to 6 feet in depth, and all the mules had to be unloaded, the baggage ferried across on the *tutins*, and the animals themselves, as well as all our horses, swam across. By good luck the camels with the tents were able to cross as they were at a ford some 300 yards below, where the water just came up to their saddles but not over them. Otherwise the delay would have been much greater. As soon as the mules had been loaded up on the far bank, on we went again.

For the next seven miles our route lay through dense tamarisk jungle, with small hamlets and clearings every here and there. The revenue arrangement was that the out-turn of all lands brought under cultivation by Sirdar Khan Jan Khan was to be divided into three shares—one for the Government, *i.e.* the Hashmat-ul-Mulk; one for Khan Jan Khan; and one for the cultivator—and under these terms the land was being rapidly cleared. The Helmund appeared to be very erratic in its course hereabouts. At Deh Saiyid, a small village about three miles beyond the crossing, we were told that the river some years before had swept away the old village, and that the young tamarisk through which we passed was formerly the site of the village fields. This showed how quickly land here relapsed into jungle. The second stream by which we camped was running strong, and was some 80 yards in width and 5 to 6 feet in depth, and so low were the banks that the water was within a few inches of the level of our tents. We had a good downpour of rain in the night; many of the tents were flooded, and precious glad we were to get out of the place the next day. The river continued rising, and as we had only one *tutin* to work with, it took us all the morning to get the things ferried across. The horses and mules were swum across by the Turkomans as usual, who seemed thoroughly to enjoy the fun of the thing, and larked about in the water and ducked each other like so many schoolboys.

We said good-bye to Khan Jan Khan's son and nephew here, and on arrival on the opposite bank we were met by Jan Muhammad, a nephew of Dost Muhammad Khan, Sarani, who escorted us on in the absence of his uncle at Birjand. I sent the camp to Deh Dost Muhammad, six miles on, and then rode off myself three miles up the right bank of the stream to visit the dam known as the Band-i-Afghan. There I found a succession of Bunds or embankments which turned off almost all the water of the Helmund from what the people said was its main bed into the channel we had just crossed. The old bed was locally known as the *sim* or boundary between Persia and Afghanistan, and an Afghan village named Deh Taus stood at the eastern end of the embankment.

The banks of the Helmund were almost imperceptible here, and it was impossible to tell by the eye what was the old bed of the river and what was the new. To the north of the embankment lay the district known as Warshufti, a Baluch word meaning alluvial soil deposited by a river when in flood, and I must say the river seemed to have flowed over this particular Warshufti in every direction some time or another. As it was there was nothing much to be seen but a waste of tamarisk jungle on every side, and a perfect network of canal-beds into which the water was turned when required. The water flowing on down the main bed of the river below the Bund was only a small stream some twenty or thirty yards wide and three feet deep. I rode down the left bank of this stream for a couple of miles till I came to the small Afghan village of Deh Ido, situated under some high *padah* trees on the opposite bank. Beyond this the stream divided into two, one going off to Ibrahimabad in Afghan territory, and the other to Sikhsar in Persian. We followed the latter, which brought us to our camp at the village known as Deh Dost Muhammad. This village was originally founded, we were told, by Ali Khan, Sarani, Dost Muhammad's father, some nine years previously. Before that the land was a waste of tamarisk jungle, but a great deal of this had been cleared, and the village contained 200 houses and a windmill. The value of land was apparently rapidly going up in Sistan, as we were told that the Karkun district, a portion of the Warshufti, was originally farmed out to Dost Muhammad at an annual rental of 500 tumans, but higher offers had been bid for it, and Dost Muhammad's rent had now risen to 3000 tumans per annum.

Next morning things began to look black. The river, we were told, had overflown its banks and had burst the embankment above, and also the Band-i-Afghan, and the country on ahead was under water. We could not go on to a place called Katamak as we had intended, and it was settled that we should make for Pulgi, twelve miles off—a name that in Baluchi signifies soft, loose soil. We started about eight in the morning in a bitter cold north wind, and three miles out we came to Karkun, or Kirmak as it is also called, built on a mound of old ruins. There was no cultivation near, and it was simply the residence of Dost Muhammad. Here I found the first burnt-brick ruins that I had seen in Sistan. On the top of the mound was a square plinth of large burnt bricks all in perfect order. This plinth had been brought to light when the village was built eight years before. Above it was the ruin of a dome of sun-dried brick, but possibly this was of later date than the plinth. I noticed bits of burnt brick in another mound near by, and examination there might possibly reveal what these buildings originally were. From the top of the mound I was pointed out the village of Jalalabad, and detached pieces of ruined buildings could be seen dotted about the tamarisk jungle and extending for two or three miles, which were said to be the remains of an ancient city.

Beyond Karkun the whole country was under water, and on arrival at a stream a little way on we found the water up to the men's necks at the so-called ford, and the camels were being dragged through with difficulty. A few that went early got across, but others coming later fell and left their loads in the water, which had to be dragged out by the men, while the camels themselves were all more or less exhausted. We had to stop and get an old *tutin* repaired, and then to ferry all our baggage across and swim the animals over. The camels bringing up the last relay of tents could not even get as far as the stream. They stuck in the mud and fell, and had to be left at Karkun utterly done up and unable to move. We ourselves, after getting the servants and kit across, had still to push on and make the best way we could through flooded land and dense tamarisk thickets for some eight miles more, till at last we got into Pulgi about 8 P.M., very glad of a rest after a hard day's work. We found ourselves fairly caught by the floods, and we wondered how we were to get out. The first thing next morning was to send back the mules to bring in the tents and things remaining behind, the camels being so exhausted that it was as much as they could do to drag themselves through the mud, and for them to carry a load was an impossibility. However, everything was got in by sunset.

While the things were being brought up I rode out to inspect a ruined bridge called Takhtapul, some four miles to the south-south-east. This looked like a low mound when pointed out to me in the distance; but sure enough, when I got to it, it turned out to be the remains of a low bridge of two arches with abutments on either side, all of burnt brick, and standing high and dry in the middle of the plain, the nearest branch of the river being some distance to the east. Our guides had it that this bridge was built by Shah Gushtasp (520 B.C.) on the road connecting the two great ancient cities of those days of Karkun, or Karkhushah, and Peshawaran on the way to Lash Jowain, a place described by Bellew.[1] We passed various other ruins, consisting of mounds full of burnt brick, all of the same large, square, flat shape—say a foot square by two to three inches thick—that one generally finds in very old buildings.

I also visited a place called Takht-i-Shah, some seven miles to the north-east, which apparently was the most northern possession of Persia in that direction. This gave me an idea of what life in the Naizar was like, and a curious life it was. About three miles out we got into the reed-beds or Naizar, and after working through them for some distance we arrived at a tract of tamarisk-covered land standing some six or eight feet higher than the level of the reed-beds; and keeping along this, past various hamlets of Persian *maldars*, or cattle graziers, we came to a more open plain of here and there hard clay, and in other places soft saline earth with low mounds scattered about, and this we were told was Takht-i-Shah. On examination all the mounds turned out to be full of burnt bricks of the large square pattern, and apparently the place was thickly populated in former days. These ruins were known by the name of Chahar Shahr, or the four cities. We pitched our camp for the night by a collection of reed huts inhabited by Saiyads on the left bank of the river, which was here a wide expanse of water and reeds without any current that I could see.

[1] P. 62.

Away to the east, on the opposite side of the water, were other reed huts which belonged to Afghans. The Afghan Government, I was told, took no revenue from them, but neither did the Persian Government; and in fact I gathered there was a considerable population about who paid no taxes to either side, and I could easily understand it. To levy a grazing tax in such a country was almost an impossibility. The tax supposed to be levied on these *maldars* was one kran per bullock per annum; but as one man expressed it to me, for every forty head of cattle caught and taxed, there were another forty hidden away in the reeds which no one but the owner could find; and then again, directly any tax collector arrived from one side, the people simply moved off to the other, and thus it was almost hopeless to catch them any way. These graziers had no houses or fixed residences. Reed huts sufficed them all the year round, and thus they lived a free and independent life, almost as wild as their own cattle. The Saiyáds told me that the season for shooting was over, and that they themselves had ceased netting for fowl, and this I soon found to be the case, as, except for a few pochards, there was not a duck to be seen. Coots were everywhere in hundreds, but all the wild-fowl had gone. I saw a few wild swans flying overhead, also some pelicans and wild geese, apparently the last to leave. The wild-fowl shooting of Sistan, I must say, appeared to me to have decreased largely, as nowhere did I see the numbers described by former travellers. This was due, it seemed to me, to a certain extent to the incessant war waged against them by the Saiyáds, who lived by netting them all the winter; but also, to a much greater extent, to the large number of guns of sorts in the hands of the people. Everywhere in Sistan one hears a constant banging of guns all day and every day; the ducks are thus harried from place to place, and are so wild that it is impossible to get near them. Again, in every village there are tame decoy geese which, in the season when the wild geese are about, are anchored out in the water while the gunner sits hidden in a hole or a bush close by, and although the country muskets of sorts are hardly worthy of the name of guns, still the birds, if not killed, are at any rate frightened away.

The Saiyáds at Takht-i-Shah, now that the wild-fowl had gone, were settling down to spinning and weaving and other sedentary pursuits for the summer, varied with netting for fish. I went out for a short time on a *tutin*, and I found one man busy making a trap for fish, or rather an approach of reeds stuck in the mud in two lines, converging to a point at which a net was placed. He had caught one fish about a foot long, which I bought from him, and I shot some pochards and coots to feed the servants on. From the top of one of the more northern mounds at Takht-i-Shah I was pointed out a high ruin to the south-west called Kila-i-Khamah, and a mound called Tappa-i-Shir Surkh to the west; while away across the Hamun to the east the Puzak cliffs stood out sharp and clear. The road from Karkun to Lash Jowain, between the two Hamuns, was said to be always closed by water during the flood season in spring and summer, when people had to cross in *tutins*.

On our return to Pulgi, which I should mention was simply one of several hamlets of tamarisk wattle-and-daub huts in the midst of jungle, we found that the country was being so rapidly inundated that the crops in the ground were being flooded and destroyed in every direction, and the people were hard at work throwing up embankments in the endeavour to save what they could. These floods, they told us, usually came in cycles of about seven years, and this was the seventh year.

I sent on the advance tents to the bank of the next

river that we had to cross, but in the evening a report came back that they had got to a place called Margán, some seven miles out, and were halted at the village of Ali Akbar, and could get no farther as the water there was now a mile in width, and there was only one *tutin* to work with. Sultan Abu Turab was very good, and collected and sent out men to make fresh *tutins*, and there was nothing to be done but to wait till they were ready. Provisions were the difficulty. No supplies, it was reported, were available at Deh-i-Ali Akbar, and we had consumed all there was at Pulgi, and as Sultan Abu Turab said, if we did not manage to get out of this Warshufti country and across to Jalalabad, the nearest permanent village, we should starve. At Margán, in the morning, a high north wind arose, and no *tutins* could cross, and the boatmen all bolted off to their fields to try and save what they could of their crops. The wind subsided a little in the afternoon, and we then managed to get sufficient men and *tutins* together to send the mule saddles across, and finally the mules themselves were swum over. The river by this time had risen so much that it took the *tutins* four hours to get across and back again, and the water was within a few yards of Ali Akbar's village, in which we were camped. By next morning we had managed to get about a dozen *tutins* rigged up, but they carried little, and only managed a couple of trips in the day, and that made the crossing a long and weary business. The horses were ridden across, and did not suffer in the least, but a horse that had been towed across tied behind a *tutin* the day before we found dead on the far bank. I myself was poled along through inundated tamarisk jungle in about three feet of water, till we came to the open stretch of the river on the western side, where the water was about six feet deep.

On the way I passed various mounds and marks of ancient ruins, and a good many more were to be seen to the south-west. I noticed the presence of the large square burnt bricks in these mounds, and it is only in this north-eastern corner of Persian Sistan that I saw them. All the rest of the country was covered with the remains of mud or sun-dried brick buildings which gave no clue, and it has yet to be seen whether the excavation of these burnt-brick ruins now buried in mounds of earth will yield anything of value. The hamlet on the banks of the river where we landed consisted of only ten or a dozen huts, called Dasht-i-Margún, and supplies were procured with difficulty. However, we managed to get enough grain and forage to keep the horses and mules going, and in the meantime the camels and remaining tents were got across. The flood went down a little, and unfortunately, instead of sending the camel saddles across in *tutins*, the men to save delay started the camels across with their saddles on, and the result was the saddles got soaking wet and terribly heavy, and the camels, when they landed, were much done up.

Next day we started early and did ten miles, but we took ten hours to do it. First of all we had a mile of water to wade through to get to the village of Jalalabad, in the mud of which many of the camels stuck and fell. At Jalalabad there was a crowd of villagers collected to see us pass. It was a good square-built village, with an elevated fort in one corner belonging to Sirdar Sa'id Khan, Nahrui, but he was said to reside mostly in his tamarisk hut at Khwaja Ahmad. We found there were a lot of black partridges about, but how it was they were not exterminated I could not understand. The local Shikaris, of which there were many, had a yellow-coloured canvas screen fixed on two crossed sticks, with a hole in the centre to shoot through, which they carried in front of them, and the black partridges, for some reason only known to themselves, would run up quite close to this screen and were shot by the men behind at only a few yards' distance. The men declared they generally killed ten or a dozen every day they went out—all cocks, I believe, which was curious.

Jalalabad was formerly one of the principal settlements of the Kayanis, the ancient ruling race in Sistan, as described by Bellew in his book,[1] but the village being now under the Nahruis, we found that most of the Kayanis had left and the tribe was much reduced. Malik Abbas Khan, the head of the tribe, had been removed to the settlement at Persian Sarakhs; his brother, Gulzar Khan, we were told was living at Bahramabad, and the number of Khawanin or respectable families left in Sistan was said not to exceed forty.

Beyond Jalalabad again we found another stretch of water more than half a mile in width, and varying from two to four feet in depth. This was too deep for laden mules, and all the baggage had to be put on the camels. Our servants who were mounted on the mules had to strip and wade, and the short, fat, Goanese cook, wading almost up to his neck in water, was a comical sight, and I doubt if he had ever had such a wash before.

The next day we made a march of eight miles past the village of Boli, but the road was so bad and the crossing of the various canals caused such delays that the camels did not get in till sunset. The camel saddles by this time had all been so thoroughly soaked that we had to halt to let the camelmen take out the wet stuffing and put in fresh. Before this was done, news came in that a northern road by which we had hoped to get out was flooded, and that our only way was to get round the inundations at their farthest point to the west as quickly as possible. We travelled south-

[1] P. 148.

west for some twelve miles through various inundated places to the village of Afzalabad, and the next day we got out of Sistan by rounding the end of the flood water and then striking the Kucha, the long straight hollow or lane some 10 or 12 feet in width and 2 feet in depth which we had formerly traversed. This was fortunately still dry, and we thus got through the reed-beds without difficulty. On either side stood the thick banks of reeds, then low and nothing but rough stubble, but ready to spring up directly the water reached them. The latter part of the way took us within a mile or two of the Mil-i-Nadiri, the pillar that here forms such a prominent landmark, and we passed along a piece of gravelly ground that looked as if it formed the beach when the Hamun was in flood.

It was now the middle of March, and the sun we found was getting hot, far too hot to continue marching at midday as we had been doing. Flies and insects were becoming daily more plentiful, and some apple-trees we had passed were already in blossom. Right glad, therefore, were we to be out of the swamps. At Bahrang we camped about a mile from the site of our former camp, close to the low walls of an enclosure marking the foundations of the fort that the late Amir of Kain meant to build but did not live to complete, unfortunately, as shelter for travellers is here much needed. The waters of the Hamun stretched from our very feet right away to the horizon, and it looked as if the lake would overflow in a day or two and thus close the road entirely till the overflow became deep enough for *tutins* to ply.

At Bal-i-kamab, our last stage in Sistan territory, Sultan Abu Turab, the Hashmat-ul-Mulk's Pesh Khidmat, who had done us so well, took his leave and departed. His arrangements for supplies and everything had been perfect, and he had served us excellently throughout.

CHAPTER IX.

THE PERSIAN-AFGHAN BORDER.

We marched through Bandan to the little village of Zainulabad, a couple of miles beyond, where I was met on arrival by a regular cavalcade of brothers and cousins, mounted some on horses and some on donkeys. The village consisted of nothing but a small fort containing about twenty families of cultivators, but there were no less than five brothers, connections of the Shaukat-ul-Mulk, sharing the possession of it. From here I determined to take a line to the east of that by which we had travelled down, and to march back to Mashhad along the Afghan frontier. Instead of, therefore, turning off to the west to Neh we went north to a place called Gisha, under the guidance of Darwesh Khan, the chief of the brothers at Zainulabad. Gisha contained no inhabitants, and we had to take all supplies with us and also drinking-water, as what we found in a shallow nullah was only fit for animals, and in fact was so brackish that they would hardly drink it. The country was open and level, with *tahgaz* bushes dotted about. The 21st of March 1894 (the Persian New Year's Day) saw us at Chah-i-Ziran, in the same level shrub-covered plain surrounded by low hills as before. The ground was green and covered with countless little flowers, showing the approach of spring, and the heavy rain we had showed that too. Chah-i-Ziran was so named from a thorn-bush called *zir*, which was plentiful about the place. Here, also, there were no habitations and no supplies. There were only a few black tents of Bahluri Baluchis scattered about. These men said that they had emigrated from Baluchistan seven generations ago. Their Kadkhuda had some 400 families under him, about a third of the tribe, the others living farther north in Kain and Khaf. The country seemed devoid of game. The partridges had all paired and vanished, and the only birds that I saw were flocks of pintailed sand-grouse flying overhead on their way north.

At Mahkunik we entered the Sunnikhana Julga or valley, as it is locally called, all the inhabitants being Sunnis and not Shiahs like the Persians. Here we found nothing but a few huts in a ravine, inhabited by some twenty dark-coloured families of Arab origin. They were very poor and wretchedly clad, and evidently a distinct race. They told us that owing to their proximity to the Afghan border the Kajars, as they called the Persians, had never been able to make them Shiahs and did not interfere with them.

Tabas, the headquarters of the Sunnikhana district, was a village containing some 150 houses, and standing out in the open in the centre of the valley, with a row of thirty or forty windmills some little distance off. The water here was derived from *kanats*, bringing it in underground channels from the foot of the hills, and the chief of Kain owned most of these *kanats*. The arrangement under which the land was cultivated was that he supplied the seed and bullocks and paid the Government revenue, and took three-fourths of the produce, leaving one-fourth for the cultivators.

The Tabas fort had been a strong place in its day.

The walls and bastions stood high on the top of a lofty rampart, all round which were the remains of a double row of *shirazis* or loopholed shelter-trenches, with a deep ditch in front, the scarp and counterscarp of which were still in good condition. The place was garrisoned by a small detachment of Kain infantry. Gazik, a large village of some 500 or 600 houses, was the northern point of the Sunnikhana district. Beyond that our road led across a stony slope immediately under a range of hills, and there was not a sign of life. Hills and plain were equally deserted.

At Ahangaran we found only ten families living in an old fort. The place was said to have been a settlement of iron-workers in former times, who worked the mines in the neighbourhood. From there we crossed a sandy plain dotted with *ták* and other bushes to Shahrakht, at the foot of another range of hills. It contained some 200 houses in a walled enclosure.

The next day we did twenty-four miles over hot sandy country, to a pool of water under a rocky gorge on the northern face of some hills called Chashma-i-Nuhur. Koki Sirdar, the chief of our Turkoman couriers, knew the place well as an old raiding guide. He said that they never could be sure of getting water at it in the raiding days, as one man with a gun on the rocks above was sufficient to keep a whole *alaman* at bay, and I could quite understand it. Turkoman raiders, though a terror to defenceless villagers, never risked the chance of any hard knocks in return, and thus naturally gave these sort of places a wide berth.

The 1st of April 1894 saw us at Mijnabad, a village of some sixty families, which, with the adjoining villages of Husainabad and Karyan, formerly belonged to Darwesh Ali Khan, Timuri, governor of Khaf, but he sold them to the late Amir of Kain for 7200 tumans, at the rate of

200 tumans per plough. Mijnabad was said to have been founded by Manija, the daughter of Afrasiab. It certainly was an ancient place, as the ground all round was strewn with broken bricks, and there were also the foundations of a burnt-brick tower.

Next day we camped at a reservoir a little off the road, and there I was met by an official deputed to attend me on the part of the Nusrat-ul-Mulk, the chief of the Timuris, by his deputy-governor of Khaf. Under his guidance we went on the next morning to Sangán. Four miles out we passed another reservoir, the Hauz-i-Mulla, and shortly after the Sangán cultivation commenced. Passing through various *báyhs* or walled enclosures full of trees, principally pines, we camped by some running water, close to the walls of an enclosure said to have been built by Nadir.

On nearing the village I was met by the Naib and his brother, the chief Mulla, and the principal elders and head-men of the village. They came out on foot, explaining that at this time of the year all their horses were sent into the hills to graze, and except the one ridden by the Naib there was not another horse in the village. This custom of turning horses out to grass in the spring is general throughout the country. The principal place of note in the village was the mausoleum of Sultan Mir Saiyid Ali, brother of the Iman Raza of Mashhad, said to have been built in A.D. 828, but the building had been long in ruins. The village itself contained some five hundred houses, of which one hundred were Timuris and the rest Tajiks. It was walled in the time of the Turkoman raids, but since then the walls had been allowed to go to ruin. The ark or citadel, which was the place of refuge in former days, was still standing, and towered over the rest of the village, but was no longer inhabited. The rows of pine trees which formed such a prominent feature were said to be the great protection of the tobacco and other crops, which without them would be destroyed by the high winds which prevailed in summer. A regular gale of wind blew all the afternoon and night while we were in the place, quite sufficient to convince us that the Sangan wind was not a myth. Next morning we proceeded on to Khaf, twelve miles beyond, passing through the villages of Barabad, Mehrabad, and Khargird. The road led over an open plain, but the mist was so thick that we could see nothing, and the bitter cold wind continued blowing.

At Barabad I was met by the priest in charge of the mausoleum there of Sufi Abdul Karim, said to be a descendant of Abu Bakr, the successor of Muhammad (632–634). This priest I found had a large number of followers amongst the Timuris of Herat and Khurasan, and was a man of considerable influence. After a short talk I went on to Khargird, where I was taken to see the ruins of the ancient Madrasah or college. This building was double-storeyed, and built round a centre courtyard some twenty-five yards square. It was well worth seeing as a fine relic of the old tilework, or rather I should call it of the mosaic work on plaster similar to that which formerly covered the Musalla at Herat. The whole of the arches and interior walls of the building were formerly covered with this glazed mosaic work, and the remains of the Musalla at Herat having been levelled to the ground by the orders of Amir Abdur Rahman in 1885, this Madrasah was said to be one of the few remaining examples of that beautiful work now left in these parts. A good deal of it was defaced by time and weather, but much of it was still perfect; and as mosaic work cannot be taken out and carried away like tiles, it ought to remain as long as wind and weather permit.

The entrance was on the east, with the Musjid opposite

and a lofty archway at either side, and each quarter contained ten rooms, five above and five below. From a tablet in the western recess it appeared that the building was constructed by Abul Muzaffar Bahadur Khan, son of Shahrukh Shah Uzbeg, in A.D. 1444, the mosaic-workers having been Shirazis. An old city was said to have existed in the neighbourhood, and I was shown a silver coin in the possession of a Hindu which was found near the Madrasah, and bore the name of Shahrukh Shah and the date 828 A.H. (1425).

After leaving the Madrasah I was met by the deputy-governor of Khaf and a party of some thirty sowars, by whom I was escorted in. On arrival at Khaf I found the Shaikh-ul-Islam or head-priest, the Kazi, the Rishsafeds or elders, and leading men of the place all drawn up in a long line to receive me. After a few words of welcome the whole party escorted me on to my tents, but there I had to dismiss them, as being Ramzan, the month of fasting, they could not even partake of a cup of tea. The Naib came to pay his formal visit in the afternoon, and I returned it in the evening.

Riding through to the citadel I was much struck by the deserted and desolate appearance of the town. We passed through the old walls, and thence on to the gate of the present town, and through what is called the bazar, but more than half the houses seemed to be in ruins. This was said to have been caused to a great extent by the exactions of the late governor, and also to have been due to the usury of the Hindus, of whom there was a colony of about twenty in the town. These Hindus all belonged to Shikarpur, in Sind, and had been established at Khaf for the last century, fresh men continually coming and going. Their chief trade, I found, was money-lending, though they had some small shops for the sale of groceries, cloth, tea, indigo, &c. They were said to charge from forty to fifty per cent., and to renew their bonds every four or six months, so that a man who once fell into their hands rarely got out again.

The town of Khaf, consisting of the citadel, avenue, bazar, bath, &c., was said to have been built by Amir Kilich Khan, Timuri, the powerful and semi-independent chief who ruled these frontier districts in the early part of the nineteenth century. It contained about eight hundred houses, and the people were all Sunnis. There were numbers of windmills, and the gardens produced all sorts of fruit, which was sold very cheap. The silk industry had almost entirely died out owing to disease, and the cultivation of opium had taken its place. Tobacco also was largely cultivated, 2000 kharwars being exported annually. The total revenue of the district was estimated at 18,000 tumans (£3600) in cash, not including the sheep-tax, which is a large item in all these frontier districts.

At Karat, some twenty-five miles farther on, I was met by a nephew of the chief of the Hazarahs in Khurasan, Mir Panj Ismail Khan, the Shuja-ul-Mulk, and received by him with much hospitality.

Some 5000 families of these Sunni Hazarahs were brought over from Kala Nou, in Badghis, by the Hisam-us-Sultanah after the last Persian siege of Herat in 1857. They were first of all allotted lands in the Jam and Bakharz districts, under their chief Yusuf Khan, who was given the rank of Sartip or colonel. Soon after some 2000 of them returned to Herat, and the Persian Government then moved the remainder away from the frontier to Isfarain, where they remained some years and lost numbers by cholera and disease. From there the survivors were moved to Khanagusha, near Mashhad. In 1877 Yusuf Khan was appointed governor of Bakharz, and built the village of Muhsinabad and settled a number of the families there. He died soon after, and his son, Ismail Khan, succeeded him as chief of the tribe. He was made an Amir Tuman and granted the title of Shuja-ul-Mulk by Nasir-ud-din Shah in 1894, and in 1896 he was appointed governor of Bakharz, but he lived at Mashhad himself, and his brother, Sartip Muhammad Raza Khan, acted as deputy in his place. On their first arrival the Persian Government gave the Hazarahs a service of 700 sowars, but after the defeat at Merv, in which the Hazarah sowars were present, this number was reduced to 500. In 1888 they were sent on service against the Yamuts and were again defeated, and the strength was further reduced by another 100 men, but 50 of these were restored in 1893, and the total number employed is now 450. The total strength of the tribe now in Persia is estimated at 1200 families.

Karat consisted of a little fort some 80 yards square, all in good repair, with ditch and parapet all round, and containing some 30 families. Outside, on a mound above the fort, stood an ancient pillar of burnt brick which could be ascended by a spiral staircase inside, but the foundations had been so worn away, and the upper portion of the pillar was so out of the perpendicular, that when I did get to the top I felt anything but safe. What the pillar was built for no one could say. There were the ruins of an old *robat* or rest-house some distance beyond, and there was said to have been a city here in former days, but nothing remained of it. Walking round in the evening I came across a curious collection of kestrels. There must have been eighty or a hundred of these little hawks all assembled on a tree together, and I wondered what they were doing.

My next march was to Hashtadan, a place formerly in dispute between Persia and Afghanistan. This dispute was settled and the boundary demarcated by General MacLean, the British consul-general at Mashhad, in 1891, and riding out due east along the Herat road across the open plain for some twelve miles we came to the line of boundary pillars, which we followed northwards till we arrived at the Hashtadan Tappa, which, like most of the artificial mounds of this country, was covered with bits of brick and pottery. The plain around was covered in the same way for far on every side, showing that the city that once stood there was of large extent. We found some Bahluri Baluch nomads scattered about, and riding across the plain we passed the carcasses of many dead sheep, a great number of which were said to have perished throughout the district owing to the excessive cold and snow in the winter. The wild asses that only two or three years before were plentiful on the Hashtadan plain had all disappeared. A shepherd we met reported that he had seen one with a small foal at heel, which the Hazarahs said they would go after and try to capture, but I never heard whether they succeeded or not. A young wild ass is no great catch, though, as of all that I have come across I have never seen one that became really tractable, or could be put to any use.

Hashtadan was evidently thickly populated at some time or other, and the tradition is that it once contained eighty *kanats* or underground water-channels; hence the name, from *hashtad*, eighty. Whatever the number was, there is no doubt that the whole plain is still dotted with lines and lines of little mounds marking the sites of the former *kanat* shafts, and nothing but the expenditure of money is required to make the place a flourishing settlement again. But no one dares to put money into anything in Persia.

From Hashtadan we marched thirteen miles to Taiabad, a village of about a hundred houses, mostly of Sunnis. The Naib met me at the village. Poor man, his intentions were good, and he was on his way to meet me a mile or two outside, but the night before having been the Id or feast at the end of Ramzan, he had evidently had a night of it, and my arrival was a bit too early for him. No one who has not lived in Persia can understand how utterly everything is disorganised there during this month of fasting. Night is turned into day and all business is practically at a standstill, and it is impossible to get anything done. At Mashhad two guns are posted in the citadel square, and these are regularly fired at sunset and a little before dawn throughout the month. Everybody is waiting at sunset with pipes lit and cooling drinks poured out, ready to fall to the moment the gun goes. Later on commences the serious eating and drinking, and this goes on all through the night. The shrine is thronged, and the whole town is *en fête*—all police regulations are at a standstill. There is no bugle call or curfew bell four hours after sunset as there is at other times of the year, and people are free to go about as they please all night.

Towards the morning another enormous meal is partaken of, and not till the morning gun has gone do the people think of sleep. The result is, not a soul scarcely is to be seen about all the forenoon, and it is only as the afternoon wears on that the people begin to get up, and even then those that can afford it simply loll about till the evening. I could therefore pity the Naib so ruthlessly disturbed in his slumbers by my early advent. On meeting me he took off his Persian astrakhan hat, a form of salutation that is daily becoming more common in Khurasan, and shows how Russian habits and customs are gradually being adopted. I have noticed that numbers of Persians who have been across the frontier into Russian territory have adopted this European form of salutation. The Persian in this respect is much more European than the Indian; and then again the Persian of Khurasan who crosses into Transcaspia meets there the Caucasian and the Russian peasant, who all dress and live in much the same style as himself, and with whom he mixes and lives on equal terms, and thus naturally becomes imbued with their habits.

In the evening I walked out to have a look at the Mazar or shrine that stood to the south-west of the village. I found that the saint's grave was placed in front of a high arched portico, still covered in parts with the remains of the tiles and glazed mosaic work that once adorned it. There was a fine Musjid at the back, and it was a pity to see such a building falling to ruin. Inside I found a party of Heratis, with whom I had a chat. They declared they had all been driven out of Afghanistan by oppression. Possibly they were partisans of Ayab Khan or of the Sher Ali dynasty; but whatever it was that caused them to leave, when I said good-bye they all took off their turbans and expressed their prayer that the English might soon take Herat, presumably under the idea that they would then be able to return there.

No one can travel about the Afghan-Persian frontier without being told the most extraordinary stories of what the English or the Russians are going to do, and so curious very often are these stories that one wonders how people came to invent them. Go where you will, the people are full of yarns. I was told that a priest, and a particularly holy priest too, had assured the people that he had himself heard a firman of the Amir's read out in Herat stating that he had given Kandahar and Herat to the English in exchange for Peshawar and Lahore, and that the English would arrive shortly to take possession, and no opposition was to be offered to them. Implicit reliance was placed in this Mulla, and no one would believe that the whole thing was ridiculous. Equally extraordinary stories wère told of the Russians, and it was not the slightest good trying to persuade the people that they were pure fiction.

From Taiabad we rode across the open plain to Riza. There were two villages here, one Mashhad and the other Riza, and the two together were known as Mashhad-i-Riza, so called from the shrine and mausoleum of Shahzada Kasim, a descendant of Abu Bakr, who was said to have been murdered by some unbeliever while conducting prayers here. I walked over to the shrine in the evening, and found a ruined tomb and Musjid in an enclosure containing a lot of pine-trees. The only man in the place was a Kandahari Fakir, a wild, matted-haired fellow who seemed to have wandered all over Afghanistan, and had lost his big toe in the snows of Turkistan. The walk from one village to the other was a pleasant one. The fruit-trees in the gardens were all in flower, and the other trees were sprouting, and everything looked green—a pleasing sight in such an arid country.

Shahr-i-Nau, a village of some two hundred houses, and the headquarters of the Bakharz district, was our next stage. The deputy-governor met me two miles out and escorted me in, and sent me presents of barley, sheep, and other things in the most hospitable manner. The village of Shahr-i-Nau was built by Muhammad Khan Beglar Begi, a Hazarah chief who formerly had charge of this frontier, but the high walls required in his day were rapidly falling to pieces, and almost the whole population was settled in hamlets outside. The place was well watered, and the numerous gardens and orchards were said to produce every kind of fruit known in these parts, with the exception of pomegranates, for which the climate was too cold. The place was full of magpies, all building their nests in the fruit-trees. Shahr-i-Nau also boasted of a shrine under a big pine-tree, and there was also a *tappa* or artificial mound, with the remains of a high citadel in the centre and walls around, which must have been lofty and commanding in ancient days.

Our route now led up the valley in the centre of the Bakharz district. We passed through continuous villages and cultivation, and the stream flowing down the valley, with the springs and grassy sward along its banks, gave a look of fertility to the place that one rarely sees in Persia. Bakharz was devastated during the time of the Turkoman raids, and the total revenue in 1894 was said to be only 3400 tumans (£680) in cash and 1800 kharwars of grain, but the country seemed capable of great improvement. The population was comprised of Persians known as Bakharzis, with a small proportion of Hazarah, Timuri, and Afghan settlers; and in years of good spring rains a large quantity of unirrigated grain was produced and exported.

Shahu-i-Bala and the neighbouring village of Aliak at the head of the valley belonged to Baluchis, but these men being confirmed nomads would not live in them; and it was curious to see the landlords living in their black sacking tents near by, and the village itself populated by their tenants, consisting of some fifty families of Karai cultivators.

We had a long march out of the Bakharz Valley over the Kalla Minar pass, marked on the map as 7120 feet, to the village of Gandusha on the other side. We sent the camels with the advance tents on ahead at sunrise, but they did not get in till sunset. We just touched snow-level, and the air at that height was delicious. Gandusha was inhabited solely by Barbaris, as Hazarahs from the Hazarajat in Afghanistan are called in Persia. They cultivated the land and paid rent at the rate of half the produce, the arrangement being that the landlord supplied the seed and paid the Government revenue, while the tenants provided the bullocks and labour—terms rather more favourable than usual to induce men to settle in the place. The emigration of Hazarahs from Afghanistan into Khurasan has latterly greatly increased, and large numbers of them have now found employment there as cultivators. They are more hardy and work for less wages than the Persians, and are adding materially to the prosperity of the country. At the same time they must be a great loss to Afghanistan, but so long as the present persecution of the Shiahs goes on in that country it is only natural that every Barbari who can will do his best to escape it. One man we met, a Barbari Saiyid in a blue turban, came out to ask, "Why did not the British Government do something to help the Barbaris?" and after talking over the matter for some little time he went on to say that the British Empire was defended by an army consisting half of Goras (English soldiers) and half of Gurkhas, who always fought side by side, and that as the Gurkhas and the Barbaris came from the same stock, the Barbaris, if enlisted in the British army, would become just as good soldiers as the Gurkhas. This idea of the origin of the Hazarahs was new to me, and I am not sure that it is one that is recognised by the Gurkhas, but I could quite agree with the Saiyid as to the usefulness of the Hazarahs, and I was glad to be able to tell him that some were even then being enlisted in the new Baluchistan regiments at Quetta.

Next day we made a short march to a place called Hawas, where we found some forty more families of Barbaris settled amongst the Persians. We were not more than a farsakh or so from Faraiman, on the high-road, and in the evening I rode out to have a look at the Band-i-Faraiman, a masonry dam built of stone and mortar faced with burnt brick, and about 100 yards in length and 50 or 60 feet in height. This dam must have been a fine work in its day, but it was broken by a hole in the centre, and nobody seemed to have thought of repairing it.

Here we were near home, and the 18th April 1894 saw us all back again in Mashhad after an absence of four months and eight days, during which we had traversed a total distance of 1346 miles.

CHAPTER X.

SUMMER AT MASHHAD.

On arrival at Mashhad I found that the whole town had been in an uproar. A mob of Mullas and students had first of all broken open the shop and destroyed the stock-in-trade of an Armenian dentist who was accused of making and selling *arak* or wine from the local grapes, and having thus satisfied their fanatical zeal they then proceeded to clamour against the Governor-General for cheaper bread. It soon became apparent, however, that the row had been more or less got up, and the bread riot did not last long. Even at the height of the disturbance not a word was said or any movement made against the Europeans resident in the town, and the whole thing passed off, fortunately, without much trouble.

Easter Day was now coming on, the greatest of all Russian festivals. Everybody holds a reception on that day, and all friends are expected to call. At my visit to the members of the Russian Consulate I was much struck at the beautifully-coloured Easter eggs that our hostesses had prepared to commemorate the day, a custom that one so rarely sees now in other countries.

The next festivity after this was the Queen's Birthday. In Persia it is the custom for all consuls to hold official receptions and dinners on the birthdays of their respective sovereigns. My reception on the 24th May commenced at 8 A.M. First of all came the members of the Russian Consulate in full uniform. Russian officers always seem to be well decorated, and the secretary in temporary charge of the Consulate was no exception to the rule. He wore the Persian Order of the Lion and the Sun, as well as the Bokharan Star, which the Amir of Bokhara appears to have lavished freely upon almost all the Russian officials in Central Asia; also the orders of St. Anne and St. Stanislaus, and his academy badge. The Consulate interpreter even was decorated, and had the Lion and the Sun round his neck. At 8.30 Mr. Van Lennep and Mr. Douglas of the Imperial Bank of Persia arrived, and at 9 came all the Persian officials in full uniform, and a gay sight they were. The Mir Punj, or general of artillery, appeared in the white tunic and red trousers of the Persian uniform, with the sash and stars of his rank; the Karguzars of Mashhad and of Sarakhs were similarly attired in Sartip's or colonel's uniform of the same colours; the Wazir was in civil dress, consisting of a cashmere shawl chogah with his decorations on it, amongst them the Queen's Jubilee medal, the record of his visit to London in 1887; the Hakím, Bashi, the Telegraph Sartip, the assistant Karguzar, and others were also in civil dress; the Nusrat-ul-Mulk was gorgeous in a blue tunic, with the portrait of the Shah set in brilliants round his neck. Everybody had the regulation two cups of tea, two pipes, a glass of iced sherbet, and a cup of coffee; and when the Persians left the same was gone through again with all the British-Indian subjects, pensioners, and others connected with India, who then came up to pay their respects. Each Persian official brought a crowd of men with him, who all had their tea and pipes in the garden outside, and it is astonishing what an amount of tea and sugar can be got through on such an occasion.

At the official dinner in the evening we sat down a party of twelve, viz. the Governor-General, the Nusrat-ul-Mulk, the Wazir, the Mir Punj of Artillery, the Telegraph Sartip, and the Hakím, Bashi on the part of the Persians; the acting Russian Consul-General and his interpreter, Mirza Taki Khan; Duke, Moula Bakhsh, Ghulam Murtaza Khan, and myself. About the middle of dinner the Governor-General got up and proposed the health of her Majesty the Queen of England and Empress of India, and in reply I drank to the health of his Majesty the Shah of Persia and of all sovereigns and chiefs of states friends and allies of her Majesty, both toasts being given in Persian.

The garden and gateway were lit up. The Persian band played outside, and there was quite a crowd of people to see the illuminations. The same thing was repeated the next night, when I had a second dinner-party, consisting of the Karguzari or Persian Foreign Office officials and others, amongst whom was the artillery Sarhang whom I had met at Birjand, and who turned up unexpectedly and announced that he had been relieved—a relief that he described as an escape from hell. He was very full of a trip he had made to Herat. He went there, he said, in the garb of an Afghan to an Afghan friend of his, and spent three days in the town seeing everything, and was very proud of his exploit. At this dinner the Karguzar of Mashhad proposed the Queen's health, and I replied as before. The third night was the last of our festivities. The Consulate was again illuminated, and I had a dinner to all British-Indian subjects, traders, agents, &c. For them the tables were removed and a Persian dinner was laid out on the dining-room floor. The party there numbered twenty-eight all told, and amongst them were the head of the Persian merchants in Mashhad, an Afghan banker, British merchants and traders from Peshawar, the Derajat and Peshin, the office clerks, and others, while in the tents outside there was a dinner for all the orderlies, Turkoman postal sowars, servants, and everybody connected with Great Britain, in fact. Dinner was prepared for over one hundred men, and at least that number must have sat down.

The next big day was on the 14th June, when the Persian festival of the Id-i-Kurban came off, and the whole town was *en fête*. Every good Muhammadan on that day kills a ram to commemorate the sacrifice, and our stables had been full of fatted rams for some days beforehand, and great was the feasting thereon. This, though, was only the sacrifice of each private household. In the town a camel was publicly sacrificed. This animal was led about for days beforehand, covered with small looking-glasses and decked up generally with paraphernalia of sorts by an impecunious Shahzadah or Persian prince, who collected money sufficient, I hope, for him to live upon for the rest of the year, as I believe he had no other source of livelihood. With him were some of the Governor-General's running footmen in their scarlet coats to give *éclat* to the proceedings, and on the morning in question the camel was solemnly led out and its throat was cut by the Shahzadah, and then the whole crowd rushed in and there was a free fight for the flesh. Some thousands of people passed the Consulate on the way to the citadel with the flesh, and I was told that the man who got possession of the camel's head and succeeded in taking it up to the Governor-General got the first prize, and that the possessor of each leg got something too. Shortly after the arrival of the people the customary salute was fired in the citadel square. The day was wonderfully cool, the thermometer in my hall not going above 72° F., and I don't think it rose above 76 all the month.

The fruit now began to come in, and by the end of June the garden was full of apricots and cherries. Plums, too, came in to the bazar in large quantities.

The beginning of July ushered in the Muharram, that month of mourning for the death of Hasan and Husain that is so religiously observed by all pious Shiahs, and Persians are nothing if not religious, at any rate outwardly. For ten days the town of Mashhad was full of processions, and all work was practically at a standstill. These processions attracted large crowds, and completely blocked the narrow streets, and for a European to be caught by one would have been most unpleasant, and might have been dangerous. The members of the Russian Consulate left the town and went out into the country for the time.

It is not in the rural districts in Persia that fanaticism is to be feared. The villagers are generally quiet and friendly and perfectly inoffensive. It is only in the towns, where religious students and people of that class congregate, that outbreaks occur. Consequently the members of the two Consulates had hitherto left Mashhad at Muharram time. As for myself I saw no necessity to move, and so remained at home, and everything passed off without the slightest fanaticism or the least show of antipathy to Europeans on the part of the mob.

The processions commenced in a small way, simply two or three banners leading, followed by twenty or thirty boys with their backs bare and bunches of small iron chains in their hands, with which they belaboured themselves. Then would follow more banners, and a crowd of traders, &c., all yelling and beating their breasts. They brought their right hands all down at the same time on to their left breasts with such sounding force as to discolour the flesh, and in many cases to abrade the skin. Truly the Shiah religion appeared to be a wonderful and fearful form of worship on these occasions, and yet no one could help being impressed by the scene. As the time went on and the fatal day, the 10th of Muharram, drew nearer, the processions got bigger and bigger. Each sect or race had a procession of its own; but the palm was, I think, by universal consent assigned to the Azarbaijani Turks, who occupied the quarter of the town next to the British Consulate. They went in for it all with by far the greatest zeal, so much so that on the ninth day I went over to the Bank premises on purpose to see their procession, which was to pass down the street in which the bank was situated on its way back from the shrine. By that time, of course, the procession had been robbed of a good deal of its freshness, and many of its followers had deserted it; but still it was a most striking sight. First of all came a double row of flags borne by men in black. Then came the boys, also in black, with their backs bared, and beating themselves with chains which they swung over their shoulders alternately to the right and left to the time given by a man with a pair of brass cymbals, and singing a solemn sort of refrain or dirge all the time. After the chain-boys came Saiyids, Turk traders, and others. After them again came the main body of the procession, consisting of men in black with their chests bared, and all beating their left breasts with their right hands in time to the same solemn dirge. The breasts of the men were deep red, and in many cases the skin was broken; but they beat away in perfect time and the effect was most solemn, and there was not a man of us who witnessed the procession who was not impressed by it, more so than I could have believed possible had I not witnessed it. The manager of the bank had a couple of sheep ready, and on the arrival of the head of the procession at the bank door, their throats were cut and the blood allowed to flow in front of the men, one on either side of the road. The leading Saiyid in charge of the procession then halted it in front of the bank, and having stopped the singing, spoke out and said that the Imperial Bank of Persia had offered a sacrifice, and their sacrifice was accepted and God would bless them for it; after which the bodies of the two sheep were lifted up and carried away, and the procession moved on again.

The next day was the *Katl*, or day of the murder, the final day of the festival, and I went down to the house of our Turkoman camel contractor to see the procession pass on its way to the shrine. I had already seen one representation of this festival in the Persian Embassy at Constantinople, and I found that at Mashhad, as at Constantinople, the black dress of the day before had been discarded and the processionists on the final day were clad in white. The result, though, did not strike me as being so solemn or impressive as it was the day before. First of all came a double line of men in single file, facing inwards and walking sideways up the street, with sticks or swords in their hands, chanting and swinging the sticks to time. Then came the central figure of the procession. This was a man stripped to the waist and covered with daggers, horse-shoes, little looking-glasses, and such like things, stitched into his body. For instance, he had a pair of crossed daggers on his breast and back, the points stuck into the skin and the handles stitched on. His arms and shoulders were heavy with horse-shoes stitched on through the skin, and he also had various padlocks about him, the hasp being passed through the skin and the padlock then locked again.

Immediately following was the procession of men in

THE MUHARRAM AT MASHHAD—SOME OF THE MEN IN THE PROCESSION.

white with bare heads, and all armed with knives and daggers, with which they cut themselves on the forehead and on the top of their heads, the blood running down over their faces on to their white shirts below. They all chanted a dirge in cadence, and were a gruesome sight to behold. I had a huge bowl of sherbet prepared, and it was served out to them by my orderlies and servants as they passed, and they drank it greedily and seemed very grateful for the attention. Some 20 lbs. of sugar was melted down, not to mention other ingredients, and though it was an occasion of mourning, it was said to be permissible to offer the mourners such consolation as one could in the shape of reviving drinks, so my men ladled out with a will. After the men in white who were cutting themselves came a lot of quite small boys also in white, who curiously enough cut and hacked themselves with even more vigour than the men. I well remember the last of all, a small child in arms of about three years of age, who also had his little knife in his hand, and was cut all over the head, and both his head and face were a mass of blood, but still he held on to his knife bravely as he was carried past. After these came the merchants and others, all dressed in black, and figuratively beating their breasts, but with a mild and gentle pat. They passed on with saddened countenance, and after them a horse was led past covered with what was apparently intended to represent horse-armour of ancient days full of arrow shafts. Then followed a troop of the regular professional breast-beaters, bare to the waist, and beating their breasts hard and in earnest, as I saw them the day before, and the crowd brought up the rear. Too soon they had passed, and the whole thing was over. All our *farashes* and servants and everybody had a holiday, and went off to the shrine, where the sight must have been a wonderful one. In the afternoon they all attended the *shabib* or religious play in the citadel, where each day's story had been acted day by day, and where the death and martyrdom of Imam Husain was to be acted that day. I was told that the man who represented Husain was finally knocked down, covered with something on which the operation of cutting off his head was performed, and finally a sham head was brought out, put on the top of a lance, and marched off amidst the tears of the audience. I watched the crowd returning from the play in the evening, and I was astonished to see how many women there were amongst them. It appeared that women were allowed to attend all the shows during the Muharram, and they took full advantage of the permission. All were completely veiled, of course.

On the 8th of August 1894 came the Shah's Birthday, the annual entertainment given by the Persian authorities. The Persian band had been hard at work for some time practising the English and the Russian National Anthems, and great arrangements had been made by the Governor-General to do honour to the occasion. The 8th was the day of the Shah's birth, but the Persians reckon the preceding night as the night of any given day, not the following night, consequently the Persian entertainment came off on what we reckoned as the night of the 7th. The Governor-General had a big Persian party in his garden from 8 till 11 P.M., the band playing away the whole time. The square was filled with people, and about 11.30 the fireworks began. Nine o'clock in the morning of the 8th was the time fixed for my reception, and at that hour I paid my visit in full uniform, accompanied by Duke and Moula Bakhsh, and duly offered my congratulations on the auspicious occasion. For the dinner party in the evening the Governor-General had his garden beautifully lit up with lanterns, of which there were hundreds. We were received in a large *shamiana*, well carpeted, and adorned with a suite of drawing-room furniture which had lately been imported from Bombay, and which, strange to say, had arrived comparatively uninjured after more than 900 miles on camel-back from Bandar Abbas. Dinner was served in an open tent, and the weather was so cool that our full-dress uniform was not oppressive in the least. We sat down a party of ten, consisting of the Governor-General, the Wazir, the Karguzar, and the Hakím, Bashi; the acting Russian Consul-General and his interpreter, the manager of the bank, Duke, Moula Bakhsh, and myself. I duly proposed the Shah's health, and the Governor-General proposed the health of the Queen of England and Empress of India in reply, followed by that of the health of the Tsar of Russia and the kings of the world.

After dinner we adjourned to the *shamiana* to smoke, and finally went up to a balcony overlooking the square to see the fireworks, and also the performances of a couple of dancing boys, who seemed to attract the crowd greatly. These dancers as a rule belong to a tribe called Fayuj in Arabic and Gharibzada or Karishmar in Persian, the latter being a corruption from Ghair-i-Shumar, or out of the count. They are scattered all over Khurasan, and are said to have been brought from India by King Bahrangur to act as singers and dancers. The whole of the tribe is under the Shah's Shatirbashi, or the chief of the running footmen, who collects their taxes and rules them through his deputies in the various provinces. Their chief in Khurasan was a Sartip, a relative of the Shatırbashi, who lived at Mashhad.

The Shah's Birthday was the last official entertainment on hand, and now that the hot weather was coming to an end, I made preparations for a tour through Northern Khurasan.

CHAPTER XI.

KALAT-I-NADIRI AND DARAGEZ.

On the 24th August 1894, just as I was leaving Mashhad, who should arrive to call but a couple of Austrian officers, Captains Müller and Goiginger, who had been on duty in Russia, to learn Russian, for the past year, and at the conclusion of their course had been on a trip to Samarkand and back! They had arrived in Mashhad the day before, having ridden over from the railway station at Doshakh with simply a Turkoman guide to show them the way, and had put up in a caravansarai in the town. They were returning via Kahka, and I was able to ask them to accompany me on the march and to arrange for them to join me in camp next day. This settled, I rode out to Pul-i-Shahi, the bridge over the Kashaf Rud, five miles to the north of Mashhad, where I found the camp ready pitched. I had with me my assistant, Khan Bahadur Moula Bakhsh, and also Mirza Muhammad Khan, a boy of fifteen, the son of the late British agent at Mashhad, Mirza Abbas Khan, C.M.G., C.I.E, a well-known man to all British travellers in Khurasan in former days, when consul-generals had not yet been thought of. An English and Persian writer and a hospital assistant completed the party. This time I took no camels with me, and I had all the tents and baggage on mules. The only really armed men of the party were

THE VILLAGE OF KARDEH, ON THE ROAD FROM MASHHAD TO KALAT-I-NADIRI.

my three Indian cavalry orderlies, as the Persian soldiers with their useless muskets and no ammunition could hardly be called fighting men, and the Turkoman postal sowars had only their swords to keep watch with at night and to protect the post from robbers on the road. On taking a muster of the camp, though, I still found our numbers amounted to 70 men, 73 mules, and 21 horses. Of these about a dozen were private servants, including cooks, table servants, bakers, washermen, &c. Another dozen were *farashes* or tent-pitchers, and another postal sowars, while the orderlies, ghulams, Persian guards, grooms, water-carriers, and hospital dresser, &c., with some 20 muleteers, brought up the total to 70; so difficult is it to cut down numbers when travelling in Eastern countries. In the West one can find accommodation on the road; in the East one has to take one's house and everything belonging to it with one.

At Rizwan, eleven miles farther north, the two Austrian officers joined us. They had nothing with them but the clothes they rode in, and were by no means comfortable on Turkoman saddles; but it was wonderful how they had got through as they did, and they deserved every credit for the way they had done it. We supplied them with all the spare bedding we had, and made them more comfortable for the night, I hope, than they otherwise would have been.

From Rizwan we entered the mountain range that bounds the Mashhad Valley on the north and east, the highest peaks of which run up to a height of 9000 and 10,000 feet. A couple of miles up the valley brought us to the defile or Zu-i-Andarukh, the narrow part of which was about a mile in length, with precipitous rocks some 300 feet in height on either side. Four miles beyond we passed the village of Kardeh, and finally camped by the side of the stream some five miles farther on at a small picturesque village named Ál, inhabited by some twenty-five families of Chulais. All the villages in these hills between Andarukh and Balghur are known by the name of Chulai Khana, the district taking its name from the tribe inhabiting it.

The Chulais are of Turk origin, but speak both Turki and Persian, and are said to have been moved from Turkistan to Khurasan during the time of the Mongol Dynasty (*c.* 1221–1335). They numbered about 500 families all told, under their chief Abul Fatteh Khan, who lived at Marish, and was the hereditary governor of the district up till 1896, when he was superseded. According to my aneroid there was a rise of some 1400 feet in our day's march, and we had a pleasant camp amongst trees and verdure. Here we lost the company of our two Austrian travellers. They rode the march with me in the morning, but were obliged to push on, and in the afternoon they started to ride on to Balghur, where my advance tents had been sent to, and dined and slept in them, and proceeded on their way to the railway at Kahka next morning.

I myself went off up the hills after oorial, but without result. A local Shikari, however, brought in a deer and some partridges. We ascended another 1200 feet in the eleven miles on to Balghur, and found ourselves at an altitude of something like 6000 feet in a climate so cold that grapes would not grow. Many of the mules slipped their loads on the way, and the rocks on either side came down so close at one place that a laden camel would hardly get through.

There is an inscription on an overhanging rock in this pass, partly in Persian and partly in Arabic, near a small hamlet called Panjmana, which I did not know of at the time and did not notice, but Mr. Ney Elias heard of it afterwards and sent Mirza Abdulla to copy it. A translation of it by Khan Bahadur Moula Bakhsh was afterwards published by Mr. Elias in the Royal Asiastic Society's *Journal*, and it runs as follows:—

"By Divine favour and grace, and by Providential assistance, his Majesty, Lord of the happy conjunction, the Emperor, Conqueror of Countries, the Implorer of aid of the aiding God, Abul Fath Muhammad Shaibani Khan, the Learned of the World, and Viceregent of the Merciful—may the days of his glory be perpetuated, and may the skirts of the exigencies of his generosity be prolonged. God has given precedence to warriors with their riches and souls over people who go not to war. On the 2nd day of the month of Shawál, in the year nine hundred and fifteen (A.D. 1410), turned his glorious reins from Marv-i-Sháhiján towards Dasht-i-Kibchák, and at the stage of Kindilik . . . Ulughtágh defeated a multitude of infidels and deviators and enemies of the faith and religion, and having taken a large number of that community as captives, marched them to Dar-ul-Islám and honoured them by leading them into the road of Paradise, and on the 22nd day of the month of Safar, in the year nine hundred and sixteen, arrived in the suburbs of the city of Yádgár-i-Khâni, which has been built by the arhitect of his Imperial magnanimity; and from the beginning of [his] departure to the end of [his] return, a period of four months and twenty days [his Majesty] traversed so many stages and marches that the quick-flying bird of conception and the swift-paced steed of imagination are impotent and powerless to conceive and imagine their survey. May God perpetuate the shadow of his Viceregency over the heads of true Believers, and strengthen the standard of his victory by the truth of Muhammad, on whom be blessing and peace."

According to the Persian historians this victory was really a defeat, but Persian historians were generally apt to gloss over any reverse. There is no doubt, however, it was the commencement of Shaibani's decline of power, as towards the end of the same year he was trampled to death under the hoofs of the horses of his own cavalry in the confusion which ensued in the fort at Marv-i-Shahijan during Shah Ismail Safavi's invasion. The locality of Dar-ul-Islam is not known at present, but presumably it meant either Khiva or Samarkand, where the captives were apparently converted to Islam.

The next day found us over the pass and encamped at Bardeh on the other side, a march of thirteen miles. The road was a difficult one. We had two narrow gorges in the first five miles, in which many of the mules fell and caused great delay. We reached the watershed after a rise from Balghur of some 1500 feet. Beyond this, instead of the narrow rocky defiles we had previously gone through we found ourselves in an undulating open country, dotted thinly with small junipers on the top of the hills known as the Karadagh Range, and the road ran along this, crossing ridge after ridge, and finally ascending to a second pass known as the Shutar Gardan or camel's neck Kotal, the road up which was very rocky and difficult for laden mules, and impassable, I should say, for camels. We did not see much game on the road, except partridges. One of these was killed for us by a large dark-coloured eagle that suddenly swooped down over my head into a bush on the opposite hillside, followed immediately by its mate. I could not see what they were after, but thinking they must have got something, I sent a man up who drove off the eagles and found a freshly killed partridge with its head nipped off. I presented the bird to the man for his trouble, and then commenced the argument as to whether it was *halál, i.e.* lawful food for a Mussulman, or not. I argued that if any of them cut off the head of a bird I had shot it was *halál*, which they acknowledged, as they did it every day; but the point was, if an eagle did it for them, whether it had the same effect, and that was a knotty point that lasted them for the rest of the march. I never heard what the result was, but I think that if that partridge had not been eaten I should have heard of it.

The descent on the northern side of the hills was very steep. We first had a sudden drop from an elevation of something like 6400 feet to about 5000 to the bed of a nullah, and thence down the latter between scarped hills on either side for another 800 feet to the camping-ground on the Istiksu or warm-water nullah, a total distance of ten miles. I found the pass full of partridges, and the village Shikari declared the hills were full of ibex, but though I had a climb with him up a rocky gorge in the afternoon, over one jagged scarp after another, not a sign of an ibex did I see.

The next day we marched six miles down to the main entrance to Kalat-i-Nadiri, but even in those six miles the aneroid marked a further descent of 1000 feet, making the height of our camp about 3300 feet. The road joined the valley at the foot of the southern face of Kalat, and ran west down this valley till we came to the break of the perpendicular scarp in the hills forming the natural fortress of Kalat known as the Darband-i-Arghunshah. We found a picket of Persian soldiers posted at this defile, and no one was permitted even to approach the gate that here guards the entrance, so jealous are the Persian Government of the entry of any foreigners into this curious natural fortress. Kalat-i-Nadiri has a great name as the mountain fastness of the great Nadir Shah, but beyond the natural structure of the place there is nothing nowadays of great interest or importance about it. Imagine a gigantic saucer some sixty miles in circumference, elevated from 500 to 1000 feet above the surrounding country and bounded outwardly on all sides by a continuous ridge of scarped rock, perpendicular at the top and then sloping steeply down, with only a break at five places. One of these breaks was the Darband-i-Arghunshah, at which I was encamped, so called after Arghun (1284), the great-great-grandson of Changiz Khan. Here two streams, one from the east and one from the west, join and enter the Kalat saucer, and passing through it, emerge on to the plains of Transcaspia through another defile on the north-eastern side. From the hills opposite the Arghunshah gates I had a good view of the interior, which here slopes down on all sides to the banks of this stream. I heard that there were inscriptions on some rocks inside that could not be got at, and the Shujah-ud-Dowlah, the Timuri chief, subsequently told me that he had tried to read them with glasses but could not make them out. Mr. Elias also wrote to try and get copies of them, but they were reported to be illegible.

My brother, Major A. C. Yate, the author of "England and Russia Face to Face in Asia," the last traveller permitted to enter Kalat-i-Nadiri, describes the interior in his account of the place, written on 5th July 1885 and published in the *Daily Telegraph* a month or so afterwards, as consisting of a confusion of lofty abrupt spurs of which the highest points were Bala Kumaili, ten miles to the south-east of Gugumaz, and a nameless eminence a mile north of Khisht overhanging the northern wall. Gugumaz was a village within the fortress four miles from the Arghunshah entrance, the headquarters of the local commandant, and Khisht was another village four miles to the north of that again, near which was Nadir's usual residence. The narrow valley extending from Arghunshah to below Gugumaz was everywhere cultivated by irrigation, the cultivation consisting of rice, wheat, lucerne, vineyards, orchards, melon and cucumber beds, &c., while the level summits and gentler slopes of the spurs throughout the whole interior were cultivated as *daima* or rain land. The relics of Nadir were described as, firstly, an ingenious arrangement for conducting water in pipes from the Harazu spring near Arghunshah to Gugumaz, now long since out of repair. Secondly, the Makbara-i-Nadir or Nadir's tomb, built under Nadir's orders, though never used as his mausoleum. This is a simple but not inelegant edifice of red sandstone. The central chamber, which was once domed, is encircled by a number of small chambers, and below it is an extensive cellar. Not far from it stands a small Musjid completely encased in *kashi* or painted tiles, known as the Bulut Gumbaz. Thirdly, the Nakhara Khana, that is, the building in a city or the spot in a camp from which is sounded reveillé, retreat, last post, &c., on drums and trumpets, situated on the red-coloured eminence two or three miles east of Gugumaz. Fourthly, Nadir's residence at Asiabad, now simply indicated by some uninteresting remains of walls, and the water tanks below Khisht. Fifthly, the remains of a wall and tower constructed under Nadir's orders on the southern face. Such is the sum total of all that remains to remind the world of the once widespread fame of the great Nadir Shah.

The inhabitants of Kalat are Jalair Turks and Ardalan Kurds. The Jalairs were brought to Khurasan by Amir Timur, and numbered some 400 families. The Ardalans were moved to Khurasan from Kirmanshah by Nadir Shah, and numbered about 300 families. Kalat-i-Nadiri till within recent years had its own hereditary chiefs of the Jalair tribe, who held the fortress as feudatories of Persia. Owing to the strength of the position they were able to maintain a large share of independence, and one of them, Yalangtush Khan, gave much trouble in the time of Muhammad Shah (1835–1848), but was reduced to submission by force. His son obtained the restoration of his father's lands and chiefship, but died in 1883; and his son again, another Yalangtush Khan, was a man of no ability, and was deprived of the chiefship two years later. That was the end of Jalair rule.

From Mashhad to Kalat we had followed the Persian telegraph line, and found it very badly put up, the line broken and poles continually down. From Kalat we followed the extension to Daragez, and this was just in the same condition, or even worse. The total length of these two lines is 72 miles to Kalat and 40 on to Daragez, and when I came to inquire I found that communication between Mashhad and Daragez had been interrupted on an average for 194 days out of the 365, which shows of itself how useless such lines as these, worked entirely under Persian management, are to the Persian Government. The local governors in these outlying tracts are callous about the telegraph, to say the least of it, as it is to their interest to keep the lines down as much as possible, to prevent complaints being made against them; while the lines themselves are run up anyhow, with bad poles and no insulators, and the staff is insufficient to keep them in repair. Small wonder that they do not work.

At Charam, our next stage from Kalat, I found the people all living in wooded enclosures under the shade of fine large walnut-trees, which extended for more than a mile. I inquired the price of walnuts, and they told me that they took them down to the railway at Kahka and sold them there for two krans, or about ninepence, a thousand. The Kadkhuda of the village came to meet me, and had many tales of former travellers. He remembered Captain the Hon. George Napier, who visited Kalat in 1872. There was no mistaking his description of him as the man with the measuring wheel. He also related how Sikandarfin Sahib put up for two days at his village. This name puzzled me for a time, but eventually resolved itself into Alexander Finn, the consul at Resht, who was on duty on this frontier in 1885. He could also tell of another English traveller, whom he had escorted from Mashhad in the same year, and this turned out to have been my brother, Major A. C. Yate. The trees in the ravine in which the village was situated were full of wood-pigeons, just the same sort of bird to look at as the English wood-pigeon.

As we neared the Turkoman frontier, the Persian *sarbazes* or soldiers on duty with me gave us many stories of former days. The nearer they got to the Turkomans the more they dwelt on them. One old man I well remember. He had been a *sarbaz* for thirty years, and had served at Shiraz and at Bandar Abbas as well as in Khurasan. He was born at Shahrud, and both he and his two brothers were all taken prisoners and carried off by the Turkomans in their youth. His brothers were taken to Khiva, and had never been heard of since. He himself was taken to Ashkabad, and his father succeeded in ransoming him there for the sum of ninety tumans. Many a man could tell a similar tale along this frontier, and the Persians have much to be thankful for to Russia for putting the Turkomans down. Nothing remains of the former fear of them now but the memory of past raids, but that memory is an abiding one, and will be long in dying out. The only thing to be said for the Persians is, that if they had had the pluck to resist they would never have suffered as they did. The Kurds and other frontier tribesmen never seem to have had the same dread of the Turkoman that the Persians had. Turkomans, so far as my experience goes, are neither good swordsmen nor good rifle-shots, and had they had any one to deal with but Persians they could never, I think, have maintained the terror over Khurasan that they did.

Our next march to Igdalik took us within a few miles of the village of Archingan, where a Russian and Persian Boundary Commission was said to be then engaged in the demarcation of the frontier between the two countries.

At Igdalik the hills rose precipitately to a great height above the village, and at the back of all lay the mountain known locally as the Koh-i-Sistan, which the villagers declared was full of shikar. Starting off at 2.30 A.M. the next morning in the dark I rode up as far as possible, and then after a steep climb up the mountain side, which we managed easily by holding on to the ponies' tails, we found ourselves at the top of the first range by sunrise. Peering over the crest we soon discovered a flock of ibex down on the other side, but there was not a head amongst them worth shooting. We then climbed a second ridge, but all to no purpose, as by the time we got to the top we found that two Mirgans or village Shikaris were advancing from one side, and another from the other side, and all chance of getting a shot was gone. Then, and not till then, did I get the Shikari to confess that there were no big heads on the hill. The higher ranges of the Koh-i-Sistan contained some, he said, and he pointed out to me the Hazar Masjid range, and told me that the only place to get really big ibex was on those hills and on two others called by him Ahuzar and Kurkhan, but that so wary were the old bucks that they only left the holes in the cliffs in which they lived by night. The Hazar Masjid he described to me as a beautiful mountain, with a flat top and full of springs, and covered with the remains of ancient buildings of some unknown age. The mountains I climbed I found to be thickly covered with grass, so thick in fact that I almost lost sight of the ibex in it when they were crossing the bottom of the valley. Wild briars and brambles abounded, while hawthorns and small junipers were dotted about higher up.

Looking north from the top of the hills, the white buildings of the Transcaspian railway station at Kahka were visible away in the distance beyond the mass of hillocky ground that here intervenes between the mountains and the plains. The Shikari pointed out to me the different places in sight, and the line of the new frontier. He told me that in former days the people here mostly lived by rice cultivation, and he complained bitterly of the Russians having not only stopped all that, but of having even prohibited their wheat cultivation as well. All irrigation whatever, it seemed, had been put a stop to in these Persian frontier villages, so that the water might run down into Russian territory, and the people were thus left to depend on what rain crops they could grow on the hillsides. These people, however, in thus complaining seemed to forget that no cultivation whatever was possible in these hills till the Russians put down the Turkoman raids, and that they ought to be only too thankful that their lives were no longer in danger, without clamouring for the water which they could not use when they did have it. The morning air on the top of the mountains was delicious, and the marvel to me was that Russia had not taken anything more than the water. I could not help thinking that it must be terrribly aggravating to the Russian officers grilling away in the plains below, to see the cool mountains above them and yet not to possess them; at least I felt sure that such would be my feelings were I a Russian officer quartered in Transcaspia.

In the afternoon I went on to Rubat-i-K̓hakistar, an old ruin standing on the banks of the Lain stream, which was here some ten or twelve feet in breadth and a foot in depth, with a strong flow. The water all ran down untouched to Kahka, in Russian territory. At Pulgavird we came to the end of the Kalat district, and at Shamskhan, nine miles beyond, I was joined by Haji Ali, the British agent in Daragez. We came down nearly 1000 feet in the march, and the heat increased accordingly, the thermometer rising to 88° F. in the shade at 4 P.M. Shamskhan stood on the banks of the Rudbar stream, which, like the Lain, took its rise in the Hazar Musjid range, and, like it, ran untouched down into Russian territory. The villagers at Shamskhan were entirely prohibited from touching the water, and their supply depended on a small spring. The Kadkhudas and head-men of various villages around were loud in their grievances against the Russians for having been deprived of the use of their water, but considering the state the country was in before, Russian rule in Transcaspia has proved a blessing, not only to Transcaspia, but to all the districts around; and if the water is necessary to enable the Russians to hold the plains below, then local wants must naturally give place to Imperial necessities.

I caught a few small fish in the Rudbar stream, and I also bagged some teal, with the help of a pair of large white-breasted hawks whom I found in hot pursuit, whose aid came in most opportunely.

Our next march took us out into the Daragez plain, where we camped at a large village containing some 400 families of Kurds and Turks, named Chapashlu. The Khan of the village, a young man named Kurdu Khan, a cousin of the Beglar Begi of Daragez, met me some two miles out with about a dozen sowars and escorted me in. All the villagers had turned out to see us arrive, and I found the customs of reception very similar here to what they were in Sistan. First of all came a man with a tray of grapes; then another man burning some aromatic seeds on a tray, which he put down on the ground in front of us, the only difference being that in Sistan this was generally done by an old woman. What the origin of the custom is I have never been able to ascertain, but it is said to keep off the evil eye. Finally, on arrival at the village a sheep's throat was cut and the blood allowed to flow just in front of us, the bleeding head being drawn across the road just in front of our horses' noses. I rode through the village, and found that Turki was the language spoken by all.

In the evening the Khan and his followers came to dinner. Not being able to sit down to table, he was dined in Persian style by Moula Bakhsh with my Indian clerks and the British agent, while all his men had dinner in another tent by themselves.

The 7th September 1894 brought us to Muhammadabad, the capital of Daragez. The road led through the gap in the line of low hills that runs down the centre of the Daragez plain, known as Kirkhkiz, the Turki equivalent of Chihal Dukhtaran, or the forty maidens. The same old story was told me here as at almost every other Chihal Dukhtaran that I have visited. Forty girls out for a party were just going to be seized by a band of raiders, when the hill opened and permitted them to escape. For some reason or other forty girls seem to be associated with almost every freak of nature that one comes across in either Persia or Afghanistan. This particular freak or gap in the hills I found to be green and pleasant, with a lot of water running through it turning a succession of water-mills, while gardens and vineyards commenced immediately below it, and continued all the way to Muhammadabad. Some two miles out I was met by the Beglar Begi or hereditary governor of Daragez, Mir Panj Muhammad Ali Khan, accompanied by his brother, son, and brother's sons, the Persian Karguzar and some forty or fifty sowars, and we all rode in together. The chief himself was mounted on rather a good-looking half-bred Arab horse. He told me he did not now go in for horse-breeding, and that mares were getting much scarcer than they used to be in the olden days, when raids and forays were of daily occurrence, and he himself had 1000 sowars at his beck and call; now he had not a tenth of that number. Those that were out with him ranged themselves in a line in front of the tent while the chief was drinking his tea. They were mostly Turks, but not Turkomans, though their dress was much the same as that of the latter. They were armed with old muzzle-loading guns slung over their backs; but their horses, though serviceable, were nothing much to look at. In olden days, so the chief said, they got many of their horses from the Turkomans, but since the Russian occupation of the Akhal their intercourse with the Turkomans had almost entirely ceased. O'Donovan in his book gives a vivid description of life in Daragez in 1880, but doubtless times have greatly changed since then.

During the day we found the heat considerably greater. We had come down another 500 feet, and the thermometer in the tent at 4 P.M. was up to 90° F. In the evening the Beglar Begi came to pay his visit, accompanied by the Karguzar and by his brother, son, and nephew, and they all remained to dinner. The old Ilkhani talked merrily, and seemed to enjoy himself. He said: "We are all wild Turkomans here. The Shah told us when he came that we ought to retain our Turkoman habits, so we have done so. If we make any mistake at table, please excuse us;" and then he fell to with a will. He was perfectly natural all through, and seemed an honest, kind-hearted man, devoid of the pretensions and nonsense that most Persian officials are so full of.

Next morning I rode out some way to the north of the town, as far as the gorge in the low hills through which the road runs to Lutfabad and the Akhal territory. I was surprised to find such a mass of gardens and enclosures, and I enjoyed the ride in the shade of the trees. Lutfabad is the Persian frontier town, and although Daragez is so close to the frontier, I was surprised at the little intercourse with the Russians that seemed to exist. A Russian agent, by name Mehdi Beg, a Karrabaghi from the Caucasus, lived in Daragez, and came to call upon me, but he said he had few friends or associates. He had lost his wife and child in the cholera epidemic, and was left all alone. Russians seemed rarely to come to Daragez, and the chief himself said that though the Russian railway station was not a couple of thousand paces from his own village of Lutfabad, yet he had never even seen it.

Muhammadabad itself had apparently been well fortified against raids. The outer portion of the town was surrounded by the remains of a wall and ditch enclosing an old *tappa* or artificial mound at the north-west corner. Inside was an inner town with its own gates, walls, and bastions, and inside that again was the ark or citadel, the residence of the chief and his family.

The chiefship of Daragez was, however, of no great date. It was of Turk origin. The first chief, Baba Khan, was said to have been a petty Khan of Karshi, in Bokhara, and to have migrated to Khurasan with a few hundred men of his tribe, the Chapashlu, and to have received a grant of land from the governor of Abivard, in Daragez. Baba Khan became a favourite of Nadir Shah's and accompanied him through all his campaigns, being rewarded with the governorship of Herat, and subsequently of provinces in Persia. He was killed at the siege of Bokhara. His nephew, Behbud Khan, one of the commanders of Nadir Shah's troops in Bokhara, was appointed governor of Abivard, but was killed by a Turkoman. His son, Agha Muhammad Khan, succeeded to the governorship and occupied the district of Daragez, where his successors have since maintained themselves, and of which they have remained the hereditary governors. They were evidently in possession of considerable power in the early part of this century, when Beglar Khan Chapashlu came frequently to notice.

Abbas Kuli Khan of Daragez was appointed Beglar Begi of Merv, and went there with 150 sowars to assume the government in 1852, but before the year was out he was besieged by Muhammad Amin Khan, the Khan of Khwarism, and died during the siege. Muhammad Ali Khan, my host, was still locally styled Beglar Begi, though the title of Mansur-ul-Mulk had been conferred upon him by the Shah in 1893. He lost the governorship subsequently in 1897, and was succeeded by his next brother, Kara Khan Agha, the governor of Lutfabad.

Muhammadabad itself did not strike me as a busy mart; in fact business seemed slack. Not half the main street, running between the two gates on the north and south faces of the town, was occupied, and though I saw lots of shops full of red chintzes and such like things, I saw little else. The population was said to amount to only about 1000 families. When I rode through the town to pay my visit to the Beglar Begi I found the people most civil. The chief's Farash Bashi and Yasawal and some twenty Farashes, met me outside the town. The Kalantar and Darogha of the town, with their men, met me at the *chaharsu*, or central cross-roads, and the streets had all been swept and watered for the occasion. The people all stood up and bowed as I passed, and the chief himself received me outside his reception-room and conducted me in. Talking of Daragez, the chief said that many *tappas* or ancient mounds existed, showing that it had been thickly populated in ancient times, but that Changiz Khan had made a clean sweep of the country, and it had never recovered. The present population of the district he estimated at 10,000, but there was ample room for double that number. The name Daragez, he thought, was derived from Dara, or Darius, who was said to have founded Muhammadabad. During the day there was a large exodus of people from the town, and I found that I had just come in for the departure of the pilgrims to Karbala. The roads had been closed by cholera and other things for the past two years, and consequently there was an extra large contingent going. I first of all heard the wailing of women who were assembled in a large crowd by the gate of the town, and then the people gradually broke up and came away, passing my tents, the men crying just like the women, and wiping their eyes with large handkerchiefs.

From Muhammadabad our route continued westwards along the frontier. At Naukhandan I went off with the British agent's son, the Mulla Bashi, as we called him, as his father's desire was to bring him up as a priest, to visit the gardens and vineyards which Haji Ali owned here. I was astonished at the acres and acres of grapes that I saw, mostly of the small, white, seedless kind, which the people dried in the sun and sold as raisins. They had a splendid crop just being gathered, and enormous quantities of grapes were spread out on mud floors to dry. The year before their raisins had fetched 12 tumans (£2, 8s.) a kharwar (649 lbs.), but this year there had been such a largo crop that the price had gone down, and they did not expect to realise more than 10 tumans per kharwar. The raisins were all exported to Ashkabad, and so also were the peaches, some fine specimens of which I found in an adjacent garden—the last of the season. These, the men said, they packed in baskets and despatched on donkeys across the hills to the Baba Durmaz station, and thence by rail into Ashkabad, where they sold at from one to three krans per man (6½ lbs.), according to the season. A good deal of wine, I was told, was also made, but it was not good and would not keep. Large numbers of wild pig were said to invade the gardens every night from the hills to the north, and scarecrows were rigged up everywhere. Pheasants used to be plentiful in Daragez, but were almost extinct, and I saw little or no game of any sort. The rise in the day's march was about 500 feet, and the next day we went up another 600 feet in our march of eleven miles to Zainuddinlu, passing through an almost continuous succession of gardens and vineyards all the way. We were shown cotton sown this year for the first time from American seed given by the Russians, and it seemed to be doing well.

Another twelve miles the next day, with a further rise of 500 feet, brought us to the end of the valley at the village of Jan-i-Aziz. The Russian boundary pillar was pointed out to us on the hills to the north, the watershed immediately over the valley apparently being the boundary line. The speciality of the place was potatoes. Fields and fields of these were to be seen, all of which were grown for export to Ashkabad. There were also a number of *sinjad* trees in full fruit, covered with their little dry berries, for which I confess I could never get a liking. We passed through a continuous succession of villages, half inhabited by Turks and half by Kurds. At each village the Kadkhuda and head-men came out to meet me, and the people were most civil all through. One curious mode of making raisins I noted in these villages, and that was the dipping of the green grapes in boiling alkali. The grapes dried in the sun turn black, but those dipped in alkali retain their green colour and are more prized in consequence. The village

Shikari brought me in a doe ibex on arrival, and the Naib told me that in olden days there used to be quantities of ibex about, but that now they were by no means plentiful. Another Shikari came in with half-a-dozen partridges, and a third with a huge horned owl.

The Daragez district ended at the head of the valley above the Mazar of Jan-i-Aziz, and here accordingly I dismissed the Naib of Duringar, as the sub-district is called, after the sect of Kurds who inhabit it, and also Haji Ali, the British agent in Daragez, who had hitherto accompanied me. The latter, an old man of sixty-six, had been employed as British agent for some seventeen years, and being a connection of the Beglar Begi's and owning considerable property in the district, was comparatively well-to-do. He was to start at once on a pilgrimage to Karbala, the almost only travel open to Persians, and their one great form of enjoyment. I had now to cross over to Bajgirha in Kuchan, the Persian frontier village on the high-road to Ashkabad. I followed the route taken by M. Vlassow, the Russian consul-general, when travelling along this frontier two years before, and though the distance was only nominally fourteen miles, it took me seven hours to do it, so bad was the going. We commenced with an ascent of 1275 feet according to the aneroid, straight up the side of a steep hill. Thence we wound up and down, in and out of various ravines along the southern slopes of the hills to the foot of the Kotal-i-Chubast, the crowning difficulty of the whole march. Here we had a climb up the almost perpendicular face of a hill for some 400 feet, and then a passage along a narrow rocky ledge with a steep declivity below, and nasty rocks jutting out above every here and there, just so placed as to catch the loads on the mules and to send the animals over the cliff. The horses got through without much damage, but it took an hour and a half to get the Abdari mules that were with us over this pass, and at one place we had to lay down felts on the rocks before we could get them up at all. The baggage mules which started at 5 A.M. did not reach Bajgirha till 4 P.M., many of them with cut and bruised legs and heads from their frequent falls on the rocks. Fortunately none were killed.

A mile beyond the small village of Shamkhal we struck the high-road at the huge caravansarai, which was erected by order of the Persian Government as a frontier fort, but which, like most things of the sort in Persia, was left unfinished as well as ungarrisoned.

Some two miles to the north of this we reached the village of Bajgirha-i-Irani, or Persian Bajgirha, as it is called, to distinguish it from the Russian Bajgirha, now known as Goudan, on the opposite side of the frontier. The village consisted of nothing but a few huts in a hollow of the hills and some small shops on the road-side for the benefit of travellers. The water was scarce and brackish, but new rooms were being built to let to travellers, and the place was increasing in size owing to the increasing traffic. Walking up to the frontier at the top of the pass about a mile above the village, I could see the Russian guardhouse half a mile down on the northern side, a well-built, serviceable-looking building, consisting of a double-storeyed barrack, with stable and sheds opposite, closed at each end with high walls and with a circular bastion at opposite angles, the whole loopholed all round. A non-commissioned officer and twelve Cossacks, I was told, originally formed the garrison, but were subsequently withdrawn, and the post was standing empty. When the Russian customs cordon was established along the frontier all authority was centred at the customs-house a little farther down in the valley. Here also were located the settlement of Molokáns, that curious Russian sect whom Leroy-Beaulieu[1] calls the "pioneers of Russian civilisation." The water supply was limited, and there was no native population of any kind whatever.

It was curious to see some of these Russian peasants driving into Persian Bajgirha to buy straw, the men in the ordinary Russian black cap, and the women sitting on the top of the load with nothing on their head beyond a red cotton handkerchief. Sunstroke, I believe, is almost unknown amongst the Russians in Transcaspia. The troops at any rate never seem to suffer from it, and they wear nothing but a white cover to their caps in the summer.

In Persian Bajgirha there was no garrison and no authority of any sort that I could see. The passport officer was simply the servant of the man who farmed the right of selling passports, and the customs officer the same, but no one seemed to disturb the peace. The height of the village according to my aneroid was about 5500 feet, and the air was cool and pleasant, the thermometer not rising above 83° F.

I had now to follow the Ashkabad-Mashhad high-road, the one great artery of trade and traffic between Khurasan and Transcaspia. A continuous line of camels and donkeys, waggons and phaetons drawn by four horses abreast, was continuously passing along it. From Bajgirha we had to ascend for some ten miles to a height of about 6500 feet, and then descend again for another five miles to Durbadam, a little village of some fifty houses of Kurds at a height of about 5200 feet on the banks of the Duringar stream. Another rise of 600 feet brought us to Imamkulia, eight miles beyond, and after this we crossed the watershed at a height of about 6800 feet, and then commenced a gradual descent of some

[1] "The Empire of the Tsars," vol. iii. p. 443.

1400 feet down to Zubaran, a total distance of sixteen miles.

We passed various consignments of wool on camels on their way from Sabzawar to Ashkabad, and also a consignment of tea on donkeys for the same place. The cheap green tea used by the Turkomans is almost entirely Indian, but the new Russian customs duties and the opening of the sea route via Batoum have almost killed the trade in it through Persia. Large consignments of wheat and cotton on camels also passed through on their way to Ashkabad, and the curious part of it was that the Persian Government had not only issued orders prohibiting the export of grain, but had even deputed a special official some three months before to this very frontier to enforce those orders, and yet, despite all this, the export of grain was going on as briskly as ever. The special official, we were told, had returned to Teheran after making over charge of his duties to the customs collector. What this meant was clear to all. The latter was simply the customs contractor's servant. He could get nothing by preventing the export of grain, and it was his interest to make all the money he could by permitting it to pass; in fact, the prohibition was an extra profit to him, as, instead of having to levy at a fixed rate, he could levy what he pleased.

The same thing happened in connection with cattle. I saw cattle being driven across the frontier daily in droves *en route* to Ashkabad, and I was told that the Russian Commissariat contractors obtained almost all the meat for the Russian troops in Transcaspia from Khurasan. The Persian Government issued a notification prohibiting the export of cattle and mules, but without the slightest effect so far as Khurasan cattle were concerned. Regarding mules the case was different. Khurasan is not a mule-producing country, and what mules there are mostly come from the south. There the prohibition of the export of both wheat and mules from the Persian Gulf ports was enforced by the help of the British Resident, and not a single mule or ton of wheat could be shipped. The result of the orders therefore was that while Russia continued to got as much wheat and beef as she liked in the north, the British trade in wheat was completely stopped in the south, and so was the supply of Persian mules.

CHAPTER XII.

KUCHAN.

FROM Zubaran we rode in to Kuchan, a distance of eight miles. The road ran down hill the whole way, a further descent of 1000 feet. Some four miles out from the town I was met by the deputy-governor and the Mustaufi, with a led horse and a carriage-and-four, and an escort of a Yasawal and twenty sowars. The Shujah-ud-Dowlah, as the hereditary chief of Kuchan is styled, had sent out his Abdarbashi or head-steward the day before to see that we had all we required, and he sent me over a cooked breakfast soon after my arrival, and came himself to pay me his visit in the evening. Our conversation naturally turned on the earthquake of 17th November 1893, which had destroyed the town. The chief himself was absent at the time, and none of his family were killed by the earthquake, but his horses and servants almost all perished.

Kuchan itself was a most curious sight. I went all through it, and traversed the whole length of the bazar, and found it just recovering from the effects of the earthquake and in process of being rebuilt. Outside the town the gardens and trees were all standing. The vineyards had in no way been damaged, and this it was that made the people averse to leaving the place and to building a new Kuchan as had been proposed. It was not till

I had got through all the gardens and had arrived at the town itself that I realised what ruin had been done. Every house had been thrown down more or less, and the walls of the town had been levelled all round. It was a second Jericho in that respect, and nothing remained but one huge mound to mark the site. The dome of the Imamzada, the shrine of the place, was, I think, almost the only building left standing: 12,000 people, and enormous numbers of horses, cattle, sheep, and goats, were said to have been buried in the ruins. The remainder of the population, said then to number about 10,000 people, were still mostly housed in wigwams and shanties which had been run up by them after the earthquake, with the old timber poles leant together and plastered over with mud, on the sites of their former houses or wherever they liked, without reference to order or regularity. Shops were being constructed of wooden posts, with the interstices filled up and plastered over; the posts being all jointed and tied together to make the building as firm and yet as light as possible, with a view to future earthquakes.

Many were the stories I was told of wonderful escapes. but there was one thing that all who witnessed the earthquake were agreed upon, and that was that the shock came suddenly, like a flash of lightning, without any warning, and that immediately after it not a sound was to be heard and the place was as silent as a city of the dead. The survivors were all struck dumb apparently; dead stillness prevailed, as if the end of the world had come; not a soul moved or spoke for at least ten minutes, and then, all of a sudden and with one accord, the whole town broke out into one fearful wail. Everybody left alive in the town seems to have been overcome by this same loss of sense and power, and it was only after a considerable interval that they recovered. Then it was that those entangled and half buried in the ruins called out for help; and what a scene must have ensued! The telegraph Sartip told me that he was in the upper storey of his house when the earthquake came on. The upper storey fell, but not the lower, and he was saved from being crushed by falling under some crossed beams, and was only buried up to his waist, and was thus pulled out unhurt. His servants, he said, who were outside and unhurt, were so dumfounded that not a man of them moved or spoke like himself for quite ten minutes, and it was only after that that he could get them to come to his help.

The postmaster had similar experiences to relate. When the earthquake took place he was ill in bed, and what happened he knew not; but when he came to his senses he found himself lying with his head out and the fallen house all around him. He was able to extricate himself and to pull out the rest of his family, though the last of the latter, a small boy, was not got out till seven hours afterwards, when he was found alive and well under an iron cot. One woman whom he knew was dug out alive on the third day; and I also heard the story of another woman and child, who were in a grocer's shop at the time of the shock, having been found alive on the fifth day. They had lived on raisins all the time; but many another must have perished miserably. This earthquake was the third, so the people said, that had overtaken Kuchan in forty years. One had occurred in 1852, when 2000 people were said to have been killed; and another in 1871, which also did great damage. Poor Kuchan, though, was still to suffer a fourth in January 1895, and then, and not till then, did the people finally give way and consent to move to safer quarters.

One of the sights of the town of Kuchan was the shrine over the grave of Sultan Ibrahim, said to have been a son of Imam Raza. The original building was said to have been constructed by Sultan Muhammad Khwarism Shah. The dome, which was the marked feature of the place, was destroyed in the earthquake of 1852, but was rebuilt by the Ilkhani. It was again damaged by the earthquake of 1871; but it was taken down and rebuilt by the Ilkhani's mother, and it escaped altogether in 1893. It was utterly destroyed, though, in the final earthquake of 1895, and with it perished, I fear, the wonderful manuscript leaves of a Koran that were therein preserved. I never saw this Koran myself, but I often heard of it. It was not perfect, but what leaves there were, were of enormous size—some 9½ feet by 5½ feet—and beautifully illuminated. The handwriting was said to have been that of Mirza Bai Sangar, son of Mirza Shahrukh Kurkan, and the story is that when Nadir Shah conquered Shahr-i-Sabz, some of his savage people removed this Koran, which was preserved on the tomb of Amir Timur, and scattered its leaves about. Nadir Shah heard of this, and ordered all the leaves to be collected and bound up. The chief of the Kurds, though, hid them in the pack-saddle of a camel and brought them to Kuchan, and this accounted for most of the leaves being torn. Amir Timur in his lifetime is said to have had this Koran drawn in front of his army on a cart. I could hear of no trace of it after the earthquake of 1895. After that a new Kuchan was founded at Haihai, eight miles farther east, and is now being gradually populated.

I remained encamped at Kuchan from the 17th to the 22nd September 1894, and during almost the whole of that time life was rendered a burden by a violent wind and dust storm. It commenced on the 16th by blowing down the valley from the east, the temperature falling suddenly from 84° F. in the tents at

4 P.M. one day to 64° the next day. On the 17th it blew up the valley from the west, but went down at night. On the 18th it commenced again from the east and blew worse than ever, and so it went on. Life in the tents was a misery from the clouds of dust that could not be kept out. One could neither read nor write. Everything was so quickly covered with dust that one could hardly tell the writing-paper from the table-cloth. It was impossible to make a pen travel on paper, and often the only place where I could find refuge was in bed. I was told these storms were of frequent occurrence.

On the evening of the 19th September 1894 I returned the visit of the Shuja-ud-Dowlah and remained to dinner. The chief had built a small single-storeyed house for himself entirely of wood. His ancestral house had been levelled to the ground, and he and his family were living scattered about in huts and in *kibitkas* or *alajiks*, as the Kurd and Turkoman felt tents are here called. A crowd of people were assembled to see us arrive, and even the women were out looking over the low wall round their camp, and comical sights some of them were, in their white tights and very short red petticoats.

The chief received us in the front room of his house, which we found to be a well-built structure of pine planks imported from Russia. Shortly after our arrival the inner doors were thrown open and we were ushered into the dining-room beyond, which was decorated with numerous glass chandeliers, while the walls were covered with the mirrors and pictures of gaudily dressed women so dear to the Oriental eye. Our party consisted of the chief and myself, Moula Bakhsh and Muhammad Khan. Mustapha Kuli Khan, the Naib or deputy-governor of Kuchan, and Sartip Ramzan Khan, formerly deputy-governor under the late Shuja-ud-Dowlah, were the only other guests, while my clerks, mirzas, and escort, &c.,

were all entertained outside. Dinner was enlivened by Kurd singing and music, and a guard of Kurds was drawn up outside, armed with the guns with large two-pronged rests commonly used in these parts. At dinner the chief gave us some very fair white wine, made in Kuchan, and two years old he said. He himself drank Russian brandy, and that copiously. On the following night the chief came to dine with me, bringing the same two old Naibs with him, and in fact they were the only men of the place I was permitted to see during my stay. Not a single one of his relatives accompanied the chief, nor did I once see either his nephew or his cousins who were in the town. During dinner the chief spoke in high praise of his Ulang or grazing-ground down the valley, and it was arranged that I was to make my first stage out there to see it. Before leaving, various presents were brought in and presented by the chief in return for those I had given to him, amongst them a Persian and Turkoman carpet, some Resht embroidery, and Kurd silk wrappers and socks and gloves, and specimens of the work of the country.

Kuchan territory commences on the east at the village of Yasaki, which divides it from Radkan, and before the advent of the Zafaranlu and Shadillu Kurds, who now inhabit the Kuchan and Bujnurd districts respectively, the whole of this part of the country, including Jajarm and Khalpush, was inhabited by a tribe of Turks called Garaili or Garaitili, whom the Kurds drove out. According to the Sani-ud-Dowlah, the Garailis were a powerful tribe, neighbours of, and of the same origin and religion, and speaking the same language as, the Mongols. They are said to have excelled the latter in civilisation—that is to say, in the dwelling in towns, as the word may be more correctly translated, and the city of Karakoram, the capital of Ung Khan, the king of the Garailis, was a civilised place before the Mongols took possession of it.

The story is that Changiz Khan, when his father died and his tribe and people rebelled against him, went to Ung Khan to seek for help. Ung Khan protected him, and treated him with such consideration that Ung Khan's own sons became jealous and poisoned their father's mind against him. Ung Khan decided to put Changiz Khan, then known by the name of Tamarchin, to death, but he escaped and returned to his own tribe, where gradually, owing to the wisdom and sagacity of his mother, he rose to high rank, and eventually declared war against Ung Khan, defeated and killed him, and took possession of his kingdom. From that time Karakoram became the seat of the government of Changiz Khan and his descendants. The Garailis therefore, so the Sani-ud-Dowlah thinks, must have come to Persia after the time of Changiz Khan, probably with Halaku Khan, who moved ten per cent. of all the Mongol tribes. The Garailis, however, did not go on as the others did to Syria and elsewhere, but remained in Khurasan till scattered in comparatively recent times by Kara Khan. Their graveyards are still to be seen all over North-West Khurasan.

Of the ancient history of Kuchan the accounts are very mixed. The Sani-ud-Dowlah compiled what information he could collect from ancient Persian authors, and according to them Kabushan, as Kuchan was formerly called, was originally described as a small town, the capital of Rastakustava, in the Nishapur district. It is said to have been called Ustava because it was situated on a high place, as verily it is, standing as it does at a height of over 4500 feet just on the watershed that divides the drainage of the Caspian on the west from that of the valley of the Hari Rud on the east. Halaku Khan is said to have rebuilt the town, his grandson Arghun to have added to it.

The ancestor of the Zafaranlu Kurd Ilkhanis or chiefs

now ruling at Kuchan was one Shah Kuli Sultan, who had the title of Amir-ul-Umara conferred upon him by Shah Abbas I. (1585–1628), and was settled by the latter in Akhal with 40,000 families of Kurds as a barrier against the Uzbegs. During the reign of Shah Sultan Hussain the Kurds of Akhal, worn out by the raids of Urgunjis and Bukharans, were driven into the mountains to the south. They ousted the Garailis then in possession of Kuchan, Shirwan, Bujnurd, and Simalghan, and acquired the land for themselves.

Kara Khan, their chief, established his headquarters at Shirwan, and settled the whole of the 40,000 families of his Kurds, in which were included the Zafaranlu, Shahdillu, Kiwanlu, Amarlu, and Karachurlu sections, in the districts of Kuchan, Shirwan, and Bujnurd. (1) Kara Khan was succeeded by his son (2) Sam Beg, and the latter's son, (3) Muhammad Hussain Khan, was the man who received the title of Ilkhani, and was appointed chief of the Zafaranlus by Nadir Shah about the year 1740. There is a story that Nadir Shah in his youth wanted to marry a daughter of Sam Beg, Kabushani, but that Shah Tahmasp forbade the marriage. This displeased Tahmasp Kuli Khan, as Nadir Shah was then named, and he openly displayed his hostility to Shah Tahmasp by besieging Kuchan, and eventually compelling the relatives of the girl to give her to him. It was also near Kuchan that Nadir Shah met his death in 1747. The Kurds there are said to have risen in rebellion at his continued oppression, and to have stolen his horses in the Radkhan Chaman. This so enraged Nadir that he started off at once for Kabushan, but was murdered *en route* in his tent at a place called Fathabad. The exact site of the murder is undecided. Between Fathabad and Haihai, the site of the present Kuchan, there is said to be an artificial mound called Khalisa Tappa and also Tappa Nadiri, and it is supposed that it was on the top of this mound that Nadir Shah was sleeping at the time, but nothing is known for certain.

Muhammad Hussain Khan was succeeded by his son (4) Amir Guna Khan, and he again by his son (5) Raza Kuli Khan. This man seems to have flourished in the early part of the nineteenth century, as he is mentioned in connection with Ishak Khan, Karai, in 1813, and as having attacked Ismail Khan, Sirdar of Damghan, who had been sent against the Khurasani nobles at Khwajah Rabi in 1814, when he had to retire with the rest. He rebelled against the governor, Wali Muhammad Khan, in 1815, but was defeated. In 1827 he seized Halaku Mirza, the governor of Khurasan, and carried him off to Kuchan. This was avenged in 1832, when Abbas Mirza, the heir-apparent, besieged and took Kuchan, and sent Raza Kuli Khan a prisoner to Mashhad.

His son (6) Sam Khan was then appointed Ilkhani, but the district of Kuchan is said to have been entrusted to one Nur Muhammad Khan, Dawillu. At the time of the Salar's rebellion of 1849 Sam Khan met the Hissam-us-Sultanah at Sabzawar on the latter's appointment as governor of Khurasan, and gave in his submission.

In 1852 Sam Khan was sent by the Hissam-us-Sultanah to assist the Wali of Herat against Kohndil Khan, and in 1854 he helped to defend Sarakhs against the attack of Muhammad Amin Khan, Shah of Khwarizm, On Sam Khan's death, his son Khan Baba Khan was a minor. Khan Baba Khan was appointed chief with his uncle (7) Amir Hussain Khan, his father's youngest brother, as deputy-governor in charge. The latter, however, soon got all power into his own hands, and eventually was recognised as chief. The title of Shuja-ud-Dowlah was conferred upon him by the late Shah Nasir-ud-Din, when he visited Kuchan on his way back from Mashhad to Teheran at the time of his first visit to Khurasan in 1867.

Amir Hussain Khan died in 1893, and was succeeded by his second son, the present chief (8) Muhammad Násir Khan, then about thirty years of age. His elder brother, Abdul Hasan Khan, had died of cholera at Teheran just a year before his father's death, leaving a young son about fourteen years of age. Muhammad Násir Khan succeeded to his father's title of Shuja-ud-Dowlah, but was dismissed from the chiefship by the Shah not long after my visit, and his cousin Khan Baba Khan, Muzaffar-us-Sultanah, the son of Sam Khan, then some forty years of age, was appointed in his stead. This arrangement, however, did not last long. Muhammad Násir Khan had the command of the most money, and he was reinstated in the middle of 1895.

From Kuchan I marched to Kharkan, ten miles down the valley. We passed three villages, all of which had suffered by the earthquake, and were being rebuilt. The shock, however, did not extend beyond them, as Kharkan had been hardly damaged at all. There I was joined by Nur Muhammad Khan, Sirdar of sowars, the man deputed by the chief to accompany me round the frontier. He was the head of 400 families who were originally brought from Akhal by Raza Kuli Khan, and given three villages free of revenue on the service of supplying eighty sowars.

Our camp was pitched in the midst of the Ulang or Chaman-i-Laili, of which the chief had told us, the grass-covered plain from which Kuchan derived all its fodder. The grass, which was said to grow nearly a yard high, was dried and twisted into long wisps, and thus transported on donkeys to the town. Several stacks of hay were standing on the Chaman itself, while numbers of fine black cattle were grazing around, having been lately let in after the hay had been gathered. The word Chaman, so expressive in Persia and Afghanistan, is a difficult one to translate. The terms meadow and pasture, usually given to it, hardly convey the full meaning. In these arid countries anything green is usually unknown except where there is irrigation. Chaman is a level marshy extent of land where there is no irrigation, but where the water is sufficiently near the surface to keep the grass constantly green and to afford continuous pasture. This particular Chaman afforded a fine large expanse of grassy land, and formed one of the great features of Kuchan. Chamans generally belong to the chief or the Government, and rarely to private individuals. They resemble commons in so far that certain people have certain rights in them and they cannot be encroached upon, but still the chief, I believe, has certain powers of alienating them, as for instance at Quetta, where the Chaman that now forms the racecourse and the polo, cricket, and general recreation ground, was a personal gift from the Khan of Kalat to Sir Robert Sandeman, and thus it is that succeeding generations of Englishmen enjoy the use of that grand open space rent free.

We next moved on through the hills to Kuran, where we camped between two villages, one of Kurds and the other of Turks. From there we had an ascent of some 2000 feet to the top of the pass, and a gradual descent again on the other side of some 1400 feet into the Aoghaz Valley, which turned out to be fertile and well cultivated, containing six villages and possessing a hereditary Beg of its own, who came out to meet me. We met lots of donkeys on the road laden with juniper wood from the Tarkharan hills for the Kuchan market, and we also met a Mulla who had accompanied Lieutenant Conyngham on his trip along this frontier a year or two before, and my orderlies lost no time in giving a dinner in his honour. I found that the nomad flock-owners all went across the border into Russian territory for the winter, paying a grazing tax of from ten to fifteen krans per hundred sheep. Eggs, fowls, ghee, and such like things were also all taken to Ashkabad for sale. The people said that they used to take these things formerly to Kuchan, but that the Persians there always tried to cheat them, and they preferred to deal with the Russians.

From Aoghaz we had another rise of about 1000 feet up the hills on the north-west to the top of an easy Kotal, and then down again into the Tarkharan Valley, which contained some 400 families. The height was about 5600 feet. Large flocks of wood-pigeons were to be seen, but nothing else. At Milanlu, some twelve miles beyond, we found ourselves in a delightful upland, with the weather beautifully cool and the air exhilarating. The Jiristan Baluk which we were now in contained fifteen villages, with a total population of 400 Kurd families, and all the villages were prettily surrounded by walnut, apricot, willow, and pear trees, especially the latter.

A mile or so before we came to Milanlu we passed a small settlement called Churma, where forty of tho families lately evicted from Firuzah had been located. Firuzah is the frontier village handed over under treaty to Russia by the Persian Government as a sanatorium for Ashkabad in exchange for some other village on the Caucasian frontier. The conditions were that the Persian inhabitants were to be removed by the Persian Government, the Russians undertaking not to people it with Turkomans. The evicted villagers were loud in complaints of their losses, and according to thoir accounts Firuzah was a sort of small earthly Paradise. We can all sympathise with people turned out of their ancestral homes, but the Russians grilling in the plains of Ashkabad were equally entitled to sympathy, and in this case the villagers had to give way to Imperial needs. That they were entitled to liberal compensation goes without saying, but according to their account this was not granted them. The Shah had certainly ordered ten tumans (£2) in cash and two kharwars (1298 lbs.) of grain to be given to each family evicted, and so far as I could gather this had been actually paid to them, but even this did not nearly compensate the people for the loss of their houses and gardens.

From Milanlu there was a direct and well-worn road to Ashkabad, and we met some people all the way from Shirwan taking fowls and eggs to Ashkabad for sale. None of these men had passports, but they were allowed to come and go with perfect freedom, the Russian officials apparently relaxing their passport rules in their favour.

We had a steep climb over the range of hills bounding the Jiristan district on the north to the village of Sarani, a distance of twelve miles. The rise from Milanlu to the top by the aneroid was nearly 1900 feet, making the height of the Kotal some 7700 feet. This pass was known as the Yanikara in Turki, and the Kharparan in Persian, a word that I can only translate as "sending donkey flying," a by no means inappropriate name. It was a hard march; but my men were now well trained when going up a steep hill to march in Indian file, each one leading his own horse or mule and holding on to the tail of the animal in front of him. We thus wound up a hill like a huge serpent in one long continuous line, and got up to the top in the quickest possible time and with the least fatigue to both animals and men.

The view from the summit over the hills to the south was very fine; but the range to the north, known as Chupan, blocked the view in that direction. The whole of this higher range and the deep valley between the two ranges was thickly wooded with small juniper, and the hillsides were covered with grass, a rare sight in these parts. The descent on the northern side was very steep in places. After a climb of some four miles down a long spur, we got into the bed of a stream and found the ravine suddenly entirely blocked by a huge landslip of apparently ancient date.

We had a long and rough climb down this landslip, and below it the valley was again blocked by a succession of other slips, making the final descent very steep. At last wo found ourselves in the little basin at the head of the Firuzah defile in which Sarani stands. The height of Sarani I made by the aneroid to be about 4900 feet, giving a fall of 2800 feet from the top of the pass. The village only contained some thirty-five families of Kurds, and I found them all very bitter against the Persian Government for having surrendered Firuzah to the Russians. Had Firuzah been handed over people and all, I doubt if there would have been hardly any outcry. As it was, much bitterness had been aroused. The new Firuzah boundary, moreover, had not yet been demarcated, and the Sarani villagers were ovidently by no means sure that they too might not have to share the same fate as their brethren of Firuzah. They said that the Russians had come and inspected their springs, and had told them that, as the water drained to Firuzah, the springs belonged to Russia. The Russians, by thus steadily promulgating the idea along the Khurasan frontier that all water draining north into Transcaspia belongs to them, are gradually instilling the idea into the minds of the people that the northern slopes of the mountains are destined to fall under Russian rule, and the people are beginning to look on the transfer as inevitable.

Eight miles to the west next morning brought us to

the Persian village of Khairabad, standing on the edge of the mountain plateau. We passed over pleasant undulating uplands, with lots of partridges flying about. Khairabad itself turned out to be a dirty little village, within a few yards of the Russian frontier, consisting of a small fort and a few huts containing some twenty families of Kurds and Turks. It was said to be entirely snowbound in winter. The Khan of the village came out to meet me with half-a-dozen sowars. The little fort in which he lived had been burnt down some years before by Abdul Hasan Khan, the late Shuja-ud-Dowlah's eldest son, in one of his numerous fits of rebellion against his father, but had been rebuilt. Subsequently, when Russian Khairabad came to be occupied by the Russians, the Persian Government ordered a frontier post to be built on their side of the border, and a new fort, consisting of a mud enclosure on a stone foundation some forty yards square, had been erected near by; but it had never been garrisoned, and when I arrived I found that it was already falling into decay, and that its only occupant was the customs contractor's collector, who levied dues on the trade between Bujnurd and Ashkabad which passed by this route. It is curious to see how seldom the Persian Government complete anything they commence. They build numbers of places like this only to leave them to fall into decay, a monument of wasted energy.

Russian Khairabad, which lies a mile or so to the north of the Persian village, was rather a bleak-looking place, as the houses stood on the open plateau without a tree or a garden or an enclosure of any sort. I could see nothing but a couple of long, whitewashed, single-storeyed buildings without verandahs or outhouses, and a low, red-painted wooden house and two or three smaller buildings, a shed for horses, and also two or three *kibitkas* or Turkoman felt huts. I was told that the water supply was scanty and there was no cultivation. A few families of *moujiks* or Russian peasants had been located in the place, but they were cattle-owners, not cultivators. A solitary Turk who kept a shop, and a few Turkoman Jigits comprised, I was told, the whole population. No supplies were procurable in the place itself, so presumably everything was obtained from the neighbouring Persian villages, and so far as I could judge the relations between the Persian villagers and the Russians appeared to be most friendly, and spoke well for their treatment by the latter. The difference in climate between Ashkabad and Khairabad in the summer must be great, Ashkabad being only about 800 feet above sea-level, while Khairabad, according to my aneroid, must be something more like 6800. I found it cold for the end of September, the thermometer marking 63° F. at 10 A.M., 61° F. at 4 P.M., and 45° F. at 9 P.M.

From Khairabad I made my way south to Yangikala, the headquarters of the Kushkhana district of Kuchan. We descended some 900 feet from the edge of the plateau to the village of Zidar, where the young Khan of the place met me with a kind invitation to stop to breakfast, which I was sorry not to be able to accept. We had a little talk about the shikar of the district, but according to his account there was little or none. At Khairabad I had seen a pillar of oorial horns, some of which were very fine, so there must have been animals about there, but the whole character of the country had suddenly changed. Instead of the steep, rocky, and wooded mountains to the east of Sarani, we had come to open, undulating, and cultivated upland country, without a tree in the place. We wound our way down through this, descending another 1300 feet, till we arrived at Yangikala, where I was met by the Hákim of Khushkhana, a pleasant and agreeable man, who dined with us in the evening. Kushkhana comprised the villages, some thirty-three in number, stretching along the Russian frontier from Sarani on the east to Gifan on the west, and thence south to the Bujnurd border, which we struck at a heap of stones sixteen miles farther on.

Three miles beyond we came to the first village in Bujnurd, named Chahar Burj, perched nearly on the top of the hills. All the men were assembled outside to meet us on arrival, and were most civil, asking us to stay and take breakfast with them and offering their hospitality in every way. The children, too, all swarmed out and thoroughly enjoyed a scramble for some coppers. Leaving them we had a steep descent to our tents, which we could see from the top of the hills standing pitched for us in the Garmakhan Valley, some nine miles below. The next valley we came to had a spring full of fish which were called *aziz* or dear, and were fed and tame. The spring belonged to some saint, and the fish were consequently preserved. At Garmakhan the Attrak had to be crossed by a shaky wooden bridge, the river running between high steep banks, and being some twenty-five or thirty feet wide and two or three feet in depth. The Beg of Garmakhan, who came out to meet me on arrival, said that he had received orders from the Saham-ud-Dowlah to give me every assistance, and all the villagers were assembled and salaamed and greeted us with a cordiality that promised well for our stay amongst the Shadillu Kurds. Garmakhan was a small level valley containing some half-dozen villages with a total of about 150 families, and apparently only some 3000 feet above sea-level. It was well watered from the Attrak. I tried fishing, but the water was too muddy to do much. The one fish I did catch was about two pounds in weight and had scales, and was of quite a different sort to those I had hitherto caught in the streams having no outlet to any sea.

YAR MUHAMMAD KHAN, SAHAM-UD-DOULAH, CHIEF OF BUJNURD.

CHAPTER XIII.

BUJNURD.

THE 2nd October 1894 brought us into Bujnurd. Our road led over the low hills to the south-west of Garmakhan till we struck the Bujnurd stream, here some ten feet broad and two feet in depth, and following that up through more hills we emerged on to the Bujnurd plain. It came on to rain just after we started—the first sign of winter—and we all got a good wetting. Some two miles out of the town I was met by Sarhang Sultan Kuli Khan, the Hákim of Gurgan, with a carriage and four and a led horse, and an escort of sixty Bujnurd Kurd Cossacks. These latter had been raised by the Saham-ud-Dowlah from his own tribesmen, and were dressed in imitation of Russian Cossacks, and armed like them with Berdan rifles carried slung over their backs. They were mounted on small Goklan Turkoman horses. The Sultan, or Risaldar, wore Russian shoulder-straps and badges of rank, and looked quite smart. The Saham-ud-Dowlah had kindly prepared his garden-house for me, but my tents were ready pitched on the Chaman just to the north of his residence, and I preferred to stay there, nearer at hand. Directly after my arrival a note came in from the chief himself asking me to name the time for him to come and call, and I fixed 4 P.M., at which hour he duly appeared, and I found him to be a pleasant and courteous man of fifty-seven years of age. He drove down by himself in a small victoria without any of the following that usually accompanies a chief in these parts. We had a long talk about Bujnurd, its people, and its district. He described the northern portion of his territory as almost entirely unpopulated, and was much averse to my risking myself by travelling there, as he said he would not be answerable for my safety. However, he eventually agreed to draw out a route for me through the most advanced villages, and with that we parted for the time being.

This northern portion of Bujnurd territory, bordering on the Goklan and Yamut Turkoman country, was almost entirely unknown, and was the country of all others that I was most anxious to visit. The chief was as good as his promise about the route, and when I returned his visit on the following day he presented me with a sketch and itinerary of the trip he proposed I should take. The Yamuts, he assured me, were all fighting, and it was impossible for me to go anywhere near their country, and it was not without difficulty that I got permission from him to visit the Goklans, who were immediately under his own superintendence. My visit was a pleasant one, as there was much to see and to talk about. On arrival at the gate I found a guard of dismounted Kurd Cossacks and the band drawn up to receive me. I was met by the second son, Sartip Suliman Khan, and the fourth son, Sartip Habibulla Khan, at the foot of the stairs, and upstairs, in the reception-room overlooking the gateway, I was received by the chief himself and his third son, the heir-apparent, Mir Panj Azizulla Khan, known as the Ilkhani. The walls of the room were hung with maps, and the chief showed me a globe on the table presented to him in 1872 by Captain the Hon. George Napier.

ENTRANCE TO THE SAHAM-UD-DOULAH'S RESIDENCE AT BUJNURD—KURD COSSACKS IN FRONT AND THE CHIEF SEATED ABOVE.

He evidently took much interest in geography, and was also thoroughly well acquainted with every part of his own territory and well in touch with his people, who were supposed to number some 15,000 families. The reception-room was covered with glass, and full of chandeliers, and the floor was carpeted with Resht silk embroidery. At the back of this there was a large orangery roofed with iron sheets. This roof was then being put on to preserve the trees from frost in the winter. On the walls were hung the skins of a tiger, several leopards, a bear, two lynxes, and several other trophies of the chase, all obtained from the jungles to the north. No wonder that I was anxious to get there. Tigers and leopards, I was told, were not uncommon, and the chief had two young snow leopards running tame about the place, together with a couple of young oorial or mountain sheep, and a young maral, the stag of the country. The tiger had been shot by his second son, Suliman Khan, at a place which was afterwards pointed out to me, and I had an interesting account of how they surrounded it on horseback in a patch of reeds, and eventually killed it. The most curious of all the skins to me, though, were those of the bears and of one of the lynxes, which were both described to me as rare. The bear's skin was of ordinary Indian size, the fur of a dark rufous brown underneath, but white or grey at the tips. The lynx was much larger than the common red lynx of India, and was of a pale brown colour, with black spots something like a leopard, and very broad and thick-set, with tufted ears and only a small stump of a tail. I had never seen either skins in the East before.

During the day I received visits from the Telegraph Master and the Karguzar or Foreign Office agent. The Telegraph Sarhang, or lieutenant-colonel, I found was not a hard-worked official. It had rained in the night, and the high ranges to the south were all tipped with snow, and his telegraph line from Bujnurd to Kuchan was consequently not in working order. There were no insulators on the line, the wire being simply nailed to the posts, and the slightest change in the weather affected the working of it, even supposing that it was intact. This, however, was seldom the case. The *ghulam*, or horseman, responsible for patrolling the line and repairing breaks had, I heard, amongst other things taken advantage of the demand for wood at Kuchan for building purposes, and the high prices there ruling, to sell the telegraph posts, and under such circumstances it was small wonder that the line was not in working order.

The Karguzar was an old servant of the State, having been an assistant to his father, the Karguzar of Bushire, at the time of the Persian war of 1857. His daughter was married to the chief's second son, Suliman Khan. Both Suliman Khan and his elder brother, Nasratulla Khan, aged twenty-two and twenty-four respectively, were the sons of Goklan Turkoman mothers, and I found them occupying very anomalous positions. Both had the rank of Sartip, or colonel, but that was all. They had both been passed over for the succession to the chiefship in favour of the third son, Azizulla Khan, a boy of sixteen, who had been acknowledged as the heir-apparent, was called the Ilkhani, and had received the rank of Amir-i-Panj, or major-general, from the Shah. Suliman Khan was the one, I was told, upon whom the chief depended for all frontier work. If news of a raid was brought in, Suliman Khan was the one to go out in pursuit. Having thus to do most of the hard work, but at the same time having to take a lower seat than his younger brother, had made Suliman Khan very dissatisfied with his position, and had filled his head with the thought of leaving Persia and joining the Russian service. What happened after I left I never knew exactly, but I heard that a year or more afterwards Suliman Khan got permission to go to Ashkabad on the plea of consulting a doctor, and once there, went off to St. Petersburg, from which he did not return till the spring of 1897. He then came back to Mashhad, and happened to be dining with me the very night that he received a telegram from his father summoning him back to Bujnurd. He left me hastily, and I never saw him again. He returned to Bujnurd as ordered, and a few days after we heard of his death and burial. The rumour was that he had been strangled. All that we knew was that his father had given him an imposing funeral.

The town of Bujnurd, said to have been founded some 200 years ago by Dauli Khan II., no longer exists, having been destroyed during the rebellion of Hasan Khan Salar in 1849. The citadel, at one time the residence of the chiefs, was in ruins, the town walls the same, and the place was nothing but a large open village, with a long bazar in the centre, standing at a height of about 3550 feet according to my aneroid. It had no trade to speak of, and the shops were simply sufficient to supply local wants. Little silk bags seemed to be the only speciality of the place. I tried to get some old coins, but we could only find a few silver pieces of the Abbaside Kaliphs of Baghdad. One Greek coin alone turned up, a common one, of Arsaces, if I remember right. As a matter of fact I rarely came across any Greek coins in Khurasan.

The town was said to contain a population of 10,000 people, but from what I saw I should doubt it, and the estimate of 1500 houses appeared to me to be nearer the mark. There were no ancient remains to be seen. There was a shrine on a mound to the south of the town, containing an Arabic inscription on a stone dated A.D. 913, and there were the ruins of an old town to the north-west called Bizhan. The chief had built an entire set of new buildings for himself and his family outside the town, all of burnt brick and roofed with tiles, with gardens laid out around. The whole place was kept beautifully clean, and I never saw a better-kept residence or a more respectable set of servants in any house in Persia.

The chief and his three sons came to dinner with me in camp, and I also dined with him. He received us in his Hauz Khana or water-tank house, a building with a high dome and a tank in the centre, with rooms all round. Subsequently he took us all over the premises, even into his private Hammam, which he kindly offered to place at my disposal if I wished—an offer that I would have accepted with pleasure if I had cared for Turkish baths. In Persia the public baths are filthy in the extreme, indescribably filthy, so bad that no European can go into them; yet such is the prejudice or fanaticism of the people that any European entering one would be mobbed to a certainty; so that the chief's liberal-mindedness in this respect was all the more marked. All the buildings of the palace opened out more or less on to a large paved quadrangle with a water-tank in the centre. At the eastern side were the ladies' quarters, and away at the end of the gardens on the west was a circular summer-house, from the top of which we had a good view. Bujnurd stands in the centre of a circular valley containing about a dozen villages, with fine hills all round and a plentiful supply of water; so that it all looked green and pretty.

Dinner was served at a table. My assistant, Moula Bakhsh, was with me, and so was young Muhammad Khan, whom the chief took great notice of, saying that his father, Mirza Abbas Khan, had been a great friend of his in former days, and eventually presenting the boy with a horse and a hawk in memory thereof. Muhammad

Khan was intensely pleased at getting the hawk, and could talk of nothing but the pheasants and every other sort of bird that he was going to kill as soon as we got into shikar country. The Karguzar was also invited to the dinner, and just as we were sitting down the Najm-ud-Dowlah, the Munajjim Bashi or chief astrologer to the Shah, arrived on his way back from Mashhad to Teheran, and was received with much honour by the chief.

Next day I had a ride with the Saham-ud-Dowlah and his two sons, Suliman Khan and the Ilkhani, to his gardens to the south of the town. A straight avenue of trees had been planted all the way out, and the gardens each contained a house with a water-tank in the centre of it, and another large tank outside with a fountain in it, the water for which was brought from the hill above. From the gardens we rode on up the valley to a spring called Chashma-i-Bishkardash, some six miles out, where the Saham-ud-Dowlah had constructed a reservoir, and was building a mausoleum for himself by the side of it. He told me that he wished to be buried there, and not at either Mashhad or Karbala, as his ancestors had been. The building promised to be a fine one when finished, comprising a double dome faced with blue tiles in the centre, with a vault for himself beneath lined with brown marble, and rooms on either side for dervishes and travellers to put up in, the whole being shaded by big chenar trees. We had tea on the *band* or dam of the pool, and then rode home, doing a little hawking on the way.

We had a long chat on the way home, and I heard many local stories. One I remember rather amused me, and that was when talking of Afghan Turkistan. The chief told me that some fifty years ago a Bujnurd man had gone to Maimana and had returned with an extraordinary story about a cave where seven men, a dog, and a deer had been asleep for centuries. He was greatly astonished to hear that I had seen the place myself,[1] and he allowed that though the story of the seven sleepers of Ephesus was in the Koran, he found it hard to reconcile it with fact. Another curious story was about a wild man of the woods who had been caught by his men in the Gurgan jungles some thirty years before. The man, he said, could talk no language, tore all clothes that were given him to pieces, and by appearance looked like an African negro of about thirty years of age. He could only suppose that he had been a slave-boy carried off in some Turkoman raid and dropped on the way, and that he had lived like a wild beast in the jungles till seen and caught. He soon died in captivity.

Beyond Chashma Bishkardash, and some sixteen miles to the south of the town, the Saham-ud-Dowlah had his Yailak or summer quarters at a place called Girawan, in the Kuh-i-Salik Mountains. I was not able to get up there myself, but Duke, who had visited the chief there, described the road to me as running south-west up a valley down which a considerable stream of water was flowing into the Bujnurd plain. All along there were gardens and groves of fine trees, and where the valley narrowed on entering the mountains the gorge was filled with a mass of foliage for a long distance. Higher still the stream flowed in a narrow ravine between perpendicular cliffs of great height, and then a high valley near the top of the mountains was reached. Here the chief and his family spent the hot months in camp every year. I was sorry not to be able to visit the place myself, but summer was now at an end. The clouds were gathering, and the weather was cold and raw, with the thermometer only 54° F.

[1] *Vide* Northern Afghanistan, p. 151.

THE SAHAM-UD-DOULAH AND HIS SHADILLU KURDS IN FRONT OF HIS RESIDENCE AT BUJNURD.

at 4 P.M.—not at all the weather for an expedition up the mountains. I had to pay my adieus to the chief instead and hurry on. The Saham-ud-Dowlah presented me with photographs of himself, his sons, and his house, Kurds, Cossacks, and Band, &c., and also with a couple of horses from himself and another from his son, the Ilkhani, so that we had a good deal of interchanging of presents. I cannot say that I was much struck with the breed of horses at Bujnurd. I have mentioned elsewhere how sadly the stock of horses has fallen off in Khurasan, and yet Bujnurd was one of the places where a few of the best were supposed to remain.

Talking of his family, the chief gave me what he called his pedigree, but it was very meagre, and I had some difficulty in supplementing it. So far as I could gather there had been nine generations of the family since the Shadillu Kurds first came to this part of the country in the time of Shah Abbas Safavi, about the year 1600, viz. (1) Kurchi Yusuf, who was succeeded by his son (2) Amir Guna Khan, and so on to (3) Dauli Khan, (4) Jafar Kuli Beg, (5) Dàuli Khan II., (6) Ibrahim Khan, and (7) Najaf Kuli Khan. The latter, according to the Sani-ud-Dowlah, was one of the chiefs summoned to join Ishak Khan, Karai, in 1813, but refused to submit to him, and he was also present with the other Khurasani nobles in their attack on Ismail Khan, Sirdar of Damghan, at Khwajah Rabi in 1814. He was subsequently defeated in 1815. Bujnurd is said to have played rather a considerable part during the Salar's rebellion. In 1847 Hamza Mirza, the Hashmat-ud-Dowlah, who was first sent to repress it, arrived at Bujnurd, when the Salar fled to the Turkoman country, but returned with a number of Turkomans as soon as Hamza Mirza had left. The latter returned to Bujnurd and scattered the Salar's following. In 1849 Jafir Kuli of Bujnurd is mentioned as the man who went out to meet and to give in the submission of the tribe to the Hissam-us-Sultanah on the latter's appointment as governor of Khurasan. In 1850 Mashhad was taken, and the Salar's rebellion put an end to.

Najaf Kuli Khan was succeeded by his third son, (8) Haidar Kuli Khan, who was the first to obtain the title of Saham-ud-Dowlah from the Shah.

On the death of Haidar Kuli Khan about the year 1870, his son, (9) Khan Baba Khan, a minor, was appointed to succeed him. Out of the ten sons left by Najaf Kuli Khan, only the two youngest were alive on Haidar Kuli Khan's death, viz. Muhammad Kuli Khan, at Bujnurd, and Sher Muhammad Khan, the Hákim of Jajarm and Isfarain. The latter remained quietly at Isfarain till he died. Muhammad Kuli Khan was entrusted with the administration as guardian of Khan Baba Khan during his minority, and carried on the work for about a year. A raid was then committed on the Mashhad-Teheran high-road by a large body of Yamut Turkomans, and Yar Muhammad Khan, the son of another brother, Yazdan Kuli Khan, the sixth son of Najaf Kuli Khan, starting off with the 150 sowars he was in charge of at the time, succeeded in intercepting the raiders and in recovering the prisoners. After this Yar Muhammad is said to have gone to Mashhad, and being clever and energetic, he was enabled to succeed in getting the title of Ilkhani and the charge of the administration transferred to himself, in the place of his uncle, Muhammad Kuli Khan. The latter did not await Yar Muhammad's return, but left Bujnurd at once with all his family. (10) Yar Muhammad Khan ruled at Bujnurd as administrator for four years, and during that time entirely ignored Khan Baba Khan. Eventually he managed to obtain the formal recognition of the Shah to his succession to the chiefship with the title of Saham - ud - Dowlah. Khan Baba Khan was given an allowance of a thousand tumans a year, and lived at Mashhad till he died. Muhammad Kuli Khan was employed by the governor-general of Khurasan as governor at Turbat-i-Jam and other places for a time, and eventually attached himself to the Shuja-ud-Dowlah at Kuchan, where he died. His son, the Hákim of Kushkhana, is still there.

Yar Muhammad Khan's eldest son, Nasratulla Khan, was away at the time of my visit holding the post of Hákim or governor of Jajarm and Isfarain, so I did not see him. The fate of the second son, Suliman Khan, I have already detailed. The third and fourth sons, Azizulla Khan and Habibulla Khan, were both by the same mother, a first-cousin of their father's. Azizulla Khan, the Il-khani and heir-apparent, seemed to be full of energy and with a great taste for sport and a good rider and shot. He took Muhammad Khan out hawking, and the two boys seemed to have a rare time of it together.

Habibulla Khan, though only thirteen, had already received the rank of Sartip, and had been given by his father the command of the Shadillu Cossacks, and dressed accordingly in Cossack uniform. The remaining three sons were quite small. There were also five daughters, but the Saham-ud-Dowlah told me himself that no less than sixty-two other children of his had died, mostly from smallpox, so that the total number he had had amounted to seventy-four—a goodly family indeed.

On leaving Bujnurd our route led north over the low range of hills bounding the Bujnurd Valley in this direction, rising some 400 feet, but descending nearly 1000 feet on the northern side into the valley of the Attrak, here a stream some 15 feet in width and 2 feet deep, running between steep banks 20 feet below the level of the land on either side. On our way we passed a flock of sheep that had just been attacked by wolves. Several were lying dead, and many others had been mauled; wolves always seizing and lacerating the tails of the sheep, and doing much wanton damage in that way.

The Saham-ud-Dowlah sent the Yawar or Risaldar major and a party of ten of his Shadillu Kurd Cossacks to escort me through his territory as far as the Goklan frontier, where fresh Goklan sowars were to take charge. The chief seemed terribly exercised in his mind as to the danger that not only I was incurring for myself, but that he too was incurring on my behalf, and Taghan Sirdar, his chief Goklan Turkoman guide and his great stand-by in all expeditions, was specially summoned in and sent with me, with many injunctions to keep me safe out of the way of Yamut raids. We had a good deal of delay in getting the mules across the river Attrak. Then we struck off north up the hillsides and had a steady ascent for some 1900 feet, and then a descent again for another 1000 feet to the little Kurd village of Kalajik. On the hills we found a sort of hawthorn tree covered with yellow haws or berries, not at all bad to eat, and nearly as large as crab apples. Another variety of the same tree had the small red berry. The hillsides were largely cultivated for rain crops in the spring, and partridges were to be found in most of the ravines wherever there was any water.

Our next march took us to Katlish, the border village of Bujnurd in this direction. The road led up for some 600 feet, and then down again and up a ravine on the opposite side to the top of a second range over undulating land, well covered with grass and largely under cultivation. Finally we descended some 1300 feet into an uninhabited valley called Kuruk, down which we worked till we came to Katlish, a walled village containing some

150 houses of Arabs. These people were said to have been brought from near Karbala, in Turkish Arabia, and were originally settled by Shah Abbas in the Attrak country. They were subsequently settled at Katlish by Najaf Ali Khan, the seventh Ilkhani of the Shadillus, who built the village walls to protect them from Turkoman raids. They had quite lost their Arabic, and talked nothing but Turki. The hills about were mostly of grey clay and very bare, with very little wood, and the weather altogether was much warmer, the thermometer going up to 77° at 4 P.M.; the height apparently was about 3100 feet. We tried Muhammad Khan's hawk at the partridges, but they would rarely rise, and merely dodged about from bush to bush. Sometimes the kizil, as it was called, a speckled brown bird something like a goshawk, would dash at a covey on the ground and settle on a bush above them. The birds were then afraid to rise, and we thus got up to them with our guns. They were generally so wild, and ran up the hillsides so hopelessly fast, that without a hawk we could rarely get up to them.

From Katlish we marched to the small Kuchan village of Muhammad seven miles off, and here we began to get into more sporting country. The valley was level and full of reeds all the way up. Forming the horsemen with me into a line, I beat through the reeds in the hope of finding pheasants, but not one was to be seen. Just as we got close to camp, though, out came a fine old wild boar, who charged right through the middle of us. We none of us had a spear. I shouted to the men to use their swords, but all to no avail. We had a splendid gallop down the valley, and I and my own men were just getting in, when the Bujnurd Cossacks came up and at once commenced firing wildly at full gallop, and as nearly as possible shot Koki Sirdar and a ghulam, not to mention one or two of themselves. This was not good enough, and I had to pull up and clear out of the line of fire, and the pig made his way into a thick clump of reeds. Poor old Taghan Sirdar, our Goklan guide, going in after the beast, was at once charged and knocked head over heels, horse and all, and the boar eventually made good his escape. As it was we had a grand gallop, and could we only have restrained the wild Kurds from firing we should have had some grand sport with our swords. Coming back, one of the big white-breasted Lammergeyer eagles, known as *humar* by the Persians, settled on some cliffs above us. I got off my horse, put up the 400 yards sight, and took a shot at it with the orderly's carbine, and by some good luck brought it rolling down. I found its oustretched wings measured 8 feet 10 inches from tip to tip. It was the first time I had ever shot one, and I had no idea they were so large. Its claws were very blunt, and the Kurds all declared it lived on bones.

In the afternoon I walked a couple of miles up the valley to a spring under a clump of big trees called Karaghuch, where I was lucky enough to bag three pheasants, the first I had seen of the kind. They had no white on the wings like those on the Afghan frontier, and were more like the English pheasant, but without the ring on the neck. The country was full of magpies. I counted thirty of them on one little bush alone. The grass was pretty thick on the hills, but there was very little wood.

In our next march of fifteen miles to Mashhad-i-Ghulaman we got into undulating upland grassy country, with the hillsides sprinkled with small juniper trees. We crossed the watershed at a height of something like 4800 feet, and then descended down a low ravine in a westerly direction till we got into the open valley, in the centre of which the village was situated. Mashhad-i-Ghulaman was only populated when Gurmab and Kulkulah were vacated by the Persians, and the villagers removed on those villages being handed over to Russia under the terms of Article III. of the Akhal-Khurasan Boundary Convention of 21st December 1881. The present houses had been built just outside the ruined gateway and walls of a former town, said to have been constructed by Nadir Shah and subsequently destroyed by an earthquake. The valley was one mass of grass, and there was grazing in it for any number of animals. I found a large flock of the white-breasted lesser European bustard close to camp, and also some hares, the first we had seen on tour, some of which we killed with the hawk. The horizon was bounded on the north by the Tagharan range, and to the south by the parallel Bash Teppe range. Both of these ranges could be ridden over anywhere, and were covered with grass and small junipers, rocks only cropping up occasionally. The valley ran down in a north-west direction to Suksu, distant about eight miles, and the same distance again beyond that was said to be the Russian Turkoman village of Daina. Suksu was uninhabited, and the whole countryside looked deserted.

This was our most northern point. We now had to turn south over the Bash Teppe range, which we crossed at a height of about 5000 feet, and camped at Raz, a village of about 700 houses, inhabited by people who called themselves Sistanis and spoke a dialect of their own. The fort above the village and the walls around it were all in ruins, and the *kanats* or underground water-channels had all been allowed to fall into disrepair during the time of the Turkoman raids. Large quantities of unirrigated grapes, though, were grown and turned into raisins. Strings and strings of bunches of grapes were hanging out to dry, and were to hang for another month or more, the people said. The valley drained down to Khartut, and the reed-beds there were said to contain a tiger, but nothing would induce the Saham-ud-Dowlah's men to permit me to venture down there, and as it was only through them that I could get supplies for my camp I was helpless. The chief's orders were strict, that my wanderings were to be confined within the zone of habitation, whereas, alas, real sport was only to be obtained beyond it. I had to continue my way south, therefore, much against my will, and leave the tigers to themselves.

We crossed the Kotal-i-Pashun at a height of about 4800 feet, and then descended into the Pashun Valley, where we put up a fine old wild boar, and had a good run after him. We thought we had got him as he slowly climbed a ridge just in front of us, but he beat us completely, going down the other side. When we got to the top not a sign of him was to be seen, the rate at which wild pig throw themselves down hill in this country being something marvellous. The Bujnurd Kurds of course had out their rifles again. I saw the Yawar firing away at full gallop, and his bullets going anywhere within a radius of fifty yards of the boar, but I was able to make them sling their rifles and take to their swords. I found, though, that they had not the heart to face the boar at close quarters. Our Sarik Turkomans, on the contrary, went in with a will, and seemed to have more sterling pluck in them than the Kurds. The latter, I noticed, generally shirked beating out thick grass and dangerous places, and it was the Turkoman who came to the front when real business was on.

After leaving the Pashun Valley we had a steep climb to the top of another range, which we crossed at a height of over 5000 feet, and then a long descent of some 2000 feet to Yan Chashma, where we found the valley full of ripe blackberries, and we all stopped and had a good feed off them. These ranges of hills that we crossed were all parallel, running west by north and east by south, the ground gradually sloping to the west. The country was bare and brown, and could be ridden over anywhere, the tops of the hills being covered with small dry grass, and the sides and ravines with a sprinkling of bushes and small junipers.

We camped at a village called Muhammadabad, which had been built about twenty-five years before by the present Saham-ud-Dowlah, and then went on to Kharaki, which had only quite lately been populated by people evicted from Firuzah. Such was the fear of the Turkomans that I had great difficulty in getting even there. We took out three days' supplies with us, and camped for the first night at a place called Gazabad on the northern bank of the Attrak, which was quite uninhabited, though it had been cultivated in places by people from the Mana district, who had not yet dared to come and live there. We put up large numbers of the little bustard in the Mana plain, but they were very wild and difficult to get within shot of. I found a few pheasants along the Attrak, but the total bag for the day only amounted to one little bustard, one pheasant, one teal, and one quail, and we also saw a wolf and a boar.

Eight miles farther down the right bank of the Attrak next morning brought us to Kharaki, where we found thirty families out of the four hundred that had been evicted from Firuzah, all perfectly yellow, and in the last stage of exhaustion from malarial fever. Every man, woman, and child in the place, I should think, was up at our dispensary in the afternoon for medicine, which was liberally given them. This sickness did not look promising for the new settlement, but it was hoped that as the ground was cleared the fever would diminish. The valley of the Attrak was here about a mile wide, perfectly level, and with a rich soil covered with low reeds, camel-thorn, thistles, and weeds about two feet in height. The river ran between steep banks, and was about thirty feet in width and one to two feet in depth. It wound about continuously across the valley, and was difficult to cross. The number of old water-channels showed that the valley had been well cultivated in olden days, and once the fear of the Yamuts was removed there was no reason why it should not be so again, unless indeed Russia stepped in and prohibited further cultivation on the plea of there not being sufficient water for her Turkoman subjects lower down. As it was, the whole of the Attrak Valley from Kharaki right down to Chat was said to be uninhabited and uncultivated.

The climate of the Attrak Valley is not a severe one. The height at Kharaki was only about 1700 feet, and the thermometer at 4 P.M. 75° F., which was warm for October. The hills on either side of the valley were bare and brown, and the country generally looked hot. I could not go farther down the valley, and had to turn back at Kharaki. So crossing the river we rode up the left bank to Pishkala, a village of about a hundred houses, surrounded by gardens and vineyards. We saw a good many pheasants and little bustard on the way, and also some wild pig and a few duck and snipe on the river.

Next day our route led south across low ranges of hills into the level circular valley of Simalghan, where we were met by the Hákim, and conducted by him to Shahabad, the headquarters of the Simalghan district. The northern slopes of the hills on the southern side of this valley showed the first signs of wood we had seen, being covered with low oak trees.

As we passed the ruined village of Haidarabad, we were told that some twenty-five years before it had been attacked by Tukmi Sirdar, the famous Tekke Turkoman raider, with 600 men. It was a walled and bastioned village, and had been built only a short time before by the then chief, Haidar Kuli Khan. I asked how Turkoman raiders had been able to take such a place, and I was told that Tukmi Sirdar came down at night from the hills to the south of the village, from which direction no attack was expected, and dismounting his men, lay in wait till the gates were opened at dawn, when they rushed the village, and out of the thirty families then in it succeeded in capturing and carrying off some sixty people. The place had remained uninhabited ever since. The appellation of Sirdar, I may say, has not the meaning of chief or noble that we attach to it in India, but is the title given by the Turkomans to those who have proved themselves fit to be leaders and guides of their raiding expeditions.

The Hákim of Simalghan told me as we rode along that the valley contained thirteen villages, with an aggregate of some 700 or 800 families of Shadillu Kurds. They caught numbers of pheasants and partridges during the winter, he said, when the birds were driven down from the mountains by cold. The plan was to get them out in the plain, and to cut them off from the hills and then to gallop after them on horseback. Both pheasants and partridges, he said, after a couple of flights invariably tried to hide themselves in the snow, in which they were easily tracked down by their footmarks and pulled out of their hiding-places by hand. The wonder was that with such indiscriminate slaughter in the winter, any birds were left at all to breed in the summer. I could find none myself, and the only game I came across were some flocks of little bustard.

Our next march took us up the Darkash Pass. The ascent was gradual and the road easy, but the difference in temperature was great. Leaving Shahabad at a height of about 3100 feet, with the thermometer at 4 P.M. 83° F., we rose some 1900 feet in the twelve miles, and found ourselves on the top with the thermometer at 4 P.M. only 59° F. Our camp was pitched by a spring in a long upland plain, almost quite level, and known as Chaman-i-Bid. The Allah Dagh range terminates at the Darkash Pass, and the Kurkhud range is said to commence there and extends eastwards, gradually rising in height. At first the hills bordering the pass had no wood on them, but junipers gradually commenced to show till at Chaman-i-Bid the range was pretty thickly dotted with them. Hearing that oorial were plentiful in the hills, I spent the afternoon in a climb up a thickly wooded ravine, working right up to the lofty cliffs of the Kurkhud range, but I saw nothing but does and young. Looking south from the top there was nothing for the eye to rest on but a large upland plain.

Next day we marched thirteen miles to Rubat-i-Karabil, a little village of ten families built near the ruins of an old stone *rubat* or rest-house. We passed along the northern side of the bare desert plain, and the only thing we saw was one solitary big bustard. I spent the afternoon again after oorial, but without effect; though the local guide told me that he had slept out for three nights in the same hills shortly before, and during that time had shot four, which he had cut up and dried for winter use. There were no rocks and no cliffs as in the Kurkhud range, so we were able to ride all about.

Our next march, and our last one in fact, through the dry upland country took us seventeen miles in a westerly direction to the village of Dasht, at the head of the Gurgan defile. There we found some fifty families of Gandar Turks and supplies in plenty. These fifty families I found provided a guard of twenty-five sowars, who were employed to watch the roads by which the Yamut Turkomans crossed the Karategin Mountains to the north, and came down on the Shahrud and Bostam districts. They were all armed with Werndl rifles. The Saham-ud-Dowlah got a grant of 600 of these rifles from Teheran when they were first purchased from Austria by the Persian Government, and he had distributed them in this manner amongst his various frontier villages.

Dasht was the place where the Saham-ud-Dowlah had promised me excellent pheasant-shooting. He told me that he had carefully preserved there, and that I was at liberty to shoot as much as I liked. Alas! the hopes thus raised only led to the greater disappointment. The reeds I found had all been grazed down and the pheasants driven away. Old Taghan Sirdar made me beat down the whole valley for the last five or six miles, assuring me that pheasants were there, but not a bird was to be seen, and except for a couple of sand-grouse, and a magpie killed by the hawk, we should have come in empty-handed. The only place I could find any pheasants in at all was a small patch of reeds below the village, a sort of refuge too deep in mud for any one to be able to drive the birds out. Here, with the help of a village dog, I managed to bag a few, and also a woodcock and some snipe, but it was toilsome work, and poor fun on the whole. Not only had the pheasants vanished, but the game in the hills, described as so plentiful by General MacLean in 1888, seemed by all accounts to have greatly diminished too, and I fancy the general distribution of rifles amongst the frontier villages will soon tend to its complete extinction. The mountains to the north and north-west of Dasht were wooded on their upper slopes with *mazu* or oak. Below them small junipers were sprinkled here and there, but these ended here, and were not to be seen farther west.

CHAPTER XIV.

THE GOKLAN TURKOMANS.

THE moment we entered the Gurgan defile we came into quite a different country. Instead of the arid upland country we had been passing through, we found the banks of the stream and the sides of the ravines thickly covered with brambles, thorns, bushes, and trees of sorts.

From Dasht at the head of the pass, which lay at a height of something like 3200 feet, we had a gradual descent of 1100 feet in our first march of eleven miles to Ishaki, a little village inhabited by some twenty families of Turks. The lofty hills on either side were wooded to their summits with *mazu*, a kind of oak, and the valley itself, which as a rule did not exceed 200 yards in width, was full of trees of various sorts, all in their autumn tints and more or less covered with moss, lichen, and mistletoe. The road itself was stony in places, but in others, to judge from the holes, it must be very muddy in wet weather. The jungle was so dense that nothing but a pack animal could get through, and a road would have to be cut through the wood before the defile could be made passable for wheels. Laden camels, indeed, could only get through with difficulty. The tracks of pheasants could be seen on the road most of the way down, but the jungle was too thick to be able to get at them. We came on a sounder of wild pig grubbing up acorns under a grove of oak, and the Cossack Bashi, as he was called, the Duffadar of the ten Shadillu Kurds who were with me, shot one with his Werndl before they could get away up the hill. All being Mussulmans, no one would eat the flesh, and I felt sorry to see so much good meat left to rot. The forests on either side were said to contain maral as well as pig, but I had no opportunity of testing this. The whole range of mountains seemed to be uninhabited. The stream that flowed down the centre of the defile was only about twelve feet wide and a foot in depth at Ishaki, but it was explained to me that this was not the main stream of the Gurgan River, as shown by the maps I had, but only an affluent called the Ab-i-Dahana or water of the pass; the main stream taking its rise at a spring called Yalli Chasma at the foot of the Guli Dagh range farther north.

From Ishaki we worked our way down the pass through thick wood for another fourteen miles to Shaghal Tappa, or Obah-i-Subhan Kuli Khan, so called after the name of the head-man of the settlement. The trees on the hillsides were of fair but not of great size, but the oaks in the valley rose to a height of what I judged to be 100 or 120 feet, with a circumference of 14 and 15 feet at the base. In addition to the oaks there were species of beeches and sycamores and a dozen other kinds of trees, and the glades were full of brambles, ferns, and bracken — a rare treat to sore eyes after residence in the arid country above.

Some four miles below Ishaki the defile gradually widened, and the narrow pass came to an end. Beyond that the road passed through an old cemetery said to have belonged to the Garaili Turks, the former inhabitants of the country. Two miles beyond that again we came to the first Goklan Turkoman *obah* or village, consisting of some thirty *alachiks*, as the felt beehive-shaped tents or huts of the Turkomans are here called. Beyond this the hills on either side widened out and decreased in height, and we passed through an open grassy valley, where I found some pheasants and black partridges. Near Shaghal Tappa we were met by the head-man and a dozen or so of his Goklan sowars, who escorted us in. The settlement, I found, consisted of two villages—one, the felt *kibitkas* of the Goklan Turkomans, numbering some fifty families, on the north bank of the stream, close to which my camp was pitched; and the other, the reed huts of some thirty families of Farsiwans, as people of Persian origin were here called, on the south bank. These latter people had been settled here by the Saham-ud-Dowlah some three years before, on fleeing from over-taxation in Astarabad. Each family had a platform elevated on poles and roofed over for sleeping on in summer to escape the flies and insects, which were a terrible pest. The heat, too, they said, was great in summer. I made the height of the place to be about 950 feet by the aneroid. None of the people seemed to be in the habit of going up into the hills for the hot weather, as was the general custom elsewhere in Persia. The Goklans did not have elevated platforms to sleep in like the Farsiwans, but they had got so far as to have some uprights and cross-beams with shade to sit under opposite their doors—a thing that I had never seen in a Turkoman settlement before. Moreover, their *alachiks* or *kibitkas* were pitched all in one straight row. As a rule Turkomans pitch their *kibitkas* anyhow, and have no accessories whatever, and their settlements look extremely bare.

I found a young maral in the Turkoman village which had been caught in the spring and tamed, and I was also shown several pairs of fine maral stag horns which had been sold to a trader at the rate of 5 krans per man weight ($6\frac{1}{2}$ lbs.). I heard, too, that an enterprising Armenian had been at the village some little time before and had done a good trade in pigskins at 3 krans apiece, and also in the melted-down fat of the animal at so much a pot. The Turkomans apparently had no such holy horror of the unclean animal that they would not make money by it if they could.

Our road the next morning led on down the valley, here an open grassy plain a mile or more in width, and gradually widening till at Chakur the hills came to an end, and there was nothing beyond but a vast plain gradually sloping west. Almost the whole valley was uncultivated. The soil was excellent and required no irrigation, but owing to the want of population miles and miles of beautiful land were lying waste. This was not the case formerly, as five miles below Shaghal Tappa we passed the ruins of Shahrak and another old cemetery said to have belonged to the Garailis. There were also various old *tappas* or artificial mounds about, marking the sites of ancient villages, but wherever the Turkomans have settled themselves they seem to have brought a blight on the land.

Eight miles beyond Shaghal Tappa we came to Chakur, the headquarters of the Gurgan district, as the land of the Goklans is called, and the residence of the local governor. I was met on the road and escorted into camp by Sarhang Sultan Kuli Khan, the Saham-ud-Dowlah's Hákim of Gurgan, with about a hundred Goklan sowars. These men were all armed with Russian Berdan rifles, purchased, they said, at the rate of about 20 tumans (£4) per rifle. They had some difficulty, I was told, in getting sufficient ammunition, but the Yamuts got it from the Russians and the Goklans got it from the Yamuts, and somehow or other they seemed to have no lack of it.

We formed quite an imposing procession as we neared

Chakur. Fresh parties of Goklans from the various villages kept continually dropping in, and I was much interested to see them all. They seemed to me to be of a rather different type to the Tekkes, Sariks, Ersaris, and other Turkomans that I had seen before. Some were rather fair, and others of an unhealthy sort of yellow colour, but all seemed to have more beard than either Tekkes or Sariks. They were fairly but not particularly well mounted as a rule, and they wore sheepskin hats rather flatter and larger than the usual run. They struck me at first sight as rather cadaverous-looking men, and not so manly as other Turkomans. Their colour may have been partly due to opium, as I was told that they had taken largely to opium-smoking of late. Even the women were said to smoke it, and if true this will soon reduce them all to wrecks, I fear.

Chakur I found consisted of nothing but forty or fifty *kibitkas* belonging to the Chakur section of the Goklans. The place lay low, only some 650 feet above the level of the sea, and the heat must be great in summer. As it was, the thermometer went up to 89° in the shade at 4 P.M., which was indeed hot for the end of October, while the flies were still a perfect nuisance. In the summer the flies were said to be a regular plague.

On my first arrival the governor overwhelmed me with terrible tales of the atrocities of the Yamuts, and so rebellious or *yaghi*, as he called it, were they that he could not possibly let me camp anywhere else than under his immediate eye at Chakur. I might ride out three farsakhs, he said, as far as the Gurgan River and see it and return, but I could not be allowed to camp there, and as to my going up the Gurgan Valley or anywhere else he was dead against it, and said he dare not let me go. There was nothing for it, therefore, but to wait and trust to luck to get on.

First and foremost I determined to put myself entirely in the hands of the Turkomans and see what that would do, and I never had the least occasion to regret my decision. I paid up my escort of Shadillu Kurds, gave them a final dinner and started them back for Bujnurd. They all rode up the valley with me as I was going out shooting, and we parted the best of friends. They had done me well during the three weeks they had been with me, and had proved themselves good handy men.

Riding back after saying good-bye, I had some good sport in a patch of newly reaped rice-fields, where I managed to bag about a dozen pheasants, rather a good bag in such a country where it was so difficult to catch the birds before they got into thick jungle.

I found the Goklans to be cultivators, and not at all nomadic in their habits like other Turkomans. They lived in the ordinary Turkoman *kibitka*, but apparently they seldom changed the site of their *obahs*, and the consequence was that their settlements were filthily dirty. The interior of their *kibitkas* was even dirty too, and they had none of the cleanliness and fine carpets and wall-bags of the Tekkes and Sariks. Not that the people were poor. On the contrary, they seemed to be well off, and the head-men were notoriously wealthy, so much so that Subhan Kuli Khan, the head of the Shaghal Tappa *obah*, was said to possess three wives for whom he had paid 1000 tumans (£200) apiece. The ordinary price was 100 tumans for a girl and 400 tumans for a widow; the latter having an extra value as they were supposed to be trained and ready to look after the house and cattle, which a young girl was not.

The governor numbered the Persian Goklans, *i.e.* the Goklans settled in the Gurgan district under the government of the Saham-ud-Dowlah, at from 900 to 1000 families. Others, however, reckoned that they numbered from 1700 to 2000 families. The revenue assessment of the Gurgan district was fixed at 6031 tumans (£1202) per annum, and this sum had to be collected by the chief of Bujnurd, and after deducting the pay and allowances of the 200 Goklan sowars kept up at a cost of about 3000 tumans (£600) a year, the balance was paid by the chief to the credit of the Astarabad treasury.

So far as I could see, the Goklans seemed to live in constant dread of the Yamuts. In the field every man had his gun or rifle beside him, and in fact never moved out without it. At night the villages were regularly guarded by a cordon of watchers, who, if they did not sleep themselves, apparently did their best to prevent any one else doing so, to judge by the noise made by the twenty men who were posted round my camp every night to ensure my safety. Even in the daytime our mules were not allowed to graze out of sight. These precautions were doubtless justified, as a Goklan of Chakur had been waylaid and shot by Yamuts for the sake of his rifle only two days before my arrival, and a mare and foal were stolen from the village the night I arrived, This latter event seemed to make little stir, as the Goklan owner simply set out to steal another horse from the Yamuts in return. Nothing was heard of him for a couple of days, and then the third night I was suddenly awoke by the firing of guns in the village, and this I learnt was to announce the successful return of the man with a horse. That little matter was thus soon squared, and probably the case of the man and the rifle was squared too in due course.

The second day after my arrival a horseman arrived with a note from the Saham-ud-Dowlah, announcing that he had received the title of Sirdar-i-Azam from the

Persian Government for his services on the Yamut border, and that his son, the Ilkhani, had been promoted to the rank of Amir-i-Tuman, the first instance I had known of a boy of sixteen becoming a general. I at once wrote to the Sirdar to congratulate him and his son, and we had a big dinner in camp to the Hákim and his Mirza and all his men, to celebrate the occasion, and it was then settled that we should hold a Turkoman race meeting for the Goklans, for which I should give the prizes, in honour of the event. After this the Sarhang ceased to offer such strenuous objections to my visiting the outlying portions of the Gurgan country as he had done at first, and eventually it was arranged that we might go up to the source of the Gurgan River at Yalli Chashma, which was something. The Sarhang gave a dinner to my men, and I myself made an excursion with him to the Tukht-i-Rustam, a curious mound half-way up the Nilah Kuh hill to the south of Chakur. There was nothing particular to see at the mound itself, except a sort of well in the rock, which was supposed to be artificial, but we had an excellent view over the Gurgan plain, and I was able to get a general idea of the lie of the country. The most prominent feature that caught the eye was the famous tower known as the Gumbad-i-Kábus, standing up in the plain away to the west. The wood and jungle ended with the hills near Chakur, and there was not a tree in the plain beyond, which was covered with low reeds and grass. The whole of the land in the plain was rich and fertile, and only required population to cultivate it to make the district one of the richest in Persia. No irrigation was required except for rice, the rain supply being ample for all other crops. Indeed the whole country was as green then in late autumn as other parts of Persia were in early spring.

Looking at the names marked on the map along the

course of the Gurgan River, I found that these were not fixed places or villages as I had thought, but were the names of various sections of the Yamuts. They were doubtless intended to represent the sites of the *obahs* or settlements of those sections, but as the Yamuts were continually moving about, the sites could not be permanent.

The country between the upper valleys of the Gurgan river and the Attrak above Chat was said to be entirely uninhabited. It was very certain there were no Goklans there, and in fact the Goklans themselves said that they were not strong enough to dare to show themselves north of the Karnava hills, which formed the watershed between the two rivers, and what Yamuts had been there had left.

The last night we had a final dinner in camp to the Hákim and all the Khans of the various Goklan sections from the settlements about, but we did not get away without one final attempt being made to steal our mules. We were roused in the middle of the night by much shouting and free firing on the part of the Goklan guards. A thief it turned out had been spotted creeping up to the mules, and no sooner was the alarm raised than mounted men were discovered on one side of the camp and a party on foot on the other, and bullets were soon hissing and tearing through the reeds after them in all directions, but without result, except that the thieves vanished in the darkness and did not repeat their visit. The Goklans from the village all turned out to help, and we had quite an excitement for the time, and such was the terror of one or two of our Persian *farashes* that they petitioned at once to be allowed to return. They were absolutely blue with fright at the idea of entering the Turkoman country, such a terror does the very name, much less the sight of a Turkoman, still possess for the Persian mind.

In the morning the Hákim and the Goklan Khans all rode out with me till we were met by the ten Goklan sowars who had been specially told off as our escort. Our road led north over bare, undulating country covered with dry grass round the foot of the hills, till we struck the Gurgan River at the twelfth mile. For the next four miles we followed up the banks of that river to the headquarters of the Baindar section, our camp being pitched near the *obah* of the chief or Khan, who came out to meet us on arrival. Goklan *obahs* were scattered about all along the road, mostly of the Kirikh section. Like all other Turkomans, the Goklans had neither trees, gardens, water, nor fields anywhere near their settlements, their *kibitkas* being simply stuck down in the middle of the bare, dry plain, the only difference between the Goklans and other Turkomans, as I noticed before, being that the Goklans seemed to have a partiality for pitching their *kibitkas* in straight rows, which the others had not. The women of all Turkoman tribes have always to fetch the water from the nearest supply, whatever the distance.

The Gurgan River, where we crossed it, was some twenty to thirty feet in width and six inches in depth, but it flowed very low down in a large, deep bed some quarter of a mile in width, and, I should think, quite a hundred feet below the level of the surrounding country.

The Baindar settlement at which we were camped consisted of five *obahs* containing from 100 to 140 families, and occupied both banks of the Gurgan just after it issued from the hills. Baindar, consequently, was not the name of any fixed spot, and going to Baindar simply meant going to any of the *obahs* occupied by the Baindar section. We had a dinner in camp for the Khan and his men in the evening, and they all seemed to enjoy themselves. The dispensary was thronged with men, women, and children all the afternoon, and Amir-ud-Din had a busy time of it treating their various ailments. The fact that we had a doctor in camp seemed to become rapidly known, and the opportunity of medical advice gratis was readily seized by all. All the people seemed very civil and obliging, and I was able to move about amongst them as freely as if I had been in India. The absence of all *purdah* or concealment of the women invariably tends to freedom in this respect, and none of the Turkomans that I have ever met veiled their women in any way.

From Baindar we had a march of ten miles up the banks of the Gurgan to Arkakli, a settlement of some hundred families of the section of that name. The river valley rapidly closed in, and we soon left the open plain for the hills. Wherever the bed of the river widened out sufficiently, rice crops had been sown, but the slopes on either side were generally dry and bare, with a light, friable soil. Only once did we get a glimpse of the forest, and that was about a mile from Arkakli, when we passed the mouth of the Kai Valley on the south, through which we had a view of wooded hills; but the forest seemed all to have been left behind as we came north.

The Kai stream joins the Yalli Chashma stream, and both flow together into the Gurgan, which may be said to commence as a river at the head of the deep ravine forming its bed, where these united streams issue from the hills into the plain at the Baindar settlement. Of the Arkaklis I found that fifty families had migrated to Chandir, in Russian territory, five or six years before, and it appeared that since Russia had occupied the Akhal several migrations of Goklans had taken place.

When the Tekkes ruled the Akhal no Goklans dared to go there, but now there were said to be some 400 Goklan families at Karakala and 200 at Chandir. One section of the Goklans, the Garkas, numbering about 200 families, were said to have gone over bodily, and detachments from both the Kai and the Arkakli sections had followed suit, the reason given being that in Russian territory they had greater security and better pasturage. The Persian story was that they had left owing to a quarrel with other sections of the tribe, but whatever was the cause, the loss of so many families in such a thinly populated country was a serious one for Persia. Some seventy or eighty families of the Kai section were said to have subsequently returned to Persia owing to the Russians having taken forced labour from them, and these were settled by the Saham-ud-Dowlah at Incha. Some hundred other families were also said to have returned from Khiva and to have been settled at Chiklik at the head of the Karabil Khan Valley. All this showed how constantly moves were still taking place.

The ascent from Baindur was not very steep, only about 50 feet per mile, Baindur being about 600 and Arkakli 1100 feet above the sea; but in the six miles on to Yalli Chashma there was a rise of 100 feet per mile. Our road led on north-east up the valley past an old Garaili cemetery and various little *obahs* of Arkaklis and Kais till we camped at Yalli Chashma. I found, though, that this spring was not, after all, the actual head of the water, as riding on I came upon another spring a mile and a half farther up the valley under some fine chinar or plane trees, and half a mile beyond that was the final head of the water at a spring called Dilma. These three springs formed the permanent source of the Gurgan River, but the valley continued, I was told, for some two farsakhs beyond in a general north-east direction, the road through it running first to Sugha and thence to Incha, Simalghan, and Bujnurd. The Guli Dagh, at the southern foot of which the Yalli Chashma and other springs rise, is a low range of dark rocky hills. It has no wood on it, but the hills to the south have a small sprinkling of oak and other trees, and we were evidently on the northern confines of the wooded region. The last Goklan settlement was at Dilma, and the Goklan territory apparently ended there in that direction.

While I was at Yalli Chashma a Goklan Shikari turned up with the skin of a snow leopard which he had shot in the hills. From his account it appeared that he and the leopard stalked the same herd of oorial at the same time, unknown to each other. The leopard got in first and seized an oorial, and the Shikari came up just in time to save the latter's life, as he shot the leopard and the oorial escaped. The man refused to sell the skin for less than ten tumans, as he said he could get that for it from the Russians.

Next morning, the 2nd November 1894, I turned back down the Yalli Chashma Valley for four miles, and then crossed over the hills to the north by a low *kotal* into the Karabil Khan Valley. The country was arid, consisting of low but steep hills of a light friable soil. We camped at the first *obah* we came to, which turned out to be known as Arab, the name of a branch of the Karabil Khan section. We found ourselves between the Dugh and the Karnowa ranges, in a rough, hilly, bare, waterless district. Had I not visited the northern portion of the Goklan country, I should have left with the impression that it was all as green and as wooded as that at the mouth of the Dahana-i-Gurgan. The farther north one goes, though, from the mountain range to the south, the more arid the country becomes, and the hills forming the watershed between the Gurgan and the Attrak are bare and brown, and almost entirely destitute of water.

Shortly after my arrival at Arab I received a visit from Kurban Khan, one of the Khans of the Karabil Khan section, who rode up with some twenty sowars to pay his respects. They were all regaled with green tea and refreshments, and then rode back again. In the meantime Moula Bakhsh had ridden off up the Karnowa Valley to pay his respects to Kilich Ishan, the head-priest of the Goklans. The Karnowa Valley runs into the Karabil Khan Valley from the north, and is in fact the most northern settlement of the Goklans. It is inhabited by the Shaikh Khojah section, who are all Saiyids or descendants of the Prophet, and number some two hundred and fifty families. The Ishan's *obah* pays no revenue, and the others only pay at the rate of some 2½ tumans per annum, instead of about 4½ tumans, which is the general rate per family.

Kilich Ishan was a man of great influence over all the Goklans, both those living in the Gurgan district in Persia as well as the others away at Khiva and at Kara-kala and Chandir, in Russian territory. He told Moula Bakhsh that he had been at Khiva some fifteen years before, and that the portion of the tribe located there numbered about five hundred families. When Moula Bakhsh arrived he found the Ishan busy superintending the building of a *madrasah* or school near his *obah*, the only permanent building, I suppose, in the whole Gurgan district. There were only two masons, and they had to burn the lime and make the bricks as well as to build the school; so the work was progressing but slowly. The priest had rather a good library in his *kabitka*, chiefly Korans and religious books presented to him by his various followers, but also containing several Bombay-printed books said to have been purchased in Bokhara, which were of more than questionable character.

From our camp at Arab we marched some fourteen miles down the Karabil Khan Valley into the plains again. The upper portion of the valley was filled with small mulberry-trees grown for silk, the only sign of silk cultivation that I saw amongst the Goklans. Lower down it became arid and bare, like the plain beyond it. We camped at Gokcha, the name of a branch of the Kirikh section, and their *obah* was situated upon the open plateau near the junction of the Sarisu stream, coming down from the Karnowa and Karabil Khan valleys, with the Gurgan River just below Baindar and on the high ground between the two. To the north and north-west of Gokcha lay a low range of hills called Tapashi, extending from the Karnowa range on the east and gradually sinking into the plain on the west, beyond which was Yamut country. The whole country to the north of the Gurgan River looked utter desert, and in fact is known as *chul*, and is apparently waterless. The Sarisu stream is the limit of the water supply on the north, and except for a few springs, there was said to be no water all the way to the Attrak.

Our camp was pitched close to the Turkoman *kibitkas*, and in the evening, when Moula Bakhsh and the clerks and Muhammad Khan visited the village, the Turkoman women all seized on Muhammad Khan and called him their boy, and frightened him to such an extent that he simply fled. Moula Bakhsh's red Turkish fez was also a subject of great curiosity to them, and they insisted upon taking it off and examining it, and proved themselves a thoroughly inquisitive lot. Evidently European-cut clothes and Turkish fezes were a rare sight in these parts.

While this was going on in the village I was engaged examining the long hollow or trench that ran past our camp in one continuous straight line, across the plain from the foot of the hills near Baindar on the east, to where it dipped into the Sarisu ravine on the west. It appeared again, so the Turkomans told me, on the other side of the ravine, and was to be traced down the right bank of the Gurgan River all the way to the Caspian Sea. This hollow was some thirty feet wide and ten feet deep in the centre, and looked at first sight as if it was the mark of some ancient highway, as most roads are worn into hollows in the light soil prevailing in this country. I found, though, that enormous bricks were buried in the soil along the southern bank of this trench, and I traced a line of wall, by the bricks in the soil, running westwards in the same straight line along the crest of the Sarisu ravine to the ruins of an old fort, some hundred yards square, situated near the extremity of the tongue of high land dividing the bed of the Gurgan River from that of the Sarisu. The bricks were all of large size, and must have been of great age. The Hákim of Gurgan told me that this wall, or the *alang* as he called it in Turki, could be traced to Tejend and Chaharjui, and that it extended all the way to China in former days. I had heard mention of a wall myself when in Daragez, and the people called it there the boundary wall built by Alexander the Great to mark the limits between Iran and Turan, but this was the first time that I had actually seen it. From the bricks it looked as if there had once been a second wall of China along this frontier.

From Gokcha we made a march of ten miles to Ai Darwesh, *i.e.* the house of the Darwesh or religious mendicant, but how that came to be the name of a section of the Goklans I did not learn. This place had been fixed upon as a central spot for the Turkoman race meeting which I had promised to hold, and here I was met again by the Hákim, who had come out from Chakur on purpose. The country had apparently been thickly populated in olden days. *Tappas* or mounds were scattered about in the plain, and the hillsides were marked by long lines of ancient terraces, showing how every bit of land had once been cultivated. The Turkomans, of course, put everything down to their predecessors the Garailis, but probably these remains were of a race prior to them.

The Hákim on first arrival had shown himself again most anxious to see me safe out of his district, and had even proposed that I should march straight on to the Persian village of Sangar, simply stopping to hold the races on my way, but that did not suit me at all. Eventually I got him to agree to my going to the Goklan settlements, on the Yamut side, on the plea that the Yamuts were also anxious to race. It was doubtless true, as he said, that there were lots of thieves about anxious to steal our horses and mules; but then they were equally ready to steal anybody else's, and we were no worse off in that respect than our hosts themselves. We heard that Yamuts had come to Chakur to revenge the loss of the horse stolen by the Goklans, but that the only thing they had been able to come across was a little girl whom they caught while leading her blind mother, and they had carried her off, expecting to be able to get a good ransom for her. To their disgust, however, she turned out to be the child of a Khojah or Saiyid, and was afterwards given back to her father free when he went to fetch her. The code of honour was a very curious one amongst the Turkomans on this point. Everything belonging to a Khojah or Turkoman Saiyid was considered sacred by them, and when anything belonging to one of these reputed descendants of the Prophet was stolen by inadvertence at any time, it was always at once restored.

Any Turkoman Saiyid can go to and fro amongst the tribes as he likes; and the only Goklans who live on the northern bank of the Gurgan are Khojahs, and they, by reason of their sanctity, are never molested by the Yamuts. This veneration of their Saiyids is about the only mark of religion that I ever noticed amongst the Turkomans, who as a rule are singularly deficient in the outward observance of the tenets of their faith.

The 5th November 1894 was the day fixed for the races, and all the morning people were gradually collecting from the outlying villages, till by noon we had an assemblage of some 150 mounted men, with many others on foot. Altogether 80 men had brought horses to race, some of them from the most distant settlements. The prospect of the races had excited the greatest interest throughout the whole Goklan country, and one old Yamut had even turned up as well, to try his luck from their settlements farther west.

My only experience of Turkoman racing had been amongst the Sariks of Panjdeh, but they were children at the game compared with the Goklans. The Sariks managed to get through their races without absolute disorder; but as to the Goklans, they quarrelled, they cheated, and were up to every devilment. I left them to arrange their own programme and to manage their races in their own fashion, and a very rough one it was, as it afterwards turned out. The arrangement was that the horses were to race in fours, the first race being the longest, and the others being successively shortened in distance. The men could thus each choose which race to enter for, and the arrangement would have been excellent could the programme have been carried out; but with such an unruly mob all order and regularity, I found, was soon lost.

The prizes were:—

1st Race	. . . . .	5 tumans.
2nd „	. . . .	4 „
3rd „	. . . .	3 „
4th „	. . . .	2 „
5th „	. . . .	1 „
6th „	. . . .	8 krans.
7th „	. . . .	4 „
8th to 20th Races	. . .	2 „

by which arrangement every man of the eighty present was to have a run for something, but I don't think all succeeded in getting it. Directly I arrived on the ground, the four horses for the first race were brought up and despatched to the starting-point with the starter, called the Vakil, whose duty apparently was not only to start the race but to fix the distance as well, and also to gallop back along with the racers to see fair-play on the road. The distances were so great that the horses started out of sight. They had no arrangement for running in a circle. The horses were simply taken away straight into space, and took their own course back to the winning-post. The Vakil had to ride in with the race, and then to take back the next lot and repeat the performance. His horse, I must say, had a hard day of it. The first three or four races were run in good order. I was able to keep the competitors under a certain amount of restraint by drawing them all up in line and taking them out four by four, but before the two-kran races had been run off the excitement became so great that the men lost all control and broke ranks, and before any one could restrain them the mob had closed in and the various competitors were racing each other wildly up the course, quite regardless of starter or anybody else, and the proceedings had to be brought summarily to a close. It was quite impossible to tell who was a winner and who was not, and so clamorous did the men become that the Hákim fairly fled. I drew off the head-men with me to my camp, and thus broke up the assembly. Turkomans one and all are so excited over a horse-race that they get quite out of hand, and require most careful management to keep them within bounds. As soon as the races were closed, the principal men were entertained at a feast which I had prepared for them in my camp, and after that they wished me good-bye and rode off to their homes.

The next day I moved my camp twelve miles to Yankak, the frontier or most westerly village held by the Goklans on the Yamut side.

Yankak is the name of one of the main sections of the Goklans. We camped at the *obah* or settlement of Karadish Khan, which contained about 100 families and was situated on the left bank of the Gurgan, about a mile to the east of a large mound known as Yas Tappa.

Karadish Khan was considered the warden of the marches, and he was the man who had to watch the Yamuts. I found, too, that he also got an allowance for protecting the Garailis at Sangar-i-Hajilar, one of the Persian border villages, and in this latter capacity he took the opportunity, when in charge of my advance camp on his way back from the races, to drive off several cows belonging to the Goklans at Ai Darwesh, in satisfaction for some cattle that had been stolen by the Ai Darwesh from Sangar. The Ai Darwesh pursued and recovered their cows, and the incident did not seem to create the least ill-feeling between the parties concerned. Cattle-stealing was a recognised occupation on both sides, and seemed to be considered as a sort of national pastime.

During the night I was at Ai Darwesh four ponies were stolen by Yamut thieves from the *obah* close to my tents, but unfortunately for the thieves the ponies were the property of a Khojah or Saiyid, and had to be given back on the owner going for them. Presumably the thieves came to see what they could get in my camp, but finding it too well guarded, took what they could from the village. The villagers on their part treated the loss with perfect unconcern, as no one for a moment doubted that the ponies would be returned at once, directly their ownership was known.

On the march next morning I saw large quantities of little bustard, but it was impossible to get near them. We also saw huge flocks of the white-breasted pin-tailed sand-grouse, called here in Turki *kilgairak.* They were all flying westwards, and the Sarhang told me that they came down in thousands every autumn, from China he thought, and that they were often so tired on first arrival that the people could knock them over with sticks. What we saw were the first arrivals of the season.

At Yankak I was able through Karadish Khan to arrange with some Yamut Khans to conduct me into the Yamut Turkoman country. These men were Naubat Khan and Malik Khan of the Kanyukmaz Charwas, and Karakishi Khan of the Igdar Charwas, and they expressed their readiness to escort me right through the Yamut country. I accepted their offer there and then, and decided to march with them to the Yamut settlement nearest to the Gumbad-i-Kabus. The thing was done before Sarhang Sultan Kuli Khan could even remonstrate. I went at my own risk, I told him, and his responsibility for me ended when I left his district. This reassured him, and the matter was settled. We had a big feast in camp that evening. The three Yamut Khans, together with Karadish Khan and some twenty of the elders of the Yankak Goklans, as well as the Hákim and his two Yuzbashis and other men, all had their respective dinners, and nothing could have been more friendly than the behaviour of all. The Yamuts generally, I had every hope, would turn out to be friendly too. It was risky, of course, to trust oneself entirely in their hands simply on the word of these three men, who might not even have the power to protect us for aught I knew, but I felt confident that the Yamuts as a tribe would have a certain sense of honour regarding the sanctity of the stranger within their gates, and in this I was not mistaken.

The Persians in my camp were in a terrible fright, notably a Yezdi *farash* and some Yezdi muleteers, but fortunately they were just as much afraid to turn back as they were to go on, otherwise they would have bolted to a man.

While at Yankak I managed to get some good sport with the pheasants. We were camped quite away from the forest district, and well out in the plain, but the river-beds about were full of reeds, which afforded grand cover for pheasants. I also came across enormous flocks of pin-tailed sand-grouse, which had just arrived. They were simply in thousands, and covered the ground in many places for hundreds of yards at a time, but always in the open, where it was difficult to get near them.

The difference between the northern and the southern banks of the Gurgan was very marked here, and I had plenty of opportunity for observing it. The north side looked bare, barren, and dry, whereas on the south there was excellent soil, covered throughout with grass and low reeds, and requiring nothing but peace and population to till it. The numbers of *tappas* about showed how thickly the tract between the Gurgan River and the mountains had been populated in ancient times, and the wooded slopes to the south made the scene a very pretty one.

I visited Yas Tappa, or the mound of despair, and found it covered with broken tiles and pottery, and made use of, as is generally the case, as the local graveyard. Amongst the tombstones I noticed the roughly-carved capital of a stone pillar, which looked as if there had been stone buildings in the place of old which were now buried in the ground, the only instance of the sort that I came across.

The climate at Yankak I found to be very variable. One day the heat was great for the time of year, and the thermometer at 4 P.M. 89° F.; the next day there was a thick mist and moist atmosphere, and the thermometer only 73°. The summer throughout the Gurgan district was said to be very hot, and during that time apparently the Goklans were left more or less entirely to themselves. The Hákim as a rule only resided in Gurgan for four or five months in the year, during the winter time, the Yuzbashi being left in charge for the rest of the year.

The Yuzbashi, as he is called, literally the commander of a hundred, and the head of the local Goklan sowars, by name Rustan Beg, was a Kurd, not a Goklan. The second Yuzbashi, Mehdi Khan, was a Khan of the Kirikh section of the Goklans, and took charge of the sowars when Rustam Beg acted as deputy in the governor's absence, but with this exception almost all the other subordinates in the district were Kurds, not Goklans. The latter seemed to obey the Kurds without demur, the Goklans being the subject race, although they refused to give their daughters in marriage to Kurds or any other strangers. The Goklans did not appear to me to be such an industrious race as their brethren the Tekkes or the Sariks. They made no carpets, and only a few coarse rugs. Felts apparently were their only manufacture, and the Hákim told me that if he could not get cash he often took revenue in felts, which were sent to Bujnurd and used for the chief's horses. The Hákim seemed to me to have nothing to do but to collect the revenue, as he did not appear to interfere in any of the cases of raids and thieving that were going on. As for the Goklans, they seemed to be at constant strife, not only with their neighbours the Yamuts, but also with the Garailis and other Persian subjects in the Findarisk district of Astarabad, and in fact there seemed to be little to choose between any of the various tribes in these parts. For instance, while the head-men of Chakur were escorting me to Yankak, the Garailis of Sangar-i-Hajilar took the opportunity to swoop down and drive off a flock of sheep from Chakur, and the last I heard was that the Goklans were in hot pursuit, and that an engagement was going on near the hills. The different parties, however, in these little encounters seemed to meet again without animosity, and no general disturbance of the peace resulted.

When the Goklans first settled in the Gurgan country I have no idea. The only mention of them I have come across in Persian books are two letters quoted in full by the Sani-i-Dowlah, written by Ahmad Shah Durani in 1747 to the Goklan Turkomans, inviting them to join him in a religious war for the capture of Mashhad, the Goklans, like the Afghans, being Sunnis as opposed to the Shiahs of Mashhad. Whether the Goklans joined him or not when he finally took Mashhad a few years later is not stated. However, it is clear that they were settled in Gurgan at that time. The country they now occupy is a comparatively small tract at the head of the Gurgan River, stretching from Yas Tappa on the southern bank of the Gurgan River on the west to the source of the Gurgan at Yalli Chashma, and to the mouth of the Dahana-i-Gurgan at Yangaran on the east. The watershed of the Gurgan limits their territory on the north-west. They do not dare to cross into the valley of the Attrak, which was occupied by the Yumats as far east as Chinaran. There is thus no continuous Goklan territory extending up to and beyond the Attrak, as shown in the maps, and the Goklans at Karakala and Chandir in Russian territory are just as much separated from their fellow-tribesmen in Gurgan as those in Khiva are.

As to the total numbers of the Goklans, Moula Bakhsh did his best to get a correct estimate, and I have a list showing the ten different sections of the tribe. These are subdivided again into nearly a hundred branches or sub-sections. The main sections are as follows:—

Kirikh	400	families.
Baindar	140	„
Yankak	100	„
Sangrig	100	„
Kai	300	„
Arkakli	100	„
Karabalkhan	200	„
Ai Darwesh	200	„
Chakur	200	„
Shaikh Khojah	260	„
	2000	„

This, I think, may be taken as a fair estimate of the numbers.

CHAPTER XV.

THE YAMUT TURKOMANS.

WE were now to leave the Goklans and to launch ourselves amongst the Yamuts, into a *terra incognita* in fact. No one that I knew of had ever entered their country from the eastern side, and even the Goklans and Kurds could not say what our reception might be. We were entering absolutely independent country, where no Persian dared set foot, although it was nominally Persian territory. The neighbourhood of Astarabad and the western portion of the Yamut country bordering on the Caspian Sea was comparatively well known, but we were going plump into the wildest and most lawless portion of all. Hence the doubts and uncertainty on the part of our Kurdish hosts. The Hákim of Gurgan and the Yuzbashi and others of the Goklans rode out with me as far as Yas Tappa, and there we said good-bye, and I rode on with our Yamut escort, the three Khans before mentioned. At the fifth mile we came to the first Yamut *obah*, on the banks of a stream known as the Hurhur, consisting of some thirty *alachiks* of the Igdar section. Here we were asked to see a man who had been shot through the leg, and going in I found a man with a fractured knee, who had been lying with his leg still unset for nearly two months. He told us that he got the wound quite by accident, as he called it. He was out with some Yamuts, and incautiously approached too near some Goklan flocks, and the shepherds thinking they were robbers, opened fire and shot him through the leg. The wound was dressed, and Amir-ud-Din arranged to get a splint made for him in camp, and to return and fix him properly up on the morrow.

After leaving the Igdar hamlet our camp was pitched at the *obah* of Murad Chala, near Gumbad-i-Kabus. As I rode along I was met by parties from all the different *obahs* we passed, and last of all I was met by Murad Khan himself, the head of the Chamurs of the Kanyukmaz section, from whom the *obah* or village took its name. Murad Khan, to mark the event, took out a bundle of coloured handerchiefs on meeting me, which he distributed to his horsemen, and they then raced each other for possession of them. The man to whom a handkerchief was given at once went off with it at full gallop, and any other man who was able to overtake him and to seize the handkerchief from him kept it for himself.

The people of both the Idgar and Kanyukmaz sections also appeared with offerings of bread, which apparently was a regular custom amongst them.

We passed within three or four miles of the Gumbad-i-Kabus on the road. This tower is the one fixed object in the plain, and is visible for miles on every side. Such a well-known landmark does the tower afford, and so visible is it from afar, that the story was told me as I rode along, of a certain chief in olden days who was coming from the direction of the Dahana-i-Gurgan, and had nearly done his day's stage when he saw this tower in front of him. Thinking it was close by, he ordered his men to go on and pitch his camp there and get his dinner ready, while he came on behind. When he followed he found to his cost that he had some thirty miles to travel before he got in, and so cross and tired was he on his arrival, that he ordered the instant demolition of the tower, to prevent other people being similarly deceived. Fortunately the tower proved strong enough to resist his efforts to destroy it.

We had amost imposing entry to our camp, as all the various parties of horsemen who had met us on the road accompanied us in. The one question on all sides was, "When are we to have the races? Are they to be to-day?" There seemed to be the greatest excitement about these races, and most of the men wanted to race there and then. Each section wanted to have the races to itself before I went on to the next. It was most amusing to watch their eagerness, but I had to curb it as best I could. I was not particularly keen on races at all, as I could not see how I was to possibly control such a lot of wild spirits. I feared that races might possibly do more harm than good, and my only plan, therefore, was to postpone the day as long as possible.

The first thing was to examine the Gumbad-i-Kabus. We rode north-north-west for three miles to the banks of the Sumbar stream, which we crossed. We then found ourselves in the midst of masses of broken brick, the sole remnants of the once great town of Jurjan. It was difficult to tell how far the town originally extended. The surface of the plain was sprinkled with fragments of pottery in all directions, far beyond the limits of the broken bricks, but the plain where this pottery lay was perfectly flat, and there was nothing to show that it had ever been built upon. The only building that was standing was an old domed mausoleum, mostly underground.

On the tongue of land just above the junction of the Sumbar stream with the river Gurgan, and between the two, were the ditch and mounds marking the ruins of an irregular-shaped fort which presumably was once the citadel of the place. Jurjan, itself, though, did not look as if it had ever been a walled city. A few gold coins were said to have been found, but nothing else. One of these I saw, and it turned out to be a coin of the Abbaside Khalifa Kadirbillah (991 to 1031 A.D.), the Khalifa who, according to the Rauzat-us-Safa, conferred the title of Falak-ul-Ma'ali upon Kabus's son, Manuchihr, and appointed him to succeed his father.

The Gumbad-i-Kabus stands on a mound about two miles to the north-east of the ruins of Jurjan and half a mile to the south of the Gurgan River. It is not what is generally known as a dome, as its name would imply. On the contrary it is a large fluted brick tower, circular inside and at the base, and ten-sided outside, with a circumference of about sixty paces and a diameter inside of ten paces. The height is certainly equal to the circumference, if it does not exceed it. The tower is hollow all the way up to the top, and the inside was once covered with plaster. There are no signs of there ever having been any stairs or means of ascent, and neither inside nor out are there any marks or holes for scaffolding. The tower is pointed at the top like a pencil and is roofed with large bricks, though how the latter have stuck on at the slope they stand in all this time is a wonder. The door faces to the south-east, and the only light in the building is a small window in the roof to the east. The floor is covered with some five or six feet of bats' dung, which has been set fire to at some time but never cleared away. Under this lie, I presume, the bones and possibly the tombstone of Kabus, as the Rauzat-us-Safa says that he was buried here. The doorway and parts of the tower adjacent to it have been much defaced. The bricks have been cut away, and the building is more or less undermined all round. Near the doorway it has been more than half cut through, apparently wilfully, but whether by the chief of whom the story is told or by whom is not known. That the tower should be still standing in this condition 900 years after it was built shows how well the work was done, and I can only trust that some one will rise up and repair the damage before it is too late. It is sad to think that a unique building of this sort should be lost to the world, all for the want of a little repair.

At the summit of the tower immediately under the eaves of the pointed roof, and again above the doorway, a duplicate Arabic inscription in Kufi character, made of projecting brickwork, goes right round the building. This was most difficult to decipher. The letters were well formed, but the raised brickwork of which they were composed had in many places fallen away. Moula Bakhsh and Mirza Abdulla spent the best part of two days puzzling out the words, and the inscription being in duplicate, their efforts were eventually crowned with success. I do not give here the Arabic inscription, but the following is the English translation, viz.: "In the name of God, the merciful, the compassionate. This high palace by Amir Shams-ul-Ma'ali, the Amir, son of the Amir, Kabus, son of Washmgir, was ordered to be built in his lifetime. Year 397 lunar and year 375 solar." 622 added to 375 gives the year 997 A.D., which is the date that Kabus regained the throne of Jurjan on the death of Fakhr-ud-Dowlah of the Dailami dynasty. Shams-ul-Ma'ali was the title given to Kabus by Eltayah Lillah, the Kalifa of Baghdad, who ruled from 973 to 991 A.D. Who the inhabitants were of Jurjan at that time is nowhere stated that I know of. According to the Rauzat-us-Safa, a Persian history compiled by Muhammad Khavand Shah towards the end of the fifteenth century, Jurjan was a flourishing country and an independent Khanate about the year 1000 A.D. under Kabus, whose family ruled there for over a century before and after him. Kabus was deposed and killed by the Jurjan nobles, who placed his son Manu Chihr on the throne. Manu Chihr was married to a daughter of Mahmud of Ghazni, but no clue is given as to what tribe he belonged to.

The banks of the Gurgan were entirely deserted, but the people, I was told, were to move back there for the winter very shortly. The Igdar were to occupy the ground near the Jurjan ruins, and the Kanyukhmaz were to camp in the desert between the Gurgan and the Attrak. Both sections had stored a lot of firewood for winter use, and this was lying piled up around the old mausoleum, where they said, owing to the sanctity of the place, it was safe from being stolen by any other section. I had thought that the Yamuts all held together, and were not divided by intertribal feuds and jealousies, but this I found was not the case. The Igdar and the Kanyukhmaz were on friendly terms, but both declined to go into the district of the Kujúks, the next section to the west, with whom they had a feud, and not a man apparently dared to move from his own *obah* to the next without his rifle, and all were armed with Berdans.

These feuds formed one of the difficulties in connection with the proposed races. Directly I arrived amongst the Igdars they wanted to have races then and there for themselves, and no sooner did I get amongst the Kanyukhmaz than they refused to race with the Kujúks.

I have mentioned that Murad Khan was the head-man of the Chumurs of the Kanyukhmaz section. I should here explain that the Yamuts are divided into two divisions, the Chumurs and the Charwas. The Chumurs are the cultivators who form the more settled portion of the tribe, and live more or less in permanent settlements. The Charwas are the cattle-owners and nomad portion of the tribe, and are more independent and move about.

They are the people who are said to give all the trouble. Owing to the scarcity of grass out in the plains, the Charwas were encamped on the outskirts of the forest that extends into the plain at the foot of the hills to the south, but directly rain fell they were to move out again into the open country between the Gurgan and the Attrak. The Gurgan River at Gumbad-i-Kabus had lost all traces of the wide deep valley that distinguished it higher up, and I found it running in a narrow bed some thirty feet deep and quite invisible at even a short distance. The banks on both sides were steep and bare, and there was nothing but a few trees here and there to mark its course. The water was only four or five feet deep and some twenty feet in width, but it was only fordable at certain places.

The great difficulty I now had was in getting supplies. The only forage we could get for our horses was green reeds. There being little cultivation in the country, no *bhoosa* or chopped straw was procurable at all, and as to bread, most of the Yamuts had to bring flour from a distance for themselves, and they had none to sell to us. The cost of bread and all food was thus excessively high. The Yamuts were none of them accustomed to retail supplies, and they had no small change of any sort. The smallest coin in the country was a kran. They had no coppers, and refused to take them even as a present. The consequence was that a kran was the minimum charge for even the smallest thing, and the Persian servants, what with fright and hunger, had a bad time of it.

I gave a dinner-party to Murad Khan and his greybeards, and the joke of the evening amongst them all was that a party had set out to raid Yankak, the Goklan village which we had just left. Whether the three Khans who had come to meet me there had spotted some likely plunder or what, I don't know, but directly they got back to their own district a party was despatched, and just as we were leaving they returned successful, with two horses and two captives. What ransom was to be demanded for the latter I did not hear.

I myself turned south-eastwards to visit the Charwas, and camped close to a mound called Kaplan Tappa, eight miles away, at the *obah* of Naubat Khan, a Kanyukhmaz Charwa, situated at the edge of a fine oak forest about a farsakh to the west by north of Sangar-i-Hajilar. Much of the wood had been burnt. The ground about my camp was covered with the charred trunks of trees, and from what I could gather I should say that the forest was being rapidly destroyed. The Yamuts regularly fired the grass and undergrowth for grazing purposes, and were perfectly callous as to the destruction of the trees.

We had heavy rain on the march, and it rained again all the night, and everything was so wet that it was impossible to move. No supplies were procurable, and I had to send a party of mules all the way back to the Goklans at Yankak to purchase flour and rice. Being so close to Sangar I naturally proposed to send there, but the Yamuts told me that supplies were as scarce there as they were with them, as the people had had to sell almost all their grain to pay their revenue to the Persian Government, and had hardly anything left for themselves. In addition to this, not one of the Yamuts dared to go to Sangar. One of their men had been murdered on the road not long before, and none of the others cared to follow in his footsteps.

An Igdar Yamut Khan was procured to act as escort to the mules going back to Yankak, and off they went. On their return the muleteers were full of the dangers they had passed through. First of all they had met a party of Goklans driving off Yamut camels. They were much afraid they would be attacked, but their Yamut escort discreetly vanished into a patch of high reeds till the Goklans had passed, and the raiders allowed the muleteers, whom I presume they recognised as mine, to pass without a word. Farther on they came across a Yamut party on the foray. This was too much for their nerves, and they bolted straight for camp and came in breathless. No sooner had we got our bread and rice than a sheep was killed, and a feast was prepared for Naubat Khan and his men. Under the influence of this Naubat Khan confided to Koki Sirdar that an *alaman* or raiding party was starting out, but nothing further was said, and the secret of its destination was well kept.

Early next morning we were startled by Turkomans galloping up to the village, all firing off their rifles as hard as they could. Two of our Persian soldiers, who happened to be in the village at the time, came flying to camp as hard as they could run, but the firing of the rifles was simply a sign of success on the part of the returning raiders, and the whole village was soon in a state of jubilation. The main body of the men soon appeared, driving the captured sheep, and then we heard the whole story. It appeared that news had been received that the Goklan flocks had come down near the frontier to graze, and it had been determined to raid them. The leader of the raid was our friend Murad Khan, our host of the day before, whose settlement we had just left, and a party of no less than 66 horsemen was collected for the purpose, composed of 50 Yamuts of the Kanyukhmaz section, both Chumurs and Charwas, and 16 Hajilar Garaili Turks from Sangar. The Charwas or Yamut nomad graziers were generally supposed to be responsible for the raids in neighbouring districts, but this instance showed that the Yamut Chumurs and also the Persian subjects of the Astarabad frontier districts were just as ready to harry their neighbours. Only three men, it turned out, went from Naubat Khan's *obah*, at which we were encamped, the rest of the number having been made up from the other settlements about. It showed how good was the Yamut organisation, and how quickly they could collect a body of men together even from a distance of eight or ten miles. The spoil consisted of two flocks of sheep—a flock was supposed to number 800 sheep, but these, it turned out, did not come up to that number, as each man's share only came to 20 sheep—a total for the 66 men of 1320 instead of 1600.

The raiders had surrounded these two flocks, killed one shepherd, and captured and disarmed the other. The shepherds of the other Goklan flocks near by collected and endeavoured to come to the rescue, but they could do nothing against so many, and the flocks, which the Yamuts thought belonged to the Kirikh section of the Goklans, were driven off. The captured shepherd escaped in the melée, and no one was there to say who the sheep actually belonged to. All was jubilation, therefore, till they arrived at our village. No sooner had they begun to divide the sheep, however, than doubts arose and gloomy looks prevailed, and soon it was whispered about that the sheep on examination were found to have a brand upon them that was suspected to be that of a Khojah or Saiyid. Sure enough this turned out to be the case. The first thing we heard the next morning was that the aggrieved owners — veritable Khojahs and no mistake—had turned up at Murad Khan's *obah* and had demanded restitution. Murad Khan at once gave back his share of the sheep, with many cries of "Taubah, Taubah" (repentance, or remorse), declaring that he had given up raiding long ago, and that he much regretted he had consented to join in this; and I could quite imagine that his regrets were real. We left the various other participators restoring their respective shares; and one poor man, who had rashly spent the night in feasting upon one of the Khojahs' sheep, had to give up one of his own in its place. That was all he got by the raid.

The dread that the Turkomans have for their Khojahs is a curious one. It is dread pure and simple that makes them restore property stolen from Saiyids in the way they do, sooner than incur the wrath or the curse of the owner. Many a story was told me of the calamities that had overtaken the wicked raider who had refused to restore some Khojah's goods, and no sooner had the Yamuts with me restored their own share than they began to discuss the question as to whether those irreligious Garaili Turks at Sangar, their partners in the foray, would restore their shares too or not. The Yamuts professed to be religiously inclined, and the Khans with me said their prayers with the utmost regularity several times a day—a thing I had never seen done amongst Turkomans before. It was amusing thus to see some of the biggest ruffians of all gravely discussing the piety of their neighbours the Turks. Whether the latter did or did not restore the sheep I did not stop long enough to hear.

The clouds by this time had cleared, and the mountains to the south-west shone out clear, largely covered with fresh snow. The Turkomans in the village were busy preparing to move, and I moved too. The Charwas of the Igdar and Kanyukhmaz sections seemed to be all on the march to the northern bank of the Gurgan, and parties with laden camels could be seen trooping across the plain in all directions. There they were to halt for some weeks to plough and sow some crops, and then were to move on to Akband, at the foot of the Gokcha Dagh hills, to remain there for the winter and spring, returning in time to reap the crops they were now about to sow. The grain when reaped is buried, they say, and they then return to Akband and only come to the south of the Gurgan late in the autumn. The number of Charwas of all sections said to be collected near Akband in the winter months, according to Malik Khan, amounted to about 800 families.

The forest, wherever it had been cleared, in the vicinity of Kaplán Tappa showed marks of canals and of former cultivation, and there could be no doubt that the district had at some time been thickly populated. The land was excellent, and it was clear that if it was only in the hands of any but Turkomans the district might be one of the richest in Persia. I naturally asked Naubat Khan why they did not cultivate the good ground where they were, instead of the poor land north of the Gurgan, and I was surprised to hear that this land belonged to the Goklans, and that they only came here to graze. The Yamut land, he said, lay west of the Gumbad, and so they cultivated there. This was a point of honour that I was not prepared for, considering that no Goklan dared to show his nose anywhere near Kaplán Tappa, much less to cultivate the land there. The consequence was that these Charwa Yamuts, who only encamped along the edge of the forest facing Sangar and Naudeh for a short time in the autumn of each year, neither cultivated the ground themselves nor yet permitted others to do so; and hence what might be a perfect garden remained nothing but a wilderness. The scenery was lovely walking about in the forest, but the only animals I saw therein were a jackal and some pigs—outside there were large flocks of little bustard, and huge flights of pin-tailed sand-grouse were continually flying overhead. The great feature of the place, though, were the thousands and thousands of wood-pigeons that were about. They were too wild to let one get near them, but they were flying all around in numbers, and had I only had cartridges to spare I might have had the finest shooting possible. In the evening they were settling by thousands in the trees to roost. Pheasants and partridges were scarce.

I was not sorry for the extra day or two's delay caused by the rain at Kaplán Tappa, as I wished to get my weekly post-bag from Mashhad before moving any farther into the Yamut country. Our Sarik Turkoman postal couriers did not like the idea of trusting themselves very far alone amongst the Yamuts, and so I determined to wait for the bag then due and to order the next to be sent round to meet us by Astarabad. Not that I feared the Yamuts would rob my post. So far as I could gather they had a high respect for the bonds of hospitality in their own country, however much they might rob abroad. The Yamuts were said by all to be upright in their dealings. There was a Russian Armenian, whom I saw, who, I was told, gave the Yamuts large advances for felts, skins, and sheep, &c., to be delivered later on, and they never attempted to cheat him in any way, albeit that he was quite at their mercy. These good traits of the Turkoman character, though, in no way lessened the unreasoning dread of our Persian servants for their Yamut hosts. Some men in our camp, notably the Yezdis, were absolutely ludicrous in their fear, and they hardly dared to move out of their tents. They were not only blue with funk, but they got quite thin with funk. Yezdis are proverbial amongst Persians for cowardice, so much so that they were found to be too cowardly even for the Persian army, and a regiment of Yezdis that formerly existed was accordingly disbanded. The story, as told by the Persians, is that as soon as the regiment had been disbanded, the men petitioned the Shah for an escort to take them home, on the ground that they were 800 poor lone creatures who could not travel without one. Yezd is in the south of Persia, but the three men of the Shahrud Regiment, quite in the north, that I had as my escort, were almost as bad. Considerable amusement was caused by the way these men flew for their lives from the village at the first sight of the horsemen returning from the raid, without stopping to reason why or wherefore they ran, and the same sort of thing might be expected to happen again in any Persian campaign against Turkomans, just as it has happened in the past. The Kurds and Turks are the only people in Northern Persia that I have seen who are fit to be trusted in any way against Turkomans.

From Kaplán Tappa I moved to Yarim Tappa, eight miles to the west, and there on the 15th November 1894 I held the promised Yamut races, but only some thirty horses appeared at the post. Most of the Kanyukhmaz, they said, were so busy changing quarters and ploughing their land after the recent rain that they could not get away, and only some three or four men of the Igdars appeared, as the remainder, being camped immediately on the Goklan frontier, did not dare to leave for fear of their *obahs* being raided in their absence. We thus had a quieter meeting than I had anticipated. The races were arranged by the Yamuts themselves, just in the same way as the Goklans had done it, and my duties were simply to judge the winners and to give the prizes, which were fixed as follows:—

1st Race	4 tumans.
2nd "	2½ "
3rd "	2½ "
4th "	1 "
5th "	6 krans.
6th "	4 "
7th and 8th Races . . .	2 "

As soon as the races were over all the competitors, and all the men and boys in the village, between sixty and seventy in number, had a feast in my camp and seemed to thoroughly enjoy themselves. I was amused at an old greybeard who was passing with his camels on the march to fresh quarters in the afternoon, and came in to have tea. The old man said his hair was now white, but never in all his life had he seen such a thing as a white tent in the country, and the appearance of white tents now was a sign that their country had gone from them. He was assured that we were only touring about, and had no intention of taking the country, but he would not be reassured.

Yarim Tappa was a Kanyukhmaz Chumur *obah,* so called from the *tappa* or mound close to it, half (Yarim) of which had been washed away in course of time by the Karasu stream at the foot of it. A good section of the mound was thus exposed, and I spent some time in examining it. I found a lot of round earthenware pots called *khum* in Persia, similar in shape to the Indian *chati,* buried in the mound at the level of the banks of the stream, and at least thirty feet below the top of the mound, but these contained nothing but earth. Few bricks were to be seen, but any quantity of broken jars and bits of pottery were exposed, and the whole mound seemed full of these from top to bottom. Bones too, apparently human, were visible here and there, and also layers of ashes, but there were no signs of any stonework. If Yarim Tappa may be taken as a sample of the numerous artificial mounds scattered about the Gurgan plain, it does not appear that they would repay excavation.

I found that after the Yamuts left this part of the country the Sangar and Naudeh villagers sent their flocks and herds to graze out on the plain during the winter and spring, a privilege for which they paid the

Yamuts at the rate of one kran per head of cattle, and half the wool of the sheep, Murad Khan in addition getting an annual payment of 50 kharwars of rice from each village, in return for which he was bound to protect the villages and to make good any losses they might suffer.

Neither Igdars nor Kanyukhmaz paid anything whatever to the Persian Government in the way of revenue. These were the two easternmost sections—the farthest removed from the seat of the local government at Astarabad, and consequently the wildest and most independent portion of the tribe. The farther west one went the more the influence of the local government apparently was felt. For instance, our next march from Yarim Tappa was eight miles to Kujúk, the habitat of the next section of the Yamuts, and there I found that the Chumur cultivators were paying revenue at the rate of 12 krans per family per annum.

Murad Khan rode out with me for the first three miles, but then begged leave and returned, as owing to a blood feud with the Kujúks he did not dare to go any farther. This was an illustration of life amongst the Yamuts that reminded me more of the Afridis than of any other people I knew of. The three Khans who were escorting me came up to apologise for Murad Khan, and to explain that his leaving me as he did was not his fault. I asked them if it was not Murad Khan's duty to escort me as his guest from his own section in safety to the next, and they acknowledged that it was, but pleaded the force of circumstances. When I came to inquire into these I found that the feud had arisen in a curious manner. Murad Khan, as I have mentioned above, was responsible for the safety of the Hajilar sheep, and these had been raided by the Kujúks. Murad Khan and his men went out in pursuit, and in the fight that ensued three Kujúks and two Kanyukhmaz were killed.

Consequently the Kujúks were one man to the bad. The Kanyukhmaz had offered them 400 tumans as blood-money, and a girl in addition, to settle the feud, but the Kujúks had declined the offer, and demanded blood. Consequently, till a Kanyukhmaz man had been killed by the Kujúks the feud could not be closed. Presumably, therefore, the Kujúks meant to shoot the first Kanyukhmaz they could get a chance at, and Murad Khan had no wish that he should be the man. It was supposed that he would be safe so long as he was actually in the Kujúk *obah,* but that he would be waylaid to a certainty on his way back. There was nothing for it, therefore, but for him to return before the Kujúks caught sight of him.

The road we followed led across the open plain, already fairly green after the recent rains. Everywhere there were marks of ancient cultivation, but there was not a man to be seen for miles. The little bustard and the pin-tailed sand-grouse held the ground to themselves in large flocks, generally consorting together, and being thus very difficult to approach. The sand-grouse by themselves were much easier to get near. We crossed two streams flowing down from the mountains on the south to the Gurgan, and like all the streams in these parts they ran in deep, narrow beds, and could only be crossed at certain places where shelving banks gave access to them.

The Kujúk section of the Yamuts occupy all the land to the north of Findarisk. We found the people busy ploughing up the plain in all directions. Oxen were mostly used, but one man we saw ploughing with a pair of horses. He had no proper collars or traces for them, and had simply fastened the ordinary wooden yoke for oxen across their necks by means of ropes and felts. Takan Khan, the chief of the Kujúk Chumurs, was absent when I arrived, having had to follow up a drove of cattle that had just been raided by his neighbours the Daz, but he returned before long, and came up at once to make his salaams, and he and his companions all remained to dinner. These dinners were curious functions. The Turkoman comes to dine, not to talk, and as soon as he has got his dinner he wipes his fingers on the nearest tent-peg and goes off without a word. It was only the Khans who came to say good-bye.

In the evening I went out shooting, accompanied by Takan Khan and his men, but though they did their best to beat for me, I only got a couple of pheasants. He told me that there were no habitations near them on the banks of the Gurgan or on the southern bank of the Attrak, and that the country between the two rivers was all *chul*, and it was impossible for one to cross to the Attrak from there.

On my return from shooting I found a curious individual in the camp, who gave his name as Haji Abdulla of Baghdad, and called himself a trader. His whole stock-in-trade, though, went into one *khurjin*, the small carpet-bags carried slung across a horse's back behind the saddle, and consisted of nothing but a few beads, combs, thread, and spices, and some tea and sugar, and by his indifference to gain it was clear that he did not live by his profits as a pedlar. It turned out that he spoke Osmanli Turki as well as Turkoman Turki, and also Persian and Hindustani, and he said that he had been travelling for sixteen years, of which several had been spent in India. According to his own account he had visited Ajmer and all the Rajputana native States, as well as Haidarabad and the Punjab States. He had then gone to Kashmir, and on to Gilgit, Hunza, and Nagar, Chitral and Kafiristan, where he wore long hair, he said, and dressed as a Darwesh, his stock-in-trade there being hemp drugs, charras and bhang. On the Kafiristan frontier he was arrested by the Afghans, but was subsequently released and turned back by them. He then went to Kashgar, obtained a Russian passport, and travelled with it across the Pamirs to Khokand. He again tried to enter Afghan territory from the north, but was again turned back, and so went to Tashkand, Bokhara, and Merv, and eventually by rail down to Uzunada, and thence by steamer down the Caspian to Astarabad. He went to Mashhad for a couple of months, and returned, and was now going back there again, he said, and thence he meant to make his way down to Sistan and across Baluchistan to Quetta and down to Sindh. He seemed to be well off, but where the money came from for all this travelling was the mystery. Amongst his papers he showed us an envelope addressed to a foreign Legation at Teheran, and signed in the corner as from Saiyid-i-Biabani, or the Saiyid of the Desert, an excellent name for such a traveller. He said his companion to India was to be a Punjabi then amongst the Jafarbai Yamuts.

From Kujúk we made a march of fourteen miles to Badrak, the name of a branch of the Diaji section. Our route lay straight across the open plain about half-way between the forest at the foot of the mountains to the south and the Gurgan River on the north. All the Yamut *obahs* lay to the south of our road, and the country to the north along the river continued entirely deserted. We passed a large shallow tank full of pelicans and wild duck. The embankment was of considerable length, and evidently of ancient construction, and the marks of former canals led off from it in various directions. Takan Khan accompanied me as far as this tank, but took leave there, as he could not go beyond. He said that some of his Kujúks had recently stolen some camels from the Kuchaks, and he did not dare to trust himself amongst the latter. I asked him why the Yamuts thus quarrelled amongst themselves, and he at once said, like all the rest, that it was because they had no supreme chief to keep the various sections under control. The Turkomans themselves all seemed to me to feel the want of some central authority. Without it every man had to take the law into his own hands, and the result was a perpetual state of feud.

Our next move was one of eight miles to Daz, where we found ourselves in the midst of the most thickly populated country we had yet seen. We found the people hard at work ploughing in every direction. Here they used one pony to each plough, and the system was of the simplest. The man jumped on his pony, took his plough up in front of him, and rode off to his field. There he dismounted, fastened the plough on to the near side of the pack-saddle by a girth or surcingle, and ploughed away till it was time to ride home again.

On my arrival at the village I was met by Yuzbashi Ata Murad and some sowars, who came galloping up firing off their rifles in the air, as is the usual custom amongst them. Sultan Khan, the head of the Daz section, was absent at the time, but turned up later on. He told me that his brother's wedding was to take place the next day, and he invited me to be present at the *toi* or entertainment he was to give to celebrate the occasion; an invitation that I gladly accepted. I found that Sultan Khan had a service of sixty sowars, with three Yuzbashis under him, and that each sowar received twenty tumans per annum as pay from the Persian Government, a fresh sign of Persian influence as we went on.

The best part of my day at Daz was taken up in the reception of the succession of Khans, Kadkhudas, and Rishsafeds or greybeards of sorts who came to make their salaams. The first of these was Karli Khan, the chief of the Chumurs of the Diaji section. He explained his absence whilst I was passing through the Diajis by saying that he had gone to the hills to get lime to repair the dome of the mausoleum of the prophet Zakariah, which was situated in his lands on the south bank of the Gurgan. He told me that there were the ruins of some old town around the tomb, and a number of mounds containing bricks were scattered about. The number of offerings that were brought to me of sheep, lambs, bread, water-melons, and such like things became almost embarrassing, not to mention the fact that they cost me double their value in return presents. However, that was part of the life.

Next morning, the 20th November 1894, was the day of the wedding, a wedding, too, in high life so far as the Yamuts go. We had only three miles to ride to Sultan Khan's *obah*, and people were already assembling from all directions as we rode in at 7 A.M. Sultan Khan and his men came riding out to meet me, and he distributed handkerchiefs to his sowars, who raced each other for them with much spirit. Sultan Khan first took us in to tea in his *kibitka*. We then went out and witnessed the first of the sports, which was the wrestling. The men wrestled by twisting their hands in each others *kamarbands* or waist-cloths, but the throw came at once as a rule. Very few kept up the struggle for more than a minute. The first three prizes were coats of sorts, but after that handkerchiefs and bits of longcloth were distributed to each man who threw his neighbour. Some of the contests caused great merriment. A man on being thrown would sometimes jump up, half mad with rage, and immediately challenge his thrower to another turn; and one couple I saw rush at it four or five times over, one after the other, much to the delight of the onlookers.

After the wrestling the shooting commenced, and while that was going on I was taken back for more tea.

Both of Sultan Khan's wives sat with us the whole time with their children, and the only sign of veiling themselves that they made was the drawing of the scarves they wore on their heads across their mouths and chins. Both looked rather elderly, as Turkoman women soon age, but one, the mother of the boy, was evidently the favourite, as she had a green mantle and much more jewellery than the other. Turkoman jewellery is much the same everywhere, and consists of massive heavy silver pieces set with cornelians.

After tea the horse-racing commenced, and went on till about 2 P.M. The prize for the first race was a horse and a shawl, and for the second and third two cows and a coat, and for the remainder small things such as bits of cloth, &c. Sultan Khan told me that he had purchased 60 tumans (£12) worth of cloth and coats to give away in addition to the horse and cows, but he himself did not appear to do anything in the way of feeding his guests. That was apparently done for him by the people of his *obah*, and the whole of them were busy, each *alachik* entertaining many of the guests and spectators. A large iron pot full of rice was to be seen ready in every *kibitka*, and Sultan Khan's relatives sent me a cooked breakfast over to my tent as a special mark of favour.

About noon, in the middle of the sports, the bride arrived, seated under a white canopy, on the top of a pony. All the women of the village collected to meet her at the door of the *kibitka*. Sultan Khan's wives and relatives scattered sugar and fruit amongst them, which they all scrambled for with great glee, and then the girl and her property were taken down into the *alachik* and we saw her no more. She was plainly dressed, without any ornaments, and as her dowry which she brought with her consisted simply of a couple of small carpets or rugs, she evidently was not an heiress. Sultan Khan told me that his young brother, the bridegroom, was twelve and the bride ten years of age, and that he had paid 100 tumans or £20 for the latter, which was apparently about the usual sum given by them for a girl. I had no idea that any Turkomans married their children so young, but early marriages are apparently allowed amongst the Yamuts. I was told that in this case the bride was to return later in the day to her father's house for another year or so, till her husband was old enough to take her; and when she did go finally to her husband her father was supposed to give her some felts and materials for her *alachik*.

I was now joined by the British agent at Astarabad, a Persian named Mirza Muhammad Taki Khan, who came to accompany me into the more open and more settled districts on the western side of the Yamut country, occupied by the Atabais and Jafarbais. Our first move was to the *obah* of Mullah Hatim, on the banks of the river Gurgan. Sultan Khan with a lot of his men rode out with me and escorted us in, and Mullah Hatim met us on arrival. The Yamuts here struck me as quite different from what I found them on the eastern frontier, and much more civilised. They were of a different complexion, too. Amongst the Dáz were many fair young men with blue eyes; and one, the Akhund's pupil, was a red-headed lout who might have belonged to any country. Our route led straight across an open grassy plain, now getting quite green, where the little bustard and the pin-tailed sand-grouse still had the ground all to themselves, the only other things that I saw being a few peewits and starlings. We crossed the Gurgan River and pitched camp on the northern bank. The ford was firm and good, and the water only up to the mules' girths. The Gurgan here was about thirty yards wide, running in a narrow bed with steep banks some fifteen feet below the level of the plain; but there were no trees or reeds or anything in the river-bed to mark its course, and it was invisible till one was close upon it.

We found ourselves only four or five miles to the east of Ak Kala, the one Persian fort in the Yamut country, then garrisoned by 300 Persian sarbaz and 20 gunners. Ak Kala commanded the bridge over the Gurgan, thirteen miles north of Astarabad, and the only time the Persian governor at Astarabad had ever ventured into Yamut territory was when he once visited this fort, and he did not even dare to do that without an escort of 500 sowars.

From the Gurgan I determined to make a trip across to the Attrak, which here in the lower part of its course formed the boundary between Persian and Russian territory. Our route led north by west across the open plain. With the exception of a small rise some thirty feet or so in height about nine miles out, the whole plain was flat and mostly soft, and covered with marshy plants. Camels belonging to the Jafarbais were to be seen grazing about, but there were no other signs of life. We camped by a shallow pool of rain-water some eleven miles out. Round the water there were marks of deer having come to drink, and I also saw a flock of what I took in the distance to be curlews.

Three miles out from the Gurgan we came to the Kizil Alan, as the depression and line of wall was here called, that we came across before at Gokcha in the Goklan territory. Here the depression was shallow and not so well marked, but on the southern bank of it stretched a long, low mound, extending in one straight line to the horizon on either side, and our Turkoman guide told us that it continued in this same straight line to Gumish Tappa on the west, and to the Goklan country on the east. This mound was full of the same large, thick bricks that I met with before, and there can be no doubt that it marked the remains of an ancient wall. Some few hundred yards to the east of where we crossed it I could see a square mound in the line, marking the site of what I presume was a guardhouse in olden days, though whether the remains of such guardhouses exist at regular intervals all along the line of wall I cannot say.

Two miles beyond the Kizil Alan we crossed what evidently had been the bed of a large canal from the Gurgan, showing that this plain was not always the desert that it is now.

Next morning our route led north across the plain for the first five miles, and then, passing along the western edge of some rising ground, we crossed a muddy, wet stretch of land for seven miles more, full of low weeds and sedgy grass, till we came to the Attrak. The Astarabad agent told me that when he came here with Colonel Stewart in 1891 this was a large swamp, full of wild-fowl, but that since the Russians had constructed the *bund* or dam at Gudri, turning the water of the Attrak into the northern channel, this swamp had dried up.

Beyond this we were met by Shaikh Nazar Atabai, at whose *obah* we camped, on the southern bank of the Attrak, three miles west of Gudri. With Shaikh Nazar came the heads of the neighbouring *obah*, just across the water in Russian territory, and their respective grey-beards, to all of whom we gave a dinner in the evening. In the whole march across from the Gurgan to the Attrak I saw only one small *obah*, about a farsakh from the Gurgan. These were camel-owners, and their camels were grazing about, and they drew their water from the Gurgan. Practically speaking the tract here between the two rivers was uninhabited.

Shortly after my arrival, up rode a Circassian with some seven or eight Russian-Turkoman Jiggits, who described himself as the Yunker or sub-lieutenant of the

Turkoman militia, in charge of the Russian frontier post near the Gudri Dam. He was a fair, lightly built, active man, some five feet ten inches in height, with a reddish-brown beard, light-coloured eyes, and good Caucasian features. He told me that Russia had then 1500 Turkoman militia, in fifteen separate *sotnias* of 100 men each, all under the command of a Russian colonel. Each of these *sotnias*, he said, had four officers, and of the total of these sixty officers, some four or five were Russians, and four or five were Turkomans, but all the rest were Circassians. The men, he said, were paid at the rate of 25 roubles a month, which, at the then rate of exchange, equalled about 42 rupees. This, of course, included horse, forage, food, clothing, and everything.

Talking of Circassians, I cannot help remarking what a useful body of men Caucasians seem to be, and what excellent soldiers many of them make. In India the impression got abroad, owing to the Muhammadan names such as Alikhan, Tarkhan, and one or two others of the same sort that came into notice, that the Caucasians in the Russian army were much the same as the Muhammadans in our Indian army, and comparisons came to be drawn between the two Governments of England and Russia as to the different manner in which they treated their respective native subjects. It was said that the Russian Government made their Asiatic subjects colonels and generals, while no Indian could rise to such rank under the English Government. The question was widely talked about, not only in India, but all over Central Asia. One of the highest officials in Afghanistan expressed the greatest surprise when I told him that a mutual Indian friend of ours had been made a colonel, and said he had always been told that such a thing was impossible under English rule. I was glad to be able to assure him that such was not the case.

The point which was lost sight of in India was, that the Russians in conquering the Caucasus conquered a people as fair and as European as themselves, and that the Caucasian, though a Mussulman, is not an Asiatic. The Russian soldier serves as naturally under a Caucasian as he does under a Russian officer. The English soldier does not serve under the Asiatic officer, and there can be no comparison between the two services. Under Russia, except for the Turkoman militia, there is no military service whatever open to the natives of Central Asia, whereas in India two-thirds of our army are natives. Under Russian rule there is little or no education and no civil employment for natives in Central Asia, whereas under English rule in India the natives of the country obtain the highest education in Government colleges at almost nominal cost, and are admitted to employment in every branch of the service. On looking over the Punjab Civil List, I notice that of the 2500 names entered in the index of gazetted officers 1500 are Indian, and only 1000 European, and this in the list of simply the high appointments in the province. This means that for every two Englishmen employed in the higher administration of the Punjab there are three natives similarly employed. Under these, again, are thousands of subordinates and clerks in addition, not mentioned in the Civil List, who are almost all natives of India.

In Transcaspia and Turkestan there is nothing of this sort. Hardly a single native is employed, and almost every appointment there, down to the lowest clerkship, is held by a Russian. This is the case not only with the administrative officers in Central Asia, but the customs, postal, telegraph, railway, and every other sort of official is a Russian, and in Russian Central Asia the native has practically no share in the admistration of his country.

In the whole of Transcaspia I have only heard of one or two natives of the country who have been given civil employment, and that only as interpreters on small pay. The Turkoman interpreter to the Governor-General, and one or two more with other officers, and a few Kazis for the administration of Muhammadan law, are the only native officials that I know of.

Now the 1500 natives of India mentioned in the Punjab Civil List are holding appointments as judges, magistrates, deputy and assistant commissioners of districts, revenue settlement officers, police, postal, telegraph, and forest officers, inspectors of schools and professors of colleges, civil surgeons and superintendents of jails, engineers in the Public Works Department, examiners of accounts, traffic superintendents, engineers and stationmasters on the railway, &c. Thus in every branch of the service the native of India is to be seen working side by side with the British official, and on very much higher pay than what the Russians themselves are getting in Russian Central Asia. Not to mention the Indian Judge of the High Court and his 3500 rupees a month, the 1499 other Punjab native officials are all in receipt of pay ranging from 100 to 1000 and even 1600 rupees a month, according to their respective appointments, and the average emoluments of the whole 1500 will probably be more than treble the amount of what the one or two Russian native subjects are in receipt of in Transcaspian territory.

This is only in one of the many provinces of India. In Bengal, Madras, Bombay, and other provinces the numbers of natives employed in the administration of the country will be much greater than in the Punjab, and the total number employed must be enormous. To counterbalance this, a few Muhammadan Caucasians have risen to the rank of colonel in the Russian army, but these are comparatively few and far between, and the total number is very small. India has not yet realised what the country would be under the Russian system of government, with every appointment held by a Russian, and employment in the public service practically closed to all native Indians.

The 1500 Turkomans who were said to have been enlisted in Transcaspia have been since, I believe, reduced in numbers, and it is reported that they are still further to be reduced, and that Russian soldiers are to be employed as frontier and customs guards in their place. The Russian soldier is a conscript, and costs nothing but his clothes and his keep, his pay being hardly sufficient to purchase his tobacco. For the Turkomans and other natives of Central Asia there is therefore little chance of military employment. The few Turkomans that are enlisted rarely rise to commissioned rank, and in fact only four or five have done so.

As to the Caucasian officers, many of them tell how their fathers fell fighting against the Russians, and relate with pride how long they held the Russians at bay, although armed, as they say, with nothing almost but swords. They claim that the Russians have learnt much of their riding and their fighting, and that they have got their best saddlery, equipment, and clothing generally from them since they conquered the country. The Caucasian *bashlik*, that peaked head-covering with the long ends that wrap round the neck, has been adopted throughout the Russian army, and I hope some of these days to see it adopted in our Indian army, where for frontier service in cold climates it would prove a grand protection. The *burka* or round felt cloak and Circassian saddlery are all in general use amongst the Russians; but it is not so much in clothing as in men that I think the Russians have gained from the Caucasus, and even the Russians themselves had probably little idea, at the time when they at last succeeded in subduing the Caucasus, what a useful body of men they would eventually obtain from these hardy and, so to speak, European Turki-speaking Muhammadans for their future contests with the Turkomans and other Central Asian races.

While at Shaikh Nazar's *obah* I rode some three miles up the river to a small rising ground called Tangli, just opposite to the *obah* on the northern bank of the river in which the Russian post was located. From the top of this rise a large sheet of water lay spread out before us, surrounded by reeds and full of wild-fowl. I heard a shot in the distance, and saw a man poling himself about on a reed-raft. Unfortunately my cartridges were running short, or I might have had some excellent shooting on that same raft. Wild-fowl seemed to be very plentiful. I saw a wild swan, but I was told they were not common here, though geese and duck abounded. On my return to camp I found some Turkoman Shikaris waiting for me with eight wild geese and as many mallards, which they had just shot and brought in. They said it required a good deal of wading about in the water to get at the birds.

Next morning I marched nine miles down the left bank of the Attrak, and camped opposite a place called Taushan Kir, just where the river turned off to the north. The Attrak, though, here could hardly be called a river. It was a miserable little bit of a stream hardly ten feet wide, and even when in flood after the recent rains it was only two or three feet deep, and the bed was so shallow that the water was almost on a level with the bank. Yet all declared that this was the Attrak. We did not see a soul the whole way down the river, and so far as I could gather, of late years there had been hardly any Persian settlements on the southern bank. Had I not visited the Attrak myself, I should have left the country with a very mistaken idea as to the real state of the frontier. I had supposed that the south bank of the lower Attrak was thickly populated by Persian Yamuts, and that *obahs*, or settlements, were dotted about in continuous succession all the way down the river. On arrival I found that there were only about twenty families all told on the southern bank, viz. one small *obah* at Tangli, and another under Shaikh Nazar, at which I camped, three miles to the west of it, and it will be necessary for all future travellers like myself to make sure beforehand that there is a Persian settlement in existence on the southern bank to go to before crossing the waterless tract north of the Gurgan, or else they may find on arrival that there is no place from which they can obtain supplies without crossing into Russian territory, for which a special passport and permit would be necessary.

At Taushan Kir we found a settlement of Khojahs on the north bank of the river, who came over to make their salaams. Persia swarms with Saiyids, a lazy, worthless set of men as a rule, who do no work and expect to be fed by others, and the Turkoman Khojah is much the same. One of these was very irate, that though he held an ancient *sanad* or grant exempting him from taxation, the Russians gave no heed to it and made him pay like the rest. In India there are whole tribes of Saiyids and others who, on the strength of their supposed descent, or of a grant from some former ruler, enjoy immunity from taxation which they have done nothing to deserve, and were we to treat the Saiyids in India as summarily as the Russians do in Transcaspia, and make them pay their share like the rest, the revenues of India, I fancy, would be considerably increased.

Our next camp was eleven miles farther west, at a place close to the telegraph line, four miles south of a low ridge called Sangar Tappa. This ridge was nearly two miles in length, running almost east and west, with a few broken bricks, the remains of what was supposed to have been a boundary pillar, at its western end. I could see no signs of the Attrak River from it, and although it is shown on the frontier map as running within 600 yards of the mound, no channel or depression was visible in the plain below, and apparently the river had changed its course and ran considerably farther north. I was told that when the Russian and Persian boundary was demarcated in 1882 the Attrak flowed into the southern bed, and the northern bed was dry. The southern bed of the river at that time, from what I could gather, was one huge swamp. Some two years before my visit the Russians were said to have dug a channel connecting the northern with the southern bed, and to have constructed the dam across the latter at Gudri, and by these means to have turned the whole of the water of the river, except when in flood, into the northern channel. Persian subjects on the southern shores of Hasan Kuli Bay were thus cut off from all fresh water, and could no longer reside there.

Formerly, I was told, there was a large population on the lower Attrak. The Atabais and Ak Atabais were the section of the Yamuts to which the land belonged, but years ago they quarrelled, and it was finally decided that the Ak Atabais should hold the land to the north of the river, and the Atabais to the south. Some time after that the Atabai Charwas, or graziers, to the number of something like 1000 families, moved off to the Balkan district in Russian territory, where they still are. They were great camel-owners, and the grazing south of the Attrak did not suffice for them. Since then the southern bank has practically remained untenanted, and apparently will continue so.

There is not a single Persian Yamut now anywhere on the river from Saikh Nazar's little *obah* near Gudri, where I camped, right down to the sea at Hasan Kuli Bay, and the course of the river having changed, there is nothing to show where the boundary is. The soil along the river is said to be salt and unfit for cultivation, so the land is not of much value except for grazing in summer. In the winter the grazing is best to the north of the river, and the few Persian subjects there have been in the habit of taking their cattle to graze there. For this they were taxed at the rate of 6 roubles per *alachik*, the same as Russian subjects, and they told a story of how the pious old Haji Shaikh Nazar on his first arrival in 1893, not understanding the rigour of Russian rule, settled down in luxury with a couple of *kibitkas* divided between his four wives. But when the tax-collector and his Cossacks arrived and sternly collected an extra 6 roubles for the second *kibitka*, he promptly sold the latter and was content to abide in one, despite the number of his family.

During our march we put up a hare, which showed that there were a few about, and I found and bagged a woodcock on the top of Sangar Tappa, but otherwise, beyond a few stray crows, rooks, jackdaws, starlings, and peewits, there was nothing to be seen. Deer-tracks were numerous, but the deer themselves had vanished, and a pool of rain-water I found was too salt even for the horses to drink.

On the 29th November 1894 we continued our march fourteen miles to Gumish Tappa, on the shores of the Caspian, the chief settlement of these parts. The Russian Chikisliar-Astarabad telegraph line, which we here left, was well set up with large pine poles brought by sea, I was told, from Astrakhan, and on by carts from Chikisliar, and formed a great contrast in this respect to the Persian telegraph line from Astarabad southwards. Our road led across the level plain, and we passed large numbers of camels out grazing. About the tenth mile we came to the *obahs* of their owners, Jafarbai Charwas. These people were living some eight miles or more away from the nearest water, and took their sheep and camels to the Gurgan to drink every third day.

On arrival near Gumish Tappa I was met and escorted into my camp by Haji Mullah Khwaja Niaz, a Turkoman, who boasted of the title of Amin-ur-Riaya and a gold medal from the Shah, and acted as sort of Persian government agent in the place. The Turkoman *obahs* were scattered about pretty thickly on all sides; and passing through them we came to Gumish Tappa itself, which was a curious-looking place from the distance, but on closer inspection turned out to be an ordinary Turkoman settlement, with the addition of wooden shanties. These had been built by the traders for their warehouses, and were raised above the ground on wooden piles, some of them being two storeys high, painted white, and roofed with tiles; while inside could be seen rolls of the bright red cloth worn by the women, and other such like commodities. I was taken all through the settlement, and at my tents I found a large crowd collected of the best-dressed people I had seen for long.

Travelling from east to west, we had gone through three distinct varieties of the Yamut Turkoman race. First came the wild, lawless, and poor Charwas or graziers round Gumbad-i-Kabus. These were poorly dressed, and had nothing but bare necessaries in their *kibitkas*, such as bedding and an iron cooking-pot. Next we came to the cultivating Chumurs amongst the Daz and Diaji sections opposite Findarisk and Katul, where the people were better off. I there noticed the prevalence of fair complexions and light eyes. Finally we arrived amongst the Jafarbai Chumurs, the sailors, fishermen, and traders of the tribe. These were the best off of all. Their *kibitkas* were well and even luxuriantly furnished, and the teapot and sugar-bowl were everywhere in evidence;

the women were well dressed and covered with silver ornaments and kran pieces, and they and the children were mostly fair-complexioned. The men as a rule seemed all well-to-do. All of them looked comfortably off, wore cloth clothes, and many of them were even dressed in fur-lined overcoats. The majority of the traders spoke Persian, played chess, and showed various signs of civilisation. They kept their own accounts, and even had a school for their children, and in fact reminded me of nothing so much as of a Borah settlement from Karachi or Bombay. Raids by all accounts were here unknown, peace and security apparently prevailed, and we no longer found every man armed with a rifle as we had hitherto seen them. Like all the other Yamuts, however, the Gumish Tappa people acknowledged no authority. There was no one head-man in the place, or any one whose authority was generally obeyed. So far was this the case that the so-called Persian agent, when asked to engage watchmen for my camp at night, was unable to detail any one for the duty, and eventually spent the night, with his brother and son, watching over the camp himself.

I found that, excluding the Charwa *obahs* scattered around over the plain, the settlement or village of Gumish Tappa itself consisted of some 300 to 400 *kibitkas* stuck pretty close together, and stretching for about 300 or 400 yards along either bank of the old bed of the Gurgan. Some eight years before, it was said, the Gurgan River had changed its course, and the water had flowed into the sea at Khojah Nafas, nearly five miles to the south. The consequence was that all drinking-water had to be brought from there either by boats or camels, and how Gumish Tappa had managed to exist at all under such circumstances was a marvel. The prosperity of the place had naturally considerably decreased, and the people would probably have deserted it altogether had it not been for their shops and sheds, which they could not move without great expense. In addition to the wooden sheds there were two or three houses built of bricks dug up from the mound at Gumish Tappa, and the sight of all these so much delighted my Goanese cook that he was heard to exclaim with a sigh of relief, as he rode in on his mule, "Thank God! here are bungalows at last." Bungalows to his mind were the one visible mark of safety, and I have no doubt that not only he but many in the camp slept sounder that night than they had done since they entered the Turkoman country.

The shops, I found, were mostly full of Russian broadcloth, chintzes, Turkey-red and coloured handkerchiefs, samavars, sugar, teapots, earthenware, and wooden bowls. There were no facilities, though, for the landing or shipping of goods. The village stood a mile and a half from the sea, and the old river-bed between the village and the sea was not so big as an ordinary canal, being only some ten feet broad and a foot or two in depth. All goods had to be laden and unladen outside and towed up and down this channel in the dug-outs called *taimul.*

Near the sea a large thatched shed on piles marked the Russian fish-curing establishment. Here some two or three Armenians from Astrakhan were engaged in salting fish and preparing caviare for the Russian market. They had the monopoly of all fish caught under a contract with the contractor for the whole Persian coast.

The mound known as Gumish Tappa, which gives its name to the place, lay about a mile to the northwest of the settlement, and was a mass of broken bricks.

Those taken out .whole were some fourteen inches square and three and a half inches in thickness. The mound was not visible at any distance, being small and hardly more than twenty feet in height. The principal portion of it consisted of two irregular low flat mounds, some six or eight feet in height, which ran out on either side to the north and south of what looked as if it had been a small point or promontory jutting out into the sea, and then, curving round some 300 yards apart, gradually sank down into the plain on the east, so gradually, in fact, that it was difficult to tell where they ended.

This fort, or whatever it was, at Gumish Tappa is said to have been formerly connected with the Kizil Alán or ancient wall that I mentioned before. On looking up the Persian history known as the "Násikh-ut-Tawárikh," I found it there recorded that Naushirwan (A.D. 530–578) built a wall on the ruins of an ancient wall said to have been built by Alexander (336–323 B.C.) as a barrier against the inroads of Kipchák Turks, Turkomans, and other tribes. Gurgan and Astarabad were both mentioned in connection therewith; but whether the Kizil Alán was Naushirwan's wall or Alexander's wall, or what, I do not know.

The marks of this wall for some distance to the east of Gumish Tappa have now vanished, and it is said that they were washed away by the sea, which at one time extended inland. At present the sea is a good half-mile from the mound, and the local idea was that the Caspian is gradually drying up. On my way from the village to the mound I was shown a slight beach which the sea was said to have come up to not so very long ago, and the whole plain was so dead level that it looked as if it must have been under water at some time or another. On the other hand, there was a report that bricks were to be found under the water some distance out in the sea, and that, if true, would seem to show that dry land at one time extended even farther west than it does now. The seashore is all mud, or rather the ordinary soil of the plain, which becomes very sticky when wet with salt water. There is no trace of any sand. On the mound I saw no signs of stonework, except a few slabs which had apparently been used for tombstones.

I rode over to Khojah Nafas. We first followed up the banks of the old bed of the Gurgan for a mile or so to a bridge, the channel being far larger above the settlement than it was below it, and filled with sea-water, some twenty yards or more in width and some three feet deep. A ride of five miles due south across a dead-level plain, largely under cultivation, brought us to the banks of the new Gurgan River, which was some thirty or forty yards wide and three feet deep. The Khojah Nafas settlement turned out to be a prosperous-looking place about double the size of Gumish Tappa, and it extended for nearly half a mile down both banks of the river. There were only a few shops and sheds to be seen, though. A mile or so below the *obah* stood another Russian fish-curing establishment, twice the size of that at Gumish Tappa.

The river was deep enough for unladen *lutkas*, or small sailing-boats, to come up; but, as at Gumish Tappa, all these boats were anchored away out at sea, two miles below the settlement. At Gumish Tappa I counted some forty *lutkas* anchored outside, and the people said they owned a hundred of them altogether.

On our way home from Khojah Nafas we came across a fine old wild-boar careering across the plain, pursued by a Turkoman boy on a pony. We promptly joined in the chase, and had a grand run, and eventually killed the boar with our swords after a long and hard fight, just at the edge of the reeds he had been making for. What brought this boar out into the open plain I cannot think, but there he was, and fine sport he gave us. He ripped one of our Sarik Turkoman's horses rather badly, owing to the man having more valour than discretion, but that was our only casualty. We might have fared worse, as a couple of Yamut guides who were with me would insist upon opening fire with their rifles at full gallop. As a matter of course they never hit the boar, nor went near it, but they very nearly shot my little terrier, and it was not till I had succeeded in making them put up their rifles that I could take a run at the boar myself without danger of being shot. Even then, when one could give one's undivided attention to the boar, he was a difficult beast to make any impression on with a sword, and nothing but severe whacks over the snout prevented him from making good his charges. He fought game to the last, and I eventually killed him on foot by a cut at the back of his neck.

The firing of Kurds and of Turkomans on horseback I have seen a good deal of, but the more I have seen of it the more useless I think it for real effect. Cossacks, Afghans, and all Central Asian people seem particularly fond of it, but it requires a very skilled hand to be really effective. I remember being out with a party of Afghans after some wild pig one day in 1887, and they shot one of their own men at the first start, and my only wonder was that they did not shoot more.

At Gumish Tappa we had a dinner party for old Haji Mulla Khwájáh Niáz and the head-men and greybeards of the various sections in the place, and after dinner they all came up to me with a representation that they said they wished to make. This was to ask me to bring to the notice of the Shah the way they were suffering from want of water, and to beg that steps might be taken by the Persian Government to bring fresh water back into their channel of the Gurgan. They said that when the river first left them they telegraphed to the Shah, and the Shah telegraphed to the governor of Astarabad, but that neither that governor nor any other governor had ever come to Gumish Ṭappa, nor had anything ever been done for them, and from what I know of Persian governors and Persian government, I did not think it likely that anything ever would be done for them.

The real fact was that the people were suffering because they would not help themselves. Each family spent on an average half a kran a day for water. If they had only had some one in authority to induce them to combine and deepen the channel of the river for themselves, they would probably have got water down at comparatively small cost, but so impossible was it to bring them to joint action that they preferred to go on with their perpetual daily expenditure rather than combine to stop it once and for all. Like all the rest of the Yamuts, they were suffering from the want of some central authority, and they even acknowledged the want of this themselves.

On leaving Gumish Tappa we marched thirteen miles up the right bank of the Gurgan, crossed the river by the bridge at the Obah-i-Anna Khan, and camped there. There were three bridges across the Gurgan—one at Ak Kala, the one we crossed, and one at Obah-i-Muhammad Khan, about four miles farther down. The latter two were slight wooden structures, built on high piles, on a level with the banks. They were erected by a Russian carpenter from Astrakhan at a cost, it is said, of 250 tumans, or £50, each. The river here ran between perpendicular banks in a deep bed about thirty yards wide, some twenty feet below the level of the plain. There was nothing to mark its course, and so sudden was the drop that a hundred yards off no one could tell that the river was near. At one time the Gurgan found its way to the sea down an old bed to Baish Yúska, five or six miles to the south of Khojah Nafas. This was left high and dry, and some forty years ago the Persians made an attempt to turn the river back to it by building a dam across the stream at Anna Khan's *obah*, where the sight of the fort they then built to guard the dam was still visible. The first flood, though, carried the dam away, and no attempt to turn the river had ever been made since. The old bed was visible some ten to fifteen feet above the present level of the water. After that the river continued to flow in two channels—one to Khojah Nafas and one to Gumish Tappa—till within the last eight years, when the latter branch ran dry.

On our march we crossed the bed of what I was told was a lagoon in former days. Twenty years ago, so our guide told us, the whole country was mostly under water, and covered with reeds and swamps full of fish and fowl. Now these had all dried up, the ground was being brought under cultivation, and men were to be seen ploughing with either a camel or a pony in all directions. The soil was wonderfully good, and rain crops could be grown everywhere. The river never overflowed its banks nowadays, they said, but whether the channel was deeper or the water was less was not apparent. The Turkomans complained of the latter.

This south-west corner of the Yamut country was far the most thickly populated of any that I had seen. *Obahs* were dotted all about. The Jafarbais in Persian territory were said to number 3000 families. Of these about 500 were Charwas or graziers, and were located on the right bank of the Gurgan, within a radius of eight or ten miles from the river. Of the Chumurs or cultivators some fifty families were said to have settled at a place lately left dry by the sea, called Tázahábád, some ten or twelve miles to the north of Gumish Tappa; but with that exception all the remainder were either at Gumish Tappa or to the south of it, between the Gurgan and the sea. None of them extended east of the telegraph line. They were large camel, sheep, and cattle owners. The sheep and wool all went to Russia, and also some cattle. Camels and buffaloes were bought, it was said, by Turks from Azarbaijan, who came every year to purchase them.

Our Turkoman friend, the so-called Persian agent, accompanied me from Gumish Tappa, and I was met some miles out on the road by Anna Khan and his men, and escorted by them to camp. Anna Khan had the rank of Sartip or colonel from the Persian Government, and a service of fifty sowars, who were supposed to get 22½ tumans each per annum, but the men complained that the governor at Astarabad wanted to pay them in rice, and this they had refused to accept. I could not quite make out the point at issue, but I gathered that it hinged upon the market price. Rice is the staple product of Astarabad, and the price had risen during the last two or three years from two tumans (eight shillings) to five tumans (£1) per Astarabad kharwar (585 lbs.). The fixed Government rate was two tumans, and as the Crown lands alone in the Astarabad district were said to yield 12,000 kharwars per annum, and the value of this had only to be credited to the Government treasury at the fixed rate of two tumans, the governor had apparently been pocketing a nice sum for the difference.

Although the country here looked peaceful, it was not so in reality. I heard that the various Khans or headmen of the different sections had refused to obey the governor's summons at Astarabad, and it was evident that relations were very much strained. The Dáz section had turned out and raided the Persian village of Katul, and had carried off five flocks of sheep, and two Persians had also been carried off on the road to Ak Kala. The quarrel between the Jafarbais and the Atabais was also still going on. The original cause, I was told, was the complaint on the part of the Jafarbais of constant thefts of their cattle by Atabais, and eventually, after appealing unsuccessfully to the governor of Astarabad to put a stop to it, they took the law into their own hands, and attacked and drove away the chief offenders, numbering about a hundred families, burning their *alachiks* and looting them of everything they could get hold of. The Jafarbais told me that thefts still continued, and that they intended to punish the Atabais again after their crops were sown; and consequently it did not look as if peace was likely to be restored amongst them for some time to come. My two guides of the Kanyukmaz section who had escorted me throughout expressed themselves as rather doubtful as to how they were to get home again. So long as they were with me, they said, they had nothing to fear, but going back alone, whether through Persian territory by Findarisk or through the Dáz or other sections, was dangerous, and they thought it quite possible that some one might be on the lookout to have a shot at them on the way. So far as I could gather, the Yamuts themselves seemed to be beginning to tire of these inter-tribal feuds, and the majority of them would, I think, welcome any settled government which could control the various sections, and protect them from the consequences of everlasting reprisals. All the Yamuts, Charwas as well as Chumurs, appeared to be cultivators more or less. Even the wildest of Charwas cultivated some land, and they only required a firm and just government to give employment to, and thus gradually to check the lawlessness of, the wilder parties among them, to reduce the whole tribe to comparatively peaceable subjects.

The numbers and power of the Yamuts in Persian territory appeared to me to have been considerably over-estimated. They have been variously numbered at from

7100 to 15,000 tents. Of these the lower estimate is, I think, the most nearly correct. The following list, showing the names of the various sections and the estimated numbers of families in each, compiled by my assistant, Khan Bahadur Moula Bakhsh, gives a total of just 7000 families:—

Igdar	300	families.
Kányukhmaz	300	„
Kúchak	300	„
Dáz	1000	„
Atabai	350	„
Diaji	600	„
Kujúk	300	„
Jafarbai	3000	„
Yilghai	350	„
	7000	

Of these, 4600 are said to be Chumurs or cultivators, and 2400 Charwas or graziers. These nine sections belong to two branches, the first five being known as Chuni and the remaining four as Sharaf. All these sections again are subdivided into sub-sections, of which I have the names and numbers of no less than ninety-one on my list. Of the whole 7000 families the really lawless characters were estimated to me at only about 300. Were, therefore, these 300 men given regular service under a competent governor, I see no reason why they should not be brought under proper control. The difficulty is to find the competent governor.

I have heard of various proposals for the building of forts and the garrisoning of the Yamut country with Persian troops, but not one of these proposals has ever been carried out by the Persian Government, nor are they likely to be carried out, and to my mind they would be futile if they were carried out. No Persian troops that I have seen are fit to be trusted in Turkoman country.

Those at Ak Kala are said to be practically prisoners within the walls of their fort, and they cannot even ensure the safety of their communications with Astarabad, although they are actually within sight of it. The Kurds are the only people on the Khurasan frontier that seem to have held their own in any way against the Turkomans, whether Tekkes or Yamuts, and to my mind they are much more fitted for service in Turkoman country than any Persians. The employment of Turkoman levies by the Persian Government is doubtless a step in the right direction, but is of little use so long as the levies cannot be controlled.

CHAPTER XVI.

ASTARABAD AND THE CASPIAN SEA.

On the 2nd December 1894 I marched the twelve miles in to Astarabad, and thus brought my tour amongst the Yamuts to an end. Anna Khan and his men escorted me as far as the little bridge over the Karasu, five miles out from Astarabad, which forms the boundary between Astarabad and Yamut territory. The channel of the Karasu was dry and mostly overgrown with grass, and only some fifteen feet broad and four or five feet deep, so that it could hardly be dignified here by the name of a river.

Beyond that we passed through level plain mostly cevered with reeds and quite uncultivated, till we were met by the *istikbál* or reception party sent out by the governor of Astarabad to meet me, consisting of the Sartip commanding the Persian artillery, a Sarhang and twenty sowars, with led horses, &c., who escorted us through the town to our camp outside the Chihal Dukhtar gate on the southern side. The sun was hot, yet we could not start early in the morning, as it was not till after 9 A.M. that the dew on the tents began to dry. The dew here was so heavy at night that the tents were soaking wet in the morning, and too heavy for the mules to carry till the sun had dried them.

The climate of Astarabad is certainly a curious one, and

very different from that at Mashhad. We all felt the heat of the sun greatly riding in at noon, probably owing to the change from a dry to a moist climate, and yet only a few hundred feet up the sides of the hills were covered with snow, and at the same time the oaks and other trees around us were still in full leaf, and orange and lime trees were all in fruit. As we came along we saw numbers of heads of wild pig stuck up in the trees. These were the trophies of the crop watchmen, and showed how they had been doing their work, much the same as the mole-catcher in England impales all the moles he has killed on the nearest thorn-bush. By the number of heads we saw, wild pig must be very plentiful round Astarabad. The country was wonderfully green all about, and though dampness reigned supreme, still the temperature in the shade was pleasant, and were it not for the mud, Astarabad might be a pleasant winter residence. It rained and snowed more than once during my stay, but the snow did not lie, and I was told that it never did lie for more than a day or two, and one could hardly expect that it would, considering that the rose-bushes were in full flower in the gardens about the town.

In riding through the town I found tho bazar bigger than I had expected. There were a lot of shops and people at work, but the boughs and sticks stretched across the top of the bazar were so low that it was difficult to ride through, and the place was deep in mud. The town itself was one vast waste, and not a quarter of the space within the walls appeared to be inhabited. The walls were said to be three or four miles in circumference, but they were all in ruins, and one could ride in and out almost everywhere.

Outside a large number of Turi and Bangashi tribesmen from Kurram, on the Punjab frontier, were waiting to meet me. These men all claimed to be and were treated as British subjects, and enjoyed considerable privileges accordingly. When they first came to Astarabad I cannot say. Some stated that they were born in Astarabad, others were quite new-comers; but whatever brought the first settlers to the place, their whereabouts seem to have been well known in Kurram, and their brethren, in going their round of pilgrimage to Karbala and Mashhad, seemed generally to take Astarabad on their way. Some had remained for want of money to go farther, others because their return through Afghanistan was forbidden, and thus a colony of about 700 families had been gradually established. The men first of all worked as wood-cutters, bringing in wood for sale from the neighbouring forest. In a little time they saved enough money to buy a bullock, and so on, till they were able to cultivate a piece of waste ground on the hillsides, after which, apparently, they soon became well-to-do. They all lived inside the walls on the outskirts of the town, and seemed to be well housed as a rule. The land thus cultivated required no irrigation, as they did not go in for rice, and the only rent they seemed to pay was one-ninth share of the produce. Altogether they appeared to be a flourishing community. Being Shiahs, they got on well with the Persians, and were not looked upon as intruders. Their presence in fact was welcome, as they provided labour which was wanted, and the fact of their occupying the outskirts of the town protected those in the town from outside robbers. A party of them armed with rusty old muskets came over in the afternoon and volunteered to guard my camp at night, which showed good spirit, but the governor had already provided me with a large guard of Persian sarbazes, so I was unable to accept their offer.

My first visitor was the Mirza or Persian writer of the Russian consul, M. Kokhanovski, who was sent by the latter to inquire after my health the morning after my arrival, which I was told was the custom of the place. In the afternoon I called upon the consul himself and had a pleasant chat. M. Kokhanovski had been Russian consul at Astarabad for twelve years. General Lovett was his British colleague when he was first appointed, but on Lovett's departure British interests at Astarabad had been placed in charge of the consulate at Resht, and no Britisher had remained in residence.

The governor of Astarabad, Keumars Mirza, Amid-ud-Dowlah, paid me his official visit the next day, accompanied by his son Shua-ud-din-Mirza, a visit which I returned in due course. In Persia the word Mirza before a name signifies simply a writer or clerk, but after a name it marks royal descent. The prince had at first proposed to send a Sartip or colonel to call upon me on his behalf, and that I should then pay him the first visit; but the British agent told him that as he was neither the son nor the brother of the reigning Shah it was his duty to pay the first visit, and he did so accordingly, and was most pleasant and cordial throughout my stay. Both he and his son came to dinner, and he invited me to dine with him, accompanied by Moula Bakhsh and Muhammad Khan. M. Kokhanovski and his assistant and the Sartip of the Hashmat battalion, then quartered in the town, and a cousin of the governor's, were also invited; and we had a great party, the first entertainment of the sort, I believe, the governor had ever given in Astarabad.

The Hashmat battalion, I found, had no barracks. I was told that successive governors had drawn money from the Persian Government for the building of barracks, but the barracks had never been built. All the summer the men lived in tents, and for the winter the Sartip had put them into *takias* or religious meeting-places in the town. The battalion was only 500 strong, and there were sixty artillerymen besides, with three Austrian and nine Persian guns.

The Sartip of the telegraph office occupied just as important a position in Astarabad as in all other Persian towns.

It is a curious thing in Persia that almost all the telegraph clerks are princes. The number of princes in Persia must be legion. In almost every telegraph office one finds at least one, and the office he holds is very different from that of telegraph clerk in any other country. In Persia he controls the action of every one. He it is who has the ear of the Government. His first and main duty is to submit to his chief and to the Persian Government daily reports of all that is going on. On his good will depends the version of affairs that is sent to headquarters, and he is the man who can despatch or keep back a telegram or do what he likes with it. Secrecy is unknown in a Persian telegraph office, and the Sartip in charge is the man who knows the secrets of all, yet nobody knows what he is doing. If any information is required at headquarters the telegraph Sartip is the man that supplies it, and such a commanding position does he hold that he is often directed by the Government to inquire into, and also to adjudicate upon, cases of local dispute. Persian rank too, again, is a curious anomaly The colonel commanding a battalion is a Sartip, and so is a telegraph clerk—one is military, the other civil, but there is no difference between the two. Rank in Persia commences at a Sarhang, which has three grades, each marked by a separate star, with slight variations, worn on the left breast, and may be held to correspond with a lieutenant-colonel. Above that comes the Sartip, which may be best translated colonel. This also has three grades, each marked by a star, and the highest grade by a ribbon as well, worn over the right shoulder. By the time, therefore, that a man has risen from a third-grade Sarhang to a first-grade Sartip he is decorated with six stars and a ribbon, and one would imagine him at first sight to be one of the most distinguished men of the realm, whereas in reality he possibly has never been out of a telegraph office in his life. Above the Sartip comes the Mir-i-Punj or general of 5000, and the Amir-i-Tuman or general of 10,000, and so on, each with their stars and ribbons; and by the time a Persian gets to really high rank he generally has the Shah in brilliants hung around his neck as well—not to mention the Order of the Lion and the Sun, so that he is, indeed, well decorated. The lower ranks consist of the Yawar, which is generally translated as major, and the Sultan as captain, and the Naib as lieutenant, but these men have no rank, and correspond more to the Subadar major, the Subadar and Jemadar of our Indian army.

Maral deer, I was told, abound in the jungles around Astarabad, and three young ones had been tamed and sent to Teheran shortly before my arrival. I did not see any maral myself, but I got a couple of pairs of horns as specimens, with fine branching antlers, one of ten and the other of thirteen points. Tigers, I was told, were now scarce. Formerly the skins could be purchased for eight or ten tumans, but now, owing to the demand for them from Russia, the price had gone up to thirty and forty tumans (£15 to £20), and more.

The sport of Astarabad was woodcock. Never before had I seen so many of these birds. The place seemed to abound in them. I could go out any day and kill half-a-dozen amongst the bushes in the old moat round the town within a few hundred yards of my camp, and every evening there was a constant firing of guns just at dusk, which I was told was caused by men who lay in wait after sunset to try and get shots at the woodcock as they flew into the gardens in the town from the thickets in the hills around. One good corner was a curious mound at the west of the town. This must have been a strong place in olden times. It was scarped all round in three terraces, one above the other, and a moat encircled it below. Old tiles and bits of brick were to be seen in it, as usual, sufficient to show that it was once inhabited, and at its northern end there was an old well which looked as if it must have been very deep in its day.

My final parting was with M. and Madame Kokhanovski, whose society I had much enjoyed during my stay. I left him busy superintending the erection of a new consulate, which promised to be a good residence when done. M. Kokhanovski wisely had a Russian in charge of the work. A Persian builder, if left to himself, almost invariably manages to put a beam or two across each chimney, and M. Kokhanovski, having narrowly escaped having had his old house burnt down over his head from that cause, had determined to do his best to prevent a similar catastrophe in the new one.

For the benefit of future travellers I here note a list of prices (opposite) at the principal places visited by me along the Khurasan border from Mashhad to Astarabad.

From Astarabad I marched to Dangalan, twelve miles, and on to Kurd Mahalla, eight miles farther, the next day. The people in both villages were most civil, and had rooms cleared and ready for me to put up in. They were a fair, yellowish-coloured race, quite different from any I had met before farther east. The villages were so hidden away in jungle that it was difficult to see where the houses were. Each house was in a separate enclosure by itself, and consisted of a long building raised off the ground on blocks of oak, with a large wooden summer-house attached, elevated on piles some twenty feet above

LIST OF PRICES

Name of Stage.	Barley, per kharwar (650 lbs).	Chopped Straw, per kharwar (650 lbs).	Lucerne, per kharwar (650 lbs).	Firewood, per kharwar (650 lbs).	Ghee, per man ($6\frac{1}{2}$ lbs).	Rice, per man ($6\frac{1}{2}$ lbs).	Sugar, per man ($6\frac{1}{2}$ lbs).	Sheep, each.	Fowls, each.	Chickens, each.	Eggs, per kran.	Bread, per kran.	Milk, per kran.	Remarks.
	T. K. S.	T. K. S.	T. K. S.	T. K. S.	T. K. S.	T. K. S.	T. K. S.	T. K. S.	T. K. S.	T. K. S.	NO.	MAN	MAN	1894.
1. Mashhad	2 5 0	0 8 0	2 8 10	1 4 0	0 6 0	0 3 5	0 5 10	0 8 0	0 0 15	0 0 15	20	$1\frac{1}{2}$	$1\frac{1}{2}$	24th Aug.
2. Kalat-i-Nadiri	3 6 7	1 0 0	3 3 7	1 0 0	0 6 0	...	...	...	0 1 0	0 0 10	...	$1\frac{1}{2}$	$1\frac{1}{2}$	31st ,,
3. Muhammadabad (Daragez)	3 6 7	1 2 0	3 3 7	2 0 0	1 3 0	0 3 10	0 6 0	0 7 0	0 1 0	0 0 15	30	$1\frac{1}{2}$	1	7th Sept.
4. Kuchan	2 8 10	1 2 0	2 8 10	1 2 10	0 9 0	0 2 10	0 6 0	0 7 0	0 0 15	0 0 10	30	$1\frac{1}{2}$	1	17th ,,
5. Bujnurd	2 5 0	0 9 0	2 8 10	1 2 10	0 9 0	0 2 5	0 5 0	0 9 0	0 1 0	0 0 10	40	$1\frac{1}{2}$	$1\frac{1}{2}$	2nd Oct.
6. Goklan country	3 5 0	0 5 0	...	...	0 9 0	0 2 0	0 7 0	1 0 0	0 0 15	0 0 10	16	$1\frac{1}{8}$	$1\frac{1}{8}$	6th Nov.
7. Yamut ,,	5 9 14	1 3 13	...	...	1 3 4	0 2 16	0 7 18	1 1 14	0 1 0	0 0 10	6	$\frac{7}{11}$	$\frac{9}{11}$	1st Dec.
8. Astarabad	3 3 7	1 0 0	...	0 4 0	0 8 0	0 1 10	0 5 0	1 0 0	0 1 0	0 0 10	20	1	2	13th ,,

1 tuman=10 krans. 1 kran=20 shahis or $5\frac{5}{7}$ annas, or $4\frac{2}{3}$ pence at the exchange of 1894.

the ground, and with a thatched roof, in which the people slept in summer. The woodwork of these buildings was excellent, and so were the stake fences round the enclosures. Each village owned large herds of cattle, which mostly found their way, I was told, to Russian territory for beef.

The remaining fourteen miles on to Bandar-i-Gaz was hard travelling through deep mud, and took us five hours to do. The country looked charming. The hills above were covered with oak and sprinkled with snow, and the road below ran through masses of bracken and brambles, with wild pomegranate bushes and thorns, interspersed with oak and other trees. Hawthorns, curiously, were both in flower and in berry at the same time. Robins, chaffinches, and other small birds abounded, and ploughing was in full swing. At Bandar-i-Gaz I was put up in the house of the Sarhadhár, as the Persian local official was called, a two-storeyed building on the very edge of the sea. The village of Gaz lies some two miles inland, and the landing-place on the sea-shore is locally known by the name of Kinárah. Here I suddenly found myself in what seemed the midst of civilisation. The bazar was full of Russians and Russian-Armenians, and shortly after my arrival the Russian consular agent came to call. The little Russian man-of-war coming in from Ashurada for provisions, and a small steamer busy unloading sugar, gave quite a look of life and activity to the place. The porters who carried bales to and fro along the wooden pier were all Persians, but otherwise the population of the small bazar seemed to be almost entirely Russian. Except the Sarhadhár and the customs officer, I could hardly see a Persian in the place.

During the three days I spent at Kinárah the weather was perfect, and I had some pleasant rides along the shore, and various trips out to sea in the little dugouts, called *taimúl*, that the people used here. The sea was alive with water-fowl, but it was impossible to get near them. Wild swans were in flocks all along the coast, and many a long shot I had at them, both from my dug-out at sea and also from the shore; but only one did I bag, and it was, I think, the toughest bird that ever I tried to eat. Wild donkey, I came to the conclusion, was succulent in comparison. However, to sit in the *taimúl* and be paddled about on a sea like glass was a pleasure of itself, despite the aggravating habits of the wild ducks that would take flight just out of shot, not to mention the charm of gazing at the lovely wooded mountains above, after the many miles of arid country that one had been marching through during the last four months. A fine day in December in Mazandaran most certainly has a charm peculiarly its own.

On the 21st December the mail steamer arrived, and I got on board, but with some difficulty, as a rough sea had got up. I found that the captain and mate and both first and second engineers were all Courlanders or Baltic Province men, who spoke English, having spent most of their lives in sailing to English ports. The Kavkas & Mercury Company's boats on the Caspian are largely officered by Finns and Baltic Province men, whereas in the Russian Navigation Company's boats on the Black Sea the officers are almost all pure Russians, and speak Russian only.

We lay to for a couple of hours on the 22nd off Chikisliar, one of the dreariest-looking spots I have ever seen. Nothing was visible but a bank of sand, with a white building in the centre and a Turkoman *obah* or cluster of *kibitkas* on the one side and a few huts on the other. Steaming on, we anchored at the mouth of the Uzunada Channel the next morning, and were kept there two days taking in cargo, finally arriving at Baku, on the opposite shore, on the afternoon of Christmas Day. The Caspian Sea, so the captain told me, was drying up at the rate, it was calculated, of nine feet in a hundred years. There were two depressions in the sea, he said—one to the north of Baku, with a depth of 420 feet, and one to the south, near Enzelli, with a depth of 520 feet, while right across the centre there was an elevated ridge which it was supposed was once dry, as there were the remains of a stone-paved road running into the sea to the north of Baku, and coming out again on the eastern shore, he said, where wheel-marks worn deep in the stones were clearly visible.

The whole of the Caspian seemed to be full of oil, and I was shown specimens of paraffin dug up from the bed of it in the form of a sort of dried cake, that may create an industry of its own some day quite apart from the oil wells of Baku. This latter town had grown enormously since I first landed at it fifteen years before. The population was said to be something like 120,000, of which the larger portion was Persian. The increase in the shipping was the most wonderful of all. There were then, I believe, 180 steamers on the Caspian, many of which were to be seen at Baku lying up stern end on to the shore for the winter, while there were some hundreds of small three-masted sailing vessels in addition, mostly employed in carrying kerosene to Astrakhan during the summer months.

Leaving Baku on Christmas night, I arrived at Tiflis (335 miles) the next evening, and at Batoum, 225 miles farther on, the following morning; and after spending a pleasant day with Mr. Stevens, the British consul, I caught the boat for Odessa, and was in London in another eight days.

My next visit to Persia was to Teheran, and I did not

see Khurasan again for nearly two years. It was in November 1896 that I made the return journey. This time I took the route *viâ* Petrovsk, and leaving London on the 1st November and travelling *viâ* Warsaw and Moscow, at each of which places I spent a night, I arrived at Petrovsk (3164 miles) on the 10th, in time to catch the weekly mail steamer to Krasnovodsk. Petrovsk was not a large place, but was gradually extending. No troops were quartered in the town, at least not in any number, there were no manufactories, and the place had none of the life and bustle of Baku. The harbour, I was told, had been frozen up for three weeks in the winter, and on that account the Russian Government were extending the railway along the coast to Baku, so as to ensure open communication all the year round. When one thinks of the marvellous development of trade on the Caspian and the great increase of shipping during the last few years, one can quite understand the necessity for uninterrupted communication. The traffic across the Caspian was alone very great; the piers on both sides were crammed with goods; Astrakhan was getting more difficult to approach every year, the steamers having to unload some twelve miles out; and Petrovsk was therefore sure to develop.

I arrived at Krasnovodsk (520 versts, or 346 miles, from Petrovsk) at 3 P.M. on the 12th, and started by rail for Ashkabad the same evening. The surroundings of Krasnovodsk were not at all inviting, bare hot hills bordering it all round to the north. The houses were low but well built, and the streets all ran to the shore, where the rails were laid right down to the wooden piers. Various enclosures and storehouses were in course of erection; the railway station, a fine large building, was already completed; and the place looked as if it would soon be an important terminus.

CHAPTER XVII.

MASHHAD AGAIN.

AT Ashkabad, where I arrived on the 13th November 1896, I found myself welcomed by M. Klem, the Russian Foreign Office representative in Transcaspia, with a kind message from General Kuropatkine, the governor-general, to say that he would be glad to see me in the evening. M. Klem was kind enough to call for me at the hotel, and drove me to the general's house, where we had a pleasant talk. Next morning I drove off to the Persian frontier. Raza Beg, Ghulam, had been sent from Mashhad to meet me, and had made arrangements for the hire of a *kaliska*, a strong low victoria drawn by four horses abreast, and with him on the box, and my baggage strapped on behind, we did the thirty-two miles to the Shamkhal caravansarai in about six hours. At Goudan, the Russian frontier station, I found a couple of Russian customs officers, who passed my luggage with much civility. It was quite a small place, with only two or three low buildings in it, and there was no large frontier guard. Here I met Captain Baumgarten, who had been sent out by General Kuropatkine to meet Mr. Ney Elias, whom I was going to relieve, and both he and the customs officer came over and dined with us the next day.

The difference of cost in travelling through Russia and through Persia was here very marked. Russia is the

GENERAL KUROPATKINE, GOVERNOR-GENERAL OF TRANSCASPIA.

cheapest country in the world to travel in so far as I know. My railway ticket from Krasnovodsk to Ashkabad, a distance of 340 miles, only cost about eight roubles, and my whole journey from London to Ashkabad, a total of some 3850 miles, including hotel bills for two nights and £8 for luggage, cost only £33. Once in Persia, the case was very different. The hire of a *kaliska* for myself, and a *fourgon* or waggon for my servants and baggage, for the remaining 132 miles from Ashkabad to Mashhad cost me £9.

At Shamkhal I found Mr. Elias, with Moula Bakhsh and other old familiar faces from Mashhad, awaiting my arrival. We saw Mr. Elias off on his journey to England. He was most kindly and hospitably looked after all the way through Transcaspia by Captain Baumgarten, who did not leave him till he had seen him safely on board the steamer at Krasnovodsk. Nothing could have been kinder than the way he was treated. Shamkhal still consisted of nothing but the large square caravansarai, with a row of small domed rooms all round the inside of it, and a stable at the far end. In these buildings the traveller can reckon on four bare walls and a roof to shelter him, but bed and bedding, tables and chairs, food and cooking things, must all be brought with him, or else, as in my case, they must be there to meet him.

Having seen Mr. Elias off, Moula Bakhsh and I drove to Imam Kulia, 24 miles, slept the night in the village there, and on to Kuchan, 24 miles farther, the next day. Kuchan I found to be no longer the old town that I saw after its destruction by earthquake in 1894. A new Kuchan was being built eight miles to the east of the old town, near the village of Haihai, and walls and streets had been laid out, and houses were being built. All the traders, the people who lived on travellers, and the followers and retainers of the chief, were locating themselves in the new town, and no one but the owners of the gardens and vineyards, who were loth to move and preferred to risk the chance of a fresh earthquake, had remained near old Kuchan.

The road from Ashkabad to Mashhad is by no means the *chaussée* that its name would signify. The Russians have put some gravel on it for the first four or five miles out of Ashkabad, but beyond that it is entirely unmetalled. The portion through the mountains from Ashkabad to Kuchan is mostly zigzagged along the hill-sides, and the soil being stony, there is not so much need of metal. It is difficult, though, for carts to cross each other in places, the turns are very sharp, and the retaining walls have no parapets. The greater part of the way is either ascent or descent. From Shamkhal to Imam Kulia there is a long ascent, and then a steep descent, with many short turns and sharp corners, down to the gorge at Durbadam, where the rocks have been blasted out just wide enough for a cart to pass, but not wide enough for two to cross each other. From Imam Kulia to Kuchan the ascent is comparatively short, with a long descent which the horses did at a round trot almost all the way. We were lucky thus to get through while the road was frozen hard, and before the winter snow had fallen in any quantity. Later on I heard of some Persian travellers who were snowed up for a fort-night on this part of the road, and could move neither one way nor the other. So late as the end of March the deep snow rendered the road almost impassable, and Duke, who was then travelling on it, was snowed up for two days, and got through with the greatest difficulty; and no heavily laden vehicle could have got through at all. I mention this to show that a journey during the winter months along this road is a risky matter.

Servants are often a careless class all the world over,

but for absolute inability to take care of themselves in strange countries I think the native of India stands pre-eminent. Many of us can call to mind the apparently persistent efforts of the native follower to kill himself when on service on the frontier or in Afghanistan, and I noticed the same trait in my Indian cook during this very drive. He had been given a *postin* or sheepskin coat to keep himself warm with, but instead of wearing it, as all of us did when driving through the cold and snow, he carefully packed it up and sent it on ahead in the waggon, and spent the day on the box of my carriage, blue with cold and with a rapidly increasing cough, which took a long time to cure.

At Kuchan we spent the night in the new caravansarai then being built. Next morning we were up early and drove on twenty-four miles to Maksudabad, over a very rough road, which would have been impassable had it been wet. From Kuchan the road runs through the alluvial soil of the plain, and in wet weather during winter and spring this portion of the road would be just as impassable as a black cotton-soil road in Central India during the rainy season. The mud would have been at least a foot deep when we passed, but fortunately the weather was fine and clear, and the mud had been frozen hard, and we thus bumped over it without sticking.

Next day the road was better and smoother, and we did our twenty miles to Chinaran in little over three hours. We had to make a long detour to a village named Saidabad, to avoid a broken bridge; and the story runs that whenever this bridge is repaired—and that is seldom under Persian management—the grocer at Saidabad promptly breaks it down again, to obtain the custom that accrues to his shop in the village from travellers passing to and fro through it.

Chinaran belongs to Zafaranlu Kurds, and was at one

time an important place. During the reign of Fateh Ali Shah it came into prominence under Mamesh Khan, who raised himself from a petty head-man to the position of an independent ruler. The possessions of the tribe then extended up the valley as far as Kuchan, and down to Gunabad, within twenty miles of Mashhad. After Mamesh Khan's death the family of the chief gradually lost its importance. His sons and grandsons were deprived of their possessions, the greater part of which fell into the hands of the chiefs of Kuchan and Radkhan. The last mention I can find of the family is of one Hasan Khan Chinarani, who attacked the citadel of Mashhad during the Salar's rebellion in 1847 and was killed. The Kurds of Chinaran now number about 800 families, and have no recognised chief, only head-men of sections.

From Chinaran we travelled to Kasimabad, twenty-eight miles. There I received a post from Mashhad with the programme of the *istikbal* or official reception that was in store for me in the morning, similar to that which had greeted me on my arrival at Mashhad in September 1893. My first post had met me on the road some six or eight miles north of Kuchan, carried by one of our Turkoman postal couriers, and afforded another instance of what excellent men they are. Leaving Mashhad in the evening, the man had ridden the eighty-four miles to Kuchan straight off, arriving there the next night, and after resting his horse had started on again to find me wherever I was. On meeting me he turned and rode back with me into Kuchan, and after a few hours' rest for his horse, started off to Mashhad again the same afternoon with my return post, thus doing his 184 miles almost straight on end, on the same horse, within three days, without thinking of it, and curiously enough this man, though dressed as a Turkoman, was in reality a Persian. He had been carried off when a boy by Sarik

Turkoman raiders to Panjdeh, and grew up a Turkoman. When the Afghan Boundary Commission under General Sir Peter Lumsden arrived at Panjdeh in 1884 he took service with the Commission as a postal sowar, and he had remained in the British service ever since. On coming to Persia he traced his relatives in a village in the Turbat-i-Haidari district, and was recognised by them from certain marks on his body. They gave him a wife and tried to induce him to stay with them, but without effect. He did not care for their village life, and preferred to remain in the British Consulate, where no one would ever take him for a Persian.

Turkomans I should not call the best material for soldiers. They never showed any conspicuous bravery in their ancient raids that one reads of; on the contrary, they generally seem to have retired at once when any real resistance was offered. Though excellent horsemen, I doubt if they would make good regular cavalry. The Russians, at any rate, have not attempted to utilise their services in that way. As irregulars, though, they are excellent. They are handy, willing, and obedient men, inured to hard work and long distances, with open, honest countenances as a rule, and with a great sense of honour—a commodity so rare amongst the people they live amongst. The Bokharans to the north and the Persians to the south have neither of them the sense of honour and loyalty to their employer that the Turkoman has. If a Turkoman says he will do a thing he will do it, and say not a word. With a Persian it is just the contrary; a thousand excuses will be forthcoming, and the work not done. The fertility of the Persian mind in inventing reasons for not doing anything is truly marvellous.

The morning of the 23rd November 1897 saw me driving in the last twelve miles to Mashhad in full uniform, and cold work it was, English uniform not being calculated for winter wear in Central Asia. The reception tents were pitched near the road, about a mile outside the town, and there the Persian reception party were assembled. I was met on the road by all the Consulate establishment. At the reception tent, in addition to the Persian officials, were the British Indian subjects residing in Mashhad, traders from Peshawar, Dera Ismail Khan, and Peshin, as well as old Reuben the Jew, here known as Haji Abdar Rahman, Jadidi or Mussulman convert, a British pensioner from the old days at Kabul in the first Afghan war, when his father did service.

The traders had a sad tale to tell me. They said that the Russian customs dues lately imposed on the frontier had put a stop to all their trade. English piece goods, they said, were rigidly excluded; muslin, tea, and indigo were the only things admitted, and these were taxed so highly that little profit was to be made. Altogether, they said, they were in a bad way.

After duly partaking of tea and sweetmeats, &c., with the Persian officials, we all mounted our horses and rode in through the town to the British Consulate. The procession was a motley one. First came the Persian cavalry sowars, dressed as Cossacks, in long, red coats; then all the mounted Persians, followed by Turkoman couriers, Indian cavalry and Indians generally, with some twenty of the Governor-General's *farashes* and Persian infantry soldiers walking in Indian file on either side of us. The incongruous part of the whole thing to our eyes, though not to the Persians, was the raggedness of the Persian soldiers' uniforms. These men were out at elbows, out in the seats of their trousers, out in their boots, out everywhere, not only those marching alongside of us, but the various city guards in the streets, who were all turned out for the occasion. However, every Persian goose is a swan in the eyes of a Persian, and a little raggedness in their soldiers was nothing to them, and by no means detracted from their appearance in their eyes. At the Consulate the Persian officials had their tea and pipes, and after their departure an English-speaking Persian *muhandis* or engineer, educated at Teheran, arrived with the usual trays of sweetmeats to inquire after my health on the part of the Governor-General. During my absence the Muaiyid-ud-Dowlah had left, and the Asaf-ud-Dowlah now reigned in his stead. The latter received us in full uniform, with his stars and sash on, and the portrait of the Shah in brilliants round his neck, and returned my visit in due course. He was the chief of the Shahsun or Shahsawand tribe of Turks scattered about in the Teheran, Kazvin, and Zinjan districts. His father, the Shahab-ul-Mulk, had been Governor-General of Khurasan in 1873–74, but was recalled, and died soon after at Teheran. His eldest son succeeded him in the chiefship, and was given the title of Shahab-ul-Mulk in his father's place. He had been at times governor of Mazandaran, Kirman, and Arabistan, and was appointed Governor-General of Khurasan in 1895, and also received the title of Asaf-ud-Dowlah.

It was pleasant to meet my old colleague M. Vlassow again, and it was not long before I found myself seated at his hospitable table once more.

The first official function after my arrival was the Czar's name-day, on the 18th December, the festival that corresponds in Russia to our Queen's birthday. So far as I can understand the actual birthday is never kept in Russia, but the saint's day after whom the person is named, and the Russian Church permits no name to be given to any one except that of a saint.

M. Vlassow held his official reception in the forenoon,

and received us in full uniform. Russian officers are generally well decorated, but Russian diplomatic and consular officers appear to be more than usually so. The diplomatic and consular services in Russia are not separate as in England, but are all one. In Russia, too, the diplomatic and consular appointments in the East are considered higher and more important than those in the West. Special training is considered necessary for dealing with the Oriental, and an appointment in Europe is considered child's play after one in Asia. This is just the opposite to what it is with us. A consul-general in Russia ranks as a major-general, and wears the uniform, such as the white trousers, &c., pertaining to that grade. All precedence in Russia goes by military rank, and every civil official has relative rank and takes precedence accordingly. Apparently the nobility have no special precedence in Russia as with us in England. A man takes precedence according to the grade in which his official position puts him, and the system more corresponds with our Indian table of precedence than with that in England.

M. Vlassow's morning reception was followed by the customary official dinner in the evening. The governor-general sat on M. Vlassow's right and I sat on his left, with the Karguzar opposite. Then came the Wazir, the Persian artillery general, the telegraph Sartip, the members of the Russian Consulate and of the Imperial Bank of Persia at Mashhad, my assistant, Moula Bakhsh, and the Russian telegraph clerk, who appeared in a gorgeous uniform for the occasion and was apparently an officer of rank, something like the Persian telegraphists. The Governor-General proposed the health of H.I.M. the Czar, and M. Vlassow, in reply, proposed the health of H.M. the Shah of Persia and of H.M. the Queen of England and Empress of India. The consulate gardens were prettily illuminated, and we all had a pleasant evening.

After this came Christmas, and this in Mashhad was doubly merry, as we had two Christmases and two New Year's Days to celebrate, the Russian and the English respectively. It was on New Year's Eve at the Russian Consulate that I had my first introduction to what M. Vlassow called his *zzonka* or *jonka*, a speciality of his own in the way of liquor for festive occasions. The making of this was an anxious business, and commenced about half-an-hour before midnight. First of all, a large copper cooking-pot was brought in and put upon the stove. Into this was emptied a bottle of claret and a bottle of burgundy. When they were heated up a bottle of grave and another of sauterne were added. Then on the top of the pot were laid three broad iron spits—in military circles these would have been officers' swords. On these was placed the top end of a large loaf of sugar, a piece some four or five inches in height, and over this was poured, by spoonfuls at a time, a bottle of brandy and another of rum. The wine below was heating up all this time. The sugar was finally set on fire, and kept on fire by constant additions of brandy and rum till it was nearly all melted and burnt away. The burning spirit dropped into the boiling wine below, which was kept constantly stirred with a big ladle, and eventually the whole mass took fire. Two pots of jam were then emptied into it to sweeten it still more, and at midnight M. Vlassow ladled out his mixture into glasses, and we all drank to a happy new year.

The new year was a cold one. The thermometer went down very nearly to zero, and we all settled down to a quiet winter life. I and my orderlies used generally to scour the country around every morning. Mashhad, although such an unpromising-looking place for sport, generally produced something for us to have a shot at. The sand-grouse went off to warmer regions in the south before the extreme cold commenced, and did not return till about the Persian new year, the 21st March, but a few partridge and *tihu* or little hill partridges were generally to be found in the hills about, though how any partridges were left in the country at all was a mystery to me. In the winter the bazars of Mashhad were full of them, and apparently they were trapped and shot in hundreds when driven down from the hills by the snow. In the summer, too, they had no rest. The Shikaris had a fatal way of potting them from behind a screen in the same way as they did in Sistan. The man starts out armed with his screen of dirty yellow cloth, say six feet by four, generally patched and streaked with other colours, and stretched on a couple of sticks like a kite. Unrolling this, he fixes it up by fitting the points of the sticks into each corner. Immediately over the crossed sticks in the centre is a round hole about the size of a cricket ball for the gun to go through. Above that again are two small holes for the man's eyes. Holding the screen close in front of him and looking through the eyelet holes, the man stalks up to his birds. The latter, for some reason best known to themselves, are attracted by the screen and allow the man to circle round and approach them within a few yards. They generally collect together in a lump, and then the man shoots them through the gun-hole. Duke told me the black partridge behaves differently from the red-legged partridge, as he once watched the whole performance from a steamer going up the Tigris. He saw a man creeping along behind a screen. Suddenly a black partridge ran up the bank, stretched out his neck, and fluttering his wings along the ground, approached the screen by a succession of short rushes. When quite close a puff of smoke appeared, and poor blackie was seen rolling down the bank. What excites the curiosity or wrath of these birds I cannot think, but apparently the *chakor*, though not as much affected by it as the black partridge, still falls a victim, and so does the *tihu* or *sisi*; and considering that guns of sorts can be bought in Mashhad for two or three tumans (eight to twelve shillings), and that the number of shooters is legion, not to mention the hawks, the marvel is that any birds at all remain.

The Kashaf Rud River, five miles to the north of Mashhad, was a sure find for an odd duck or a teal or two, while, as the weather got colder, large flocks of the big European bustard appeared. They were very wild, being constantly shot at by native gunners, and it was impossible to get near them in the open plain, but my orderlies soon became comparative experts at driving them, and they were often able to send them over my head as I lay low in some hole in the ground.

The first I shot scaled 17½ lbs., and the next 15 lbs., while the smallest specimen I saw weighed 11 lbs. They were capital eating.

At the approach of spring, in the beginning of March 1897, Mashhad was startled by the arrival of Russian officers, doctors, and Cossacks to patrol the Persian frontier, so they said, against the plague which had appeared at Bombay. There was no plague in either Baluchistan, Afghanistan, or Persia, but despite that, some 150 Russian Cossacks were sent into Persia and posted as a military cordon all along the Persian-Afghan frontier, from Zulfikar southwards to Hashtadan, with doctors at Karez and Turbat-i-Haidari, and all traffic was forbidden between Persia and Afghanistan or Baluchistan. Not only was no one permitted to cross from Afghanistan into Persia, but no one in Persia was permitted to return to Afghanistan. The roads were entirely blocked, and all trade between the two countries was brought to a standstill. This, of course, gave rise to much dissatisfaction in Mashhad, which had a large and old standing trade with Herat, and was dependent on the latter place to a large extent for various commodities, which rose greatly in price accordingly.

So strict was the régime that my post-bag from Quetta through Kandahar and Herat was stopped, and was only allowed eventually to pass after the bag had been opened and every envelope snipped and fumigated, a ridiculous precaution, considering that it had been three weeks on the road from Quetta alone, whereas ten days was the limit for all quarantine. The result of the blockade was that, under the plea of plague, British Indian trade with Mashhad was put a stop to entirely for the time, and the Afghan trade was diverted from Persia into Russia through Panjdeh. The merchants in Mashhad lost heavily, many became bankrupt, and the state of things was very unsatisfactory.

The first Russian officer to arrive in Mashhad was Captain Benderoff, a Bulgarian who was said to have been concerned in the abduction of Prince Alexander of Battenberg, and had been given a commission in the Russian army. He took charge of the Persian-Afghan frontier, and remained in charge all through the year. The Russian Cossacks under his orders practically took possession of eastern Khurasan. They were subsequently relieved by men of the Persian Cossack Brigade from Teheran, but these were also under a Russian officer, and to all intents and purposes were Russian troops. In fact the Cossack Brigade at Teheran may be said to answer very much to our Haidarabad contingent in India.

The squadron of the Persian Cossack Brigade that I saw at Mashhad were wonderful in comparison with Persian troops. They were drilled, disciplined, clothed, paid and looked after, and reflected credit on their Russian officers for having made so much out of such material. The men were mounted, though, on ponies that evidently would not stand the wear and tear of a campaign. In fact their march from Teheran to Mashhad alone had told heavily on them in this respect, and, though valuable for the preservation of order in Teheran, the men did not look to me as if they would be of much use on hard service.

On the 21st March came the Nouroz, or the Persian New Year, the great Persian festival, and the only national festival the Persians have, one may say, that is unconnected with religion or mourning of some sort or another. All servants and dependents come up on that day to make their salaams, and every man expects his present. It is the Persian Christmas, in fact, and the festivities connected therewith are supposed to last into April.

On the thirteenth day after the Nouroz the whole of Mashhad migrates in a body outside the town—that is to say, the whole of mankind. Women, for some reason or another, are rigidly excluded from this day's outing. When I passed the Suráb gate, going out for my ride in the early morning I found a special guard posted there. I asked them the reason for it, and they told me that they were there to prevent any women leaving the town. This order, I was told, was issued at the instance of the priests, who, when powerful enough to get their wishes enforced, always prevent the women going out to participate in the festivities of this particular day. As a rule the women get out despite the priests, but this year the latter were too much for them, and they were all shut in, and were limited in their revels to the gardens inside the walls of the town. It is a fixed custom in Persia that everybody must leave their own house and go out on this day, otherwise ill-luck and misfortune will overtake them.

On my return from my ride I found men and boys flocking out in hundreds, and carts and waggons were busy plying outside, taking people up to Koh-i-Sangi, which seemed to be a favourite place of resort. My orderlies celebrated the day by tent-pegging and lime-cutting, which attracted large crowds, so much so that I feared some accident would occur. However, fortunately we escaped any contretemps of that sort, and we were able to continue the practice regularly every week all through the summer. The Turkomans used to join in with a will, and their efforts always caused much amusement. Nothing that we could do would induce them to sit down in their saddles and ride at their peg. A Turkoman galloping is all legs and boots, which go flying about in every direction. They are by no means good swordsmen either, though always keen.

Spring at Mashhad is a charming time, and the whole country seems to blossom out. Birds of all sorts appear to breed. The blue jay or Indian roller—the Kulagh-i-Sabz or green crow, as it is called by the Persians—comes in hundreds and takes possession of almost every nullah bank, closely followed by that gay bird, the European bee-eater, which similarly lays its eggs in a hole in some bank. Almost every Kanat well has its pair of pied wagtails, the sky is full of swallows and swifts, and the Persian nightingale sings and breeds in the gardens. At one time I had two nightingales' nests and six or seven nests of a little tree-warbler in my garden, all within a few yards of the front-door steps. Soon after the middle of April the quail appear, and the cock birds are netted in large numbers, by means of calls, in the young wheat-crops, and sold in the bazar at the rate of six for a kran. They breed around the town, and towards the end of July, after the corn is cut, young quails are to be found in the grain-fields, and are excellent eating. Another bird that breeds in Khurasan in large numbers is the rose-coloured starling, the Sár, as the Persians call it. The Koh-i-Sangi to the south-west of the town is a favourite resort of these birds; large flocks gather there, and breed amongst the tumbled mass of rocks and boulders that forms the western end of the hill. In June, when the young birds are fledged, men and boys go out from the town with baskets and catch them in numbers. It is a curious sight hunting about the rocks for the nests. The old birds sit around, jabbering away as hard as they can, almost every one of them with either a grasshopper or a white mulberry in its mouth for the benefit of the young birds that, alas for them, are being ruthlessly carried off.

The 24th of May found us busy again with our Queen's birthday festivities, the same as those described before in 1894. I held my reception in the morning. The first to appear were the Shaukat-ud-Dowlah, the Timuri chief, and the chief of the post-office, both in full uniform, one resplendent with the star and sash of Amir-i-Tuman, and the other with that of a Mir Panj. Next came the artillery general, with the Motamim-i-Lashkar, a sort of paymaster-general, decorated with the portrait of the Shah round his neck. After him came the Karguzar, the telegraph-general, the passport officer, the colonel of the Firozkoh Battalion, the protector of the health, and various others. After them came all the British-Indian subjects, and finally M. Vlassow and all the members of the Russian Consulate. We sat down a party of fourteen to dinner in the evening, and twelve the evening after.

On the 26th May we all rode out to Zachariah, a little village at the foot of the Koh-i-Sangi hills, to a picnic in celebration of M. Vlassow's birthday, the last that we were to celebrate together, as shortly after this M. Vlassow was summoned to St. Petersburg to take up his appointment as Russian Minister to Abyssinia. On the morning of the 12th June we saw him and Madame Vlassow off on their way to Doshakh, the nearest and most convenient railway station for Mashhad for those who are not compelled to drive.

This year Mashhad had again to experience a change of Persian governors, and the Asaf-ud-Dowlah had to give place to H.R.H. the Rukn-ud-Dowlah, the youngest brother of Nasir-ud-Din Shah. The change was a very sudden one, and typical of Persian ways. A telegram was received one day to say that the Asaf-ud-Dowlah had been recalled and the Rukn-ud-Dowlah appointed in his place, and from that moment the Asaf-ud-Dowlah and all his officials were out of power. The Beglar Begi, the police magistrate of the town, when appealed to in some case, said he was out of office and could do nothing, and the highest in the place were at once nobodies. A nominal deputy-governor was appointed, but nothing could be done by anybody; and as to the Asaf-ud-Dowlah, his sole anxiety seemed to be to pack up and get away as quickly as possible. It was not till nearly a month afterwards that the Ain-ul-Mulk, the eldest son of the Rukn-ud-Dowlah, arrived at Mashhad to take over charge on the part of his father, and the latter himself did not arrive till the autumn.

I duly paid my visit to the Ain-ul-Mulk. His Highness received us in a tent in the citadel garden, and returned my visit the next day. His father, as the brother of the late and uncle of the reigning Shah, did not return visits, but the nephews and cousins of the Shah had no such privilege, and his Highness returned the visits of M. Vlassow and myself without the slightest demur. His rank, however, was the cause of much etiquette amongst the Persians, and at my garden party reception on the 22nd July 1897, the day of her Majesty the Queen-Empress's Jubilee, none of the Persian officials could come in till after his Highness had left, as none of them could sit in his presence. Official receptions are rather hot affairs in the East in the height of summer, and from the middle of June to the middle of August the heat in the town of Mashhad was often great; still, the British Consulate being situated at the highest point of it, close to the citadel, and with open ground and gardens all round it, escaped the closeness that enveloped the rest of the town. I was often advised to go out into camp in the hills at this time, but I found it more comfortable on the whole to remain at home. The rays of the sun are so hot in the extraordinary clear climate of Persia, and they beat down so unmercifully on an unprotected tent; whereas with a double-storeyed house the lower storey is always comparatively cool, and the thermometer in my hall, with doors and windows open, rarely rose above 75° or 77° Fahrenheit. Only once do I remember it going up to 80°, and that was in a hot week just at the end of July.

Mashhad in this respect was a great contrast to Transcaspia. While we were well and cool we heard that last year's fever had broken out again in Merv. The Russian infantry had been sent away to Krasnovodsk on the Caspian Sea, and the Cossacks to Yulatan, and the whole place was more or less deserted. Doctors were sent up to try and combat the outbreak, but with all their efforts it was said there had been a total loss of some 24,000 lives since the fever first appeared. No wonder that the Russians in Transcaspia should look with longing eyes on the healthy temperate uplands of Khurasan, when their life in the sandy plains below is such a burden to them. Panjdeh boils, Merv fever, and Ashkabad heat are all hard to bear. The houses, too, at Ashkabad and elsewhere are all built more or less on the ordinary Russian pattern, without upper storeys or verandas, and with small rooms and little windows. They are well calculated to keep out cold, but not to keep out heat, and consequently the residents suffer more than they otherwise would in the hot weather.

On 9th July 1897 M. Ponafidine, the new Russian Consul-General, arrived with his wife and family. He was met and escorted in by the same Persian *istikbal* that I was received with on arrival, and had the same round of ceremonial visits to go through. M. Ponafidine was already known by name in India, having been a member of the Pamir Boundary Commission, and before that Russian Consul at Baghdad. Speaking English well, our circle at Mashhad was thus pleasantly maintained.

M. PONAFIDINE, RUSSIAN CONSUL-GENERAL AT MASHHAD.

CHAPTER XVIII.

HISTORY AND ANTIQUITIES OF MASHHAD.

It was not till I had been for some time a resident at Mashhad that I began to get hold of its history, and to realise what it was that gave the place such a hold upon the Persian mind. At first I could get little information, but eventually Moula Bakhsh obtained a copy of the Sani-ud-Dowlah's works on the subject, and these were of great assistance to us. I have already more than once mentioned the Sani-ud-Dowlah's name, and I may now explain who he was. His real name was Muhammad Hasan Khan, the son of Haji Ali Khan, Itimad-us-Sultanah, one of Nasir-ud-Din Shah's ministers, who died about 1872. He was French interpreter to Nasir-ud-Din Shah, and was afterwards promoted to be press minister and granted the title of Sani-ud-Dowlah. He accompanied the Shah on his journey to Khurasan at the end of A.H. 1300 (A.D. 1882), when he collected historical and geographical information about the different places in the districts he passed through, and embodied it in a book called the "Matla'-ush-Shams," literally the horizon of the sun, or, in other words, Khurasan. The book was published in three volumes in the years 1301–2 and 1303 A.H. Volume i. contains an account of the Shah's journey from Teheran to Mashhad *viá* Firozkoh, Damghán, Bostam, Nardin, Jajarm, Bujnurd, Kuchan, Radkhan, and

Túa. Volume ii. is devoted to Mashhad, and contains a historical and geographical account of the town, a description of its buildings, and a history of its notable men. Volume iii. contains an account of the Shah's return journey from Mashhad to Teheran *viâ* Nishapur, Sabzawár, Mazinán, Shahrud, Damghán, and Semnán. The Sani-ud-Dowlah was subsequently given his father's title of Itimad-us-Sultanah, and died in Teheran in 1895. He compiled altogether some two dozen books, almost all of them on geographical, historical, and other such subjects connected with Persia, but they are little known, and have never been translated. I have therefore quoted from him largely.

The town of Mashhad is generally supposed to have been populated by the gradual absorption of the people of Tús. This town is said to have been built by Tús, the son of Nouzar, the son of Jamshid, Peshdadi, who gave it his own name. It is generally supposed to have been gradually deserted, but how far this is the case it is difficult to ascertain, as it appears that the town gave its name to the district, and that it is in that sense that it was mentioned by the Arab geographers. In Ouseley's translation of Ibn Haukal, amongst the places depending on and bounding Nishapúr, Tús is mentioned as "to the north of Nishapour, where is the Meshid of Ali-ben-Mousa-al-Redha, on whom be the blessing of God. There also is the burial-place of Haroun." To this Ouseley adds a footnote that "the Khalif Haroun Arrashid died in the year of the Hegira 193 (A.D. 808.)." This is the only mention that I can find of Tús in Ouseley's Ibn Haukal, and in that the word Tús apparently refers to the district, Mashhad being some sixteen miles to the south-east of the ruins now known as Tús. The Sani-ud-Dowlah, however, gives the following quotations, which he says are also from Ibn Haukal, viz.:—

"Taking Tús as a dependency of Nishabur, its towns are Radkhan and Tabiran, Bazdghur and Nughán. The tomb of Hazrat Ali, son of Musa Raza, is in Nughán; so is the tomb of Harún-ur-Rashid. The dome of Hazrat Raza is at a distance of a quarter of a farsakh from the town, in the village of Sanabad."

In another place he adds:—

"Both tombs are situated in a fine building in a village called Sanabad, and round this village is a strong wall; and a large number of people believe in this Mashhad (place of martyrdom)."

The exact date when Ibn Haukal wrote is unknown, but Ouseley places him in the beginning or middle of the tenth century, between the years 902 and 968 A.D. Tús, however, was a flourishing city when the poet Firdúsi died there in 1021. It is related that before his death the poet vowed to devote the reward due to him by Sultan Mahmud of Ghazni, for the writing of the Shah-nama, to the bringing of water to Tús for the benefit of the city. He died before the reward came, but his daughter eventually received it, and she dutifully expended the money in carrying out her father's intentions. The water she brought was that from the spring now known as Chashma Gilas, which issues at the foot of the hills on the eastern side of the valley some fourteen or fifteen miles above Tús. The original name of this spring is said to have been Gulasb, and it was here that Yazdijard was kicked by a horse. Gulasb has now become corrupted into Gilas. The water was taken by a canal from the spring to Tús. After the ruin of Tús it was brought on to Mashhad by Amir Ali Sher, Wazir of Sultan Hussain Baikara (d. 1506), in a canal which is said to be twelve farsakhs or forty-eight miles in length. This is the canal that now enters Mashhad at the Bala Khiaban gate, and flows right through the town to the shrine and out again at the Pain Khiaban gate.

The Sani-ud-Dowlah quotes various histories mentioning Tús and the battles that have been fought there from the early Muhammadan times up to the year 1381, when Amir Timur arrived at Tús and took possession of Khurasan. He then relates that in 1389 Haji Beg Jani Kurbani, one of Timur's nobles, rebelled at Tús, strengthened the town, and struck coin in his own name. Timur, when he heard of this, sent his youngest son, Miránshah, against Tús, the siege of which lasted several months. At last Haji Beg fled the town, which was taken by Miránshah, and pillaged by his troops. It is said that 10,000 people were massacred, the place was converted into a desert, and no trace of the town was left. At the present moment Tús consists of nothing but the ruins of a large domed building, surrounded by the remains of the walls of the town, which enclose a space of about a mile square. These walls are of mud, and are said to have beeen 17 feet thick at the base, and to have contained 106 bastions and nine gates. All the ground formerly covered by the town is now under cultivation, and nothing is to be seen in it but bits of broken brick. The ruins of the citadel lie to the north of the walls, and mark the site of a fort some 230 yards square, which was formerly surrounded by a moat. All buildings have entirely disappeared except the one structure in the centre. What this was it is impossible now to say. The building measures 14 yards each side, and is square up to a certain height. The dome in olden days was double, but the outer dome has been destroyed, and only the inner one now remains.

The extracts quoted from Ibn Haukal are the first mention we have of Mashhad. At the time Ibn Haukal wrote, Mashhad consisted of nothing but the village of Sanabad, not a sign of which now remains but the name, which still clings to the Kanát or underground channel that supplied it with water, and which now supplies the

THE RUINS OF TUS, THE ANCIENT CAPITAL OF KHURASAN.

Suráb or north-western quarter of Mashhad. The town of Nugán has also disappeared. Nothing remains of that either but the name which it has given to the quarter and the gate on the north-eastern face of the present Mashhad.

The construction of the fortifications of Mashhad and of the dome of the shrine are attributed to Suri, governor of Nishapur in 1037 A.D., during the reign of Sultan Mas'úd Ghaznavi (1030–43); but later on, during the reign of Sultan Malik Shah Saljuki (1073–92), a disturbance is said to have taken place, when Mashhad was looted. After this, in 1121, a wall was built round the town, and this saved it for a time. In 1153 the whole of the Tús district was ravaged by the Turkoman tribe called Ghaz, with the exception of Mashhad and a few other walled villages. In 1161, however, the Ghaz returned and took and plundered Mashhad, but spared the shrine. In 1207 the whole of Khurasan passed into the hands of the Khwarazm Shah Sultan Muhammad (1200–20). In 1296, when Ghazan (1294–1303), the great-grandson of Halaku Khan, ascended the throne, a number of Tartar princes rose against him; and one of them, Daoud, son of Borah, came with a large force from Mawará-un-Nahr to Khurasan and plundered most of the towns, Mashhad included. Mashhad is mentioned by Yakut, and also by Batuta, who travelled in Khurasan in 1334, and describes how he went from Jam to Tús and Tús to Mashhad-i-Raza, "a large town and full of people." In 1418 Sultan Shah Rukh (1408–46) made a pilgrimage to Mashhad and presented the shrine with a golden candelabrum weighing 500 oz., and in the same year the mosque that his wife Gauhar Shád had commenced to build was completed. Shah Rukh is also said to have built a palace to the east of the town to live in when visiting the place, but of this no trace now remains.

In 1507, during the reign of Shaibani Khan, Mashhad was taken and a large number of the inhabitants killed by the Usbegs; and again in 1525, at the commencement of the reign of Shah Tahmasp (1523–76), Ubaid Khan Usbeg took Mashhad after a siege. Tahmasp retook it in 1528, but the city walls not having been finished he lost it again, and did not finally secure it till 1530. Ubaid Khan again besieged it in 1535, but the walls and bastions being then very strong, he failed to take it, and had to retire to Herat. It is recorded that the commander in Mashhad, Súfián Khalifa, was absent at the time of this siege, but that his wife conducted the defence, going round the walls on foot day and night, till Ubaid Khan was compelled to retire. Finally, in 1544 Mashhad was taken by Muhammad Sultan Usbeg, who made a general massacre of the town.

It was again besieged in 1579 and 1581 by Ali Kuli Khan, the guardian of the minor Shah Abbas. During these sieges, Murtaza Kuli Khan, Parnak-Turkoman, who had been appointed governor by Shah Ismail II. in 1577, tried to raise money in the town, but failed. He then took the golden candlesticks from the shrine, melted them down, and coined money with which to pay the troops; but all to no avail, and in 1585 Mashhad became the headquarters of the young Shah Abbas, prior to his assumption of the reins of government at Kazvin.

In 1589 Mashhad was taken by Abdul Momin Khan, governor of Balkh, after a siege of four months. A general massacre ensued, and it is said that even the priests and Saiyids were not spared. They took refuge in the shrine, but were seized and murdered. The shrine was plundered, and it is recorded that the gold, silver, and jewelled candlesticks and lamps, of which there were great numbers, also carpets, utensils, and china, and the library, which had a collection of old books from all countries of Islam, all fell into the hands of ignorant and savage Usbegs. The massacre and plunder lasted for three days, and only a few people escaped. On leaving, Abdul Momin took with him the gold pillar that had been put up by Shah Tahmasp over the dome of the shrine; and amongst other valuables carried off by him was a diamond, said to have been the size of a fowl's egg, which had been presented to the shrine by Kutb Shah of the Deccan (1512).

In 1598 Mashhad was reoccupied by Shah Abbas, on the flight of the Usbegs. He repaired the shrine, and then returned to Irak. The same year some Usbeg princes arrived at Isfahan with presents for Shah Abbas, amongst whom was one Yar Muhammad Mirza, who presented a large diamond. It was discovered that this was the same diamond that had belonged to the shrine, and had fallen into the hands of Abdul Momin Khan. By the advice of the priests Shah Abbas sold this diamond in Turkey, and remitted the proceeds to Mashhad to be expended in the purchase of land for the shrine. In 1601 Shah Abbas made another pilgrimage to Mashhad, walking the whole way on foot from Isfahan, and it is said that he then extended the courtyard and made other improvements in the shrine, besides putting up a pair of jewelled doors and having the dome gilt. He also constructed the Khiaban, or main street. In 1652 Shah Abbas II. is said to have faced the shrine with glazed tiles, and in 1695 Mashhad was visited by Akbar, who presented the shrine with a gold candlestick weighing 30 oz. and also a chandelier, and at the same time gave three hundred English pounds to the shrine officials, though where this English gold came from is not stated.

In 1722 Malik Mahmúd Sistani occupied Mashhad, and in 1726 Shah Tahmasp II. marched against him with Fateh Ali Khan Kajar and besieged the town. It was during this siege that Nadir Kuli Beg Afshar first came to notice. The siege is said to have lasted two months, when the gate of Mir Ali Ambia, a gate that no longer exists, was opened by treachery, Nadir was let in, and both the town and citadel fell into the hands of Shah Tahmasp II. Malik Mahmúd Sistani was put to death.

In 1729 Mashhad was again besieged by an Abdali Afghan force from Herat, and Nadir's brother, Ibrahim Khan, who was defending the place, was defeated, and had to shut himself up in the town till Nadir himself came to the rescue, and drove the Abdalis away after a thirty-one days' siege.

In 1747 Nadir was assassinated, and was succeeded by his nephew, Ali Kuli, who took the name of 'Ádil Shah, possessed himself of all Nadir's jewels and treasure at Kalat-i-Nadiri, and murdered all his descendants except the one boy, Shah Rukh, aged fourteen, whom he imprisoned. Ali Kuli was, however, deposed and blinded the following year, and when Shah Ruhk was put on the throne he killed both Ali Kuli and his brother, Ibrahim Khan. A year after, though, in 1749, Shah Ruhk was taken and blinded by Mirza Saiyid Muhammad, the Mutawalli or guardian of the shrine, who assumed the title of Shah Suliman. He is said to have removed the jewelled railings, that Nadir Shah had made for his own tomb, from Nadir's mausoleum to the shrine. I may here mention that all trace of this mausoleum has disappeared. It is related that the bones of Nadir Shah were removed to Teheran and buried under the entrance to the palace with those of Karim Khan Zend by the Shah, Aga Muhammad Khan (1794–97), and apparently the mausoleum must have been destroyed at the same time. Makbara-i-Nadir still gives its name to one of the quarters of the town, but that is the only trace of it that remains.

Shah Suliman in his turn was blinded and deposed, and Shah Ruhk again came to power, but the remainder of that prince's reign seems to have been principally taken up in the quarrels between his two sons, Nasrulla Mirza and Nadir Mirza, who alternately got the upper-hand. Both in turn plundered the shrine. Nasrulla seized all the gold and silver articles he could find, and turned them into money. Nadir took the gold plates off the dome and the jewelled crown that was fixed on the top of it, and also the jewelled doors, and finally is said to have burnt a carpet worked with gold valued at 7000 tumans for the sake of the metal, which only realised 700 tumans.

Mashhad was taken by Ahmad Shah Abdali of Herat, but he left Shah Ruhk in possession, which he nominally retained till he was finally deposed by Agha Muhammad Shah in 1796, soon after which he died. Nadir Mirza, who was in command at the time, fled to Herat. He is said to have returned the following year, after Agha Muhammad Khan's death, and was subsequently appointed governor. In 1802, however, Mashhad was besieged by the Kajar troops. Nadir Mirza again plundered the shrine and melted up the candlesticks and lamps, but despite all his efforts the Kajar troops effected an entrance, and Nadir Mirza was sent a prisoner to Teheran, where he was put to death by Fateh Ali Shah.

In 1813 there was a rebellion on the part of the Khurasan nobles. Various chiefs are mentioned, viz. Ishak Khan, Karai; Raza Kuli Khan, Zafaranlu Kurd, of Kuchan; Najaf Kuli Khan, Shadillu Kurd, of Bujnurd; Beglar Khan, Chapishlu, of Daragez; and Sádat Kuli Khan, Bagháirlu, of Jahan Arghián. In 1814 Ismail Khan, Sirdar of Damghan, was sent against them, and pitched his camp at Khwajah Rabi, where the chiefs attacked him, but were driven off, and Ishak Khan and his son were afterwards killed. In 1818 Fateh Ali Shah came to Mashhad and built the new court of the shrine known as the Sahn-i-Nou. In 1825 Khurasan was raided right up to the gates of Mashhad by Ali Kuli Khan, son of Muhammad Rahim Khan, the ruler of Khwarazm, and again in 1828, while the intervening years seem to have been mainly occupied in internal squabbles between the various chiefs. Finally, at the end of 1828 Abbas Mirza invaded Khurasan with a large Persian force, restored order at Mashhad, and then marched against Raza Kuli Khan of Kuchan, and subsequently against the Salar Turkomans of Sarakhs. He died in 1833, and was buried in the shrine.

At the end of 1837 the siege of Herat took place under Muhammad Shah in person. The Sani-ud-Dowlah discreetly avoids all mention of the fact that Muhammad Shah failed to take Herat. Any failure or reverse on the part of the Persians is always thus glossed over by him throughout, as by other Persian historians.

In 1839 took place the rising in Mashhad against the Jews. Owing, it is said, to an insult offered by the Jews to the Mussulman religion, the people of the town attacked the Jews' quarter and killed 200 of them. The rest accepted the Muhammadan religion, and were not further molested. These Jews are now known by the name of Jadid (*i.e.* new, or converts). They are Mussulmans only in name, and still have their own Jewish quarter, and follow their own religion in secret. They number about 200 families.

In 1845, for the first time, it is said, the appointment of Mutawalli, or guardian of the shrine, was conferred on the governor in addition to his own duties, and Allahyar Khan, Asaf-ud-Dowlah, held both posts for the space of a year. The custom of combining the two charges seems to have become general since then, and the present Asaf-ud-Dowlah when governor-general was also the Mutawalli Bashi of the shrine, as his predecessor was before him.

In 1847 came the rebellion of Hasan Khan Sálár, the son of Allahyar Khan, Kajar, Asaf-ud-Dowlah, the maternal uncle of Muhammad Shah. The Hashmat-ud-Dowlah, who was sent against the Sálár, seems to have occupied Mashhad, but to have been driven out again by a rising of the townspeople, who killed 700 of the Persian troops and beat back the remainder into the citadel, where they were besieged by the Sálár and a number of Turkomans. Great scarcity is said to have ensued, the price of bread going up to two tumans per man weight of 6½ lbs. What the value of a tuman was fifty years ago I cannot say. Twenty years ago, when the kran was a franc, the tuman was valued at eight shillings and fourpence; in 1885 it was worth about six shillings and eightpence, but by 1898 its value had gone down to four shillings.

The Sálár's rebellion has been oftened mentioned, but the Persian accounts of it that I have come across are so mixed that it is difficult to form a connected narrative. The "Mirat-ul-Buldan"[1] gives one of the best accounts, but even that seems a confused jumble of names. One thing seems certain, though, and that is that at the time of Nasir-ud-Din Shah's succession, Khurasan was entirely out of hand and was practically independent. In 1848 Haji Nur Muhammad Khan, Sirdar, and Suliman Khan, Afshar, were appointed to restore order in Khurasan, but the Sálár refused to listen to the advice of his uncle, Nur Muhammad, and next year Sultan Murad Mirza, the Hisám-us-Sultanah, was despatched from Teheran with a Persian army to subdue the country. It

[1] Vol. ii. p. 7.

is difficult to follow the moves of the various chiefs, but it would appear that on the arrival of the Hisám-us-Sultanah's troops at Sabzawar, they could do nothing against the town, and were thinking of retiring to Shahrud from want of provisions, when Sam Khan, the chief of Kuchan, withdrew from the Sálár's party, and joined the Hisám-us-Sultanah's camp with 600 sowars and various other tribal chiefs. He induced the Persian troops to proceed to Kuchan instead of to Shahrud by the promise of supplies, and marching through Sar-i-Valayat they took Safiabad, and made the Bughairis submit to terms. The Hisám-us-Sultanah afterwards moved to Isfarain and thence to Jagatai. The Sálár here attempted to aid Allahyar Khan, Juwaini, but was defeated and had to retreat, and the Hisám-us-Sultanah took both Jagatai and Ak Kala. He then went on to Sabzawar, pitching his camp at Khusrogird. The Sálár had left his brother, Mirza Muhammad Khan, and his son, Amir Aslan Khan, to guard the fort at Sabzawar, and fighting went on for some days between their sowars and the Hisám-us-Sultanah's troops. At last Mir Yahiya Khan, Tabrizi, arrived from Teheran with a reinforcement of 2000 sowars, three guns, and treasure and decorations for Sam Khan, Ilkhani, and the other chiefs who had rendered service to the royal cause. The Hisám-us-Sultanah was thus enabled to invest the town. Mustaffa Kuli Khan, Turbati, who was in command of the citadel, surrendered it, and Sabzawar was then taken. The Sálár's son, Amir Aslan Khan, managed to break out and escape. The Hisám-us-Sultanah then advanced to Nishapur, where the governor handed over the town.

Finally the people in Mashhad, owing to the scarcity, turned against the Sálár, and the town was taken. The Sálár was driven to take refuge in the shrine, from which he had already appropriated the candlesticks and broken up the golden railings and silver doors to coin money. He was seized, and subsequently executed by order of the Shah, as well as his brother, Muhammad Ali Khan, and his son, Amir Aslan Khan, all of whom are buried in the garden at Khwajah Rabi, where their tombstones lie in a very neglected state.

In 1853 Faridún Mirza, an uncle of the Shah, was appointed governor-general of Khurasan. He repaired the shrine, the Musjid, and the colleges, but died in 1855, when Sultan Murad Mirza, Hisám-us-Sultanah, was appointed to succeed him, and in 1856 the attack on Herat took place. In 1858, on the recall of the Hisám-us-Sultanah, Hamza Mirza, Hashmat-ud-Dowlah, was appointed to succeed him, and he it was who built the fort at Sarakhs. In 1859, by order of the Shah, the Mutawalli of the shrine put up the golden door and established a guest-house in the shrine for pilgrims and poor.

In 1866 the Shah appointed his son, Jalál-ud-Dowlah, a minor, to the government of Khurasan, and started himself on a pilgrimage to Mashhad later on in the same year. On arrival at Mashhad he went straight to the shrine, to which he presented the Jika or jewelled aigrette in his hat, and then took up his residence in the citadel, with his camp outside. In 1868 cholera appeared at Mashhad, and the Jalál-ud-Dowlah died of it and was buried in the shrine.

In 1871 came the famine which devastated the whole of Khurasan. In 1876 Mashhad was connected with Teheran by telegraph. In 1881 a miracle is said to have been wrought in the shrine, when a woman who had been paralysed for fifteen years saw the Imam in a dream. He told her to get up; she woke, and, it is said, found herself cured. In 1883 the Shah paid a second visit to Mashhad, and in the same year Suliman Khan, Sahib

Ikhtiyar, the Persian commissioner arrived at Mashhad to demarcate the Russian and Persian frontier. At the end of 1884 the British commissioner, General Sir Peter Lumsden, arrived at Mashhad for the demarcation of the frontier between Afghanistan and Russian territory, and in 1889 came the establishment of the British and Russian consulates-general, followed in 1891 by that of a branch of the Imperial Bank of Persia.

THE SHRINE OF IMAM RAZA AT MASHHAD—GENERAL VIEW, WITH THE KATLGAH CEMETERY IN THE FOREGROUND.

CHAPTER XIX.

THE TOWN AND SHRINE OF MASHHAD.

THE town of Mashhad averages about a mile and a half in length by a mile in breadth, and is surrounded by a mud wall and dry ditch. This wall is said to have been built by Shah Tahmasp (1523–76) and to have 141 bastions. It is kept in sufficient repair to prevent people getting in and out, and stands about 20 or 25 feet high, looking quite formidable from the outside. The ditch, though, is now getting gradually filled up. The residence of the governor is in the citadel at the south-west corner of the town. Originally, so far as I can gather, the Chahár Bagh, a quarter of the town to the west of the shrine, seems to have been the residence of the ruler, but the present buildings in the citadel were commenced by Abbas Mirza, the son of Fateh Ali Shah, who died at Mashhad in 1833, and were completed by Muhammad Nasir Khan, Kajar, in 1876. All the southern end of the citadel, though, is still a waste.

The principal feature of the town is the Khiábán or main street that runs in a straight line right through it from N.W. to S.E., with a width of some 25 yards and a length, according to the Sani-ud-Dowlah, taking the Persian zar at 41¼ inches, of 2234 yards, from the Bálá Khiábán gate to the shrine on the west, and of 973 yards from the Páin Khiábán gate to the shrine on the east.

According to the plan of the shrine, the distance from portico to portico is 110 zars, which makes a total length of 3333 yards, or not far short of two miles. This street, though, is not available for traffic from end to end. The portion that runs through the precincts of the shrine is carefully barred off, and no animal or vehicle of any description, and no man unless a Mussulman, can pass through, but must find his way round through the narrow lanes on either side.

Almost all the business of the town is centred in this main street. The road up to the bank and telegraph office, owing to the caravanserais there in which most of the cart-drivers from Ashkabad put up, and the main streets leading to the Suráb, Idgah, and Nughán gates, show a little sign of life, but otherwise the remaining streets are nothing but dirty, narrow, winding lanes running between high mud walls enclosing the houses on either side, with a low, narrow doorway here and there marking the descent into the house below. Almost all the houses in Mashhad seem to be considerably below the level of the streets, owing to the fact apparently that everything is built of mud, and the people, not having been able to dig up the streets to get earth for their houses, have gradually cut away the ground on either side of them to build their walls with.

The town is divided into six large *mahallas* or quarters and ten small, each under a Kadkhuda or head-man. Except the shrine, which stands out prominently, the gilt dome and lofty minarets of which can be seen from afar, there are no buildings of any particular size or note in the town, and nothing is to be seen above the level of the ordinary run of mud houses but a couple of domes, one known as the Gumbaz-i-Sabz, a half-ruined mausoleum full of Darweshes near the citadel, said to be about 200 years old, and another at the other side of the town known as

THE SHRINE OF IMAM RAZA AT MASHHAD.

the Buka or mausoleum of Pir-i-Palandoz, built during the reign of Shah Sultan Muhammad Khudabanda, and which bears a date corresponding to A.D. 1577. The Musalla, about half a mile to the east of the town outside the Páin Khiábán gate, consists of nothing but a ruined portico. It has an inscription, so the Sani-ud-Dowlah says, giving a date in Abjad corresponding to A.D. 1676. The face and interior of this building, which is of burnt brick, was at one time entirely covered with fine tiles, or rather, I should say, with glazed mosaic tile-work, something similar to what was on the Musalla at Herat. A good deal of this has fallen away, and the upper part of the building is full of swifts' and other birds' nests, while the ground floor is inhabited by a colony of ragged Sistanis who are the most vociferous beggars.

Of the various Musjids and Madrasas or colleges in the town the Sani-ud-Dowlah mentions that an inscription on the Musjid-i-Shah gives the date 1451. This building, also known as the Musjid-i-Uzbakia, was erected by Amir Malik Shah during the time of the Usbeg occupation, and is used as a Sunni mosque. It is said, though, that the Kibla is not right, *i.e.* that the recess marking the direction of Mecca is not correctly placed. The Musjid near the Páin Khiábán gate, built by Shah Abbas, bears date 1641. The Musjid-i-Imam Raza in the Katlgah cemetery was built by Shah Abbas in 1602, and the Madrasa-i-Fázil was built in the same reign. The Madrasa-i-Muhammad Bákir, in the Bálá Khiábán, and also the Madrasa-i-Bahzádia, were built in the reign of Shah Sulimán (1668–94). The Madrasa-i-Dodar was originally built in the reign of Shah Rukh (1408–46), but was repaired in 1677. In the Musjid belonging to it there is an inscription bearing date 1439. The Madrasa-i-Abbas Kuli Khan was built in 1666, and the Madrasa-i-Parizad in 1680. None are therefore of any very great age. Mashhad is said to have been much improved during the reign of the Safavian dynasty (1499–1736) and the above dates would seem to bear this out. It is also recorded that during the same period the shrine was so decorated that it became full of gold and silver candlesticks and other things of that sort, and when one reads of the number of times that these articles were plundered and melted down, one wonders where they all could have come from.

According to Malcolm, Mashhad in Nadir's time (1736–47) had 60,000 inhabited houses, whereas at his grandson Shah Rukh's death in 1796 it had not more than 3000, and was then at its lowest ebb. The population at the present day is supposed to be about 60,000, including men, women, and children. The number of inhabited houses is estimated at 20,000, but this is merely a guess, and I don't think there are anything like that number. There has never been any attempt at a census.

At the head of the town is the Beglar Begi, or the police magistrate, as we may call him. He is supposed to have a force of sixty policemen under him; at least that is the establishment which I believe is provided for, but the governor takes the pay of half of these for himself, and the Beglar Begi has to do the best he can with the remainder.

The town is guarded by Persian *sarbazes*, or soldiers, one whole battalion being distributed about the town in small guards of about a dozen men each. These men never drill or do any military duty whatever so far as I have seen, and are mostly armed with old muzzle-loading muskets, which probably they have never fired in their lives, for which they have no cartridges, and which look as if they would not go off under any circumstances. A Persian soldier's pay is only a quarter of a kran, or, roughly speaking, a penny a day, with a ration of bread, but even this small pay they rarely get. I remember hearing a great noise one day, and on inquiry found that it was caused by the men of the battalion on duty in the town having risen in a body to complain to the governor-general that they had received no pay for three months. They next, as usual, besieged the telegraph office. Finally an inquiry was held, and a decision purely Persian was arrived at. It was decided that the Sartip, or colonel in command, was to refund one-third of the pay due. The remaining officers of the battalion were to pay up another third, and the men were to relinquish their claims to the remaining third. Apparently, so far as the men were concerned, it was acknowledged by all that they could not reasonably expect to get more than two-thirds of their pay. As to the officers, they at once, in their turn, besieged the telegraph office, and wired off a petition to the Shah to say that they had had no share in it at all. A day or two after the Sartip made a clean bolt of it, and that was the end of the matter.

As to the men, they are invariably in rags; they are supposed to get two suits of blue cotton clothes a year, but I doubt if they get them; and as to greatcoats, even in the depth of winter only one greatcoat is allowed to each guard-house, and the sentries have to wear it in turn. What comes of the money drawn for the remainder is pure speculation. These so-called soldiers are supposed to keep order in the town, in so far that it is their duty to stop all people passing at night after the bugles have sounded four hours after sunset. They do not interfere in any other way that I know of.

The principal disturbers of the peace of the town are the Tulabá, or religious students. These men live in the various Madrasas, or colleges, and are supported out of college funds, or else they attach themselves to different priests. They are a most unruly and troublesome lot. Students, though, is not the real name for these men, as many of them have no studies, and in fact some of them can neither read nor write. Any one, in fact, who puts on a white turban can call himself a Tálib, and may spend his whole life as such. If he cannot get into one of the colleges he joins the staff of some priest on the chance of getting fed, and helps to magnify the importance of the priest to whom he has attached himself. Every Mujtahid, or chief priest, is a civil judge, and if the Government is weak enough to permit it the priest's adherents can get a great deal of power into their hands, and the priest and his adherents naturally work together for their mutual benefit. In Mashhad, when any of the chief priests quarrel amongst themselves, as is often the case, about some endowment property or anything of that sort that they may be in charge of, the sides of each are taken up by their respective adherents, who collect round themselves all the mob and ruffians of the place, and the first thing one hears is that the shops are shut, and all business is at a standstill. Neither side, as a rule, has the pluck to proceed to blows, and nobody has the courage to interfere, from the governor downwards, but the whole town remains in a state of subdued disturbance till the matter at issue is settled, the shopkeepers not daring to open their shops for fear of being looted, and everybody grumbling, and yet not a soul daring to raise his hand against such a state of tyranny. The power of the priesthood in Mashhad is something extraordinary, and would be permitted nowhere except under Persian rule.

I remember one noted priest who caused great rows and disturbances in Mashhad for long. At last, when things had come to such a pass that all business was at a

REFERENCE TABLE.

1. Kázimkhání gate.
2. Covered passage leading to mosque.
3. Ághá Mirzá Muhammad's place for prayers.
4. Mulla Mustafa's place for prayers.
5. Minaret.
6. Passage.
7. Grocers' gate.
8. Mirza Nasrulla's place for prayers.
9. Tank.
10. Musjid-i-Pirizan or Old Woman's Mosque.
11. Well.
12. Porch of Madrasa-i- (College) Páin Pá.
13. Mausoleum of Sheikh Bahái.
14. Place for prayers.
15. Waiting-room of mosque.
16. Jái Sang-i-Chahárpa (stone showing Imam's footmarks).
17. Kafshkan-i-Musjid (place of taking off shoes before going into mosque).
18. Imam-i-Juma's place for prayers.
19. Covered passage.
20. Mulla Muhammad Taki's place for prayers.
21. Portico, with passage leading to kitchen.
22. Chaharsúk (Bazar) of the new court.
23. Aiván-i-Dákhil or The Inner Portico.
24. Gate of the new court.
25. Aiván-Khárij or The Outer Portico.
26. Place for taking off shoes.
27. Golden portico of the new court.
28. Madrasa (College) of Ali Naki Mirzá.
29. Kashik Khana or waiting-room for Shrine servants, and Library.
30. Waiting-room.
31. Tahvil Khana or treasury and storeroom.
32. Tomb of Náib-us-Saltaneh.
33. Tomb of Mushir-ud-Dowleh.
34. Tomb of Hisám-us-Saltaneh.
35. Dárui Huffáz or Place for reading Korans.
36. Tomb of Farman Farma.
37. Tomb of Jalál-ud-Dowleh.
38. Storeroom.
39. Tomb of Shaikh Muhammad Taki.
40. Gate.
41. Tomb of Motamin-us-Sultaneh.
42. Tomb of Husain Khán Sipah Sálár.
43. Dár-us-Saiyáda or place for Saiyids reading prayers.
44. Portico built by the Hisám-us-Saltaneh.
45. Silver gate put up by the Hisám-us-Saltaneh.
46. Tomb of Amin-us-Sultán.
47. Dár-us-Sáda or The Hall of Blessing.
48. Tomb of Múin-ul-Mulk.
49. Tomb of the Hashmat-ud-Dowleh
50. Hátam Khan's Gumbad (dome).
51. Dár-uz-Ziáfa or The Entertainment Hall.
52. Allah Virdi Khán's Gumbad (dome).
53. Passage leading to Gumbad.
54. The Haram-i-Mubárak or The Sacred Shrine.
55. Tomb.
56. The Golden Gate.
57. Female mosque.
58. Tomb of Mirza-i-Názir.
59. Tauhid Khána-i-Mubaraka or The Sacred Place for the acknowledgment of the unity of God.
60. Tomb of Mirza Muhammad Khan Sipah Sálár.
61. Staircase.
62. Tomb of Háji Kawám.
63. Mosque.
64. Tomb of Muhammad Wali Mirza.
65. Library.
66. The Golden Minaret.
67. The Golden Portico.
68. Place for drinking water.
69. Tomb of Sárm-ul-Mulk.
70. Madrasa-i-Parizád (College).
71. Madrasa-i- (College of) Bálásar.
72. Gate of the new court.
73. Bazar of cloth merchants.
74. Madrasa-i-Dodar (College).
75. Shrine prison.
76. Waiting-room for gatekeepers.
77. Portico.
78. Portico below the clock.
79. The Golden Reservoir built by Nádir Sháh.
80. Aiván-i-Abbási or Portico built by Sháh Abbás.
81. Golden Minaret.
82. Passage leading to Háji Mirzá Jafar's College.
83. Gate of the old court.
84. Gateway of the Nakkára Khána (drum-house).
85. Gate of Khairát Khán's College.
86. Water Reservoir.
87. Bazar of Goldsmiths.

standstill, the shops having been shut for the best part of a week, the governor plucked up courage to send his men with ladders to scale the walls of the priest's house at night, and to arrest him and send him off out of the town. That, though, was a mere flash in the pan. The students at once raised an agitation for the priest's return, the town was for some days practically in their possession, with all the mob at their back, the governor's heart failed him, and the priest was brought back in triumph.

The priests are sole judges in all cases involving points of religious law or settled by the administration of oaths. There is a Diwan Khana, or court-house, presided over by a judicial officer, who exercises civil powers for the settlement of litigation, but no Persian court can administer an oath, and consequently the priests are practically almost the sole civil judges in the land, and so long as they are allowed to assume executive authority as well, so long must power remain in their hands. It is impossible for the Persian Government to do away altogether with the right of the priests to settle civil cases, but had the Government the power to prevent them from taking the executive into their own hands, and to establish properly constituted courts for the execution of decrees, the difficulty might then be solved. At present the Persian Government have not the power to do this, and as it is, not only are the priests practically the sole administrators of all civil law, but in addition to this they are the only real protectors the people have against the rapacity of their governors.

The population of Mashhad is naturally largely made up of the priests' classes. Everywhere one sees either the white-turbaned Mullá and Tálib, or the green-turbaned Saiyid or descendant of Ali and the Prophet's daughter Fatima. Of these latter the Razavis, or descendants of

Iman Raza, enjoy special privileges, and comparatively few of them apparently work for their living.

As to the population generally, Mashhad has no peculiar race or tribe or people of its own. It is a mixture of all races, and the majority of them subsist almost entirely on the 30,000 pilgrims who are said to visit the shrine every year. The endowments of the shrine, intended for the benefit of these pilgrims and of the poor, are mostly eaten up by hordes of hungry attendants, and a system of fraud and peculation seems to permeate through all classes in the place.

As to trade, there is little or none. The new Russian customs dues have almost entirely robbed Mashhad of its former importance as a distributing centre for tea, indigo, and other Indian goods for the Central Asian market, and the Mashhad traders are most of them bankrupt. Little business is now done beyond the mere local wants of the town and district, and the local traders have by no means a high character for commercial integrity. The system of *bast*, or sanctuary, in the shrine for every kind of fraud is of itself an incentive to dishonesty, and is fully taken advantage of by all. A man once safe in the *bast* can afford to wait till he can make his own terms with his creditors. No one can touch him there. The Shah himself cannot take a man out of the shrine once he has sought refuge there. He is under the protection of the priests, and is safe from molestation. I will say, though, that this does not necessarily follow in the case of red-handed criminals. I have known a case in which a murderer who took refuge in the shrine was tried there by religious law and adjudged a murderer and unfit to remain in the sacred precincts, and was accordingly turned out. He was immediately arrested at the gate by the governor, and sentenced by him to death. I remember that coming in from my ride that morning I was inadvertently present at his execution. As I passed the citadel I saw a number of the governor's *farashes* escorting a prisoner in front of me. These *farashes* are always to be recognised by the sticks they carry, ready to bastinado any person they may be ordered to. The prisoner was taken out by them into the artillery square or parade ground, just between the British Consulate and the citadel, and there the executioner divested him of his chains and then cut his throat from ear to ear, in the midst of a crowd of onlookers. The whole thing was done so quickly that it was over before I knew what had happened. The man hardly moved, and death appeared to be practically instantaneous.

Throat-cutting is the usual method of execution in Persia. Had the murdered man's relatives been willing to accept blood-money, the murderer might have been bought off by his friends, but in this case the relatives demanded his blood and they got it. One case I remember in Mashhad, in which a bribe on the part of the murdered man's relatives to the executioner secured an extra sensational execution. I shall not easily forget the fright of a Hindu servant of mine from India when he described to me the sight he had witnessed. The criminal was tied by the heels to a tree head downwards, with his legs stretched wide apart, and then hacked in two down the middle by a sword. The poor wretch continued to yell, he said, till the sword reached a vital part; and my servant evidently wished himself safe back in India again, away from such a terrible country. Another man was beheaded, while a noted thief had his career as a robber put an end to by having the tendon of his leg cut across just above the heel. Another of the same light-fingered fraternity was similarly punished by having his fingers taken out at the joints. A holy man, an Akhund or religious teacher, who was tried and convicted by the religious court of having caused the death of a little girl, had a string put through his nose, and was led through the town like a camel by the governor's order, and his nose was subsequently cut off. The men with the maimed feet and hands duly turned up for treatment at the British Consulate dispensary. It was curious that all cases of mutilation of this sort invariably came to our dispensary to be treated. I never heard of any one going to the Persian hospital in the shrine under such circumstances, though that was the place that ought to have been open to all.

Large numbers of people, not only from the town but from the districts around, and even from Herat, used to flock into the charitable dispensary, maintained at the British Consulate by the Government of India, something like 6000 men, women, and children being treated there during the course of the year by the British Residency surgeon and his Indian hospital assistant. In the absence of the Residency surgeon the hospital assistant used to take charge, and the continued popularity of the Mashhad dispensary is an example of what excellent work is done by our Indian hospital assistants. Trained in the Indian medical schools, they are often men of ability and experience, who deserve much higher pay than they get, and I have thought that it must be hard for them, after spending several years in acquiring their professional knowledge, and with the continued anxiety of recurring examinations for each step in promotion, to see men often younger and less trained than themselves getting better pay without any further examinations, as clerks in some Government office. Personally I should like to see the pay of office clerks in India reduced, and that of more active workers increased. I know of no country in the world so ruled by clerks as India, and the contrast between England and Russia in

THE BRITISH CONSULATE CHARITABLE DISPENSARY AT MASHHAD—MEN PATIENTS AT THE ENTRANCE IN THE CENTRE AND WOMEN AT THEIR ENTRANCE ON THE LEFT.

Asia in this respect is something marvellous. In Russian Central Asia there is no such thing as the native clerk, and the Russian clerks are few and far between — a district officer may perhaps have one. The huge office establishments of the Indian district officers are unknown in Russia, and one cannot help thinking what a blessing it would be for India if there was a little more personal rule there and a little less office routine!

To give an account of the superstitions current in Mashhad would be endless. I never knew a place where more curious ideas prevailed, especially amongst the women. One custom that I was often a witness of I may here refer to. Near the Suráb gate stands an old and broken figure of a tiger, carved out of a block of stone. Riding past I often noticed a bevy of women around this tiger, and one woman in the centre seated astride of it. The tiger in question was said to have been carved by a stone-cutter some 150 years ago, and he left a will that it was to be erected over his grave as a tombstone. Presumably the stone-cutter is buried underneath. At any rate the record of his skill still remains by the roadside, and all women who want children for some reason or other make pilgrimages to this tiger, and apparently with the best results, to judge from the numbers who throng to it. The woman is seated on the stone tiger, and various incantations are gone through, such as the cutting of a string with forty knots, and other things, and the ceremony is over. I remember a similarly carved figure of a tiger in the Gazargah shrine at Herat, but I have no recollection of ever having heard of its being endowed with similar powers to this one at Mashhad.

As to climate, Mashhad, I should say, is wonderfully favoured. The town stands at a height of about 3200 feet above sea-level, in an open valley twelve to fifteen miles in width, bounded on the north-east and south-west by parallel ranges of mountains, which culminate in heights of 9000 and 10,000 feet. The returns recorded since the establishment of the British Consulate in the town give the following averages of temperature, which may be taken as a general guide:—

Month.	Degrees Fahrenheit in the Shade.		
	8 A.M.	Maximum.	Minimum.
January	26·78	40·5	22·81
February	32·72	43·20	26·92
March	44·36	59·13	38·78
April	56·57	69·3	49·19
May	68·08	79·61	56·64
June	76·64	87·45	63·90
July	80·25	89·4	65·49
August	74·49	85·56	57·38
September	65·27	78·98	54·25
October	51·25	65·43	44·13
November	41·64	56·92	36·41
December	35·61	48·10	31·67

Considering the extremely insanitary state of the town, Mashhad is wonderfully free from disease.

Of the buildings in the neighbourhood of Mashhad, the principal and almost only one of any importance is Khwajah Rabi, the mausoleum of the saint of that name, a large domed building situated in a garden some two and a half miles to the north of the town. Khwajah Rabi himself is said to have been a contemporary and associate of Ali, the son-in-law of the prophet. He accompanied the army of Islam that was sent to subdue Khurasan, and died there. There are lots of stories about the Khwajah's holiness and silence. He is said to have been one of the eight Zahids or hermits, and for twenty years never to have uttered one single word regarding the affairs of the world. According to one authority he died in A.D. 682, and to another in 689. The Imam Raza is said to have visited his tomb, and further to have stated that the one advantage he derived from coming to Khurasan was his pilgrimage to the tomb of Khwajah Rabi. The present building was erected by Shah Abbas, according to the following inscription carved on a stone over the entrance gateway to the garden:—

"The originator of this sublime edifice (firmly) founded as the sky, and the builder of this grand structure whose (pinnacles) touch the heavens, is his Majesty the King of the Kings of the World, the Sovereign of Mankind, the Protector of the Countries of God, the Defender of Men, the Shadow of God, the dust of the threshold of the Prophets, the dog of the porch of Ali, the propagator of the true creed of the Innocent Imams, the King, son of the King, the Emperor, son of the Emperor, Shah Abbas Husaini, Musawi, Safavi. Completed in 1031 H. (A.D. 1621), under the care and supervision of the most mean and humble servant, Ulugh Razavi."

Under this inscription a small stone of modern date has been let in, it is not mentioned by whom, containing the following:—

"Let it be known to the frequenters, both high and low, of this paradise-like ground, that if any of them do the least injury or damage to this holy place, either to its building or to its trees, may the curse of God and the Prophet fall on him, and may he be counted as one of the murderers of Iman Husain, and may he be deprived of his share of happiness both in this world and the next. Dated 1257 H. (A.D. 1841)."

The mausoleum is the usual octagonal structure, surmounted by a lofty blue-tiled dome. Under the centre of the dome is a wooden cover supposed to enclose the tomb of the saint, but in reality, I was told, there is nothing under it but a slab, which on being removed gives access to a vault below. This they say is never opened now, and as far as I could gather the vault is supposed to be haunted by the ghost of a Mulla or priest, who sits there reading the Koran. The building also contains the tomb of Fateh Ali Khan Kajar, the founder of the Kajar dynasty, who was killed by Nadir Shah in 1730. The whole edifice is now much out of repair; all the tiles have gone off the upper portion of the dome, and the sides of the building have been much damaged. The various arches and porticos on each side were originally lined with glazed tiles of beautiful colour and pattern, made, it is said, by men brought from Kum for the purpose; but these tiles have fallen out in many places, and no attempt has been made at repair. The revenues of the shrine are said to be considerable, but the money is not spent on the building by the Mujtahids in charge of the endowments. The place is now a favourite resort for picnic parties from the town.

The main feature of Mashhad-i-Makadas, or Holy Mashhad, as it is called by the Persians, is its shrine, and no description of the place would be complete without an account of that.

Imam Raza was the eighth of the twelve Imams or spiritual heads of Islam, and at the age of thirty succeeded his father, Musa-el-Kazim, the seventh Imam, who was killed at Baghdad in A.D. 799. His mother's name was Khezran, and he was born at Medina in 770, five years after the death of his grandfather, Jafar-us-Sadik, the sixth Imam. According to the Sani-ud-Dowlah he remained at Medina till the year 815, when he was sent for by the Kalif Mamun, the son of Harun-ul-Rashid. It is said that he was taken to Bussorah, and thence to Ahwaz, Isfahan, and *viâ* Dasht-i-Ahuan and Koh Mayamai to Nishapur, where he performed a miracle. Leaving there he went to the village of Hamrar, where a spring appeared for his ablutions, which still exists. Going on to the village of Sanabad, he passed by Koh-i-Sangi and

THE SAHN-I-KUHNA OR OLD COURT OF THE SHRINE OF IMAM RAZA AT MASHHAD.

blessed the hill, the result of that blessing being that the people then found the stone quarries which still exist there. The Imam stopped at the house of one Hamidbin Kahtaba-i-Tai, who lived in Sanabad, and there entered the Kubba or dome in which lay the grave of Harun-ul-Rashid. There he drew a line on the wall of the building and said, "This will be my mausoleum. I will be buried here." From Sanabad he went to Tús, and thence to Sarakhs and on to Merv, where he was received with great distinction by Mamun, who subsequently made him his heir-apparent in the Kalifat. According to the Sani-ud-Dowlah, Imam Raza refused to agree to this, and it was only when Mamun used threats that he consented to it. The people were then ordered by Mamun to change the colour of their clothes from black, the colour of the descendants of Abbas, the head of the family of the Abbaside Kalifahs, to green, the colour of the descendants of Abu Talib, the father of Ali, and at a public Durbar held by Mamun, the latter's son, Abbas, and all nobles, kazis, and troops made their submission to Ali Raza. Mamun then asked the Imam to give an address, but all he said was, "You have the right to be guided spiritually by us, and if you acknowledge us as leaders as well, it will be our duty to expend our spiritual guidance upon you." By order of Mamun, a large number of dirhams and dinars were coined in the name of Imam Raza, and the Sani-ud-Dowlah describes how one of these same dirhams fell into his hands at the time he was compiling his book, and gives a drawing of it. The coin is shown as containing the names of Kalifah Abdullah-ul-Mamun and of the Wali Ahd or heir-apparent of Muslims, Ali, son of Musa, with the word "Zavviri-yasatain" or double chief, *i.e.* both spiritual and temporal. At the same time Mamun gave his daughter Ummi Habib in marriage to Imam Raza, despite the fact that the Imam was twenty-two years older than Mamun himself.

Mamun drew up a long agreement regarding the appointment of Ali, son of Musa, as his heir-apparent, in his own handwriting, and the Imam endorsed a few lines on the back of it. In this agreement, which is in Arabic and is dated Ramazan 201 (A.D. 816), Mamun appoints Imam Raza to succeed him with full powers, and Imam Raza in his endorsement agrees to discharge his obligations under the deed in case he should survive Mamun; but he adds that "the Jáma-o-Jafr (a formula for foretelling events by *abjad* reckoning) says the opposite, and I do not know what will happen to me. In reality, the decree of God will come to pass."

When the news of this appointment reached Baghdad, the Abbasis protested strongly against the transfer of the Kalifat from the house of Abbas to the house of Ali, and serious disturbances arose which threatened the fall of Mamun's empire. Mamun started towards Baghdad, and when he reached Sarakhs he killed Fazl-bin-Sahl (his minister, and the man who had advised Imam Raza's appointment) in a bath there. On arrival at Sanabad in Tús, Imam Raza expired. The exact date of his death is given by Sir William Muir as August 818. The Sani-ud-Dowlah gives at length in Arabic the questions he addressed to certain *ulemas* (priests) on the subject of the Imam's death, and of their replies thereto. In these the priests agree that though there is no definite proof that Imam Raza was poisoned by Mamun, they strongly suspect he was.

The Imam was buried in Harun-ul-Rashid's mausoleum, as foretold by him, and his grave now forms the great shrine at Mashhad.

The shrine is described as a square building, surrounded on three sides by *sahns*, or large, open, paved enclosures

THE SAHN-I-NOU OR NEW COURT OF THE SHRINE OF IMAM RAZA AT MASHHAD.

or courts. The one to the south pertains to the Musjid of Gauhar Shad, that on the north is called the Sahn-i-Kuhna, or the old court, and that on the east the Sahn-i-Nau, or new court. The Imam's tomb under the gilt dome has three railings or gratings round it. The first, of steel, has no inscription or date at all. Between the first and second railing is perforated copper-work, covered with gilt, put up to protect the jewelled gate of the second railing. The second railing is also of steel, with four emeralds at the corners fixed in plates of gold. It has an inscription in two lines, in Nastálik character, stating that it was put up in 1747. The third railing is also of steel, and has the 76th chapter of the Koran engraved on it in full in Suls characters, inlaid with gold. At the foot of the tomb is a projection, behind which is the jewelled gate put up by Fateh Ali Shah. The space between the railings and the covering of the tomb, averaging about a foot and a half in width, is paved with blocks of glass. The cover of the tomb is made of wood, inlaid with gold, and bears on it the name of Shah Abbas. Around the gilt dome is an inscription which bears the date 1607. A second inscription records the fact that the dome was destroyed by an earthquake, and that Shah Suliman restored and ornamented it in the year 1675. An inscription on one of the minarets bears the date 1729.

Taking the Persian zar at 41¼ inches, the Sahn-i-Kuhnah is 98½ yards in length and 69½ in breadth; there is an inscription in it by Shah Abbas II. (d. 1649). The Sahn-i-Nau was built by Fateh Ali Shah in 1818; its length is 82½ yards, and breadth 56 yards; an inscription on the gate bears the date 1855.

The Musjid-i-Gauhar Shad was built by Gauhar Shad Agha, the wife of Shah Rukh, the son of Amir Timur (1408–46). An inscription in it bears the date 1666.

The Sahn of this Musjid is 60 yards in length and 55 yards in breadth. The mosque was repaired in the year 1642.

There seem to be few tombs of any note in the shrine, and none of any great age. The Sani-ud-Dowlah mentions that Shaikh Bahai or Baha-ul-Din's tomb stands in the south-west corner of the shrine, and that an inscription in golden letters on the building above it bears the date 1671, but most of the other inscriptions mentioned by him are less than a hundred years old. Shah Tahmasp's (1576) tomb has no inscription at all.

The revenue of the shrine from land and houses in cash and grain now amounts to 100,000 tumans, or at the present rate of exchange to £20,000 a year; but if the estates were properly administered and honestly managed it would be much more. I am told that the shrine officials practically have a monopoly of the landed estates, and get these at a rent far below what they are worth. About 95 per cent. of the revenue is derived from this endowed property, left to the shrine by wealthy people, the remainder being made up of burial fees and other small items. The whole of this sum is expended every year; nothing is saved or kept in reserve, and, in fact, there is sometimes a deficit. The whole management is in the hands of the Mutawalli Báshi or guardian appointed by the Shah, and the two secretaries. The guardian is frequently changed. Very often the duties are combined with those of the governor-general; at other times a separate guardian is appointed. There are some twenty Mujtahids or chief priests at Mashhad, and about the same number of shrine officials. For the everyday service of the shrine there are five different sets of establishments, known as Kashiks, one of which is on duty each day by turn. Each establishment or relief consists of one Sarkashik, or head-man; one Khádim Báshi, or head of shrine servants; one Durbán Báshi, or

THE MUSJID OF GAUHAR SHAD IN THE SHRINE OF IMAM RAZA AT MASHHAD.

head of gate-keepers; one Farásh Báshi, or head of attendants; and a large number of Khádims, Durbáns, Faráshes, and guards, numbering perhaps 170 men. In addition to these there are the cooks and other servants permanently employed, amounting to some thirty more. Most of the shrine officials have titles. The chief Farásh Báshi is the Hajib-ut-Taulia; various Sarkashiks are known as the Imad-ut-Taulia, the Nizam-ut-Taulia, and the Itizad-ut-Taulia. The secretary is known as the Itamad-ut-Taulia, and the Tahvildar, or treasurer, as the Nasr-ut-Taulia, and so on. Other officials include the man in charge of repairs; the hereditary guardian of Gauhar Shad's mosque; the Rais-i-Duftar, or head of the office; the Názir of the kitchen for pilgrims; and the Mudarris or librarian.

The Sani-ud-Dowlah gives the following list of books in the library of the shrine:—

1.	Korans and other documents in the handwriting of different Imams	44
2.	Parts of Korans in Kufi character	39
3.	Korans	830
4.	Manuscript Korans	426
5.	Printed ,,	116
6.	Parts of Korans	85
7.	Commentaries (Tafsir-i-Khas)	91
8.	,, (Tafsir-i'-Áma)	115
9.	Books on pilgrimage and prayer	168
10.	Original traditions (Akhbár-i-Khas)	287
11.	General ,, (Akhbár-i'-Áma)	17
12.	Original religious law (Fikh-i-Khasa)	297
13.	General ,, ,, (Fikh-i-Áma)	26
14.	Principles of law (Usál-i-Fikh)	74
15.	Science of religious discourses (Hikmat-i-Kalám)	274
16.	Commentaries (Mani-i-Bián)	37
17.	Science of logic (Ilm-i-Mantik)	67
18.	Dictionaries (Lughát)	43
19.	Medical books (Fib)	77
20.	Books on morals (Kutub-i-Rijal)	21

21.	Science of reading the Koran (Ilm-i-Karaat)	24
22.	Manners and morals (Ma'áraf-us-Akhlák)	20
23.	Arabic grammars	88
24.	Mathematics	62
25.	History and poetry	25
26.	Firmans	11
27.	Title-deeds	12
28.	Endowment deeds	75
29.	Leases	21
30.	Sanads	16
31.	Copies	122
		2896

Of the £20,000 annual revenue, the guardian first of all takes 10 per cent. as his fixed allowance; but this by no means represents the total value of the appointment, as he gets large presents in addition from the tenants of the endowed property, and from the various shrine officials whose tenure and appointments may depend upon his good-will.

The pay of the shrine officials and establishment takes up another 45 or 50 per cent. Lighting takes 5 per cent., and repairs about the same. Charitable grants to priests and pilgrims come to some 7 per cent.; the food supplied to shrine officials and servants, to 8 per cent.; to pilgrims, 7 per cent.; and miscellaneous contingencies, 6 per cent. The shrine hospital and dispensary, which ought to be the finest institution of its kind in the country, is only entered as costing about 2 per cent. of the revenues, and, as a matter of fact, does little or nothing in the way of medical relief. I am told that few of the pilgrims get the benefit of the food and medicines supposed to be given to them, and that, though a large number of people feed on the shrine, there is little charity.

THE PORTICO AT THE ENTRANCE TO THE SHRINE OF IMAM RAZA AT MASHHAD.

CHAPTER XX.

THE NISHAPUR HILLS.

At the end of August 1894, when the weather began to cool, I commenced preparations for a tour through the central portions of Khurasan, which I had not as yet been able to visit. We had the same hiring and selection of mules and the engagement of tent-pitchers and extra postal couriers as before. For the latter I had generally engaged Turkomans, but this time I took a few Mervis as well, and they proved themselves to be good men. The Mervis in Khurasan do not belong to any particular tribe, but are simply so called because they were natives of old Merv. A large number are said to be in Bokhara and a considerable number in Herat, where they are called Afshars. A number are also to be found in the Teheran, Shiraz, and Astarabad districts. Those in Khurasan number about a thousand families, and are settled in the Mashhad and Jam districts under a headman named Sharif Khan, said to be descended from Bairam Ali Khan of Merv, the man who presumably has given his name to the railway station of the present day. The Mervis were brought to Persia by Nadir Shah, and had a service of 200 sowars under the Persian Government, but the number has been gradually reduced to sixty-five. The men I had with me lived and dressed just like Turkomans, and could not have been told from Turkomans by any one who did not know them.

My first move was to Gulistan, ten miles out, with the view of exploring the range of mountains between Mashhad and Nishapur.

The village was a curious high-walled structure, standing on a mound overlooking the stream, the houses being built two and three storeys high, with the windows looking out of the high walls all round. In the cholera epidemic of 1892 Mr. Elias moved out of Mashhad only to fall into worse trouble here at this very place. The people of the village were dying of cholera, and it was found that they were washing the dead bodies in the stream above. Camp was moved at once, but, alas, it was too late. The men had already drunk the water, and the same evening one of the orderlies, a Duffadar of the Guides Cavalry, and the office Duftry, a Ghurka, both took cholera and died. Persia is just the same as India so far as sanitary measures are concerned, and nowhere in the East can one find the least care or precaution in this respect. About a mile below the village a band or dam had been built across a narrow rocky gorge, in the middle of which there was a curious well built of blocks of cut stone to take off flood water through an arched channel at the bottom, with a circular flight of steps outside the well again to permit people to ascend and descend. The village contained some seventy houses, but there was hardly any cultivation; nothing but orchards, the people living principally by the sale of their fruit and wood. Below the village the bank of the stream was one mass of walled gardens or enclosures, and although lucerne was plentiful, flour, grain, and dry fodder were scarce, as in all the hill villages on the range.

The height of Gulistan I made out by the aneroid to be about 4100 feet. From there we moved eight miles up the stream to Jághark, a pleasant march under shade almost the whole way. The mass of trees on either side of the road was unique in this country. The sides of the gorge were steep and were irrigated by numerous water-channels taken off from the stream, and the whole valley from side to side was one mass of foliage. The trees were of many kinds, apple, pear, plum, quince, peach, apricot, mulberry, walnut, poplar, plane, ash, willow, hawthorn, and various others. The stream itself, or rather what remained of it, was only six feet in width and three inches in depth. Jághark contained some 250 families, but the houses were so hid away in the trees that one saw nothing but those fronting the narrow road leading through the village. We ascended some 700 feet from Gulistan, and the difficulty was to find a place sufficiently level to pitch a tent on. There was no open space of any sort, and the only plan was to hire an orchard, but very few of them were level enough to camp in, and such as there were, were mostly wet from constant irrigation.

From Jághark we followed up the course of the stream nine miles to Rubat-i-Pai Gudar, or the hostel at the foot of the pass, the hostel, if one can use such a word, consisting of a low stone-vaulted structure used as a stable, with niches in the walls for men. The roof was the only level place we could find to pitch our tents upon, while our men accommodated themselves inside below us and the animals were tethered at the door. The road over this pass is the direct route between Nishapur and Mashhad, and is largely used by pilgrims and caravans in the summer. In the winter from November to March it is closed by snow. We met a good number of pilgrims on their way from Kúm, all mounted on mules and donkeys, the only animals that could get through. The road above Jághark we found very rough and stony, and tiring for our animals. The first half ran through thick foliage; after that the gardens and orchards gradually gave place to willows and briars, and they too ceased about two miles below the Rubat. The hills around were bare and stony, the only things on them being little thorny plants. I came across a curious sort of tailless rat which I afterwards found to be fairly common all over the range, at a height of about 6000 feet. It lived in holes under rocks, where it accumulated a good supply of bits of grass and plants, presumably for use during winter. The skins were subsequently identified as belonging to a species known as *pikas*, or whistling hares.

The height of the Rubat was marked as 6910 feet on the map. My aneroid made it about 200 feet higher. I rode up to the top of the pass, distant about three miles. The first portion of the ascent was gradual, but then came a very steep pull up the side of the hill, and after an hour's climb we landed on a ridge near a hut used as a protection for travellers caught in a storm. Another twenty minutes brought us to the summit. There was a rise of 1500 feet to the hut and of 2300 feet altogether to the summit, which, according to my aneroid, was about 9400 feet in height. The top of the range looked as if it could be ridden over anywhere, and in spring it was said to be covered with rich grass. According to our guide, large numbers of nomads came up every year in May and June. Baluchis from the Nishapur side, and Timuris from the Mashhad side, and their black tents and flocks were then to be seen in every ravine where water was to be found. The top of the pass was covered with numbers of little heaps of stones erected by pious pilgrims, who here, on a clear day, get their first glimpse of Mashhad. About a farsakh to the north-west stood a peak called by our guide the Lakki Tarsa, apparently the one marked on the map as 10,112 feet in height, and two farsakhs beyond that again, so the guide said, was a still higher peak named Lakki Shirbad—a ride along the top of the range to this latter peak would be lovely in spring.

From the pass I returned to Jághark, and leaving the main camp there I made a trip to the south-east, to see what the mountains were like in that direction. We first crossed a ridge some two miles out to Dehbar, a village of ninety houses, at a height of some 5300 feet. The road was under shade the whole way up the banks of the Dehbar stream. Not a bit of ground could be found flat enough to camp upon at the village, and we eventually pitched our tents in an orchard some way below. A steep climb of some 800 feet and a drop down again of another 400 took us on to Zaghai, a village of about 100 houses, from which there was a direct road to Mashhad through the village of Alamdasht, the distance being only five or six farsakhs. In other valleys to the east lay the villages of Mughan, Ardama, and Balandar. I was anxious to visit Mughan, but I put it off on being told that the easiest way to get there was from Turuk. The consequence was, I never got there at all, as the snow fell before I returned. The Shah, in the diary of his visit to Khurasan in 1867, mentions a wonderful cave near there, in which the dripping water is forming pillars, and where there are artificially made rooms and wells, and a pool without a bottom, and other wonderful things, but I lost my chance and never saw them. Moula Bakhsh and I spent the day at Zaghai, resting in an orchard. The orderlies bought some fowls in the village and cooked them, and we all made our breakfast off them with great relish, and then returned to our tents at Dehbar, and back again to Jághark the next morning. From there we went across the hills to Kang, a village some nine miles to the north-west, containing 200 houses, and at a height of about 5350 feet. We camped in an apple orchard on a ridge between two streams, and the place was drier than any we had yet been to. Jágharк was terribly damp. Everything was wet, and rheumatism was developed amongst us in consequence.

The next morning we went five miles up the hills to visit the ruins of an old fort called Hisar, said by the villagers to have been built by Afrasiab. We found it consisted of a curious rocky hillock standing out on the watershed between the Kang and Zushk valleys, on which a narrow fort some 200 yards in length and 50 in breadth at the broadest had been built. Nothing remained but the ruins of the walls, built of small stones, the slate of the hill. The air of the place was delicious, standing as it did at a height of some 7550 feet. From the fort a path ran straight on up to the summit of the range. The whole range appeared to be rideable everywhere in its higher parts, and the Shikaris with us said there were springs of water on the top. The summit of the range looked a pleasant place for a camp, but there would be no shade for the hot weather, and all supplies would have to be taken up from the villages below.

From Kang we made a march of seven miles across to Abardeh, below which, at the foot of the hills, lay the large village of Shandez, containing some five hundred houses. Just above Abardeh were the walls of an old fort said to have been destroyed by the Shah's troops at the time of the Sálár's rebellion. All these hill villages sided with the Sálár apparently, and after Mashhad was taken guns were brought up, the villages gave in, and were simply looted and left.

From Abardeh we had a hot march of twelve miles

farther north to Gulmakán, across open rocky country very different from the shady valleys we had been living in of late, and we found ourselves camped in the open and all but back on the plains again.

From Gulmakán I made an expedition thirteen miles up the valley to Chashma-i-Sabz, a small lake up in the mountains at a height of about 7700 feet. The march took us four and a half hours, and the baggage mules six hours, and we ascended some 3100 feet. For the first hour we passed gardens and plantations, but after that there was nothing but a line of willows and wild brier along the banks of the stream. The lake itself we found to be only 300 or 400 yards in length, and 100 to 150 in breadth, fringed with reeds and with lofty mountains overhanging it on west, south, and east. The guide told us that the lake was formerly much larger, and pointed to a ledge as a former shore. It was fed apparently by a number of springs, and contained a lot of small fish, upon which a couple of white-breasted fish eagles were busy feeding when we arrived. I watched them for some time, and they seemed to catch a good many. I caught one myself with a grasshopper for bait; but though very dark-coloured, so far as I could judge it was of the same species as those found in all the inland rivers of the country. There were lots of partridges along the valley, and the orderly with the advance tents told me that he was confronted on arrival at the lake by a big wild boar. The villagers declared there were numbers of pig in the mountains, and that in winter they came down and did much damage. There were no habitations anywhere near the lake, and all our supplies had to be brought up from Gulmakán. There were no trees either, or shade of any kind to camp under, but there was plenty of good grazing for our animals, and firewood was procurable from the willows down the stream and the thorn plants on the hills around. I noticed the water-ousel flitting up and down the stream, and sounds, said to be of otters, came from the lake at night.

The next morning, the 27th September 1897, I started early for the summit of the range, an ascent, I found, of some 3000 feet. I did not get to the top of the highest point, but the height of the path along the main ridge or watershed of the range where I struck it was about 10,700 feet by my aneroid; so that the highest peak is probably over 11,000 feet. I took my horse up without any difficulty, riding a great part of the way, and when the road was steep, dismounting and hanging on to its tail. Along the top even camels can travel, and they are brought up there by the nomads in the spring. One could evidently ride right along the top of the range from one end to the other without difficulty. On our way up the local Shikari spotted a herd of wild sheep down in a ravine below us. I was not to be tempted so far down again, but he went off and had a shot at them, though without success, further than that he drove them up the mountain side right on to the top of my orderly Duffadar Safiulla, of the 19th Bengal Lancers, and Koki Sirdar, Turkoman, who had gone out for a shoot on their own account, and who both banged away freely, as I could see through my glasses, but unfortunately without result.

On the top we all met and halted for breakfast, and then riding west for an hour along the summit, we turned and descended a spur to our camp at the lake again. The Shikari, not to be beaten by the failure of his first attempt, went on and killed an oorial after all, and brought it into camp in triumph. It rained at times, and it was cold on the top of the range, where the rain came down in the form of soft snow. Curiously enough, the whole of the top and sides of the range was covered with rat-holes. Rats seemed to swarm, to judge by the number of holes, and also by the kestrels about, though they were difficult to see. Round the lake were colonies of mice.

Next day we were glad enough to get back to Gulmakán, as it clouded over and evidently came on to rain hard up above after we left. We saw a good many wild sheep on our way back, and I was lucky enough to kill one as he stood looking at us from the fancied security of a ridge high above us. I also bagged a large solitary snipe —a bird I had never seen before, and which I took for a woodcock when it was first flushed. On the plains below Gulmakán I found a lot of sand-grouse, many of them young birds, and I bagged a couple of dozen in a very short time, and also a hare.

Our next move was across the valley of the Firizi stream to a little hamlet called Kalata-i-Dargah, on the side of the line of scarped hills that here projects from the main range, and is known as Chil-i-Shah, from the point at the end of it overlooking Chinaran. The villagers only numbered ten or a dozen families, and they were in a terrible fright at the advent of a Faringi, having never seen one before, and thinking that he must be going to take the country. There were lots of partridges and *tihu* about, and I had some good sport with them, and the next morning I started early up to the Chil-i-Shah after ibex, which were said to be plentiful, but I saw only four small ones in some holes in the cliffs. These cliffs, curiously enough, were full of fossil shells. We then moved five miles up the valley to Firizi, a large village of some 300 houses, but almost entirely empty. All the villagers were away in their gardens up the various nullahs and ravines around, gathering their walnuts, which apparently formed their principal stock of wealth.

Next day we had a long and hard day's work climbing up to the Binalúd peak, at the top of the range, and back. Leaving Firizi, which stands at a height of about 5100 feet, we struck a valley full of walnut trees, called the Zau Mang, which we followed up to its head at a height of about 7000 feet. The upper part of the Zau was full of partridges. They were running about everywhere, but the Shikari would not let me shoot them for fear of frightening the *kuch*, as the oorial or wild sheep is called.

We had a long and steep climb on to the top of the peak known as Takht-i-Naldagh, at a height of about 8800 feet. In returning we followed the crest of the range in a south-east direction, above a line of white limestone precipices, till we arrived close under the Binalud peak. We had to strike down a steep declivity, dragging our mules after us as best we could, and finally arrived back in camp at sunset, after a hard five and a half hours' going each way.

The air was delicious at the top of the range, which here, as before, I found to be rideable almost everywhere. We found a flock of wild sheep under the Binalud peak, and I caught a couple of the tailless rats or mouse hares I before mentioned, but I could not succeed in getting a single specimen of the other rats and mice that seemed to inhabit the higher parts of the range so thickly.

About two-thirds of the way up, a little stunted juniper was to be seen; but, with that exception, the hillsides were perfectly bare of wood. The summit was covered with round patches of that curious spiky plant so common in the hills of the country, looking like a round soft cushion in the distance, but which would be a terrible surprise to any one sitting down upon it. There was also another curious plant that grew on rocks like a huge limpet. This plant, also common in all these hills, is as hard as wood and sounds like wood on being struck, and has a light green surface which at times, on close inspection, is found to be covered with minute flowers. When decayed and broken, one sees that it was a plant after all; but when young and green, one would never think it was so.

The name Binalúd appeared to be confined to the peak alone. It was nowhere applied to the range itself, and, in fact, the only name I ever did hear applied to the whole range was Kuh-i-Nishapur.

Next day we rode over to a small village called Paya, some six miles away in the hills to the east. We heard there was an inscription on a rock there, but it turned out to be nothing, the date 1211 (A.D. 1796) being alone legible. Coal was said to be found in the neighbourhood. There is no doubt that there is plenty of coal obtainable in these hills, but the mines have never been worked. I tried to burn some of it myself at Mashhad, but the coal I got was only surface stuff and of little use. Wood fuel, however, is getting scarcer and scarcer at Mashhad every year, and these coal-mines will doubtless be opened up before long. Paya, like Firizi, seemed to live on its walnuts. All the ravines about were full of fine old walnut trees, and the people were all engaged in gathering the fruit. The Firizi people told me that they sold about a thousand tumans worth of walnuts a year. They disposed of them to Russian Armenians and others at Nishapur, where the walnuts realised about twelve tumans (£2, 8s. 0d.) a kharwar (649 lbs.), or three krans (14d.) per thousand. Some of their trees, they said, yielded a crop of 10,000 walnuts, which appeared an enormous number for one tree to bear, but they stuck to it that such was the case. They also told me that a couple of Russian Armenian loupe-cutters had come to Firizi two years before and purchased some walnut trees, and cut out and carried away the loupes in a cart which they managed to get up to the village. A big walnut tree, I found, was only valued at about ten tumans, or a couple of pounds.

While at Firizi I bought a huge basket of honey from one of the villagers, a rare luxury in an arid country like Persia. I had got some before in the wooded country near Astarabad, but nowhere had I seen honey in Khurasan, and I was pleased to find that the villagers here knew something of bees and were able to hive them in baskets; but, so far as I could gather, they had no idea of preserving the bees during the winter, and when they took the honey they left the bees to die.

Our next march was down the valley of the Firizi stream to the end of the Chil-i-Shah ridge, and then round that to Khurramabad, a little village of some thirty houses out in the plain at a height of about 3900 feet. My object was to explore the hills still farther to the north, but our way was barred by the Chil-i-Shah ridge. There was no path over it practicable for baggage-mules, and there was nothing for it but to leave the hills and go round. The great feature of the Nishapur range is the comparative steepness of its slopes on the Nishapur side, which go straight down to the level of the plain, whereas on the eastern side there is a large elevated tract, from 4000 to 5000 feet in height and some ten miles in width, cut up by innumerable ravines and valleys between the higher range and the level of the Mashhad plain. It is in this tract that all the villages and orchards that we had been visiting were situated, and we now had to leave it and move out into the plain to get farther north. The reason that we selected Khurramabad for our camping-ground was that we heard there was an engraved stone in some ruins close by, and, not long after our arrival, Moula Bakhsh and I rode off to explore them. There was little to be seen, however, but some low mounds and ruined mud walls, except one small enclosure which our guide assured us with great earnestness had been discovered to be an Imamzadah, or saint's tomb, by an old blind man in the village, who dreamt one night that it was so; and when they dug out the place next day, sure enough they found the tomb. The ruins were known as Manijan, and the tradition was that this was the site of a large city built by Manija, the daughter of Afrasiab, and called after her.

After wandering some time about the place I was beginning to wonder where the engraved stone could be, when suddenly the guide stopped before a large flat piece of limestone, or some light-coloured rock, lying prone on the ground, about fourteen or fifteen feet in length, six to eight in breadth, and from one to two feet in thickness. On the southern edge of this stone was an inscription in a single line in large, roughly cut Arabic letters. The stone did not give one the idea of ever having been a slab cut for inscription. On the contrary it appeared to be a natural piece of rock left lying in the middle of the plain by some freak of nature. It rang when struck like so much metal. The only words that could be deciphered were the three in the centre of the line, viz. Muhammad Khwarazm Shah. There was evidently a date in Arabic words following these, but it was illegible. On looking up the history of this Muhammad Khwarazm Shah, I found that he fled to Khurasan in the year 617 (A.D. 1220), and that Changiz Khan sent two generals with 30,000 cavalry in pursuit of him, one of whom came to Tús and Radkhan. It is possible, therefore, that this Sultan Muhammad Khwarazm Shah saw this stone in his flight and had his name engraved upon it. The samo Sultan Muhammad is also mentioned by Elias in his "Tarikh-i-Rashidi."[1] There is another Khwarazm Shah mentioned as well, but his name was Sultan Atsaz

[1] Pp. 287-289.

Khwarazm Shah, not Muhammad. He is said to have died at Khurramdara, of Kuchan, in the year 551 (A.D. 1156). Whether there is any connection between Khurramdara and Khurramabad it is impossible to say. Atsaz was the son of Muhammad, the son of Anushtagin, who was born in 490 (A.D. 1096), and possibly the inscription may have been Atsaz bin Muhammad Khwarazm Shah, and this stone was in reality his tombstone, though now so rough and chipped. If any one hereafter is able to decipher the date, the question will be settled.

From Khurramabad we marched seven miles along the plain at the foot of the hills, and then turned west for a mile or so up a gorge till we came to a large dam of stone and mortar built right across the valley, 260 paces in length and 14 paces in breadth, with a height of about 40 feet, and a sluice underneath to let the water through. There were four circular masonry wells in the face of the *band* for carrying off flood-water through arched passages some 45 feet in length at the bottom. Water, we were told, though, was only held up by this dam for a short time in spring. The tradition was that it was built by Bai Sangar, the son of Shah Rukh, the son of Amir Timur, who, according to the Sani-ud-Dowlah, was appointed governor of Tús and Kuchan in 1414 A.D. The villagers declared that there was formerly an inscription on the *band* giving the name of Bai Sangar, and also indicating that money was to be found under one of the buttresses for the repair of the *band* in case it should give way. This inscription was now lost, they said, but they gave me the lines of the rhyme in its original Persian, which, translated into English, ran as follows:—

> "Left, left, to the left of the left road,
> Seven jars of gold to the left hand;
> Whenever the band is ruined,
> The cost of the band under the left foundation."

No one, though, had as yet succeeded in finding those seven jars.

A couple of miles higher up, and after passing through a deep and narrow gorge, with solid walls of rock two and three hundred feet in height on either side, we came on the village of Aklamad, surrounded by lofty and precipitous hills on all sides. The village stands at a height of about 4450 feet, and there is a path over the hills at the back of it to Bar on the Nishapur side, but it runs up a sort of devil's staircase, and nothing but the village donkeys can get over it. Aklamad is consequently almost unapproachable except through the gorge, and there are the remains of a wall built across that about half a mile below the village. The place is noted for its apples, and it was to Aklamad that I sent to get young grafted trees for the Consulate garden at Mashhad. I did not see any game about, but there were some small oorial in the cliffs around, and the place was said to have been known in former days as Bisha-i-Gurazan, or the Wild-Boar Jungle, from the number of pigs it contained. A mile or so below the village there is a curious cave in the rocks about thirty feet up on the right side of the gorge called Palang-darra, or the Panther's Cave. The entrance is a small round hole just big enough for a man to creep in, and smooth all round. Inside is the cave some forty yards in length by ten in breadth, and five or six feet in height, containing a mass of some sort of rock-crystal quite different from the rocks around.

CHAPTER XXI.

RADKHAN, BAM, AND SAFIABAD.

AKLAMAD was the last place I had to visit in the Nishapur range. I had now examined all the eastern face of it, and I determined to strike across the Mashhad Valley and have a look at Radkhan. We rode across the plain till we struck the high-road from Mashhad to Kuchan, and then on to Mili, where we camped on the edge of the Chaman-i-Gobagh, which consists of a long flat depression or marsh some two miles in width and eight in length, covered with small yellow grass in the autumn, but in the spring full of grass a foot or two in height, affording magnificent pasturage. Gobagh, or the Ulang-i-Radkhan, as it is generally called, is the historical camping-ground of kings and armies.

According to the Habib-us-Siyar, Sultan Sanjar (1126–57) was here a great deal. Amir Timur came in 1382 and 1407, Sultan Abu Said in 1467, and many others. Shaibani Khan (1510), it was said, came here every spring, returning to Merv in the summer. Gobagh is a village on the eastern side of the marsh opposite to Mili, and presumably it ought to be spelt Gokbagh, or the blue garden, and it has been suggested that it was the site of the blue palace built by Shaibani Khan, and his favourite resort.

Turning up north-westwards along the eastern side

of the marsh for some three miles, we came to the famous tower—the great landmark of the district—known as the Mil-i-Radkhan. This is a brick building some fifty paces in circumference and eighty feet in height. The walls are some seven or eight feet in thickness, octagonal inside and circular outside. The plinth is about eight feet in height, and above that the face of the building consists of thirty-six semicircular pillars. At the top of these originally ran an inscription in Kufic characters inlaid with blue tiles, but this is utterly defaced now. Above this rises the conical top. The building is now hollow throughout, with two doors opposite each other at the bottom, but a circular staircase originally ran up one side of it inside the wall, and there were evidently interior floors and an inner dome. An earthquake or something has cracked and split the tower on both sides, so that it is doubtful if it will stand another shock. Whether it was constructed as a mausoleum, or what, it is impossible to say. One tradition ascribes it to Sultan Sanjar. Another idea is that it was built by Alp Arslan (1063), who held a great assembly of all his nobles, governors, and chiefs at Radkhan to announce the appointment of his son, Malik Shah, as his heir-apparent. A third report is that it is the mausoleum of Amir Arghun Agha, a Mongol noble, who was sent to Khurasan by Uktai Khan, the son of Changiz Khan, to repair the damage done by his father. Arghun Agha made Radkhan his headquarters, and died in 1274.

The present town of Radkhan stands two miles to the north of the pillar, and is said to have been built by Raza Kuli Mirza, son of Nadir Shah. It was surrounded by a wall and ditch, but this is now all out of repair. The ruins of former Radkhans lie to the south-east, nearer to the pillar, and their glory has quite departed. The present town does not contain more than

800 houses, despite the excellent situation and the amount of water it possesses.

The chief of Radkhan, Muhammad Ibrahim Khan, is the son of Muhammad Raza Khan, the last chief of the Kiwanlu Kurds. These Kiwanlus were brought to Khurasan by Shah Abbas at the same time as the Zafaranlu, Shadillu, and other Kurds now on this frontier. At that time they are said to have mustered 12,000 families, but the number has gradually dwindled down. The author of the diary of the Shah's journey to Khurasan in 1867 gives their numbers then at 5000. Now probably 3000 is nearer the mark. Three sections of the tribe hold the Radkhan district down to Chashma-i-Gilas, and in the summer go up into the Hazar Musjid Mountains. Five other sections live in the hills on the Daragez border; others are scattered about Khurasan, some 300 or 400 families being in the Juwain district south of Isfarain.

The Kuh-i-Imarat, as the hills on the Daragez border are called, is a well-known range, said to possess numerous villages, streams, and pastures, and also to be famed for its herbs, and to be covered with juniper trees. According to the chief, all the hills at the back of Radkhan were full of game. The number of partridges was something wonderful, he said. They shot and trapped sacks full of them in the winter when driven down by snow, and the birds sold then at ten for a kran, or a halfpenny apiece; the price while we were at Radkhan being four for a kran. There were also plenty of oorial, and the Hazar Musjid range at the back of all was full of sport, despite that it was overrun with nomads in the spring.

The Kiwanlus had no ruling chief, and Muhammad Ibrahim Khan was only their leading Khan. His grandfathers, he told me, had been hereditary ruling chiefs for generations, the same as the chiefs of Kuchan and Bujnurd, but the process that has been so surely and steadily going on all over Persia had gone on here, and the hereditary chiefship had been abolished, and a local governor appointed in his stead.

In reading up the history of Radkhan, I found that both in the Shah's diary of 1867,[1] and in the Sani-ud-Dowlah's "Matla'-ush-Shams,"[2] mention was made of the bones of a mammoth having been found at Radkhan, and of the teeth of the animal having been produced before the Shah, who handed them over to his French physician, Dr. Tholozan, in whose library at Teheran they were said to have been preserved. I inquired about this, and Muhammad Ibrahim Khan sent a man to show me the place where the bones were found. The man took me down a walled lane by the side of a small nullah through the gardens at the south of the town, and described to us how some forty or forty-five years before, when a boy of ten or twelve years of age, he and two others were returning home from some village out in the valley when they saw a great bone sticking out from a hollow in the ground that had been washed out by a flood of water. They got spades and commenced to dig, and about two feet underground found the head and bones of some huge animal. They carried the bones to Radkhan, where they soon broke up, and the pieces were dispersed and lost. Nothing was preserved but two teeth, one of which he declared weighed a man and a half, and the other a man and a quarter, or $9\frac{3}{4}$ and $8\frac{1}{8}$ lbs. respectively. The man described the skull, which he said was perfect when first taken out, and he declared, and stuck to it, that it had one horn which came out of the middle of the top of the head. He was positive of this, and he was corroborated in his statement by another old man. It would be satisfactory to know what animal these teeth belonged to.

[1] P. 310. [2] P. 172.

When returning Muhammad Ibrahim Khan's visit, I found him waiting for me at the outer door with a sheep, whose throat was cut in front of me as I arrived, and I thus stepped across its blood in orthodox fashion as I entered the gate. I was conducted to a tent in the garden, where we sat and chatted, Muhammad Ibrahim Khan told me that without doubt there was a vast swamp at Radkhan in olden days, covering the whole valley. He himself, he said, could remember the time when reeds and wild pigs abounded, though now there was nothing but a grassy plain. He had marvellous tales of enormous snakes, as thick as a tent-pole, which were still to be found in the swamp in the spring, but of this I had no ocular proof.

From Radkhan we marched five miles out into the centre of the valley and camped at Saidabad, about a mile from which we crossed the Kashafrud, here a little stream with a muddy bed not more than six feet in width and six inches deep, fed by the springs in the marsh farther up to the north-west. The ground we crossed was mostly soft, salt earth, and the whole area of the marsh in the morning was covered with a thick, low mist, and the cold was great while we were in it. The people at Mili and elsewhere told us that they never remained in their villages on the edge of the swamp in the winter, but moved out into black tents in the ravines of the hills to the north, for the sake of warmth. It struck me at first as a strange idea to move out of a thick, solid mud-hut into a thin blanket-tent in the midst of the winter snows for the sake of warmth, but I understood it well when once I got into the damp cold of that Gobagh swamp fog. The cold, however, did not prevent the sand-grouse from coming for their morning drink, and I had some capital shooting as we went along.

On arrival at Saidabad I found there were the ruins of an old fort a short distance to the south of the village, called

Kila-i-Gaur, or more correctly, Kila-i-Gabr, the fire-worshipper's fort, and while walking over it I turned to the villager with me and asked if they had never found old coins in it. This he was energetically denying as usual, it being fatal to any man to own to having found treasure in Persia, when suddenly Nafas, the son of Koki Sirdar, who was with me, turned and said, "Here is a coin," and picked up an old copper at his feet. We did our best to decipher it, but without result, and I could get no information as to who the fort originally belonged to. My servants came back from their gossip in the village *hamman* with marvellous stories of a dragon that was sitting on guard over treasure in one of the towers, and strange to say they believed the tale thoroughly. Close by the fort was another building, an old brick *rubat* or rest-house.

Near to our camp we had a large black tent encampment of Kurds, who had numbers of sheep and camels grazing on the marsh grass around. They were a cheery lot of people, and when I went amongst them I was surrounded at once by men, women, and children, who all talked and laughed away in the merriest manner. In Persian towns and villages it is so seldom that one sees any women, that the free life of the nomads strikes one all the more. The number of children these Kurds had was something phenomenal. They simply swarmed around me. I duly congratulated the men on having their quivers so full, and they all laughed and said it was their one regret that their women would not have children more than once a year; an idea which seemed to tickle the good wives immensely.

Sending on the main camp round the foot of the hills, Moula Bakhsh and I went up to take a last look at the northern portion of the Nishapur range. We camped on an undulating plateau, some 5700 feet in height, at the little village of Dash Bulagh. Beyond that undulating uplands from 6000 to 7000 feet in height, with little or no surface water, but evidently covered with high grass in the spring, continued to the top of the range. These uplands were utterly deserted at this time of the year, although the climate and air was delicious. One small pig was the only thing we came across, but, as usual, the ground was infested with rats. I caught another of the little mouse hares, but all attempts failed to keep any of them alive. They all refused to eat or drink, and soon died.

We joined the camp again at Hissar, a village peopled by Zafaranlu Kurds. As we approached all the women came out to see us arrive, a sure sign that we were amongst a different class of people from the Persian residents in the plains nearer Mashhad. The village musicians, a drummer and a fifer, played us in, and the head-boy of a local school came out and recited some composition in our honour by the village pedagogue. The boys all had a good scramble for coppers, which created much amusement.

Twelve miles farther took us to Chakana, which lay in a narrow valley, at a height of something like 5000 feet, and contained about 150 families of Bayát Turks.

Chakana was the headquarters of the Sar-i-Valayat district, which we now entered, and which extended on both sides of the Mashhad watershed, and comprised the western portion of the elevated tract of country from which not only the Mashhad waters on the east, but the waters of Bam, Safiabad, and Juwain on the west, took their rise. The district contained 62 villages, big and little, all inhabited by Bayát Turks, a tribe numbering some 15,000 families. The revenue was said to be 6000 tumans (£1200), made up of sheep-tax 1000, land revenue 2000, and house-tax (of 2 tumans per family) 3000 tumans.

These Bayát Turks said that they had been brought to this district by Nadir Shah from Irak, or somewhere in the neighbourhood of Teheran. In former times they had a ruling chief of their own, but this they had lost, like almost all other tribes.

The watershed, which we crossed about a mile out of Chakana, was very slightly marked. After crossing it, we circled round the foot of the Kuh-i-Ashik, and following up the banks of a nullah, we camped first at a village called Khwajahabad, and next at Yangija. Some two miles to the south lay a solitary peak called the Kuh-i-Mar, or Markuh, a conical peak forming a good landmark. A little way up the stream was a saint's tomb in a walled enclosure, the object of much local veneration. Inquiring into the origin of this, I was told that a man in the village had dreamt that an Imamzada had appeared to him, and had told him that if they dug in this place they would find his tomb. They dug, and found a curious fragment of polished stone. This was sufficient. A large mound was built up over the spot, the precious bit of broken stone was put on the top, a wall was built round it, and the place at once became holy and venerated accordingly. Not only the guide who told the story, but all the men with me placed the most implicit confidence in the alleged dream, and it was curious to see what a wonderful hold such stories have on the popular mind in Persia.

At Yangija we left the Amirabad stream, and passed through a stony and uninteresting country, mostly covered with wild thyme. The people that we met spoke only Turki, and were little used to strangers. We crossed a *kotal*, or pass, at a height of some 6100 feet, and descending into the valley of the Bar stream we came to Nashib, a group of three villages, two of them inhabited by Bayát Turks under the Sar-i-Vilayat district, and the third by

Bughairi Turks under the Bam-Safiabad district, which we now entered. The Bughairis struck one as a much more pleasant sort of people than the Bayáts. The latter would give nothing without being paid for it beforehand, and seemed to distrust every one in every way, whereas with the former it was just the contrary. The very children were different. Scattering some coppers amongst them to be scrambled for, each Bughairi boy as he got one at once ran up to touch my hand as a sort of thanks, whereas in other places every boy that got a coin promptly concealed it and swore that he had got nothing.

The whole of the Bam-Safiabad district was peopled by these Bughairi Turks, who numbered some 1300 families all told. Of these there were two sections, the first, under Bam, numbering 800 families; and the second, under Safiabad, 500; the latter being called Sarakhsis, because they came from Sarakhs. Both sections had chiefs of their own till within the last generation. Now the descendants of these chiefs have neither position nor power. According to the Sani-ud-Dowlah,[1] the Bughairi is a section of the tribe of Garaili Turks who were brought from Karakoram to Khurasan by Hulaku Khan (1253–64).

From Nashib we moved to Fathabad, and then crossing another pass at a height of 6250 feet, we descended 1000 feet in the next three miles to the village of Bam. The mountains rising some three or four miles to the north of Bam were locally known by the name of Shah Jahan, and this seemed to be the general name for the range. According to the Shah's diary of 1867[2] the Bam-Safiabad district is separated from the Kuchan district by the Kuh-i-Jahan Arkian, the northern slopes of which are occupied by the Zafaranlu Kurds, and the southern slopes by the Bughairi Turks. All we could

[1] Matla'-ush-Shams, vol. i. pp. 157, 158. [2] P. 314.

learn as to the origin of this name was that Arkian was an ancient town at the foot of the mountain some three or four miles from Bam, the site of which was now occupied by a village called Jahan. The Sani-ud-Dowlah gives the following explanation:—

> "It is said that on the top of Kuh-i-Shah Jahan are two mausoleums called Shah Jahan and Jahan Arkian. Therefore the skirts on this side (*i.e.* the north) are called Shah Jahan, and those on the other side Jahan Arkian, as the tomb of Shah Jahan inclines towards this and the tomb of Jahan Arkian on that side."

Whether this is the case or not I do not know. The only thing that seemed to be certain was that the Shah Jahan mountain was a range distinct from the Aladagh marked on the maps.

Shortly after our arrival at Bam, a man in the village turned up to offer himself as a guide. His qualifications were that he had been to Ashkabad and could speak Russian. In Central Asia the Persian or any other villager who goes into Russian territory learns to speak Russian. The Russians work on the same pay and on perfect equality with the Persians, Afghans, Turkomans, and all Asiatics. They dress in the same manner, live in the same way, and mix together freely. In India the Englishman can neither work on the same pay as the native, nor live like the native, nor dress like the native. Any villager, Persian or Afghan, who goes into British India never learns to speak English, he only learns Hindustani. The difference is curious, and exemplifies the different systems and modes of life.

In the evening the Shahzadah or Persian prince, the governor of the district, arrived and came to dinner. He showed me a silver coin which he said was one of the coins of the treasure-trove recently found by the Saham-ud-Dowlah at Bujnurd. It appeared to be a Sassanian coin, but I could not be certain. The reports of a wonderful find at Bujnurd had been all over the country for months, and had at last got to the ears of the Shah, who promptly despatched a man all the way from Teheran to Bujnurd to find out the truth of the matter. The man had returned to Teheran, so it was said at Mashhad, with a few gold pieces and the report that nothing more had been found. The Shahzadah, fresh from the spot, had heard a different story. This was that a boy chasing a young partridge followed it into a hole. Inside he found a cave containing a golden idol with jewelled ear-rings and other things, and much coin. The boy told his mother, the mother told the father, and the latter lived in comfort for some time by selling the coins a few at a time. At last the chief heard of the sale of these coins, and then the whole thing was up. The chief promptly traced and arrested the man, and made him show the cave. No sooner had he seen that than he killed the man, and melted the idol and everything up. Only a few of the silver coins had been saved, and this was one of them. It is something marvellous the way in which treasure-trove stories spring up in Persia. The whole country is full of them.

From Bam we had a march of seventeen miles south to Safiabad, which contained some 200 houses of Turks brought here from Sarakhs by Nadir Shah, under a chief named Safi Khan, who gave the name to the place. Its height was about 4000 feet.

About a mile to the north of the village lay a long, low, narrow hill, called by the people Tappa-i-Nauriz, a corruption from Nauzar, one of the last of the Paishdadian kings who ruled Persia prior to the Kayani dynasty, which came into power in 708 B.C. To the east of this were the ruins of a caravanserai strongly built in stone and mortar, a rare thing in these parts. The building was some sixty yards square, and contained, among other rooms, the remains of a musjid and a bath. To the east of this again were the remains of various mausoleums built in the same style. These were all, doubtless, of Muhammadan origin. The ruins of a large town were said to extend all round the hill, but the land had been mostly ploughed up, and nothing but bits of brick and pottery were left to mark the site. The hill itself, though, was full of interest. The top was covered with the remains of mud buildings intermixed with bricks and stones. It was under these that the interest lay. The hill or mound consisted of thick masses of conglomerate lying on the top of hardened mud, and it was by the merest chance that we heard of an old Saiyid who was said to have found vast underground bazars inside it. We got hold of this Saiyid, and he pointed out to us places where he said entrances were to be found. I set men to work to dig at the spots indicated, and sure enough we found that the mound, which was some 500 yards in length by 50 or 60 in breadth and some 50 feet high, was tunnelled throughout its entire length. This tunnel had been run through the hardened mud immediately under the flat conglomerate which formed the roof, and apparently in olden times was of sufficient height for a man to walk upright. Now the mud had fallen in and filled up the floor, and it was only possible to creep along, and at places the opening was barely big enough for a man to crawl through. One of my men went in for about 250 yards. I myself only got about half that distance. Apparently the tunnel consisted of a main street, with little rooms at each side. Each room had a small well in it something like those we found in the rock-cut caves at Panjdeh[1]; but the rooms were so filled up that it was difficult to distinguish what they were for. We found them tenanted solely by hyænas

[1] Northern Afghanistan, p. 193.

and porcupines, which apparently abounded in the place. One entrance was under the old gateway of the city above, about a third of the way down from the northern end of the mound, and other two were near the southern end, all on the western side; a fourth entrance we found at the northern end on the eastern side. All these apparently communicated with each other in olden days. Inside the entrance under the old gateway was a well, now only twenty feet deep, but the Saiyid declared that he remembered it very deep with running water at the bottom, and that it was only of late years that it had got filled up.

In the middle of the mound my men told me they found what seemed to have been a water-mill, and the old Saiyid was full of stories of underground streams and other wonders, having spent years, apparently, crawling about in these passages; but, so far as we could gather, without much result. The only thing we found was a curious round ball of polished marble which we came across in digging out the entrance. A low hill to the north-west was also declared by the Saiyid to have rooms excavated in it, one of which contained ten or fifteen skeletons. He pointed out where the entrance was that he had found. It was under a grave, and now blocked up. From the well under the gateway in the main mound a passage ran down to the north, and this, the Saiyid said, led underground to this low hill beyond. It was terribly hard work crawling about the passages, and all the men were pretty well done by the evening. One amusing incident happened, and that was the fright one of my servants and the Duffadar of the orderlies got when first exploring the well. They came flying out and declared that they had disturbed a dragon, and nothing would induce them to return till they had sent to camp for their swords. The governor's Naib or deputy in the village was in a great state of mind at our doings. Nothing would convince him that we had not found treasure, and he felt sure that he would suffer for it accordingly.

We spent one day in an expedition to Dakma Nauriz, or the cave of Nauzar, a ride of sixteen miles and back. The old Saiyid told us such wonderful stories of a cave in the Yarimja mountain, as he said, a farsakh away, that Moula Bakhsh and I determined to go and see it. He declared that a Darwesh had induced him to accompany him to the cave some years before, and that they had spent three nights in it, and had found rooms full of skeletons and a passage that led right through the mountain to the turquoise mines at Madan, and running water and an engraved stone; but instead of one farsakh, we went on and on till we had ridden four farsakhs, and then the old man could not remember where the place was.

At last he led us to a cave in a face of limestone rock in a ravine which turned up to the north, not far from two white mausoleums belonging to the villages of Surkh and Sangar. The entrance was very small, and invisible from below. After working our way for some distance into the hill through a narrow cleft in the rock we found the passage blocked by stones, and had to return. The place, it was true, seemed to be full of skeletons, as we found three skulls in the short distance we were able to traverse. We had no time, though, to stay long with such a long ride back to camp Several of our horses during the day were bitten by some poisonous fly, which caused a huge swelling under their bellies, which the animal would not allow any one to touch.

From Safiabad we moved on to Alas, a small hamlet of eight houses on the edge of the plain, which here stretched away to the west, and was dotted with the black tents of Zafaranlu Kurds from Kuchan, who had come to graze their cattle and sheep during the winter months. Looking south-west, the horizon was bounded by the line of hills running to the south of Tabas and Jaghatai. Between these hills and ourselves lay a long line of mounds dividing the Safiabad-Mangli plain from Juwain, and the Garmab stream at Safiabad was said to run west to Mangli, and thence to Garatai along the north of these mounds. Mangli was described to me as the ruins of an ancient town built of burnt brick.

Ten miles farther on took us to Dastgird, across the watershed of the range of hills that divides the Safiabad from the Bam valleys, at a height of about 5200 feet. I here first realised that these hills were a separate range, extending a considerable distance due west out into the plain, and that Bam had its own drainage system, separate from that either of Safiabad or Isfarain.

Two marches westward took us out of the Bam Valley into the Isfarain district. The road led west along the foot of the Shah Jahan range. The Bam nullah then swept round to the south through the low hills and ran down to Garatai, the bend of the nullah making the termination of the Bam Valley; beyond, or to the west of that, lay Isfarain. Shortly below Garatai the Bam and Safiabad streams united, and ran down together towards Jajarm, quite separate from the drainage of the Isfarain valley.

Before I visited this part of the country I had an idea from the map that Isfarain was one large desert plain, with one nullah through the centre of it. On inspection I found that it was not a desert plain at all, but rather a hilly tract, with separate valleys and streams, and full of villages wherever there was water at the foot of the hills. The Safiabad and Bam valleys at the eastern end ran parallel to each other more or less, and were divided by a mass of low hills that broadened out as it went west. The Bam Valley was the smaller of the two, being only two or three miles in width and some twenty miles in length, and lay at an elevation of 1000 to 1200 feet higher than that of Safiabad.

CHAPTER XXII.

ISFARAIN AND JUWAIN.

WE paid a short visit to Garatai—which we found only contained some forty families of Bughairi Turks, and stood at a height of about 3350 feet—then camped for the night at Kasimabad, and rode on next morning to Mianabad, the headquarters of the Isfarain district. The village was a large one of some seven hundred houses, and was surrounded by a large expanse of garden enclosures and suburbs. There was no inhabited village of Isfarain; and Mianabad, instead of being in the midst of a large plain as marked on the maps, was situated at the extreme north of it, immediately under the mountains, at a height of about 3900 feet. The valley to the south was some eight miles in width, with the ruined walls of the Shahr-i-Bilkis standing out prominently in the centre, and seemed to be one of the most fertile places I had come across. It was under Bujnurd, and was mostly peopled by Shadillu Kurds, the governor being Mir Panj Nasratulla Khan, the eldest son of the chief of Bujnurd, who was away at Bujnurd at the time of my visit, so I did not see him.

The ruins, locally called the Shahr-i-Bilkis, consisted of two parts, the citadel and the city. The citadel was some 400 yards in length and 150 in breadth, and stood upon a mound or rampart twenty or thirty feet above the plain, and surrounded by high mud walls. The place must be of great age, judging from the height of the ramparts on which the walls stand, resembling Farah and Herat in this respect. These ramparts, I take it, have been gradually formed by the constant washing down of the mud walls on them during centuries of rain, and the continued building up of the walls again by the men inside them; consequently, the higher the mound or rampart the greater the age of it. To the north-east of this citadel lay the ancient city, presumbably, of Isfarain, some two or three miles in circumference. The walls were still ten or twelve feet thick in places. The ground inside had been ploughed up and levelled, but many mounds still remained, and many coins and relics were said to be found in them. My servants all rushed off to dig in the ruins directly we arrived. They were full of tales they had heard from the people about of wonderful finds of sorts, more especially of some men who had come to dig and work the soil for gold the year before, and had paid the governor a tuman a day for the use of the water. These men had continued to dig for some considerable time at this high rate, till at last one night they decamped, and it was supposed they had found something very good and had made off with it.

I could find no coins amongst the villagers, as not a soul would confess to owning any; but at last I got hold of an old man who had spent much of his life digging about the place, and from him I purchased a bag of old copper coins at the rate of two Persian coppers for each one of his. This came to fourteen coins per kran, or a little more than a farthing apiece, which was as much as they were worth, as they were simply a mass of dirt and rust, and after much cleaning and labour we could make nothing of them. It was impossible to say to what age they belonged. The principal work of the old man seemed to be washing the soil for gold. He said he rarely found gold coins, but that he found minute fragments of gold mixed with coloured beads and other odds and ends, and from what we could gather he found sufficient to pay for his labour. Whatever coins were found appeared to be mostly Muhammadan.

Isfarain is mentioned by Ibn Haukal as one of the dependencies of Nishapur, but no details are given by him regarding it, and the only mention I have found of it about that date is the record, under the head of the notable men of Nishapur, that Shaikh Abu Ishak Isfaraini, priest and author, died at Nishapur in A.H. 418 (A.D. 1027), and his body was removed to Isfarain.

The "Zinat-ul-Majalis," written in 1595, describes Isfarain as a middle-sized town with a temperate climate and a large number of walnut trees, and says that its Jama Musjid possessed a basin the circumference of which was twelve zars. This reference to the Jama Musjid seems to point to the Shahr-i-Bilkis of the present day as the old Isfarain. The Jama Musjid building in the centre of the ruins existed within the memory of the present generation, and it had only been destroyed of late years by people carrying off the bricks of which it was built. One coin found in the ruins had the word "Isfarain" clearly marked on it in Persian character. It was difficult to ascertain how long the city had been deserted, but according to local tradition it was finally destroyed by the Afghans, presumably in the invasion of 1731. The walnut trees have now entirely disappeared, and Isfarain stands a deserted heap of low mounds, stones, and broken bricks, out in the open plain, Its height is about 3800 feet. How the name Shahr-i-Bilkis, or Shahr-i-Saba, as I also heard it called, came to be connected with it I have no idea. I never heard that the Queen of Sheba was supposed to have emanated from

Khurasan. However, Persians have the liveliest imaginations of any people I know, and they may have imagined even that.

The stories current amongst the people regarding my advent were marvellous and numberless. The first, of course, was that I was going to take the country and declare it British territory. The second, that I was to repopulate the city, there being a prophecy that the city was to be repopulated again, and its being so would be one of the signs of the coming of the Mahdi. Another idea was that I was to kill a cow on the ruins, and to cut its skin into one long thong, and as much of the land as I could encompass with that was to be British territory. A fourth idea was that the Shah had sent me to reassess the revenue. Each man apparently let his imagination run riot on his own particular fears. As to my men, they dug away in the mounds with great zest all day, but the only results were four old copper coins found by a Peshkhidmat, and three more by the Vakil or Naik of the Persian Guard. I could hear of no traces of tiles, or bowls, or china of any sort, though there were lots of fragments about.

To the south of the ruins there was a *ulang* or marsh affording good pasturage, the springs in which gave rise to a stream that watered five villages on the southern side of the valley. The whole place, though, seemed to be full of springs, and water was flowing everywhere, while the valley was said to contain no less than 50 villages altogether. The Government revenue was 6000 tumans in cash and 12,000 kharwars of grain, but the amount realised by the local governor was said to be double that, the villages and cultivation having increased of late years. Cotton and opium were both largely grown, and the people of Isfarain as a whole, men, women, and children, seemed to be almost more addicted to opium-smoking than any I had seen, and that is saying a good deal in a country where this particular form of vice is so very prevalent, and where the sad effects of it are everywhere visible. There were lots of wild duck flying about, and also some big bustards and sand-grouse.

From Shahr-i-Bilkis we marched to Fariman, and then to Chahar Burj. Here the line of low hills that divided the Bam and Safiabad valleys merged into the plain and came to an end, and the Isfarain Valley widened out, sloping down to the south-west for some twelve or fifteen miles. The plain was dotted with the black tents of Zafaranlu Kurds from Kuchan, who were here mixed up as nomads with the Shadillu Kurds from Bujnurd, who inhabited the villages. To the north lay the Behnamdeh or Saluk Mountain, well sprinkled over with juniper trees, which were said to form the principal supply of wood and charcoal for this part of the country. From the nature of the soil and the large amount of broken pottery about, it was clear that Chahar Burj had been a large place at some former period, but I could gather no information of its ancient history. From there we had a march of nineteen miles to Sankhas, as it is called, though I believe the correct name is Sangkhwast. We passed some ruins near the little village of Astain, the name of one of the seven ancient cities that the Isfarain Valley is supposed to have formerly contained. Adkan and Kuran, where two other towns are supposed to have existed, lay on the southern side of the valley.

Near Sankhas the plain was cultivated and thickly dotted with round mud towers—the refuge of the people in the bygone days of Turkoman raids. The people here being Persian-speaking, were doubtless more exposed to raids than their Turki-speaking neighbours the Kurds. Sankhas I found was noted for its wind, which blows down the valley almost continuously every afternoon. We ourselves suffered from it, and the Sani-ud-Dowlah even mentions it in his book, and endeavours to give causes for it. There are the remains of various old buildings about the village, and well situated and watered as it is from the Shughan Valley to the north, it was probably an important place in its day. Its height is about 3000 feet.

Three or four miles to the north was a large and fine *rubat* or rest-house, not far from the village of Kili, at the foot of the Behnamdeh Hills. This *rubat* formed one of the stages on the ancient high-road, which the Sani-ud-Dowlah says[1] says ran from Gurgan by Fars, Dahana-i-Gurgan, Dahana-i-Dasht, Karabil, Ishk, Kili, Karaja, Nasirabad, Sultan Maidan, Hasanabad, Chambarghirbal, Saidabad, and Shankola, to Mashhad, at all of which places there were *rubats* said to have been built by Amir Ali Shir, the Wazir of Sultan Husain Baikara, who died in 1509. I saw those up to Karabil on my Gurgan tour, and I had just seen those at Saidabad and the other end, and here we struck the route in the middle again. I could not help thinking that the *rubat* and ruined town at Safiabad were possibly the Nasirabad of this route.

From Sankhas we worked southwards to Jajarm, round a large saline deposit of soft earth. Beyond that the cultivated land was covered with Turkoman towers the same as at Sankhas. Jajarm contained about 500 houses, and, according to my aneroid, stands at a height of about 2950 feet. In the centre of it is a huge mound some 70 or 80 feet in height, the ark or citadel of former days, and now known by the name of Narin Kila. It is surmounted with the remains of walls and bastions, but these do not apparently represent the original fortifications, as below them again, and buried in the mound, are another and older series of bastions and walls. Part

[1] Matla'-usb-Shams, i. 122.

of these had been exposed on the western side, and I found them to consist of two sets of walls, one above the other. The mound is circular, or rather oval, about 140 by 110 yards in diameter at the top, and has a depression marking what was formerly the site of a large moat all round it below, with a circumference of some 400 yards. I could see no trace of any stone or brick work, nor could I hear of any coins being found in it. I was shown one silver coin which was said to have been found in the ruins, and this was inscribed with the name of the mint of Jajarm and the date 739 A.H. (1339 A.D.). The name of the king we could not read, but the coin showed that at the time it was struck Jajarm was large enough to have a mint of its own. All the other coins I saw were Muhammadan with the exception of one, a copper coin, which had a man on horseback upon it. Although so few coins seemed to be found, the villagers said that when digging out the foundations of their houses they came upon bricks and metal at great depths, which showed that the place was of great antiquity.

To the north of the village lay an old fort, said to have been destroyed by Nadir Shah, who was opposed here by the Garaili Turks. Of these only a few families remained, and they, I found, had lost their Turki, and spoke Persian. The Naib or governor's deputy in the village was a Garaili, and he was an excellent guide to all the different ruins about. To the south, at the western corner of the village, he showed us an old mud ruin some thirty-five yards square, called the Kushk. What it could have been we were all at a loss to understand, and who built it was unknown. It stood high, quite forty feet I should think, and the walls were enormously thick. The lower storey consisted mainly of four cross passages meeting in the centre at right angles. Above these on the first storey were various small rooms, not much wider, in fact, than the walls were thick. Apparently there had been another storey above these again, if not more. The whole building was of unburnt brick, and so much of it had been washed down that it was difficult to tell what it was originally like.

At the south-east corner were the ruins of buildings said to have been erected by Kazim Khan, Garaili, who was for long governor of Jajarm, and was said to have moved from Khalpush to Jajarm in the time of Nadir. Chaman-i-Khalpush seems to have been a famous place in its day, and to have been a general halting-place for kings. Alexander himself is said to have camped there. *Khal*, I believe, means a place, and *push* is the name of a flower, and according to the Sani-ud-Dowlah the jungles around contain many fruit-trees, such as pears, cherries, plums, and a fruit called kundus, while the oak forests shelter maral, tigers, pigs, and deer. Pheasants, wild-fowl, kabk, and tihu are said to be plentiful, and also a special bird called zangulabál, which is not to be found elsewhere in Persia. I was sorry not to be able to visit the place, to see what this bird of the Sani-ud-Dowlah's really was. There are also many cemeteries in the place belonging to the Garailis, some 12,000 of whom are said to have been settled there till after Nadir's death, when the Turkomans raided Khalpush and scattered them all.

In Jajarm we were shown a couple of huge mill-stones cut from some conglomerate rock, the largest being some two feet thick and eleven or twelve feet in diameter. No one could say what these stones were for and where they came from. They were far too large to be worked in the ordinary water-mills of the country.

I rode out to Kila-i-Jalaludin, four miles to the west, near the village of Garma. This fort, which stands on the top of a low hill, is remarkable by being most substantially built of stone and mortar—the rarest thing in

Khurasan, where as a rule everything is built of mud, or rather of sun-dried bricks, which soon relapse into mud so far as looks are concerned. The fort was sexagonal, with a bastion at each corner, the inside of each face being about sixteen yards in length. There were a number of large earthenware jars, of a deep-red colour and very well made, built into these walls and bastions; and the foundations of the building seemed to have been carried down to a considerable depth, another unusual thing in Khurasan, where the foundations are generally the weakest part of a building. Just below the hill on the western side was a spring, but the fort seemed to have been supplied with water from a well down a curious hole in the rock. It was this hole that drew my attention to the place, and on looking up the Sani-ud-Dowlah to see if he made any mention of it, I found that he described the fort and gave it as his opinion that the jars in the walls were for the storage of flour, not of water, as the well inside the fort contained water; but he remarked that this well had no signs of having been artificially made, and looked as if it was natural. In his time the well was filled up to within twenty zars of the top, and the water of the spring, he said, smelt of sulphur. In the "Zinat-ul-Majalis," the author, who wrote in 1595, quoted Hamadulla Mustaufi as the authority for a description of a hill called Shakak, in the vicinity of Jajarm, that had a cleft in it from which came two sangs of water, that is, water sufficient to turn two mill-stones, adding that in the "Ajaib-ul-Makhlukat" it was recorded that in this hill there was a cave in which if a man put his head, he got ill of the smell. Whether the cleft here spoken of and the well in the fort were one and the same it was impossible to say for certain, but I could hear of no other such cleft and no other spring of water similar to that at Kila-i-Jalaludin in the vicinity of Jajarm.

The well, so far as I could see, was very irregular in shape and bore no signs of finished work, and the village people also said that no one could go down it on account of the smell.

Who built the fort was not known. Jalaludin was the title of Malik Shah Saljuki, who reigned from 1075 to 1092. No mention, so far as I could judge from the extracts given, appeared to have been made by the authors quoted above regarding this stone-built fort, and if the hill and the well were the ones mentioned by them, presumably the fort was not built in their day, and the *shagáf* or cleft they wrote of has since been converted into the well.

We found that Jajarm at one time, and that apparently not so very long ago, must have been a big town. A mass of broken bricks and other ruins extended a long way out. About half a mile to the south-east stood the tomb of a saint named Khwajah Ali bin Muhammad Ziyar, in a domed brick building some thirty feet square. There was no inscription or anything, though, to testify to the name. We had a surprise in store for us here, as we found that this tomb was covered up to a height of seven or eight feet with large handsome blue tiles on which verses from the Koran had been brought out in large relief. These tiles were a foot and a half or two feet in length and over a foot in breadth, and beautifully made, and had evidently been brought from some other building and put up on this tomb, as they were fixed in upside down and any way. We could find no date on any of them. The Sani-ud-Dowlah makes mention of some tiles in the Jama Musjid at Jajarm which had also been put up irregularly, but gives no information as to where they came from. One of them, he says, had a date which he thought was 577 (A.D. 1181), but that though the 77 was clear the 5 was doubtful.

To the north of the mausoleum stood another ruined building in stone and mortar, a square room surrounded by cloisters. In the floor of the room was a hole which led down to a large whitewashed underground place, supposed to have been a *sardaba*, for living in during the hot weather. This vault was full of bones and skulls and skeletons in cloth, a ghastly place to get into. The village idea was that these bones were the remains of some army that in former days was seized with cholera at Jajarm, when the bodies of the men that died were thrown into underground chambers instead of being separately buried, though when this happened none could tell. There were many of these underground chambers all round. We could see the brickwork of some just exposed under the ground. Low mounds marked the site of others, but after my experience of the first I did not care to break into any of the others.

The Jajarm district, I found, was badly supplied with water, and what there was was used up in the growing of cotton for export to Russia through the Armenian traders in Sabzawar. The village did not even grow sufficient grain for its own consumption, and the silk industry it formerly possessed had quite died out. The inhabitants were said to be of very mixed origin, and to consist of no less than ten different tribes. The climate was hot, so hot, in fact, as to give its name to the place, Jajarm being a corruption of Jah-i-Garm, or the hot place. The district had been under the rule of the chief of Bujnurd for many years, but formerly it used to be sometimes under Astarabad and at others under Bastám and Nardin.

Bastám is said to have been a pre-Muhammadan town built by Wastam. The fort was repaired by Hussain Kuli Khan, the second brother of Fateh Ali Shah, but the place has now lost its importance owing to the rise of

Shahrud, which is a better centre for trade. It possesses a shrine in the tomb of the saint and philosopher Bayazid Bastámi, who died in A.H. 260 (874). The mausoleum was built in A.H. 702 (1303), and has a shaking tower twenty-four feet high. One of the large porticoes was built in the reign of, and is still called after, Sultan Ujaita, the fifth in descent from Changiz Khan, in A.H. 703 (1383).

Nardin is said to be populated by Alexandrian Arabs, and to be famous for its earthquakes. It possesses a shrine, on a hill to the north-east, known as the tomb of the prophet Daniel, a famous place of pilgrimage. Two miles beyond there is a large and very ancient cemetery containing tombstones cut in a peculiar shape, while some 500 or 600 trees near the tomb are attributed to a miracle by the prophet Daniel. There are no dates on the tomb, only a modern Persian inscription.

Jajarm marked the turning-point in my tour. It was the 10th of November 1897, winter was coming on apace, and I had to turn my face towards Mashhad without further delay. The ground to the east of Jajarm was soft and saline, and the country gradually became perfectly bare. At the sixth mile we crossed the combined Isfarain, Bam, and Safiabad streams, here only ten or twelve feet in width and three inches in depth, the water being perfectly salt. The stream ran in a deep bed with precipitous banks some twenty feet below the level of the plain, and it was said to be only passable at two places in summer, and in the winter not to be passable at all, so bad was the soil. We crossed the watershed at a height of about 3300 feet, and emerged into the Juwain Valley, some 300 or 400 feet below it.

We passed through large beds of gypsum in these low hills, both in the white crystal stage and in the more earthy deposits, and it was from here evidently that the

Jajarm people in olden days obtained the material for their mortar that is such a marked feature in the ruins of the buildings there. In the Juwain plain we had more soft saline earth to cross, with the Juwain stream of salt-water in the centre of it. We camped at Shafiabad, on the southern side of the valley. Looking westward towards the setting sun, the villagers said there was not another habitation for some fifty miles. A few black nomads' tents might be gathered round the spring at Rubat-i-pul-i-Abrisham, but that was all.

The Shafiabad village was watered by *kanats* brought down from the hills to the south, which here rose up in a succession of five or six rocky ridges one above the other. The villagers were all Persians, and numbered some ninety families all told. The only game about the place seemed to be ruddy sheldrakes, which were in swarms along the salt-water in the stream where I could not get near them. We saw a huge flock of pelicans flying east, and I was amused at our guide, who seemed much pleased at the sight, and assured us that this was a sign of plenty of rain in the coming winter. Whenever the pelicans, he said, came up from the Caspian Sea and went on pilgrimage to Mashhad, they were sure to have a good year.

In the centre of the valley, at the village of Azadwar, were the ruins of the old town of Juwain, from which the district took its name. These ruins consisted of the remains of a lofty building of sun-burned brick, some forty yards by thirty in diameter and forty feet in height, which in former days had three storeys, and possibly four. This was surrounded by a wall and bastions, and to the east of it lay a mass of mounds full of bricks and stones, the remains of the ancient town. I could get no coins or relics. The villagers were too afraid of being tortured on the suspicion of having found treasure to own to the possession of even an ancient copper, and no clue was to be found as to the age of the ruins.

Near Azadwar we found a colony of about 400 families of Baluchi nomads encamped in black tents, who said they had migrated to the Juwain district in the famine of 1871, and had remained there ever since. A large number of Baluchis are said to have been moved by Mahmud of Ghazni from Baluchistan to Sistan, whence they were brought to Khurasan by Karim Khan Zand (1752–79). They numbered some 3000 families all told, and are scattered throughout Khurasan, besides several thousand others still in Kain and Sistan. They have no tribal chiefs, nothing but head-men of sections, and they are everywhere under the local governor of the district.

On leaving the ruins I came upon a flock of the small Indian sand-grouse, the first I had seen in Khurasan. How they got up to Juwain I don't know. Here, too, I had a curious instance of the terribly destructive effect of hawks upon partridges. A boy assured me that there was a covey of partridges in his cotton-field. He said that there were twelve originally, but that the hawks had killed off five, and only seven were left. I asked how he knew it was hawks, and he told me he had found the feathers of each of the five in the place where the hawks had eaten them. I beat his cotton-field, and sure enough up got the seven birds. I shot one, and the question that arose to my mind was, would even a couple be left to breed by next spring? Taking this as a sample of the ordinary covey, it is marvellous how so many birds survive.

From Shafiabad we marched up through the hills by Gaurtan and Dasturan to Jagatai, the headquarters of the Juwain district. Some two miles to the south of Gaurtan there was a curious, conical, rocky hill called

Shadman, and the villagers all declared that the Shikaris who had succeeded in scaling its cliffs said there were the remains of an ancient windmill on the top of it, though how any one could have taken his corn up there to be ground, was more than they could tell. They had also various caves about, full of rock-crystal.

Our night at Dasturan was rendered lively by the free firing that went on over a raid on the village flocks. The village was *en fête*, and everybody was engaged in the festivities at a wedding, when suddenly a shepherd rushed in to say that that three mounted men and several footmen had attacked the flocks and driven off some sheep. The women screamed, the men yelled, and there was no end of a row. We could hear the party in pursuit letting off a lot of powder in the distance, but I never heard that anybody was a bit the worse, or what became of the sheep.

Jagatai was surrounded by a high wall about 600 yards in length and 400 in breadth, and contained some 600 houses of Persians and Kilichi Turks, who called themselves a section of the Garailis. The village stands at the foot of the low hills immediately overlooking the Juwain Valley to the north, and its name must apparently have been derived from Jagatai, the second son of Changiz Khan, who obtained Khurasan on his father's death in 1227, and probably settled some of his tribesmen here.

Juwain is a sub-district of Sabzawar, and was said to contain sixty-five villages and to have a revenue of 18,000 tumans (£3600) of which 8000 was collected as sheep-tax. Silk used to be largely cultivated, but silkworm disease had appeared some ten or twelve years previously, and the production had been much reduced.

At Jagatai I left the upper road through the hills and

went down into the plain, passing round the edge of the long slopes from the range to the south. Four miles out we crossed the nullah running down to Shahristana, a village inhabited by the 600 families of Kaiwanlu Kurds we had already heard of at Radkhan, and distinguishable from afar by its large and solitary chinar tree, which forms a conspicuous object in the centre of the plain. At the eighth mile we crossed another nullah running down to Khusroshir, or the city of Cyrus. Both these villages were said to be very ancient. We saw a good number of deer during the march, but they were all making off towards the hills, and I could not get a shot. The Duffadar, though, with the advance camp, was more lucky, and when I got in I found he had bagged a fine buck gazelle, which he had shot with his Martini carbine. The only thing I bagged was a solitary hubara, the first that I had seen. They do not appear to be plentiful in Khurasan.

Kumaisdan, where we camped, lay three miles south by west of Ak Kala, a place marked in large letters on the map, but which I found to be nothing but a ruin. It consisted of a high-walled, massive citadel about 200 yards square, with a deep ditch, and to the north of that, and joined on to it, a walled town from 600 to 800 yards square. The gate of the citadel opened into the town, and riding through, one found oneself in the midst of a mass of ruined buildings that must have been fine and lofty in their day. The citadel was full of ruined walls and broken-in domes and vaults, much being wantonly destroyed by people digging for burnt bricks. The town was built almost entirely of unburnt brick with the exception of a fine Musjid in the centre, sixty yards in length, which still stood almost entire. It was curious to find such a large fine place, so new-looking and so regularly built all in rectangular lines, and yet so utterly deserted. So far as I could gather, the town was built by Allahyar Khan. Its total life was said to have been only twenty-one years, when it was taken and destroyed by the Hisám-us-Sultanah at the time of the Sálár's rebellion. Allahyar Khan was a difficult man to affiliate. His descent I could make nothing of, but he was apparently a famous chief of the Kilichis, then the most powerful and active section of the Garailis, and who in fact have never had a chief of their own since. He declared himself independent in the reign of Fateh Ali Shah (1798–1834), and was at one time the independent ruler of both Sabzawar and Juwain. He joined the Sálár's rebellion in 1847 with his son and grandson, and all three were eventually captured and taken to Teheran, where they were killed or died. Some grandchildren, I believe, still survive in Jagatai, but they are in very poor circumstances and of no position.

From Kumaisdan we marched to Mihrabad and thence on to Tabas, where we had a sudden drop in the thermometer of 30°. The day before at 4 P.M. it had registered 75° F., and the next day at the same hour it was only 45°, with a bitter cold wind. Winter was evidently coming on.

The country round Tabas was much up and down, and difficult for the mules, but was well populated throughout. Tabas itself was a curious village, lying in a sort of basin surrounded by hills on all sides, at a height of about 4800 feet, and containing about 100 families. Looking back over the Juwain plain to the north, we could see a continuous line of villages along the banks of the Juwain stream in the distance, parallel to the low ridge that bounded the valley on the farther side. The Juwain plain here appeared as a long valley ranging from six to twelve or fifteen miles in breadth, the low ridge to the north of it apparently merging into the Safiabad plain to the east and into the Jajarm plain to the west. We had an ascent of nearly 1000 feet to cross the pass from Tabas, and then a descent of some 1400 feet to our camp at the village of Sang-i-Safed below. It was very cold crossing the pass. The water in our tents was frozen at night, and the horses and mules were all a bit tucked up in the morning.

CHAPTER XXIII.

SABZAWAR, MADAN, AND NISHAPUR.

THE morning of the 18th November 1897 brought us into Sabzawar. The road led straight down the long slope from the hills, a gradual descent of some 1200 feet, Sabzawar standing at a height of about 3050 feet. Approaching from the north, the old citadel stood out prominently on a high rampart, surrounded by a dry ditch, but the walls were in ruins and the interior uninhabited.

The acting governor, Mirza Muhammad Hussain Khan, Herati, met me on my arrival and escorted me through the town, entering by the Irak gate on the west and riding through to my camp, which was pitched outside the Nishapur gate on the east. Sabzawar possesses a covered bazar of brick domes stretching for nearly half a mile almost right across the town from gate to gate, and containing, it is said, 750 shops; and it was through this we rode. We formed quite a procession, with all the governor's sowars and farashes in front, and my clerks, orderlies, and servants behind; and the shopkeepers and others looked up in surprise and wondered who we all were. I heard one man whisper to his neighbour as I passed, "Is he English or Russian?" and that, I fancy, was the general question all along the line. The English and the Russians are the only two nationalities at all generally known in Persia; and though the English may be included in the general name of Faringi, or European, the Russians as a rule never are, and to the Persian the *Urús* is always a separate race.

Our camp was thronged all day by people coming to look at it. They certainly had never seen a British consul-general camped in tents there before. We found that there were no less than thirty Russian Armenians in the town, agents of firms in Russia trading in wool, cotton, and dried fruits, the export trade of which was said to amount to the value of 500,000 tumans, or £100,000 sterling a year. The revenue of the district was said to be 33,000 tumans in cash and 4000 kharwars of grain, and the population of the town to be about 12,000 people.

According to the Sani-ud-Dowlah, the Sabzawar fort or citadel was built by Amir Wajih-ud-Din Mas'ud Sarbdari after the death of Sultan Abu Said Mughul in 1335. The Sarbdari dynasty consisted of twelve kings, but only lasted for forty-four years altogether, viz. from A.D. 1337 to A.D. 1381. They came originally from the village of Bashtin, near Sabzawar, rebelled, and made Sabzawar their capital, and are said to have ruled from Astarabad to Khaf, before the twelfth and last of the race submitted to Amir Timur in 1381, when the dynasty came to an end.

The circumference of the town and citadel is said to be 3880 zars. Deducting 380 zars for the citadel, the circumference of the town is about 3500 zars, or a little over 2¼ miles. The walls were repaired by Allahyar Khan, Kilichi, when ruler of the town, and are still in good condition. Allahyar Khan also built the fort at Mazinan, the stage on the Teheran road just before Pul-i-Abrisham, where the province of Khurasan comes to an end.

The citadel at Sabzawar stands on an artificial mound, which evidently marks the site of something very old, but what that was no one knows. Sabzawar, though not so old as Nishapur, is still considered an old town. It contains at present twelve caravanserais, three Madrasas, and two Musjids. Of these, the Jama Musjid is said to have been built at the time of the Sarbdaris, but it has no date. It contains a stone inscribed with a firman of Shah Tahmasp, dated 1571, remitting certain taxes, and another by Shah Tahmasp II., dated 1723, exempting the people from the payment of presents to governors on arrival, on the ground of their having suffered so much from the raids of Afghans, Baluchis, and Turkomans.

The morning after my arrival I rode out to see the Minar or pillar of Khusrogird, a column of burnt brick which stands close to the high-road about four miles to the west of the town. The column is circular and about a hundred feet in height, with a spiral staircase inside it by which one can ascend to the top. It is said to mark the site of the ancient city of Baihak, made famous by the history known as "Tarikh-i-Baihaki," written by a resident of the town. The inscription round the pillar has long since vanished, but it is popularly supposed to have belonged to a Musjid. Nothing of the ancient city remains, and the ground around has all been ploughed up. Nearly a mile to the north, in the present village of Khusrogird, are the remains of an old sexagonal fort on an artificial mound, about eighty yards in diameter, with high thick walls, surrounded by an outer wall and ditch. This is supposed to have been the citadel.

The pillar has a solid square plinth at the bottom, which is due to Nasir-ud-Din Shah, who visited it on his way to Mashhad; and finding it much damaged and undermined at the base, like almost all ancient buildings in Persia, ordered it to be repaired, to save it from falling down—one of the only instances I have met with in Persia of an ancient building having been repaired in modern times.

Mirza Muhammad Hussain Khan, Herati, the deputy-governor, turned out to be an exceptionally well-informed old man. He came over to dinner and ate heartily, despite the fact that he was eighty years of age and had never used a knife and fork before. He told me that he was in Herat at the time of Todd's mission during the first Afghan war, and he well remembered him and also Lugin, the doctor, and Shakespeare, the assistant. He said that Todd always used to have the *nahar* or midday meal laid on the floor in Afghan fashion, and whoever was there sat down with him. He remained in Herat till the Hisám-us-Sultanah's siege, and retired to Persia with the latter in 1857, and had been in Persia ever since. He was given a pension by the Persian Government, and as Mustaufi had travelled over the whole of Khurasan and Sistan to assess the revenue, and seemed to know it better than any other man I had met.

I had now to visit the turquoise mines at Mádan, and to do this we left the high-road and struck off into the hills to the north-east. We had a rise of some 1600 feet in the first fourteen miles to cross the Kotal to the village of Aliak, and a gradual descent of some 900 feet in the nine miles beyond that to Sultanabad. Here we found ourselves in the Nishapur district, which stretches up as far as Mashkan, while Rubat-i-Gaz, four miles to the north-west, marked the confines of Bam Safiabad. The Kafilah road from Sabzawar to Kuchan and Ashkabad here turned off northwards to Mashkan. From Sultanabad we marched ten miles to Rubati, crossing the usual Persian plain from the foot of the hills on one side to the foot of the hills on the other.

Ten miles farther the next morning brought us up to

the two villages known as Mádan, which stand on some low hills at a height of about 5000 feet, and contain between them 400 houses. I was met on arrival by the two agents of the contractor for the mines, and a guard of twenty men of the Karai battalion under a Naib or Jemadar was drawn up on the road and escorted me in. Fifty men of this regiment are always on duty at the mines, being relieved every six months from Turbat-i-Haidari. The men had no uniforms, and were armed as usual with worthless old muzzle-loading muskets.

We just got into camp in time, as the weather changed and turned to wet, with sleet and rain, and before long all the hills around were covered with snow. As soon as possible I rode out to visit the turquoise mines, with the contractors' agent as guide. I found there was comparatively little to see, and yet, till one had seen it, it was difficult to realise how the turquoises were produced. The mines are situated in the small ravines on the face of a hill about a mile to the north of the village, and to my unpractised eye there was nothing different in that one hill from any of the others around. It was apparently composed of the same dark-coloured rock that is so common throughout the country, and riding past, no one would suppose that it contained minerals of any sort. The mines are worked in the roughest manner possible. The only implements used by the miners are short iron jumpers about eighteen inches in length, and a small hammer with which they drive holes into the rock, which is then blasted out with common country gunpowder. The lights used are common oil lamps, just a wick in a small open saucer, and the consequence is that the galleries are smeared all over with oil and smoke, and the atmosphere inside is stifling. When blasted the bits of rock are collected and brought out to the entrance in small baskets, and outside a lot of small boys break up the rock into little pieces with small hammers and pick out any bits of green or blue they see. The turquoises are not the smooth, round stones one is accustomed to. On the contrary they are flat and jagged and all shapes, just like irregular bits of glass mixed up in the rock. Almost every turquoise is more or less broken in the hammering out; in fact, unless it was broken the blue colour would not be visible. A man stands over the boys and collects all the coloured fragments in a bag. These are taken to the village and sent into Mashhad at the end of the week, there to be ground down into shape by the cutters.

I went to the mine farthest west at first, which was big and high. By creeping in at the small door at the entrance, which is locked at night and watched by a sentry, I got into a gallery some twelve or fifteen yards in length, and from the end of that I could see the miners at work beyond, drilling holes into the rock for blasting. The stone last blasted was brought out and broken up before me, to show me how they picked out the turquoises. I watched the operation, and looked at the turquoises found, but it was impossible to say what was good and what was bad. All the chips with the least bit of colour in them were collected and taken away, and the result was left to the cutters to determine. Subsequently I rode round to the eastern side of the hill, where a great cavity has been cut in the hillside by the quarrying of ages, and one could see old and broken shafts and galleries in all directions. The miners have no windlasses or ropes or anything to help them. They climb down the hole from one step to another, and there is hardly room to turn.

According to the Sani-ud-Dowlah, the turquoise mines are not mentioned in ancient history, and the oldest account of them appears in the "Tansuknama-i-Ilkhani," by Khwajah Nasir-ud-Din, Túsi, written during the reign of Hulaku Khan (1253–64). Up to the end of the Safavian dynasty the mines are said to have been worked by the Persian Government. During the anarchy which ensued between that period and Muhammad Shah's time they passed from one hand to another, and were worked by any local chiefs or tribes who were able to take possession of them. Towards the end of Muhammad Shah's reign they are said to have been let by the Persian Government to the miners living in the two villages for 500 tumans a year. After that the rent gradually rose to 3000 tumans per annum. In 1879 the Malik-ut-Tujjar of Mashhad got a lease of them at a rent of 8000 tumans, and worked them with great profit for three years. In 1882 the Mukhbir-ud-Dowlah, the Persian telegraph minister, outbid the Malik-ut-Tujjar, and rented the mines for fifteen years from the Persian Government at the rate of 9000 tumans for the first year and 15,000 tumans for each succeeding year. He formed a company and worked them for a time, but in 1884 the company fell through, and the Mukhbir-ut-Dowlah gave up the concession. In 1885 the Malik-ut-Tujjar again obtained the lease at a rent of 9000 tumans a year, and he held it till 1893, and is popularly supposed to have made a fortune out of it. He was then outbid and ousted by the Naiyar-ud-Dowlah, the governor of Nishapur, who increased the rent to 11,000 tumans, and held the mines for two years. In 1895 the Timuri chief, the Nasrat-ul-Mulk, and the Herati bankers at Mashhad took a lease of the mines for a term of ten years at an increased rent of 13,200 tumans per annum. This contract was signed by the late Shah, and was confirmed by the present Shah. Yet, despite that, it was cancelled at the end of the first two years, on an offer from the Malik-ut-Tujjar to raise the rent by an extra

10,000 tumans. The latter at the time of my visit was holding the mines at the rent of 23,200 tumans (£4850), but how long he will continue to hold them it is impossible to say. The most solemn contract appears to have no force in Persia, and the instability of the engagements on the part of the Persian Government has naturally been of great detriment to the mines. The contractors, not being sure of their position, have been prevented from working the mines systematically, and from carrying out any improvements, and the result is that the crude and wasteful methods of former ages still maintain themselves in full force.

The Herati bankers at Mashhad, Haji Muhammad Hasan, Mu'awin-ut-Tujjar, and Haji Ali Akbar, Mu'in-ut-Tujjar, to give them their full names and titles, are the sons of a Haji Mulla Ahmad, formerly a banker at Herat. When the Malik-ut-Tujjar ousted them from their lease of the turquoise mines, they retaliated by ousting the Malik-ut-Tujjar from his contract for the Ashkabad-Mashhad cart-road, and thus there was a general post all round, which brought no good to anybody but the Persian officials, who had the handling of the money paid by both parties to effect it. The bankers at one time enjoyed protection by the British Consulate, but they have now become Persian subjects. British Consulate protection is no longer afforded to Afghan subjects in Persia, the Shah objecting on the grounds that Persian subjects get no consular protection in Afghanistan; consequently Afghans who have hitherto looked to the English for help have now no one to whom they can appeal, and suffer in consequence.

As to the working of the turquoise mines, the Sani-ud-Dowlah has given an account, and so has General Schindler of Teheran, who held the management of them for a year in 1882.

The mines themselves are situated in seven different ravines in the hillside. In the first ravine the oldest and most important shafts have all been filled up by careless working, and are now unworkable except at great outlay, which no Persian contractor ventures to incur, not being sure of being allowed to retain his contract for the period specified. In the second one mine only is worked by the contractors, another is filled up and unworkable, and a third is sublet to the miners, who work it themselves. In the third ravine only one mine is worked, and that by the miners; the others are deserted, as it does not pay to work them. Two mines in the fourth are sublet to the miners, while the contractor is working one himself. In the fifth two mines are sublet to the miners, and the contractor there also works one himself, but it is only a branch of an old and important mine now filled up and deserted. In the sixth ravine the one mine is filled with water, and cannot be worked, and in the seventh the mines are neglected, as it does not pay to work them. This of itself shows what an unsatisfactory state the mines are now in. Five regular mines and some half-dozen minor ones are sublet to the village miners at a rent of about 1500 tumans a year, and only three mines, named respectively the Zak-i-Ulya, the Chiragh Kush, and the Gandal-i-Karbalai, are worked by the contractors themselves. These are worked for twelve hours daily, from 9 A.M. to 9 P.M., by two sets of workmen, who relieve each other at 3 P.M. Each set consists of—(1) the Zábit, or overseer, on 3 krans a day; (2) the Ustád, or workman, on 1½ to 2 krans a day; (3) the Amala, or coolie, on 1 kran a day; (4) the Fala, or boy, on ½ to ¾ kran a day. The overseer superintends the working of three or four workmen, and collects the stones. The workman excavates the rock, the coolie removes and carries it from the mine to the open, and the boys break up the rock brought out and pick out the turquoises, which are collected by the overseer. The total establishment employed on each of the three mines is only two relays of three overseers and twelve workmen each, and a total of thirty-seven coolies and boys. All these are under a head overseer, who receives 10 tumans a month, and the accounts are kept by two Mirzas or writers, receiving each 10 tumans a month. Two mounted messengers are employed on 6 tumans apiece per month to carry the stones excavated during the six working days of the week, *i.e.* Saturday to Thursday, in a sealed leather bag to the contractor at Mashhad, where they are cut and prepared for sale. The contractor has also to pay for the guard of fifty men at the mines at the rate of 7½ krans for each man per month, and the working expenses for the cost of gunpowder, oil, &c., are said to amount to 120 tumans a week, in addition to the pay of the establishment. The theft of stones that goes on in the mines is enormous, but for all that the outturn of the three mines is said to come to between 300 and 400 tumans per week, and the total outturn for the year 1896–97 was said to have amounted to 19,000 tumans. In addition to the value of the turquoises excavated from the mines, the contractors were said to have realised 8000 tumans in the shape of taxes from the 400 miners living in the two villages, and 750 tumans more from the inhabitants of the other villages of the district, besides the rent of the mines sublet by them.

In addition to the mines in the hillsides above described, turquoises are also found in the earth and detritus at the foot of the hill, and these are the best and most valuable of all, as they come out unbroken. These earth mines are much easier to work than those in the rock, and old men and boys, the weak and the lazy, seem to dig about promiscuously, and though there is no certainty about it, still, when they do find anything, it is always valuable.

Turquoises at the mines are divided into three kinds —1st, the Angushtari, or stones fit for rings; 2nd, the Barkhana, or stones fit for trappings, &c.; and 3rd, the Arabi, or stones fit for Arabia. The first are all carefully cut and polished at Mashhad, and are always sold separately. The best of these are found in the earth mines, and the majority of them are exported to Moscow, which seems to be the great centre of the turquoise trade. The second kind are subdivided into four divisions. The first two of these are largely exported to Europe, while the third and fourth are sold in Persia for the ornamentation of Kalian pipe-heads, horses' trappings, and small-arms, &c. The third kind are as a rule bad and light-coloured stones, for which there is no sale in Persia. The name arose owing to some of the miners going on pilgrimage to Mecca. They took some of these bad green-coloured stones with them, and found a good sale for them in Arabia, which is now the market for them and the origin of the name. The private arrangements of the miners for the disposal of the stones they find are not very easy to fathom. There is a body comprised of twenty-five elders or head-men of the villages who seem to purchase the turquoises from the miners in the first instance, and then half cut the stones, sufficient to classify them before disposing of them to brokers and cutters at Mashhad. Both the elders and the brokers make their profit on the transaction, and, so far as I could gather, the actual miner came off worst of all.

The cheating that goes on in the sale of turquoises is something wonderful. Stones of all sorts of sizes and colours were brought for sale into my camp, and almost everybody in it invested some of his savings in turquoises as a memento of his visit. The Indians and

Afghans were especially keen to buy. They showed with pride some good coloured stones they had purchased, and thought they had got wonderful bargains. A week afterwards all pride in their purchases had disappeared, and there were many sadder and wiser men gazing ruefully at their stones, which had mysteriously changed colour from a beautiful azure blue to some worthless light-coloured green without any apparent reason. What preparation the miners keep their stones in to preserve their colour I cannot say, but one thing is certain, and that is, it is not safe to buy a turquoise in Persia till after it has been at least a week under observation, to see whether its colour is permanent or not.

The two villages at Mádan in which the miners live are known as the upper and the lower, and the concession for working the mines not only includes the government of these, but also the whole of the surrounding district, containing thirteen other villages as well, and comprising an area of some forty square miles, with a total population of about 1500 families. Besides the turquoise mines there is a salt mine, a lead mine, and a mill-stone quarry as well in the district. The lead mine and quarry are in tho Batou hills just to the south, but the contractors did not consider it worth while to work either. The salt mine is situated four miles to the east, and is sublet by the contractors for 250 tumans a year. I visited it on my way out of Mádan, and found it consisted simply of an open cave or tunnel running straight into a hill of solid rock-salt. There was only some twenty or thirty feet of earth above the salt at the tunnel's mouth, and no propping up or supports of any kind were required. The salt was beautifully white and clear, more like crystal than salt to look at, and so firm and solid was it that it formed an arched roof of itself. The salt was blasted out with gunpowder just like any other rock, and the only precaution taken by the miners was not to work near any place where, owing to some fault or other, water had got in. Wherever they find the rock soft or wet they at once cease working there, for fear it might fall in. I was told that this rock-salt was to be found all about the district wherever red earth was to be seen, and that there were several mines similar to the one I had seen. The salt was considered superior to that obtained from salt lakes, and the Mádan mines were supposed to supply all Sabzawar, Kuchan, and Bujnurd, the price at the pit-mouth being one kran per donkey-load of say 130 to 160 lbs.

From Mádan I marched twelve miles to Hisar-i-Nau, a village standing at a height of some 4100 feet, and containing about thirty families of Amarlu Kurds. These Amarlus were brought to Khurasan by Shah Abbas at the same time as the Kuchan, Bujnurd, and other Kurds. They now number only about a thousand families, and have no chief of their own, their last man of any importance having been one Kurdu Khan, who had died a few years before. They mostly inhabit the Marush Baluk of Nishapur, which is to the north of Hisar-i-Nau, extending between Madan and Bár up to the Sar-i-Valayat district, and are partly settled in villages and partly nomad.

The 1st December 1897 brought us into Nishapur, fifteen miles farther on. This place is generally written Nishabur in Persian histories and documents, but as it is pronounced Nishapur, I spell it so. Our road led through a thickly populated and well-cultivated plain the whole way, the last two or three miles being through gardens and enclosures belonging to the town.

Some two miles out I was met by the deputy-governor with a carriage and led horsés and a party of horsemen, who escorted me through the town, entering by the Sabzawar gate and coming out by the Mashhad gate, opposite to which my camp was pitched. We traversed the whole of the bazar, half a mile or more in length, and apparently it was market day, as the crowd was great and all the shops, said to be some 450 in number, were open. The trade of Nishapur, I was told, was nothing like equal to that of Sabzawar, but there were ten or twelve Russian Armenians in the town who were said to export some 50,000 tumans or £10,000 worth of cotton, wool, and dried fruits in the year.

The town is quadrilateral and the walls were in good condition, having been all repaired by the late governor, the Naiyar-ud-Dowlah. The Sani-ud-Dowlah gives the circumference of the walls at 3300 zars, or 3782 yards, with fifty-eight bastions or towers, and I presume that is correct. The town has four gates, one on each face, and is abundantly supplied with water drawn from the foot of the Nishapur range to the north-east. The height, according to my aneroid, was about 3900 feet.

The only building of any size that I could see in the town was the Jama Musjid. It was not known when it was built, but there was a stone in it bearing an inscription regarding a bequest of land by Shah Abbas in A.H. 1021 (1612). Most of the townspeople seemed to be Saiyids, who were said to live largely on allowances from the Government, and such traders as there were, were reputed to be far from wealthy. The richest man amongst them had died a few years before, and he left only 20,000 tumans, or £4000.

On arrival at my tent I found the table covered with plates of sweetmeats and trays of melons, &c., and fowls and other things were laid out in front of the tent, all sent by the governor for my special delectation, just as had been done at Sabzawar. In the afternoon the governor himself, the Bayan-us-Sultanah, came to call, accompanied by his Peshkar and his son-in-law, both of whom had to sit upon the floor. Apparently he did not permit them to have chairs in his presence. He was an elderly man, and apologised for not having been able to come out to meet me himself on that account. Being a Mustaufi of the first class, he was at the top of his tree, so to speak, as the only promotion beyond that, that I know of, is to Minister of one of the departments of the State. He was an excellent talker, one of the best, in fact, that I had heard in Khurasan, and he spoke the Persian, largely composed of Arabic, of the educated Persian of the present day.

I halted at Nishapur for a couple of days to examine the ruins of the ancient city, which commence about a mile to the south-east of the present town and are very extensive. The Sani-ud-Dowlah gives the circumference of them at 9000 zars, or over six miles. Nothing is now left aboveground but the *tappa* or mound of Alp Arslan, on the north-east, and a line of mounds on the south-west; but the intervening ground is a mass of lumps and hollows, and though almost all under cultivation, is full of broken bricks and pottery, and wherever it has been dug into one can see that the soil is full of bricks to a considerable depth. The line of mounds on the south-west encloses a space of about half a mile in length and some 600 yards in breadth, which is said to have been the citadel of the city. The walls and bastions were evidently all of mud, as there are comparatively few bits of brick in them. The mounds themselves will all disappear in course of time, as the people have found out that the earth of which they are composed is full of phosphates or some equally strengthening substance, and are gradually clearing it away to spread on their fields.

Near the south-east corner of this ancient citadel stands the small mausoleum of Shaikh Farid-ud-Din Attar, a celebrated philosopher and author, who died in 1220, and whose books are still in much request. He was a grocer in Nishapur, and the story goes that a Darwesh entered his shop one day and had a long conversation with him on the subject of death. They did not agree, and at last the Darwesh declared that death was easy, which Shaikh Attar denied. The Darwesh thereupon lay down on the floor, said one "Allah" and "Akbar," and expired on the spot. This so appalled Shaikh Attar that he gave up his shop and became a Darwesh himself. The mausoleum erected to his memory is of the usual square pattern, with a dome in the centre. The outer dome has never been built, which gives the building an unfinished look.

Half a mile to the east of this is the Imamzada Muhammad Mahruk, in an enclosure surrounded by a wall, and this building is said by the Saiyids, its custodians, to have stood in what was at one time the centre of the ancient city. Mahruk was the great-grandson of Imam Zain-ul-Abidin, who was murdered and burnt by Yazid, governor of Khurasan, about the middle of the eighth century.

The tomb of Umar Khaiyam (d. 1123), lies just to the left of the portico of this shrine, in a small alcove of its own. It is simply a brick structure some three feet high, uncared for and without any inscription or mark. The tomb is utterly neglected by the Persians and in fact is treated with disdain, as Umar Khaiyam was a Sunni instead of an orthodox Shiah, and to be despised accordingly. So little is known of him in his own birthplace that the majority of the people of the town are ignorant even of his name, and I was amused to hear my guide, the Duzdbaghir, or Catch-the-thief, as he was locally styled, the head of the Karawals or watchmen of the town, who had been sent by the governor to show me round, gravely turn and ask if Umar Khaiyam was a Christian, as every Faringi, and especially every Englishman, he said, who came to Nishapur went on pilgrimage to his tomb. Nothing is too bad for Umar Khaiyam, according to the Persians, and he is credited by them with every vice. There are various stories about him in prose and verse, but whether they rest on fact, or are due to the hatred of the Persians for his Sunni tenets, I cannot say. At any rate they do their best to traduce his character.

The *tappa* of Alp Arslan stands some three miles to the east of the present town, near the village of Turbabad. I was astonished at the mass of broken bricks and bits of pottery that we had to pass through to get there. The *tappa* is a large flat-topped artificial mound some 200 yards square and 30 feet in height, which is said to be the site of the ancient Shadiakh built by Alp Arslan in 1073 for his son Malik Shah, whom he married to a daughter of Uktai Ka'an, the son of Changiz Khan.

According to the Sani-ud-Dowlah, nothing reliable is to be found in history regarding the ancient ruins of Nishapur, and what is recorded is apparently fabulous. It is stated in the "Bostan-i-Siyaka"[1] that the first Nishapur was built by Tahmurs Divband. That was ruined, and another town was built by Ardeshir Babakan, Sassani, which was also destroyed, and Shapur built a third, which he called after his own name. Firdosi says that Yezdigird II. often lived in Nishapur, and that in his reign the city was a very prosperous one, but the name of Nishapur rarely appears in the history of the Sassanian dynasty after his reign, and when the Arabs took possession of Khurasan the place was of little importance. The number of Sassanian coins which have been found at Nishapur, though, would seem to show, so the Sani-ud-Dowlah says, that it was an important town in the time of those kings. In 1010 a hundred thousand

[1] P. 573.

people are said to have died of famine in it. Togrul Beg, the first of the Saljukis, made it his capital in 1037, and so did his son, Alp Arslan, who succeeded him.

In 1115 it was destroyed by an earthquake. In 1153, during the reign of Sultan Sanjar, the town was taken by the Ghaz tribe, who massacred thousands of the inhabitants, and were not finally driven out till 1159. Two years afterwards, the constant quarrels between the Sunnis and the Shiahs in Nishapur came to a head, and the leaders of both sides were killed by Muaiyid Ainia, the mosques and colleges were destroyed and the libraries burnt, and Muaiyid Ainia made Shadiakh his capital. Ainia killed Rukn-ud-Din Muhammad, the last of the Saljuki kings, the nephew of Sultan Sanjar, but was himself killed in 1174 by Takish Khan Khwarism Shah. Nishapur then sank into insignificance, and was no longer called a city, and Shadiakh became the capital of the Nishapur kingdom. In 1221 the Moghul troops under Tuli Khan, son of Changiz Khan, completely destroyed the old Nishapur. They flooded the town for seven days and nights, levelled the buildings to the ground, and sowed barley on the site. In 1267 Shadiakh was finally destroyed by an earthquake, and a new town was built near by. That was destroyed by another earthquake in 1405, after which the present town of Nishapur was erected. In the early part of Shah Abbas's reign (1577–1628) the town was plundered and the people massacred by Abdulla Khan and Abdul Momin Khan, Usbegs, and after the decline of the Safavian dynasty the Bayáts, the Kurds, and the Iliks of Sistan again plundered the place. In Nadir Shah's time, too, Nishapur suffered severely, so that it has had a checkered existence all through. At present it is said to contain 3000 houses, with a population of about 12,000 people. The revenue of the Nishapur district is said to be 60,000 tumans, and the population to be about the same number, divided amongst 300 villages.

The governor, when I returned his visit, was surrounded by the Peshkar and his son, two Mustaufis, and his son-in-law, all of whom, as before, he made sit upon the floor. We had a long chat and many stories, and eventually the conversation turned upon coins. I asked what ancient coins were found in Nishapur. The governor could not tell me, but the Peshkar produced an old gold coin which was thought to have been of Hulaku, and another of Timur's. The Peshkar then sent his son off to somebody else, and he returned with three silver Sassanian coins, but I could hear of no other kinds. Sassanian coins were evidently the ones generally found.

Riding along the high-road on leaving Nishapur, I was astonished to see the number of *fourgons* and *kaliskas*, the Russian equivalents for waggons and carriages, that went past. The increase in the wheeled traffic of Persia of late years has been something marvellous. Formerly nothing but pack animals were in use, and now horses seem to be put into draught everywhere. On arrival at Buzhmehran, a small village to the north of the road, I found all the villagers assembled to meet me, and at the head of them an officious man in brass buttons, wearing a large oval silver medal with the lion and the sun on it. The villagers seemed to have a wonderful belief in my powers, as they came up with a petition for a certificate from me that their crops had suffered from floods and their revenue assessment should be reduced accordingly. The medal man was peculiarly amusing. He came up to say that he was a Vakil or corporal of Persian Cossacks, and had been on duty with the Persian Commissioner on the Russian Frontier Commission, and had thus got his medal. He said, though, that he wanted to improve his position still more with his brother villagers, who were apparently not so much impressed by the medal as he thought they ought to be, and the best way he could think of to do that was to be presented by me with a robe of honour. He was quite willing, he said, to pay for this robe if I would only give it to him, and thus increase his respect. I could not help being amused at his request, though it was a very ordinary one in Persian eyes, where every official pays regularly for the *khillat* that is presented to him to enable him to maintain his position.

The next morning we passed through Kadamgah, the inhabitants of which were all Saiyids, and seemed to be cordially hated by their neighbours and travellers alike: not a man had a good word to say for them. Kadamgah means literally the place of the footsteps, and consists of a shrine containing, I was told, a piece of hard black stone a little less then two feet square, with the impression on it of the two feet of a very large man. This stone is fixed in the wall, and the impressions, though they look artificial, are venerated as the actual footprints of the Imam Raza of Mashhad, who is said to have walked here on his way from Nishapur to Tús, and to have performed a miracle by bringing into existence, for his ablutions, the spring of water that now supplies the shrine and garden. The peculiarity of the place is the number of large pine-trees by which the shrine is surrounded, and which are said to run up to a height of over ninety feet. The shrine was built on the design of the mausoleum of Khwajah Rabi at Mashhad, by Shah Suliman Safavi, in 1680. It is 80 paces in circumference, 14 paces in diameter inside, and 58 feet in height, but is now much out of repair, and although endowed, is apparently neglected by its guardians. The dome is faced with tiles, and has an inscription in the

Suls character, but many of the tiles had been taken down and sold. No Christian is allowed to enter any of these shrines in Persia.

In the next stage to Fakr-i-Daúd, or the pride of David, we had a rise of some 500 feet, and the weather, which had been bad for the last two days, here got worse. The hills around were soon all white with snow, and I had to give up all thoughts of visiting the Mughan cave, as I had intended. At the Dizbad stream we crossed the boundary between the Nishapur and Mashhad districts. We found the caravanserai at Fakr-i-Daúd crammed full of people, travellers like ourselves, and had the storm continued, we should have found difficulty in getting shelter in it. Fortunately the weather cleared a bit, and we got up our tents, but this part of the road, owing to its elevated position, is always a dangerous one in winter, and many people have been frozen to death on it.

Sharifabad, our next stage, possessed two large caravanserais, and I put all the horses and mules in these for the night. We ourselves slept in our tents, but they were so covered with frost next morning that it was nearly noon before we could start. We reached the crest of the range at the fourth mile, at a height of some 4900 feet, and then we had a steady descent for another eleven miles all the way down to Turuk, a drop of some 1550 feet. At the ninth mile, at a rise called the Tappa-i-Salam, the point at which pilgrims get their first view of the gilt dome of the shrine at Mashhad glistening away in the sun out in the plain below, we passed a pillar bearing an inscription in Persian poetry, stating that the road had been made by Sipah Salar Muhammad, the son of Amir, governor-general of Khurasan in the year 1867. The road may have been a marvel for Persia at that time, but how waggons and carriages got over it at all in the state I found it was a marvel to me. I would not have driven down that descent for a great deal. We camped at the caravanserai by the roadside. This building consisted of two enclosures, called respectively the summer and winter courts. The latter, built by Shah Suliman Safavi in 1669, had rooms all round the sides, with stables at each corner. The outer enclosure, built in 1861, had only open arches with recesses for sleeping in in the hot weather.

A mile to the south of the caravanserai was a curious conical mound known as the Tappa-i-Nadiri, though it had nothing to do with Nadir. This mound, or rather hill, was some 550 paces in circumference and 100 feet or more in height, a most unusual height for an artificial mound in Khurasan. It had been dug into in various places, and the whole of the soil was full of bones and pottery from top to bottom. There were no bricks in it, but apparently round stones were used in the buildings of which it was formerly composed. It looked to me as if it was of great age.

Next morning, the 9th December 1897, I rode the remaining five miles into Mashhad, and found myself sitting down to breakfast with Dr. and Mrs. Duke in a house again. This brought my last tour in Khurasan to an end.

We had traversed a round of 752 miles in our three months' outing, and after so long a residence in tents the big Consulate house seemed lonely and dreary; but the winter snows outside and a warm fire inside soon reconciled one to life in a house again.

It is astonishing, though, how the fascination of tent life grows upon one in Eastern countries.

CHAPTER XXIV.

WINTER AT MASHHAD.

DURING my absence from Mashhad the Rukn-ud-Dowlah had arrived as governor-general, and in due course I received a visit from the Sartip appointed by his Royal Highness to call and inquire after my health, according to Persian etiquette, and I duly paid my official visit in return. The Karguzar, the chief of the telegraphs, and various other officials had also been changed, and I had many visits to receive and return. The 18th December brought us round to the Czar's fête-day again, and then we had the English Christmas and the Russian Christmas, and the English New Year's Day and the Russian New Year's Day to celebrate, and various Persian dinner-parties between whiles, so that the time soon passed, despite the winter snows.

My Indian servants stood the cold wonderfully well. Karim Bakhsh, the cook, I carefully clad in a suit of good thick barak, and he throve so well that he even rushed into matrimony. He came to me to ask permission to marry, and when I asked him who the lady was, I was amused to hear that my Persian cook's brother had arrived, bringing a lady with him as a wife for his brother; but the latter had declined the offer on the grounds that he already had a wife in Teheran and he did not want another, and, with great generosity, had offered to bestow the lady on his brother in the art, Karim Bakhsh. The latter told me that he had been round and taken the advice of all his Indian friends in the Consulate, and their advice to him was not to marry the woman for good and all by an *akdi* or permanent marriage, but to marry her for three months by a *sigha* or temporary marriage, and to see how he liked her first. I duly added my advice to that of the others, and, congratulating him on his luck in having such a chance, I granted the required permission, and he lost no time in establishing the lady in a room above the kitchen. This system of temporary marriages is one of the features of Mashhad life. Every pious pilgrim can be provided at once with a temporary wife by the nearest priest for a week or a month or a year, with the full consent of both the law and the Church, and the privilege is fully taken advantage of by all Muhammadans. Permanent marriages constantly take place as well. More than one of the Indian members of the British Consulate have thus found a partner of their joys and sorrows for life in Mashhad. I have even known Christians to be married in Mashhad by Mussulman Mullahs. Two Europeans who had no consuls of their own to marry them were thus united by Persian priests under Muhammadan rites, and their marriage under the laws of the land in which they were living was held to be legal, and was registered accordingly in their respective countries.

The end of the year 1897 marked a great fall in the Persian exchange. When we visited Mashhad in 1885 the rate of exchange was 240 Persian krans to 100 Indian rupees. At the end of 1897 we were getting 345 krans for our 100 rupees, and at the beginning of 1898 the rate rose to 356 krans. The sterling rate of exchange was 51½ krans to the English pound.

At the end of January the snow commenced to thaw

after lying for a month on the ground, and on the 4th February I shot my first sand-grouse, the return of which looked as if the hard weather was now to be over, but it was not so. The streets in the town became one fearful mass of slush, but no slush or anything else could keep the religious students quiet for more than a certain time, and fresh riots now broke out, and suddenly the whole town was in an uproar.

The first thing we heard was that a party of Tálibs had seized a man who was accused of being a *bábi* or dissenter, had beat him with sticks, pistolled him, drenched him with naphtha, and finally burnt him to death in the main street of the town, close to the shrine. This outrage brought matters to a climax. The question was taken up, and the Persian Government was constrained to take action. The first sign of movement was the sudden arming of the Persian troops on guard in the town with Werndl breechloading rifles and some half-dozen cartridges apiece. The Consulate guard was thus armed like the rest. Hitherto their old muzzle-loading muskets without any ammunition at all had been considered sufficient for our protection, but this was now altered. The governor-general posted guns in the town commanding the Khiábán or main street, and then plucked up courage to set about the arrest of the murderers. The Shah sent orders to the shrine officials to give up the men harboured in the shrine; the governor-general seized one of the Mujtahids, a notably disturbing element of the peace of the town, and deported him into the country, and commenced to arrest the religious students wherever he could find them. The result was a general flight. The Tálibs took off their big white turbans which they had worn so truculently for so long and hid them wherever they could, and bolting out of the town, went off to their native villages in the guise of peaceable cultivators. Quiet was restored at once, but what punishment was eventually inflicted upon the murderers I never heard, as I was ordered off to India at the time, and I left before the case was settled.

I applied for and obtained formal permission, through the British Legation at Teheran and the Embassy at Petersburg, to travel by the Transcaspian Railway from Ashkabad to the Caspian. I had some difficulty in getting a conveyance, as the road was still practically closed by snow, but at last I found a man who engaged to supply me with a carriage for myself from Mashhad to Ashkabad for 35 tumans, a sort of victoria, drawn by four horses abreast, and a *fourgon* or waggon for my servants and baggage to the frontier and back for 32 tumans more. My servants and orderlies were not allowed to cross the Russian frontier, and I had to arrange to drive on there with only one man who could travel with a Persian passport, the Russians refusing to let any one with an English passport cross the frontier. I found some little difficulty at first in getting Russian rouble-notes for my journey, but I eventually got some at the rate of 517 krans per 100 roubles.

CHAPTER XXV.

RETURN TO INDIA.

THE weather towards the end of February got very cold again, followed by a heavy fall of snow. The thermometer went down to zero, and Captain Whyte, who arrived from Teheran to relieve me, came in half frozen, saying he had never felt such cold in his life before. My last evening I spent with M. and Madame Ponafidine at the Russian Consulate, and next morning, the 1st March 1898, I said good-bye to Mashhad and started on my way to India.

I had hoped to make Chinaran, forty miles out, before nightfall, but the road was too heavy, and we had to stop at a village eight miles short of it, where I got one mud hut about ten feet square for myself, and another next door for the servants. Never shall I forget the cold of that night. The water in a bottle on the dinner-table froze into a solid block of ice while I was eating my dinner, and nothing I had would keep my head warm. Next day we did thirty-six miles, to Mirabad. The sun came out and thawed the frozen road, and it was with great difficulty that we got through at all.

The cold was as great as ever at night, and it was only by keeping my ink-bottle over the fire that I could write at all. Next day clouds came up, the thaw commenced, and the road was worse than ever. We dragged laboriously through melting snow, and got into Kuchan at noon. I halted for lunch in one of the caravanserais, where I was visited by the head of the fraternity of half-a-dozen Armenians from Erivan, who lived and traded in the place.

In the stables next door to me were a party of Russian Molokans from the settlement at Goudan, on the frontier. Their waggons, laden up with cotton and skins, were standing outside, and the men and their horses were in the stable waiting for the thaw to dry up and let them get on. It was curious to see these men in their Russian caps, Europeans in appearance, and yet living, dressing, and eating exactly as Persian peasants. They seemed to earn their living mainly by plying as cartmen between Ashkabad and Mashhad, and they plied for exactly the same hire and worked at just the same rates as the Persians, and had not the faintest idea of any superiority. The Persians never called them Russians, curiously enough —always Molokans, and seemed to look upon them as a separate tribe from the Russians, and more akin to themselves. There was apparently no fanaticism against them, and they worked on equal and friendly terms with the Persian and Turki cartmen.

Leaving them, we had a hard pull up through mud and snow for eight miles to Zubaran, where we spent the night. The snow was very bad on the high ground, and it took us seven hours to do the sixteen miles on to Imam Kulia. When I arrived at Goudan I found Captain Liffkine waiting for me. He was acting as political secretary in Transcaspia for M. Klemm, who had gone off to Petersburg with General Kuropatkin, and had most kindly come out to meet me and drive me in the last thirty-two miles to Ashkabad. We changed horses and lunched at the half-way resting-house, where a Russian and his family were doing the work that a Dak Bungalow Khausamah would have done for us in India; and on arrival at Ashkabad I found myself back again, so to speak, on the confines of Europe. Captain Liffkine installed me comfortably at a hotel, and subsequently saw me off at the station, where I found a special carriage had been reserved for me, a kind mark of attention on the part of the Transcaspian authorities. At Krasnovodsk I met our old friend Graf Armfeld, of the Kushk Commission, who kindly saw me off on board the steamer. Baron Vrevsky, the governor-general of Turkestan, with all his staff and their wives and an English governess, were also travelling by the same boat, and their society made the time pass pleasantly.

At Tiflis I found various old friends of the Afghan Boundary Commission days, and I received a cordial welcome from all. One of the first men I came across in the hotel was Cololonel Alikhanoff, whom I had last met when putting up the boundary pillar on the banks of the river Murghab, near Panjdeh, on Christmas Day 1887. I had a pleasant dinner with him and Prince Orbeliani and Colonel Kartzoff at the English Club in the evening, a club which I was told was managed on the lines of the English Club at Petersburg. There was a house dinner every Thursday evening, which I just came in for, and we sat down fifteen all told. It was astonishing how many of these could speak English. We had three generals present—the general officer commanding the Caucasian Army Corps, the assistant governor-general of the Caucasus, and the general of artillery—besides one or two other officers and some civilians. We sat talking for long, and the evening was an interesting and pleasant one. Colonel Alikhanoff told me that he was occupying his leisure, now that he was unemployed, in writing a book on Persia, describing Kuchan and Bujnurd. He explained to me the headings of the various chapters, and I trust the book may be translated some of these days, and thus rendered generally available.

The next day I dined with General Kuhlberg, the Russian Commissioner with us on the Afghan Boundary Commission of 1885–86, who had hospitably collected as many of the old members of the Commission as he could to meet me. Colonel Zakrchevski, the chief of the staff to General Komaroff at the time of the Russian attack on the Afghans at Panjdeh in March 1885, and whom I now found in Tiflis as the colonel commanding the 15th Grenadier Regiment, kindly brought a carriage to drive me over, and we sat down a party of ten altogether, including General Zelenoy, whom Colonel Peacocke and myself had last met at Tiflis in March 1888. The conversation, as on the day before, turned upon the Tirah campaign, in which at that time Russian officers took the keenest interest. They contrasted our operations in Tirah with theirs in bygone years in the Caucasus, and they described how their generals had invariably suffered in retreats just as ours had done, till they had learnt by experience to stick to the sky-line. I asked if any history had been written of the conquest of the Caucasus, by which the tactics pursued by the different generals could be studied, but they could tell me of none. They said it took them sixty years to conquer the Caucasus, and that we could not expect to conquer Tirah in six months, especially with the enormous amount of baggage that we took with us. This was a point that all Russian officers seized upon. They instanced the pictures in the *Graphic* and other illustrated papers as a proof of the difference between their impedimenta and ours. I remember one illustration in particular which they brought to my notice, in which the baggage mules were depicted coming down a pass. They said, "Look at those boxes on the mules; what are they?" I explained that they looked to me like cases of tinned meat. "Tinned meat!" said they; "why, we conquered the Caucasus on biscuits, and precious few of them." And doubtless this was true.

Another point touched upon, and strongly professed in Central Asia, was the division of Afghanistan between England and Russia. It is wonderful how almost every Russian officer one meets harps upon that. They seem to forget that England is pledged to maintain the integrity of Afghanistan, and that so long as the Amir remains loyal to his engagements with us we so intend to maintain it. Apparently Russians think that could they once get possession of Afghan Turkestan up to the Hindu Kushk, they could so improve the rich provinces of Andkui and Balkh that they would be able to raise sufficient supplies there to feed as many troops as they wanted, and they would then be able to maintain a constant menace on India, and thus, as it were, have England at their mercy. We can understand the wish of the Russian frontier officer to effect this, but England having laid down her frontier, must naturally be prepared to maintain that frontier, and this is a point the Russian does not seem to have realised as yet.

I found the wish for a railway to India just as prevalent in Tiflis as it was at Ashkabad. The junction of the Indian and Transcaspian railways is a project that finds much favour in the eyes of all Russian officers in Central Asia, and many a Russian officer has pointed out to me in glowing colours the desirability of it. They propose that they should build the line down to Herat from their side, while we should extend the Quetta and Chaman line up to Herat on ours. Their main object seems to be to get the Russian railway into Herat. Almost every Russian I have ever met has advocated this extension, but never once have I heard it suggested that the junction should be at the frontier, as it is in all other countries. On the contrary, Herat is always the place named. It is impossible for us to permit Russia to build railways in Afghanistan; but even supposing a junction was effected at the Kushk frontier, I do not see how it could pay. In arguing the point I always took the financial side of the question, and asked who was to pay for it. I said that before any company could be induced to find the capital and construct a line to join the Indian and Transcaspian railways it would have to be shown that there was some prospect of the line paying its expenses, and that so far as I could judge there was none. The new customs cordon established all along the Russian frontier in Central Asia had, I pointed out, entirely stopped what little trade with India formerly existed, and there was nothing that I knew of to be carried by the proposed railway. The Russian reply was that though they taxed all manufactured goods, there was no tax on raw products, and that they would be glad to take rice from India. That was the only product they could think of. I said rice came mostly from Burmah, and it would be cheaper to send it direct from Rangoon by sea to Batoum or Odessa, as the case might be, than to carry it by sea to Calcutta and thence all across India and Afghanistan by rail; besides, what was there for them to send to India in return? Wheat was suggested, but to that all I could say was that Transcaspia, first of all, had not enough wheat for its own requirements; and secondly, India was a wheat-exporting country itself, and did not require wheat, and if it did, it would be cheaper to get it direct by sea. In the end assafœtida was the only thing that they could think of, and one train a year, I said, would about suffice for that. Not a single Russian that I heard speak on the subject could show me that he had ever studied the subject for a moment from a practical point of view. With them the wish apparently was the father of the thought, and yet so deeply did the idea seem to have taken hold of their minds, that not one would admit the impracticability of their scheme. "It will come; it will come," was their constant cry; but I do not see that under present circumstances such a railway would benefit India, not even by its passenger traffic. It took me twelve days to get to London from Ashkabad, and with another long and weary railway journey across India and Afghanistan in addition, I fancy the present sea-trip of a fortnight to Marseilles would generally hold its own with ease. The present rate of speed on the Russian railways might doubtless be accelerated, but even then, beyond a quicker postal delivery, I can find nothing to lead me to suppose that India would gain in any way by the junction of the Indian and Transcaspian railways, nor do I see that the line would pay its working expenses; while as to the Russians, their desire for it would seem to be prompted solely by the desire to get a foothold in Herat and an open road to India, as never once have they suggested any relaxation of their prohibitive custom dues, nor have I heard them ever express any desire to foster trade with India in any way. On the contrary, I can call to mind a conversation on the subject I once had with a high Russian officer. He had been dilating on the subject of what a grand thing it would be to join the Indian and Transcaspian railways, if only to show to the world the friendship that existed between the British and the Russian Governments, and went on to say that such a railway was not a thing to be constructed by a company for the sake of gain. It was an Imperial work, to be undertaken by the Governments concerned for Imperial purposes, and he added, "Look at us; we are building the Merv-Kushk Railway, and that will never pay a cent in a century." I simply said, "Are you building that railway out of friendship to England?" The ludicrousness of the whole thing struck him at once. He saw the joke, and jumping up with a laugh, he said, "No, we are building it to protect our interests in China and the Bosphorus." The bubble was pricked, and there was the whole thing in a nutshell. We both had a hearty laugh, and parted the best of friends. I admired him all the more for his candour, though I must say it took me an hour or more to get at it.

On arrival at Batoum I found the steamer had been delayed by storms in the Black Sea, but thanks to the kindness and hospitality of Mr. Stevens, the British consul, the time passed pleasantly, and the morning of the 19th March 1898 saw me steaming down the Bosphorus into Constantinople, whence I made my way to Alexandria and Bombay, and thus found myself once more back again in India, after a longer absence than usually falls to the lot of the Indian officer.

INDEX.